CW00550205

Introduction to Corporate Finance

Edited by
Peter R. Davies FCIB

The Chartered
Institute
of Bankers

Introduction to Corporate Finance

First published 1990

Apart from any fair dealing for the purposes of research or private study, or criticism or review, as permitted under the Copyright, Designs and Patents Act 1988, this publication may only be reproduced, stored or transmitted in any form or by any means, with the prior permission in writing of the publishers, or in the case of reprographic reproduction in accordance with the terms of licences issued by the Copyright Licensing Agency. Enquiries concerning reproduction outside those terms should be sent to the publishers at the undermentioned address:

BANKERS BOOKS LIMITED
℅ The Chartered Institute of Bankers
10 Lombard Street
London EC3V 9AS

Chartered Institute of Bankers (CIB) publications are published by Bankers Books Limited under an exclusive licence and royalty agreement. Bankers Books Limited is a company owned by The Chartered Institute of Bankers.

ISBN 0 85297 210 5

© The Chartered Institute of Bankers, 1990

🅱🅛 British Library Cataloguing in Publication Data

Introduction to corporate finance.
    1. Companies. Financial management
    I. Davies, Peter R.
    658.15

Typeset and printed by Commercial Colour Press Ltd, London E7.
Typeset in 10/12pt Century; text printed on 80 gsm paper; cover on 240 gsm.

Contents

List of Contributors

Philippa Back, BA (Hons), graduated from University College London with an honours degree in geography. She joined Citibank NA in London and then, in 1979, left to work for Bowater Industries plc, where she set up and ran the cash management department. She left Bowater as Treasurer to take up the appointment of Group Finance Director at D C Gardner in February 1988.

She is a council member of the Association of Corporate Treasurers, and is Chairman of their education committee. In 1987, her first book *Corporate Cash Management* was published by Woodhead Faulkner.

John Bateman, ACIB, joined Midland Bank in the North East where he held various appointments in Middlesbrough and Newcastle before moving to London and joining the international division of the bank in 1975. There he worked in corporate finance and other related lending areas before he was appointed as Manager of the bank's Bahrain branch in 1980.

On his return to the United Kingdom he spent two years heading the division's sterling clearing operations before he became an Assistant Trade Finance Director of Midland Montagu Trade Finance in February 1986. In this role he has been actively involved in arranging export finance packages for a number of major UK companies and, more recently, has headed the department's sales team responsible for developing business in the Far East.

He is an Associate of The Chartered Institute of Bankers.

Adrian Coats, MA, ACA, ACT, graduated from Edinburgh University with a degree in economics. He joined the London office of Peat Marwick Mitchell where he qualified as an accountant in 1980 and then moved to Grand Metropolitan as Treasury Accountant in 1982. There he held a number of positions, including that of Assistant Treasurer. Recently, he has taken up the position of Treasurer of the South of Scotland Electricity Board. In 1986 he passed the examinations set by the Association of Corporate Treasurers.

Alan Colley, ACIB, DipFS, joined National Westminster Bank in 1972. After a period in domestic banking, he moved to the international division, where he has worked in the credit control, training, corporate marketing and treasury departments. He is currently a Commercial Loans Manager.

Alan Colley completed the Financial Studies Diploma in 1983, obtaining the Centenary Prize for the highest aggregate marks in the Practice of Banking papers.

Peter R Davies, TD, BA (Hons), ACIS, FCIB, has recently retired from National Westminster Bank plc, where he was Controller Correspondent Banking in corporate and institutional banking. He had previously held a number of appointments in the domestic and international side of the bank's business. He has been Chief Examiner for Corporate Finance in the Financial Studies Diploma since 1985, and has contributed articles to *Banking World* and to *The Handbook of International Finance*, and book reviews for the former. He has also been involved with training, including the development of courses concerning the marketing of financial services.

Jennifer Hopper, BA (Hons), ACIB, DipFS, is Manager, Global Systems Planning, Barclays Bank. She joined Barclays in 1981 after graduating from Oxford University with an honours degree in modern languages. During her training programme she worked principally in UK branches and at a regional office, but also served a year's attachment to the treasury department at Unigate plc, where she was involved in sterling and foreign exchange money market dealing, and the establishment of a commercial paper programme. Before taking up her present appointment in June 1988, Jennifer Hopper was a Corporate Manager at one of the bank's business centres. She is an Associate of The Chartered Institute of Bankers and, on completing the Financial Studies Diploma in 1986, was awarded the Institute's Centenary Prize for the highest aggregate marks in the Practice of Banking papers.

Robert Hudson, MSc, BA (Hons), ACIB, is Senior Manager, Balance Sheet Management, in Barclays Bank's treasury department. He is a graduate of Leeds and Bristol Universities with a first degree in economics and a Master's in quantitive economics. He spent six years working for the UK Government Economic Service before joining

Barclays Bank's economics department in 1978. From 1982 to 1985 he was Assistant Manager of Barclays Futures Limited. This was followed by a first spell in balance sheet management, and then the financial engineering unit of the bank, where he specialised in techniques of interest rate and exchange rate exposure management. He is an Associate of The Chartered Institute of Bankers.

Nigel Jump, MA (Econ), BA (Hons), ACIB, is a Senior Economist in the industry section of the economics department of Barclays Bank. He graduated from the University of Lancaster in 1975 and obtained a Master's degree in economics from the University of Manchester in 1976. Having taught at the University of Durham, he was a lecturer in economics at Liverpool Polytechnic before joining Barclays Bank in 1981. He qualified as an Associate of The Chartered Institute of Bankers in 1987.

Sarah Laws, BSc (Econ), ACA, ACT, is Financial Controller of Oppidan Estates. She qualified as a chartered accountant with Coopers & Lybrand before joining Habitat Mothercare plc. Following the merger with British Home Stores plc, she was appointed Group Financial Accountant and then Assistant Group Treasurer for Storehouse plc. She is an Associate of the Association of Corporate Treasurers and a graduate of Bristol University.

Gillian McGrattan, MA, BSc (Hons), is Research Manager in the economics department of National Westminster Bank.

She holds a first degree in medical sciences and a Master's degree in politics, philosophy and economics from Oxford. Before joining National Westminster Bank in 1986, she had spells with the Confederation of British Industry and Standard Chartered Bank working mainly in economic forecasting.

Gillian McGrattan's chapters were prepared with Dr Jan Toporowski, a former colleague at Standard Chartered Bank and now a lecturer at the Polytechnic of the South Bank.

Michael Meltzer, MBA, BA, DipM, attained a business degree in marketing from the Polytechnic Wolverhampton. In 1975 he took a Master's degree in business analysis at Lancaster University. He spent several years in the computer services industry — his final position being Manager of Cash Management Services for Automated Data Processing. His experience in banking covers the areas of account management, electronic banking and global custody. He worked for some time with American banks before moving to Lloyd's Bank in 1987, where he is now Chief Manager in electronic banking and cash management services within the corporate banking division. In this role, he is responsible for the marketing and development of cash management systems that assist Corporate Treasurers.

Len Ross, MSc (Econ), is a consultant economist and, until 1989, was Principal Lecturer in economics and business studies at the Polytechnic of Central London. He graduated in economics at LSE, where he took a Master's degree in international economics. Before joining the Polytechnic, he worked as an economist in both the public and private sectors, including the Economist Intelligence Unit, British Rail and Esso Petroleum. His main teaching and research interests are in finance and international business. He is co-author (with J R Shackleton) of two economic texts and has written widely on economic and financial topics, including regular contributions to the *TSB Review*. He has had a long association with The Chartered Institute of Bankers and is currently an assistant examiner for Monetary Economics.

Rachel Sopp, MA, ACA, ACT, graduated from Cambridge University with a degree in mathematics and operational research. She joined Coopers & Lybrand in 1980 where she qualified as a chartered accountant and then specialised in treasury management consultancy. Over a period of six years, she has carried out assignments in a wide range of companies and treasury areas from decision support systems for corporate treasurers to international financial co-ordination. These assignments have taken her to many places in Europe and, in particular, Scandinavia. She is currently based in West Germany.

She was a double prizewinner in the Association of Corporate Treasurers' Diploma in Treasury Management.

Richard Taylor, ACIB, ACT, joined Lloyds Bank in 1971 and is an Associate of both The Chartered Institute of Bankers and the Association of Corporate Treasurers. His various appointments within the bank have included a two-year attachment to the corporate international banking division in New York and a period as a Manager with the commercial service division in Reading. He is now Manager, commercial banking, at the Thames Valley and South Midlands regional executive office.

Nicholas Tonkin, MSc (Econ), BSocSc (Hons), graduated from Birmingham University in economics and statistics and also holds a Master's degree in econometrics from the LSE.

Following short spells in industry and consultancy, he spent three years in forecasting and project appraisal for the National Ports Council. He joined Barclays Bank in 1980 working as an assistant to the group economic advisor before moving to the bank's treasury division. Responsibilities there included supervision of overseas operations and assisting management of the bank's capital raising activities, and funding overseas investments. In 1986 he became a Manager in the bank's newly-formed financial engineering unit, which involved product development and advising on complex lending proposals. He is now a Manager in the bank's corporate division.

Gilly Webb-Wilson, BA, ACIB, graduated in French and German from Oxford and, after a short spell as a junior marine insurance broker at Lloyds, joined Barclays Bank in 1975. In 1978 she joined Grindlays Bank as an Account Manager in the consumer goods unit of the UK corporate bank. After a period as head of the unit, she transferred to the European corporate banking department where, as Assistant Director and Country Officer in charge of a number of countries, she specialised in the financing of short-term trade and the longer term financing of capital goods exports and overseas projects. She was also involved in sovereign risk lending and in risk syndication.

In 1986 she left mainstream banking to become an independent financial and banking consultant specialising in the preparation and teaching of training courses and seminars for bankers. She is an Associate of The Chartered Institute of Bankers.

Preface

Originally, in commissioning this book, The Chartered Institute of Bankers had sought to provide a suitable background text for the Financial Studies Diploma. The objective of the Corporate Finance paper is to develop an understanding of the role of the banker as a corporate financial advisor. The book has, however, now evolved into a text designed to have a wide use among bankers and students of finance, who seek a general understanding of the financial world of large corporates.

Each chapter evinces a variety of writing styles, and whilst each is essentially self-contained, there is some inevitable overlap since many financial instruments can be harnessed in more than one way in order to meet differing needs and circumstances. The versatility of these instruments is matched by the flexibility with which they are used in the financial markets.

With such a wide-ranging subject it is difficult for any single book to delve deeply into every facet of corporate finance, so many chapters contain suggestions for further reading. There are, however, important caveats — first, the world of finance is ever changing and therefore both student and practitioner need to follow the financial press to keep abreast of developments. Secondly, students will find that reading on its own will not be sufficient to gain a pass in the examination for, like the practitioner, they will need to understand and adapt the principles to the problems faced.

As leader of the Editorial Panel, I must express my thanks to my fellow members, Lance Moir, ACIB, David Adams, ACIB and Robert Skinner, ACIB, DipFS; to my secretary Sandra Mussett and to all the contributors for their hard work and goodwill. No less a valuable contribution has been made by the staff of the Institute, especially Brian Rawle and Uschi Gubser. Without their efforts this book would not have reached the reader.

Peter Davies

December 1989

PART A

Editor's Notes

The economic background is introduced in two chapters covering the demand for finance by corporates, and corporate financial behaviour in relation to their needs. This is followed by a chapter on multinational corporations identifying factors peculiar to that type of organisation which represents in some regards the ultimate in corporate activity.

The developments in corporates are mirrored in the way specialist financial institutions have grown in response to the needs of the major corporates, and a number of financial techniques are outlined in the way that they meet their needs. This section is rounded off by a chapter discussing some of the ways in which financial institutions are restricted in their ability to assist their major corporate customers.

Corporate Growth and the Financial Environment

Len Ross

Introduction

Corporate bankers have enjoyed an unprecedented boom in demand for their services since the mid-1980s. As Table 1.1 shows, merger and acquisition business, for example, has never been greater. Among industrial and commercial corporations there were nearly 700 takeovers in 1986, an increase of 15% from the previous year; this was followed in 1987 by a surge of two-thirds to more than 1,100. Even more impressive was the money involved. Spending on acquisitions grew rapid, or over £21 million. This fell back to £14 million in 1987 but the increase in the number of takeovers deals held up. Total expenditure is above £16 billion.

Table 1.1
Corporate finance activity
UK industrial and commercial companies

Year	Acquisitions				Capital issues (£bn)			
	Number (£m)	Expenditure (£m)	Cost per takeover	Total net issues	Of which: Equity	Debt	Rights	
1983	447	2.34	5.24	0.47	2.20	1.07	2.19	
1984	568	5.48	9.64	2.31	1.49	0.91	1.27	
1985	474	7.00	14.00	5.18	1.23	0.01	3.05	
1986	696	14.93	21.60	9.06	7.30	1.28	5.70	
1987	1,125	16.36	15.44	11.95	1.66	0.82	10.47	
1988	1,224	22.10	18.05	7.61	5.68	1.98	4.91	

Source: Phillips & Drew Statistics

Capital issues present a similar picture. New equity issues alone reached nearly £15 billion in 1987, almost double those in the previous

CHAPTER 1

Corporate Growth and the Financial Environment

Len Ross

Introduction

Corporate bankers have enjoyed an unprecedented boom in demand for their services since the mid-1980s. As Table 1.1 shows, merger and acquisition business, for example, has never been greater. Among industrial and commercial corporations there were nearly 700 takeovers in 1986, an increase of 15% from the previous year; this was followed in 1987 by a surge of two-thirds to more than 1,100. Even more impressive was the money involved. Spending on acquisitions more than doubled in 1986 to a massive £14.9 billion with a mean cost per takeover of over £21 million. This fell back to £14 million in 1987 but the increase in the number of takeover deals held up total expenditure to above £15 billion.

Table 1.1
Corporate finance activity —
UK industrial and commercial companies

| Year | Acquisitions | | | Capital issues (£bn) | | | |
	Number	Expenditure (£bn)	Cost per takeover (£m)	Total net issues	Of which: Equity	Debt	Rights
1983	447	2.34	5.24	3.33	2.29	1.04	2.13
1984	568	5.48	9.64	2.34	1.42	0.91	1.27
1985	474	7.09	14.96	5.18	4.23	0.94	3.95
1986	696	14.93	21.50	9.06	7.80	1.26	5.79
1987	1,125	15.36	13.66	15.44	14.92	0.52	10.47
1988	1,224	22.10	18.05	7.54	5.63	1.91	4.91

Source: Financial Statistics

Capital issues present a similar picture. New equity issues alone reached nearly £15 billion in 1987, almost double those in the previous year and ten times as great as in 1984. The stock market crash of October 1987 not surprisingly produced a slump in new issue activity, but by mid-1988 and into 1989 there was a recovery in share prices bringing companies back to the equity capital market. Takeover business meanwhile was actually boosted by the crash; in 1988 both the volume and value of acquisitions were actually running higher than in the year before, possibly as depressed market values made many companies more attractive to cash-rich predators.

Corporate finance is therefore a big and, though volatile, almost certainly a growing business. Management and underwriting of acquisitions and new issues are not of course the only sources of income for investment banks. Others are assisting companies with capital restructuring, provision of finance for the rapidly growing numbers of management buy-outs, and the devising and marketing of instruments such as swaps and options for the management of risk from interest and currency fluctuations.

The Scope of Corporate Finance

The term corporate finance encompasses a wide range of activities but we can distinguish two broad categories of financial decisions to be made by companies:

(a) *Investment or capital budgeting.* These decisions are concerned with the size and distribution of a company's investment in income-earning assets — fixed assets, such as property, machinery, plant and equipment; and various financial and intangible assets, such as securities, brand names, patents and technology. The overall goal of investment is usually assumed to be the maximisation of after-tax cash flows and therefore of the value of the company to its shareholders.

(b) *Provision of finance for investment.* A company raises finance essentially by selling financial assets or claims on itself — shares, bonds, bills and other securities, loans, leasing contracts, and so on. Profit maximisation is again presumed to be the aim, this time by minimising the cost of finance.

The corporate finance business of the banks and other financial institutions tends to be geared naturally, though not exclusively, to the second type of activity. Even the smallest firms normally need some element of external finance such as a bank loan or mortgage. As companies grow, whether organically or by takeovers, their demand for external capital is likely to increase disproportionately. In providing finance, banks and other lenders obviously become involved in satisfying themselves about the soundness of a company's investment plans but it is the company itself which is ultimately best placed to decide how it will use its capital resources. Lenders can and do influence investment policies but their primary role is to help the company raise finance at the lowest cost, in the most appropriate forms and with minimum risk.

This opening chapter concentrates therefore on the corporate demand for external finance and for related services, such as new issue management and the marketing of the company's shares. Also, the focus is on the company's long-term capital needs rather than on its demand for short-term finance which is introduced in Chapter 2. In turn, corporate banking is almost, by definition, mainly concerned with the needs of the larger company; in Britain the term 'corporation' tends to exclude small companies and to embrace only those with publicly-quoted equity and with a capital employed running into at least tens of millions of pounds but more usually into hundreds of millions and even billions of pounds. To get a better understanding of the demand for capital we first take a look at the nature of the corporation itself and the factors that lead to the development of large-scale business.

The Growth of the Corporation

Big corporations are found in most industries and their development has a wide range of explanations. Some of the biggest corporates are in the financial sector — the clearing banks, the largest building societies and insurance companies. Among industrial and commercial companies operating in the UK, the top ten ranked by *The Times* in terms of capital employed in 1987/88 included two nationalised industries — the Electricity Council and British Coal; the privatised British Telecom and British Gas; two oil companies (BP and 'Shell' Transport & Trading); ICI; the tobacco giant BAT (now diversified into insurance); and the conglomerate Hanson. In terms of turnover the rankings change somewhat but elsewhere in the top 20 (see Table 1.2) we find Unilever (food products, detergents, etc.); Grand Metropolitan and Allied Lyons (brewing, pubs, hotels); General Electric Company; Dalgety in food and commodities; and wholesalers and retailers, Dee Corporation, Sainsbury's and Marks and Spencer.

Table 1.2
Top 20 UK industrial companies
by turnover 1987–88 (£bn)

Rank	Company	Business	Turnover	Capital employed
1	British Petroleum	Oil, chemicals, etc.	34.9	18.5
2	'Shell' Transport & Trading	Oil, chemicals, etc.	23.9	14.6
3	BAT Industries	Tobacco, insurance, etc.	11.3	6.4
4	ICI	Chemicals, oil etc.	11.1	6.2
5	Electricity Council	Electricity supply	11.1	38.8
6	British Telecom	Telecom services	10.2	12.1
7	British Gas	Gas supply	7.6	7.4
8	Hanson	Industrial conglomerate	6.7	4.9
9	Shell UK	Oil, chemicals, etc.	6.7	3.7
10	Grand Metropolitan	Hotels, brewing, milk, etc.	5.7	3.4
11	Unilever	Detergents, food products, etc.	5.4	2.6
12	Esso UK	Oil,chemicals, etc.	5.4	3.7
13	GEC	Electrical engineers	5.2	3.8
14	Ford Motor (UK)	Vehicle makers	5.2	2.4
15	Dalgety	Food products, commodities	5.0	0.7
16	Dee Corporation	Wholesale, retail distribution	4.8	0.9
17	J. Sainsbury	Food, retailing	4.8	1.4
18	Marks & Spencer	Retail stores	4.6	2.4
19	British Coal	Coalmining	4.5	4.4
20	Allied Lyons	Brewing, drink, hotels, etc.	4.2	3.2

Source: The Times 1000 (1989 edition)

Economies of scale

Some large corporates are what economists describe as *natural monopolies*. These are found in industries with extensive economies of large-scale production and distribution; as corporates grow in size they are able to take advantage of various sources of increased productivity of labour and capital. Operating with a bigger capacity gives scope for division and specialisation of labour and for economical use of expensive capital equipment which can often be substituted for labour. Most producers, particularly those in high-volume processing industries such as food, drink, oil and chemicals, can gain important unit-cost reductions from increased plant capacity — a factory, warehouse or oil refinery with double the capacity of another usually costs substantially less than twice as much to build. The same principle of 'dimensional economies' applies to transport operations and helps to explain the development of super-tankers, juggernauts and jumbo jets.

Natural monopolies emerge when the market is not big enough to support more than one firm operating at or below the optimum scale where unit costs are at their minimum. The first firm to expand lowers its costs and is able to drive out competitors by undercutting their prices. Economies of scale explain the development of monopolistic corporations in electricity and gas distribution and in telecommunications; the capital cost of setting up the supply network is very high but once established the operating cost is low. The cost of duplicating the monopoly's distribution system is an almost insuperable barrier to new competitors which will only be profitable if they are granted access to the network. Scale economies are a major factor too in 'oligopolies' — industries dominated by just a few large organisations, such as banking, oil, chemicals, detergents, tobacco, steel and vehicles. This time the market can accommodate more than one but no more than two, three or a handful of main suppliers. Small companies survive only by specialising in production for niche markets.

Scale economies act as a barrier to the entry of new competitors. Once established, monopolies like British Telecom and British Gas have captive markets and, unless regulated by the government, can push up prices to maximise profits without fear of attracting new entrants. Oligopolists such as the oil companies are less secure but have an incentive to form price-fixing and market-sharing cartels while erecting artificial barriers against potential rivals. For example, the incumbents may deliberately invest in surplus capacity which they can use to swamp the market and cut prices to unprofitable levels for new entrants. Or they may, like the big brewers, buy up or 'tie' retailers and other sales outlets so that newcomers will be forced to set up their own distribution networks.

Not all large corporates are based on scale economies in a single product or range of connected products. Many of them, such as Hanson and BTR, are 'conglomerates' producing a wide range of goods and services sold in apparently unrelated markets. We return to conglomerates below, but a general point is that economies can arise as the organisation itself grows, independently of the scale of output in particular products. For example, if two companies merge, the new larger one may be able to cut overheads by offering common central services in administration, finance and accounting, transport, sales and marketing. Many of the costs are fixed and can be spread more thinly over the larger combined turnover. Also, the separate constituents may not have been able to justify employing their own specialist staff in, say, marketing or finance and may have bought in such services on the open market. Beyond a certain size it may pay the enterprise to integrate these activities. Some large corporations, for example, have established their own banking and finance divisions or subsidiaries to handle takeovers, new capital issues and treasury operations to avoid costs such as underwriting and broking commissions.

Integration

Integration is an important part of the growth process in most corporations whether it takes place by organic expansion or through mergers and acquisitions. Companies can be expected to integrate the market for goods or services once the costs of in-house production are lower than purchasing them from outside. Larger corporates are able to exploit scale economies in activities like finance and transport and thus achieve savings from internalisation. But both buying and selling in the external market may be more costly for other reasons, in particular because the market is 'imperfect'. For instance, the markets in which a company buys its raw materials may be dominated by a monopoly or producers' cartel charging prices above competitive levels. The company may therefore be able to source itself more cheaply by buying up one or more materials suppliers. It might also gain a competitive advantage from more secure suppliers. Similarly, companies will attempt to increase and safeguard their market share by taking over or tying buyers, retailers and other distributors of their products. Examples are the brewers and oil companies, while the acquisition of independent bakers by the big flour millers, Ranks Hovis McDougall (RHM) and Associated British Foods, can be seen as an attempt to secure their share of a stagnating market for bread.

Vertical integration

Imperfectly competitive markets provide a major incentive for companies to grow through vertical integration where firms expand by moving into earlier stages of production (backward integration) or into later stages (forward integration). Many multinational corporations (companies controlling production and distribution subsidiaries in two or more countries) developed historically by vertical integration across national frontiers. The oil majors are largely integrated both backwards from refining into crude oil production and transport, and forwards into manufacture of oil-based derivatives such as chemicals and fertilisers and into the distribution and marketing of their products.

Another reason for integration is that external markets cannot always be effectively organised. The market for 'knowledge' is a case in point. The development of many corporations has been founded on their monopoly of knowledge assets (inventions, discoveries and superior technology) produced by their own investment in research and development (R. & D.) or purchased from outside. Knowledge assets can often be patented, and to exploit them the corporation has the choice of selling a licence to other firms or of producing the patented products itself. Probably most firms opt for the second by investing directly in their own production facilities and thus integrating the market for the knowledge assets. This is because licensing is unlikely to achieve in royalties what the patent-owning firm regards as the full market value of its asset. Prospective licensees, for example, lack information to assess the market potential of the product and will tend therefore to undervalue a licence to produce it. More important though is that the patent owner will fear loss of its monopoly advantage to competitors through infringement of the licence agreement. Either way, the knowledge asset is often perceived to be more profitably and securely exploited by direct production and marketing by the patent-holding corporation itself.

Moreover, knowledge assets are not always patentable. A company producing computer systems, for example, may have a competitive advantage from the knowledge and experience of its R. & D. team and its design and installation staff. Its knowledge assets cannot be embodied in specific products and cannot therefore be sold separately; it can only exploit its advantage by producing and marketing its products directly. The same may apply to other intangible assets such as brand names. Corporations may wish to protect the reputation of their brands by controlling production and marketing themselves rather than licensing outside firms. Coca Cola, for example, sometimes prefers to establish subsidiaries overseas which produce under licence from the parent company. Franchising plays a similar role in allowing corporations to exploit their particular expertise and goodwill in areas such as retailing and services while maintaining close quality control over the franchisees.

Horizontal integration

The drive to integrate activities rather than engage in market transactions helps mainly to explain growth through vertical expansion. But corporations also grow through horizontal integration and conglomerate diversification. In the first case, companies grow with increased output and sales of products similar to or closely related in production or demand to existing products. Growth may be organic as a company invests in new capacity to meet growing demand or to establish new but related product lines and brands. An oil refiner might expand into chemical production to make use of its by-products, a brewer into lager and spirits, or a building society into banking and other financial services. Horizontal growth can alternatively be achieved by merging with or acquiring other firms with overlapping products.

The primary incentive for horizontal expansion is increased profits. Economies of scale, as we have seen, are an obvious possible source of cost reductions, particularly in industries with high-volume production like oil, chemicals, food and drink. Horizontal growth is also likely to mean greater market share and reduction of competition, allowing the firm to raise prices. This increase in market power is of course the major reason for the interest of governments in horizontal mergers; in the UK a proposed takeover may be referred to the Monopolies and Mergers Commission if it results in the new enlarged firm having more than 25% of the market for its products. A firm taking over another may also hope to increase the profitability of the acquired company by imposing better management or more advanced technology, or by applying superior marketing skills and organisation.

In industries with declining markets or facing more intense competition from overseas, horizontal mergers may be defensive rather than expansionist. Mergers in the British motor vehicle, textiles and shipbuilding industries both before and after the Second World War were often motivated by the need to eliminate loss makers and to establish larger, more efficient units able to compete with foreign producers, often in developing countries.

Conglomerate diversification

Conglomerates producing a range of largely unrelated products tend to arise through acquisitions rather than internal growth. Hanson plc has grown into a group with a capitalisation of around £5 billion (from only £200 million ten years ago) through a steady stream of takeovers of companies in the UK and USA engaged in a bewildering range of activities — cigarettes (Imperial Tobacco acquired for £2.5 billion in

1986), department stores (Allders), batteries (Ever Ready), bricks (London Brick), electrical and mechanical engineering, food products (including HP baked beans), typewriters (Smith Corona in the USA), building products, office furniture, chemicals and plastics. BTR, once primarily engaged in tyre manufacture (it was formerly called British Tyre and Rubber), has similarly grown largely by acquisition into a huge international holding company with more than 300 operating units. Its activities now include building and building materials, electrical and electronic products, automotive components, paper, sports goods (Dunlop and Slazenger), and Pretty Polly tights. The growth of conglomerates like Hanson and BTR can be viewed as a kind of portfolio investment in which the acquiring corporation maximises its returns through the imposition of superior management and financial discipline on its subsidiaries.

The dividing line between conglomerate diversification on the one hand and vertical and horizontal expansion on the other is not always clear. We may find that a company producing a range of apparently unrelated products is in fact marketing them through the same outlets (beer and peanuts) or is employing overlapping production facilities or technology (oil refining and fertilisers). Similarly, corporates with a seasonal demand for their products may move into other lines to achieve fuller plant utilisation (Wall's ice cream, pork pies and sausages).

However, corporations like Hanson and BTR come close to being pure conglomerates. The benefits of conglomerate growth are usually less obvious than those of vertical or horizontal integration but a number of possible incentives to diversification have been suggested. One is that diversification is a means of spreading commercial risks on the 'not-all-your-eggs-in-one-basket' principle. The wider the product range the greater the chance that a fall in demand for one product will be offset by growth in the sales of one or more of the others. Plausibly, this incentive to diversify is strongest when the market for a firm's staple product is already in decline. Stagnating cigarette sales, for instance, may well have led to the former Imperial Tobacco group's entry into brewing, food and snack products and restaurants as well as to diversification by BAT (British American Tobacco) into insurance and financial services (extended in August 1988 with the US$5.2 billion takeover of the Farmers insurance group in the USA).

Product diversification is likely to reduce the variability of a company's total earnings and rates of return, especially of course when there is a negative correlation between the profit rates on the different products — increased earnings on one are matched by a fall in another. But this is of no particular benefit to shareholders since they can achieve more stable returns easily through a diversified portfolio of investments in different companies. In any case, we are interested in why a corporation like Hanson should deliberately develop as a multi-product conglomerate. It is unlikely that reduced variability in returns on its own would provide sufficient incentive for a systematic programme of acquisitions of companies operating in diverse fields. One suggestion is that the more stable earnings achieved by diversification allow a corporation to increase its gearing — the proportion of its capital raised in debt (bonds, preference shares and debentures) relative to equity. There should be less chance of a diversified company making losses and therefore of default on its debt. Investors may thus be willing to lend more and on more favourable terms to a conglomerate than to a single-product firm with less stable earnings.

Ability to increase gearing may have other advantages. Interest on debt is tax-deductible but a more important benefit may arise in periods of unanticipated inflation. In the early and mid-1970s, for example, nominal interest rates failed to keep pace with rapidly accelerating inflation (reaching over 25% p.a.) as lenders consistently underestimated the extent of future price rises. The result was the emergence of substantial negative real interest rates (nominal rates adjusted for inflation). Some commentators have argued for a causal relationship between the negative real cost of corporate borrowing and the surge in debt-financed conglomerate acquisitions in the early 1970s, particularly in 1972 and, to a lesser extent, in 1973. The connection though is questionable for the merger boom evaporated in the mid-1970s when negative real interest rates rose still higher.

Ownership and control
Conglomerate expansion in any case has a more convincing and simpler explanation. It has long been noted that in large corporations there is likely to be a 'divorce between ownership and control' (a classic phrase coined by American economists Berle and Means in 1932). While shareholders own the assets of the company, the diffusion of shares among large numbers of relatively small equity holders means that they typically have little effective control over the use of their assets. Control is in theory exercised by electing the directors but small shareholders generally have little incentive to participate actively in voting and boards of directors tend to become self-perpetuating. In

turn, the company's operations are controlled largely by the executive directors and the senior managers whom they appoint. Unless managers have very large shareholdings themselves (directly or indirectly through share options) their own interests are promoted not by maximising profits for the owners of the firm but by increasing the assets which the managers control. This is because their own rewards, status, perks and promotion prospects are positively related to the absolute size and rate of growth of such variables as turnover, number of employees and the physical assets of the company. On this view, the large corporation is the private instrument of the managers of other people's wealth.

The separation of ownership from control may increase the numbers of conglomerate mergers in two potentially powerful ways. First, the rewards and security of employment of managers (including directors) are related to their company's continued existence and performance. Their interest is not so much in maximising profits but in maintaining a steady rate of profit acceptable to the shareholders. They have a strong incentive therefore to diversify the company's activities to reduce the variability of returns and the risk of insolvency. The drive to diversify, for example by taking over under-performing firms, may conflict with the shareholders' interests in profit maximisation, but shareholders, as we have seen, may be largely powerless to monitor managerial decisions. The theoretical connection between managerial control and a propensity to make conglomerate acquisitions has been given strong empirical support in a study of takeovers in the USA in the 1960s (Amihud and Lev, *Bell Journal of Economics*, 1981). They find a significant positive correlation between conglomerate takeovers and the diffusion of share ownership in the acquiring companies. Those in which no single shareholder had more than 10% of the equity (and probably therefore manager-controlled) were much more likely to engage in conglomerate acquisitions.

The Market for Corporate Control

If manager-controlled companies are more likely to be conglomerate predators, another line of reasoning is that those which underperform financially because the managers pursue their own interests will ultimately fall victim to takeover themselves. On this view, put forward amongst others by another American economist, Henry Manne, in 1965, the stock market functions as a market for corporate control. Manne argues that consistently poor management of a company will show up in a low price for its shares relative to those of companies in the same sector or to the market as a whole. To quote Manne: 'The lower the share price, relative to what it could be with a more efficient management, the more attractive the takeover becomes to those who believe that they can manage the company more efficiently. And the potential return from the successful takeover and revitalisation of a poorly-run company can be enormous.'

Manne's insight implies that the market for a company's shares affords unique protection to its non-controlling shareholders against inefficient management in the sense that managers, by running a company in their own interests, fail to achieve the best possible returns for the shareholders. Because the incumbent managers and directors stand to lose their jobs and incomes from a takeover, the threat of a 'hostile bid' as the share price falls may induce them to improve profit performance. If they do not, or if they act too late, the takeover will become a reality. This explanation of conglomerate (and other) acquisitions certainly accords well with the record of takeover exponents like Hanson and BTR. Both have concentrated on acquiring problem companies (such as Imperial Group by Hanson and Dunlop by BTR) whose profit performance has often been dramatically improved by introducing sound management and financial control and by disposing of the less viable or compatible parts of the acquired companies, usually for cash which helps to pay for the next takeover. It would be no surprise if Lord Hanson and BTR Chairman Sir Owen Green had been directly inspired by Henry Manne's 1965 observation that 'taking over control of badly run corporations is one of the most important "get-rich-quick" opportunities in our economy today'.

Management buy-outs and divestment
The boom in both management buy-outs (MBOs) and management buy-ins of recent years may have a similar explanation. In the case of buy-outs the existing managers themselves are clearly best placed to recognise under-performance of a subsidiary or division in a larger group. By acquiring control themselves, at a price often well below the valuation justified by potential profits, they can forestall outside predators and safeguard their own employment. But if poor performance is the result of weakness in the incumbent management itself, there is an incentive for a buy-in, usually by acquisition followed by replacement of the whole or part of the management team.

The rapid growth of MBOs from virtually zero since the late 1970s (see Table 1.3) is an indicator of the increasing importance of divestment whereby corporations sell off subsidiaries which they decide are no longer compatible with the operation of the group as a whole. There are various reasons for divestment. Technological change, for example, may erode the benefits from economies of scale. Products which previously shared a similar technology and plant might now be more efficiently produced by separate companies. Many divestments follow conglomerate acquisitions. Hanson, for instance, sold off much of the Imperial Group which it acquired in 1986. In doing so, it brought back about two-thirds of the £2.5 billion cost of the takeover and retained subsidiaries accounting for more than a half of the Group's profits.

Table 1.3
UK management buy-outs

Year	Number	Value (£m)	Average value (£m)
1983	233	364	1.6
1984	238	403	1.7
1985	261	1,141	4.4
1986	313	1,188	3.8
1987	345	3,218	9.3
1988	356	3,755	10.5

Source: CMBOR, an Independent Research Centre founded by Spicer & Oppenheim and Barclays Development Capital Ltd at the University of Nottingham

In a divestment, the subsidiary's existing management frequently succeeds in buying it in competition with outside bidders. This is partly because of the management's insider knowledge of the true worth of the subsidiary's assets which is partly dependent on the existing management team remaining in control. If so, banks and other financial institutions have an incentive to provide finance for the MBO often with a large proportion in debt, giving rise to the phenomenon of leveraged buy-outs. Although this gives the new company a high gearing (debt/equity ratio — see Chapter 2), the strong profit performance typical of bought-out companies gives a high degree of confidence to lenders that the debt will easily be serviced and that the surplus profits will produce a possibly substantial increase in the value of the equity stake.

Short-termism

Corporate managers have not been slow to defend themselves against charges of managing in their own rather than the shareholders' interests. A frequent line of counter-attack, in fact, is to pass the blame for poor long-term financial performance on to the shareholders themselves. Institutional shareholders, in particular, are claimed to pay excessive attention to the short-term performance of companies in which they invest. There is pressure on managers, they say, to produce quick returns which leads them to neglect investment projects and research and development (R. & D.) with a long pay-back period. R. & D. spending especially reduces current earnings and the firm's share price and thus makes the firm more vulnerable to takeover. 'Short-termism' among the big institutional investors, such as pension funds, is therefore responsible for long-term financial under-performance.

However, there is little evidence to support the assertion. Various studies in fact seem to refute it. One finding in the UK, for example, is that a company's share price actually tends to rise after the announcement of increased capital spending. A study by the American Securities and Exchange Commission confirms that effect and finds no connection between the level of institutional shareholding and the R. & D. spending of corporations while firms with high R. & D. activity were no more susceptible to takeover than others.

On the other hand, it is certainly true that there are strong and perhaps growing forces towards a short-term perspective among institutional investors. Pension funds, for example, may put pressure on their managers to meet quarterly profit targets. Stockbrokers, interested in trading volumes, may encourage buying and selling of shares to boost turnover. The short-termism claim undoubtedly has some foundation although its importance is sometimes exaggerated. It is notable that the complaint tends to come loudest from managements of companies with a poor profit performance in both the short term and the long term!

Management structure

Low profitability may result not so much from mismanagement as from an inappropriate management structure as companies fail to adapt to growth and product diversification. Smaller ones tend almost naturally to adopt a functional management organisation in which managerial responsibilities are allocated according to function — finance, production, R. & D., marketing and personnel. Since the functional heads are normally accountable to the Chief Executive and may have a place on the board of directors, control of the company's operations and decision-taking tend to be highly centralised. In a single-product company or one with a closely-related range of products a functional management structure may be highly effective. Specialisation by managers may improve productivity and the various functions can be co-ordinated from the top.

A pure functional organisation, however, is likely to break down once a company grows with product diversification. Development of new products in particular requires co-ordination of R. & D., production and marketing as well as decisions from the board about the allocation of financial resources among competing projects. If the interests of one set of functional managers, say, in production, become dominant the firm may fail to develop its products in response to market and competitive pressures. The failure of the British Leyland (now Rover) vehicle group in the 1960s has sometimes been attributed to its control by engineers with resulting neglect of marketing needs, cost and quality control and industrial relations.

An alternative is product organisation with managers primarily responsible for production and marketing of particular products or groups of products. In multi-product companies this type of structure is quite common. Fisons, for instance, has three product divisions — pharmaceuticals, horticulture and scientific equipment — each with a Chairman on the board of directors. Then again, large corporations, especially those with international operations, may organise themselves geographically with separate divisions and subsidiaries covering regions, countries or groups of countries. Most companies have mixed or matrix structures with lines of responsibility running through products, functions and regional divisions. But whatever the dominant management structure, all corporations have to strike a balance somewhere between centralised and decentralised decision-taking. Excessive centralisation, with all significant decisions on finance, investment, product development, pricing and so on having to be referred to headquarters, may lead to demotivation of product or area and regional managers. The centre itself will become overstretched and bureaucratic. Slow decision-taking may lead to lost profit opportunities when competitors act more quickly.

To go to the extreme of decentralisation and devolution of decisions to subsidiaries and divisions has other dangers analogous to those arising when shareholders have no effective control of their assets. But some corporations successfully take decentralisation to a high degree. BTR has more than 300 operating companies each with autonomy, not just in day-to-day management but also in strategic decisions on product development and marketing. The only constraint laid down by the centre (headquarters has just over 20 staff!) is through three regional offices in the form of profit and financial targets; investment projects are normally authorised only if their payback period is less than five years. BTR's financial performance has certainly not suffered from decentralisation — its profits have increased by more than seven times since 1982 to £819 million in 1988. A major factor in its success has almost certainly been the incentives it gives to managers through its share option scheme.

Multinational Corporations

Since the Second World War there has been a mushroom growth of multinational corporations producing and marketing goods and services in two or more countries. Multinationals are dealt with in depth in Chapter 3 and it suffices to point out here that their development has broadly the same explanations as we have looked at for corporate growth in general. Companies usually expand initially at home on the basis of some specific advantage — scale economies, knowledge assets, brand names, goodwill, and so on. Most large corporations, as their home markets become saturated, sooner or later turn overseas to satisfy their growth aspirations. Initially, they are likely to exploit foreign markets by exporting but, in many cases, the corporation finds it more profitable and strategically advantageous at the outset to locate production abroad with direct control of marketing of its products. With some products, transport costs rule out exports but, more important, the foreign country may erect barriers to the company's exports in the form of tariffs and other controls to protect local producers against imports. In recent years, for example, the growth of protectionism and strength of the yen have led to a surge of Japanese investment in Europe and the USA. Denied access to the markets for their exports, Japanese corporations wanting to maintain their sales of vehicles, electronic goods and so on have been forced to set up direct production inside the trade barriers.

While multinationals often establish foreign producing and distribution subsidiaries from scratch (Nissan in Britain) they increasingly expand abroad by takeover of existing companies (Nestlé's acquisition of Rowntree and BAT's of Farmers). The growth in numbers of cross-border mergers is no doubt linked to the liberalisation and globalisation of capital markets. A UK corporation like Hanson now has little if any more problem in raising finance for an American takeover than for one at home. In Europe the 'single market' in 1992 will mean the abolition of most remaining restrictions on capital movements between EC countries, while anticipation of the freer market for both goods and services is already bringing a stream of proposed and actual cross-border mergers. The international dimension of corporate finance thus looks set to grow still further in importance.

Summary

The corporate finance market has boomed in recent years with record levels of acquisitions and capital issues. The core source of demand for long-term finance is the growth of the corporate itself either through internal investment or, more frequently, by acquisitions. Some big corporations are natural monopolies based on economies of scale. Others have grown through their possession of 'firm-specific' advantages, such as their knowledge assets, brand names and goodwill, and there are often incentives to integrate the markets for these assets. Growth through diversification to form conglomerates has various explanations. A cogent one is that managers have no effective control by shareholders and are relatively free therefore to pursue their own goals of growth and diversification in order to secure their own employment and boost their rewards. However, an efficient stock exchange acts as a market for corporate control. Corporate growth has become increasingly international as the globalisation and liberalisation of financial markets facilitate cross-border mergers and takeovers.

CHAPTER 2

Corporate Financial Behaviour

Len Ross

Introduction

The central thesis of the last chapter is that the primary source of demand for long-term corporate finance is the growth of organisations, whether through internal, organic expansion or by mergers and acquisitions. Growth by any means obviously implies an increase in the corporate's capital to finance its investment in new assets. In this chapter our main concern is with how corporations satisfy their need for finance and with both the internal and environmental factors, such as inflation and tax, which influence the size and pattern of demand for capital.

Internal and External Finance

A major consideration for the financial manager is the division of the company's financing between internally-generated funds and external sources. Internal finance comes from the undistributed income of the corporation and is essentially equivalent therefore to a compulsory raising of fresh equity capital by issues of shares. The retention of £10 million of profits is no different in principle from paying out the money in dividends and keeping the company's capital intact by selling £10 million of shares. But this is not to say that the existing shareholders see it like that. Many might prefer dividends to the notionally equivalent increase in the value of their shares, some of which they would have to sell to obtain the cash.

If retained profits are equivalent to raising capital by issuing shares, then the corporate should be indifferent between internal and external finance. The opportunity cost of both is the minimum expected return on capital required by shareholders to induce them to buy and to hold the company's equity. This is the shareholders' desired rate of return. If equity investors require a minimum expected return of, say, 16% (including a risk premium, above the return on alternative riskless investments, as a reward for the uncertainty about the corporate's actual profits), then the company will have to fix the price of any new shares accordingly. Similarly, any retained earnings must promise at least the same rate of return to avoid a drop in the corporate's share price and market value as a result of equity sales by existing shareholders.

However, there are transactions costs in issuing shares (underwriters' and issue managers' fees, etc.) which can largely be avoided by increasing share capital through profit retentions. Corporate directors can therefore validly justify a high rate of profit retention and correspondingly low dividend payouts. Nevertheless, some commentators (including the distinguished American economist, William J. Baumol) suggest less transparent motives for restricting dividends. They argue that the widespread preference for the use of internal funds to finance investment projects and acquisitions is explained by the desire of managers and directors to avoid the more stringent scrutiny of shareholders in making new issues. Managers particularly like to finance their more speculative spending with retained profits. But this view seems ultimately fallacious. If projects funded internally fail to earn adequate returns, then, as we have seen, the corporate's share price will fall. In short, ignoring transactions costs, the opportunity cost of internal and external finance is the same.

Table 2.1
Sources of funds of UK industrial and commercial companies (£bn)

Year	Total income	Retained income £bn	% of total	External funds	Total funds	As % of total funds Internal	External
1983	55.8	25.0	45	7.6	32.6	77	23
1984	65.2	28.7	44	6.8	35.5	81	19
1985	73.8	31.4	43	13.1	44.5	71	29
1986	68.7	28.5	41	27.1	50.2	57	43
1987	85.3	38.2	45	36.5	74.7	51	49
1988	96.3	39.8	41	46.6	86.4	46	54

Source: Financial Statistics

Whatever the explanation, we can see from Table 2.1 that British industrial companies do have a heavy, though recently diminishing, dependence on internal funds. Between 1983 and 1988 the proportion of corporate income retained was relatively stable at between 41 and 45%. The rise in total income thus increased new internal funds in almost the same proportion, by 60% from £25 billion in 1983 to nearly

£40 billion in 1988. But external financing soared by over 500% from under £8 billion to £47 billion to give an increase in the total inflow of funds to corporations of 165% to £86 billion. As a result, there was a sharp drop in relative (not absolute) reliance on internal financing. From a peak of 81% in 1984 the share of profit retentions in total funds fell to 57% in 1986 and to only 46% in 1988. Part of the explanation is the exceptional increase in the total demand for capital to finance the boom in physical investment and acquisitions. The demand for funds in 1988 was £36 billion higher than in 1986 and, though sharply increased profits with the same retention ratio brought in an extra £11 billion, the remaining £25 billion had to be raised from outside.

This suggests some constraints on the ability of companies to increase the retention ratio. For one thing, a substantial part of gross profits is already earmarked for items such as corporation tax and payment of debt interest. In 1988 these amounted to £36 billion leaving £60 billion or 62% of gross income available for distribution to ordinary shareholders. Corporate dividend policy is better evaluated by relating dividend payments to the profits available for distribution, as in Table 2.2.

Table 2.2
UK industrial and commercial companies —
dividends from income available for distribution (£bn)

Year	Gross income	Available for distribution	Dividends	Dividends as % of available income
1983	55.8	29.8	4.8	*16.1*
1984	65.2	36.3	5.0	*13.8*
1985	73.8	39.5	7.0	*17.7*
1986	68.7	40.0	9.0	*22.5*
1987	85.3	53.9	11.9	*22.1*
1988	96.3	60.0	17.6	*29.3*

Source: Financial Statistics

Dividend policy, as our discussion predicts, hardly looks generous with only around one-sixth of available profits paid out in 1983/1985 though rising to over one-fifth in 1986 and 1987. Also there was a sharp rise to 29% in 1988. The increased dividend ratio in recent years is perhaps surprising in view of the steeply increased overall demand for finance. However, increased dividend payments at least partly reflect the greater number of shares on issue while the downturn in interest rates in 1987 until the summer of 1988 lowered the cost of new debt relative to equity. With outside funds readily and relatively cheaply available, corporate managers no doubt felt they could reward shareholders with bigger dividends, possibly to divert attention from some of their more extravagant takeover spending. American studies suggest that directors' dividend policies are dictated by a perceived need to be 'fair' to shareholders. While that probably really means that they restrict dividends to the minimum which they think will keep the shareholders happy, it is nevertheless true that different classes of shareholders vary in their preferences for dividends as against the capital growth implied by higher retentions. A major factor is the tax treatment of dividend income and capital gains.

Thus, tax-exempt shareholders, such as pension and life assurance funds (and in the UK now, private investors in Personal Equity Plans (PEPs)), should in theory be largely indifferent whether they receive their returns from cash dividends or from the increased capital value of their shares. In practice, though, fund managers may prefer the cash inflows from dividends which they are then free to reinvest in the company or place elsewhere. At times of high interest rates and depressed equity values, dividend receipts directly add to the fund's liquidity and effectively reduce shareholdings without having to record realised capital losses. In any case, fund managers may well feel that they can invest the dividend income more effectively than the company.

For non-exempt private investors, however, the differential tax treatment of dividend income and capital gains should give a preference for profit retention. In the UK the complete exemption from tax on 'small' capital gains (since the 1988 Budget, up to £5,000 of gains accruing since 1982) clearly tips the balance against dividends for smaller private investors. Before 1988 this also applied to bigger shareholders because capital gains were taxed at a lower rate than the higher marginal rates of income tax. The 1988 Budget, however, made capital gains taxable at the individual's marginal income tax rate so that only smaller private investors now receive a direct tax advantage from receiving their returns in higher share prices rather than cash dividends. But small investors account for only a tiny fraction of total equity holdings and even they are now encouraged to shift into tax-exempt PEPs.

From 1988, therefore, the tax system is largely neutral in the treatment of dividends and the implicit income from undistributed profits. The effect on companies' dividend policy, however, is likely to be slight since the big tax-exempt institutional investors are unaffected. Directors and their financial advisers will presumably continue to compromise between their own likely preference to maximise retained income and that of many shareholders for cash payouts.

Capital Structure

If internal financing from retained income is strictly equivalent to raising new share capital, the question arises as to why firms choose additional forms of financing. In particular, why do companies typically incur high levels of debt in the form of bonds, debentures and other loan stock and borrowing from banks and other financial institutions? The basic mix of equity and debt is the company's capital structure, usually described in terms of a gearing or (in America) leverage ratio which measures the amount of debt relative to equity in the firm's financing. The question of the optimum level of gearing has long been a central and controversial issue among scholars of corporate finance. The topic of gearing is also dealt with in Chapter 8. In this chapter we focus on the broad question of gearing and simplify by assuming for the most part that corporate debt consists mainly of fixed-interest bonds. However, debt can take a wide variety of forms, such as bank borrowing at variable interest rates, mortgage and other secured loans, Eurobonds with interest paid gross, and so on. The particular questions which arise from the use of particular types of debt are considered in later chapters.

For financial managers the gearing issue boils down (or should do) to choosing the capital structure which minimises the overall cost of financing the firm's assets. If debt is cheaper than equity (because lenders will accept lower returns than prospective shareholders) then gearing should be increased. This is consistent with (in fact, the same as) the prior goal of maximising the value of the firm on behalf of the shareholders. So long as the financial manager acquires finance at the lowest cost, the capital structure is irrelevant since the stream of income produced by the firm's assets cannot be affected by the choice of financing methods. So why should gearing be a contentious issue?

The conventional answer is that the level of gearing affects the financial risks to investors and therefore feeds back to alter the cost of capital to the company. This is particularly so for firms with variable and uncertain earnings and which have an inherently greater risk for investors. For example, if a company offers a guaranteed constant stream of income of, say, £20 million a year, investors should be indifferent whether they buy the company's debt or equity since market forces would equalise the yields on each, irrespective of the company's capital structure.

But if the company's profits are variable, then with the same expected earnings of £20 million a year, the level of gearing will alter the financial risk to different investors and therefore affect the relative required rates of return on debt and equity. Basically, the higher the gearing the greater will be the fluctuation in earnings per share for given changes in total earnings. This can be seen in a simple example (Figure 2.1). The company has total capital of £200 million. With all-equity capital — zero gearing — earnings per share (EPS) clearly change in direct proportion to the company's total earnings. But with 50% gearing — £200 million capital split equally between debt and equity — profits accrue to shareholders only after deduction of interest, assumed to be fixed at £10 million a year. Equity holders therefore receive no returns until total earnings reach £10 million, but get all earnings in excess of that. With only half as many shares, the EPS increases twice as fast with total earnings as in the zero gearing

Zero gearing — £200m capital; £200m shares

Earnings (£m)	Interest (£m)	Equity earnings (£m)	Earnings per share (p)
40	0	40	20
30	0	30	15
20	0	20	10
10	0	10	5
0	0	0	0

50% gearing — £100m debt at 10%; £100m equity — 100m shares

Earnings (£m)	Interest (£m)	Equity earnings (£m)	Earnings per share (p)
40	10	30	30
30	10	20	20
20	10	10	10
10	10	0	0
0	10	−10	−10

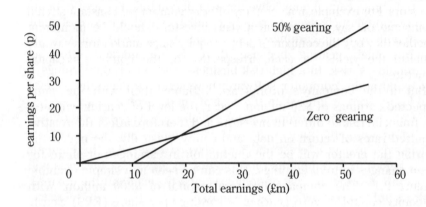

Figure 2.1 Effects of gearing

case. This can be seen in the graph in Figure 2.1. Up to £20 million total earnings, shareholders in the geared company are worse off than those in the ungeared one. At £20 million they do equally well, but as total earnings rise the gap in their favour grows wider and wider. At £40 million, for instance the EPS for the geared shareholders is 30p but only 20p for ungeared shareholders.

Ostensibly, equity holders benefit from gearing so long as the company's expected total earnings exceed £20 million. But note the meaning of 'expected' earnings. These should be interpreted as a probability weighted forecast of earnings. If there is a 100% guarantee of £20 million next year then that is the expected income with no risk of variation. However, expected earnings are also £20 million if there is a 50/50 probability that income will be either £40 million or zero. The point is that gearing adds to the uncertainty about future equity returns and therefore increases risk to shareholders. While expected returns may be the same, shareholders will now demand a premium to compensate for the risk that earnings turn out to be zero.

Gearing therefore increases the cost of equity capital since the risk premium raises the expected returns required by investors to induce them to buy the company's shares. The extra cost of equity capital will be greater the bigger is the existing variability of the company's income. This exposes the fallacy that, when debt is superficially cheaper than equity finance, companies can always gear up to the benefit of shareholders. Increased gearing, in fact, by increasing the cost of equity capital, may leave the overall combined cost of debt and equity capital unchanged. Certainly, companies with a record of stable or steadily-growing earnings — say, a gas or electricity utility — can tolerate high gearing because there is no marked effect on shareholders' risk. In a high-risk business with uncertain earnings — oil exploration, computer software, new ventures generally — even modest gearing will drive up the cost of equity capital.

Moreover, gearing beyond a point will also force up the cost of debt. The risk for debt holders is that the company's earnings will be inadequate to pay interest and, in the worst case, that the company goes bankrupt and defaults on its debts. In a low-risk business with moderate gearing the risk of default is clearly small and the company will be able to borrow at close to market rates of interest. Increased gearing in a high-risk company may significantly raise the probability of default and, like the equity investor, potential lenders will demand higher yields to offset the greater risk.

The upshot is that companies have an optimum level of gearing which minimises the overall cost of capital. Gearing should be increased to the point where the marginal cost of debt — the cost of borrowing another pound — equals the marginal cost of equity finance. The optimum gearing will obviously vary from one company to another. Other things equal, it will be lower for a risky business than for one with a stable stream of income. For a very high-risk business the optimum may be zero (except for borrowing secured against safe assets). Also, the firm's optimum capital structure will be continually shifting with changes in its business. A company, for example, which diversifies may be perceived as less risky than before and be able to increase its gearing.

But the optimum gearing for all companies can be altered, perhaps quite radically, by changes in the external environment which affect the relative cost of debt and equity and of different types of borrowing — at fixed or variable interest rates, short-term or long-term and so on. Probably the most important external influences on capital structure are the taxation of corporate income, the general level of interest rates and equity prices, and the rate of inflation. How these interact to affect corporate capital structure is extremely complex. Thus, Table 2.3 indicates large fluctuations in corporate gearing in the 1980s but it is not always easy to identify the causes.

Table 2.3
Gearing of UK industrial
and commercial companies (year end)

	1980	1981	1982	1983	1984	1985	1986	1987	1988
Broad gearing [1] (%)	63.1	64.7	60.7	58.1	55.5	53.5	49.5	47.4	49.5
Long-term gearing[2] (%)	13.4	13.0	11.8	8.8	9.6	9.2	n/a	n/a	n/a

Notes:
1 Total non-equity finance as percentage of total liabilities.
2 Debentures, mortgages and long-term loans as per cent of total net assets.

Source: Financial Statistics; DTI analysis of large companies

Both sets of ratios in Table 2.3 are at best crude indicators of corporate gearing but are broadly consistent in showing the trend. The 'broad' gearing ratio, after a peak in 1981, shows a downturn in non-equity financing from 65% of total liabilities to under 50% in 1986 to 1988. A major explanation for the growing importance of equity finance is simply the relentless rise of share prices from 1982 onwards which pushed up the value of outstanding equity and induced a huge expansion of new issues from £2.3 billion in 1983 to nearly £15 billion in 1987. Thus, at the end of the third quarter of 1987 (not shown in the table), just before the equity crash in October, the broad gearing ratio dropped to 40% from almost 50% at the start of the year. But by the end of 1987 the share slump restored the debt ratio to nearly the level 12 months earlier; a year later, the gearing ratio had fully recovered to its end-1986 level.

The long-term gearing ratio, which expresses long-term debt only as a proportion of net assets, is less sensitive to changes in share values. The ratio is available only to the end of 1985 but again shows a declining trend in corporate gearing to only 9.2% from 13.4% in 1980.

Corporate taxation

Corporation tax on profits was raised to 52% in 1973 and was held there until 1983 since when it has been successively cut to its present 35%. Its major effect on corporate gearing comes from the deduction of debt interest from profits in calculating liability to tax. The higher the level of corporation tax the greater the attraction of debt relative to equity finance. Thus, in the example in Figure 2.1 the ungeared company with £20 million income before 1983 would have paid tax of 52% or £10.4 million on all its earnings. The geared company would have been liable for tax only on £10 million of profits after debt interest so that its tax bill was halved to £5.2 million. The advantage was reduced because the debt holder then had to pay tax of, say, 30% on the interest receipts but there is still a large reduction of £2.2 million in the total tax bill on income of the geared company. (Note that the company is deemed to have paid the equity holder's basic rate tax on dividends.)

Debt finance was in principle much cheaper than equity capital before 1983. Since then though the cut in the corporation tax rate has removed much of the advantage. Taking the same example at 1988 tax rates the total corporate and personal tax paid for the ungeared company is £7 million and for the geared company £6 million. Another point is that the reduction in the corporation tax rate has been accompanied by cuts in first-year capital allowances and other changes which have boosted the taxable profits of most firms. Many companies before the changes regularly had no tax liability at all because they were able to claim allowances larger than their profits. For those companies which now have taxable profits there will be a net tax advantage from incurring debt. For the rest, the incentive to gear up has substantially diminished and this could have played a part in the observed relative reduction in gearing in the 1980s.

Inflation and interest rates
Most long-term debt in the UK is issued at fixed nominal interest rates. But, of course, the nominal interest rate is a compound of the real rate of interest (the real return demanded by lenders) and the expected rate of inflation over the period of the loan. If lenders want 5% a year in real terms and expect inflation of 10% they will require a nominal or 'money' interest rate of 15%. Changes in actual inflation inevitably feed back into expectations of future inflation. Normally, a rise in inflation will be followed by an increase in nominal interest rates. Existing fixed-interest borrowers will benefit as higher inflation erodes the real value of their debt. New borrowers, however, will face greater cash outflows in paying interest on their debt even though there may have been no increase in real interest rates. Higher inflation and nominal interest rates therefore are likely to discourage new issues of bonds and debentures and ultimately to reduce long-term gearing.

Also, if inflation is both high and volatile, as it was from 1973 until 1983, future inflation becomes difficult to predict and interest rates highly uncertain. There is increased risk in both borrowing and lending at fixed-interest rates with a likely shift therefore towards short-term, variable interest rate borrowing. In fact, UK company issues of fixed-interest securities — debentures, preference shares and bonds — virtually dried up after 1973 and did not pick up again until the early 1980s. The fall in inflation and nominal interest rates resulted in a strong upturn in 1986 and 1987. Gearing failed to rise, however, because of the boom in share prices and new equity issues.

Table 2.4
UK industrial and commercial companies —
selected sources of external funds (£bn)

Year	Equity issues	Fixed-interest borrowing			
		Debentures and preference shares	Capital issues overseas	Bank borrowing	Other loans
1983	1.9	0.6	—	1.6	0.8
1984	1.1	0.2	0.3	7.3	0.6
1985	3.4	0.8	0.8	7.7	0.9
1986	5.4	0.5	1.5	9.4	1.5
1987	13.2	0.5	4.0	13.0	2.8
1988	4.6	1.2	3.1	29.6	3.8

Source: Financial Statistics

The sources of new external funding shown in Table 2.4 give some indication of the way corporations have reacted to changes in the environment in order to adjust their capital structure. The surge in equity financing in 1987 is particularly prominent with £13.2 billion of new share issues in stark contrast with the low of only £1.1 billion in 1984. The rise in equity financing is partly explained by the large privatisation sales of shares by the UK government, but the surge in 1987 is also related to the share price boom which lowered the cost of equity capital. The result, as we have seen, was a sharp drop in gearing up to the equity crash of October 1987, which, not surprisingly, produced a slump in new share issues to £4.6 billion in 1988, little more than one-third of the 1987 total.

Fixed-interest capital issues had started to recover in 1980 and picked up rapidly from £1.6 billion in 1985 to reach £4.5 billion in 1987 and £4.3 billion in 1988. Most of the growth was in overseas issues, mainly Eurobonds, but the increase in long-term, fixed-interest borrowing was almost certainly associated with the world decline in inflation and nominal interest rates. However, variable-rate borrowing, principally from the banks, remained the most important source of finance, exceeding equity issues, even in 1987. Thus, despite the fall in inflation in 1986/87 uncertainty remained about its future course while reliance on monetary policy in the UK to manage aggregate demand and the exchange rate led to increased volatility of interest rates. In 1988 the slump in new equity issues and low interest rates until the summer combined to boost bank borrowing to nearly £30 billion, more than double the 1987 figure.

Financing of acquisitions
Another influence on corporate capital structure is the level of spending on acquisitions and the methods used to finance them. In a takeover, the assets and liabilities of the acquired firm are absorbed into the buying firm. This can affect the gearing of the combined company. The purchase of shares in the selling firm can be made for cash, equity or debt. Use of cash will tend to increase gearing since it reduces the buying company's liquid assets and the market value of its shares. Table 2.5 shows how acquisitions have been financed since 1979.

Table 2.5
UK industrial and commercial companies —
financing of takeovers 1979–88

Year	Takeover spending (£bn)	Cash	Equity	Fixed interest debt
1979	1.7	56	31	13
1980	1.5	52	45	3
1981	1.1	68	30	3
1982	2.2	58	32	10
1983	2.3	44	54	2
1984	5.5	54	34	13
1985	7.1	40	52	7
1986	14.9	15	64	21
1987	15.4	32	62	6
1988	22.1	70	22	8
1987(Q4)*	3.3	50	46	4
1988(Q1)**	6.1	71	24	5

* Q4 = fourth quarter; ** Q1 = first quarter

Source: Financial Statistics

The importance of the different methods of financing takeovers has fluctuated enormously. Overall, use of cash has been predominant but dropped sharply in the takeover boom from 1985 to 1987. Cash slumped to a mere 15% of acquisition spending in 1986 compared with the more typical 50% or more in earlier years. Cash partially recovered to nearly one-third of the total in 1987 but in both years equity financing was at unprecedented levels of over 60%. Use of fixed-interest debt issues to fund takeovers rose to over one-fifth of expenditure in 1986 (when leveraged takeovers with 'junk' bonds were at their height in the USA) but fell away to a more normal 6% in 1987. The variation in financing methods has thus largely been a matter of switching between cash and equity.

The share price boom is a possible explanation of the heavy use of equity in 1986/87. Rising share prices may have reduced the perceived, if not the actual, cost of equity capital for acquiring companies. At the same time, shareholders of the purchased companies were willing to accept payment in equity because share values seemed destined only to rise further and because cash would have made many shareholders liable to capital gains tax on the proceeds of their steeply appreciated share sales.

This seems to be confirmed by the radical shift back to cash financing of takeovers after the equity crash in October 1987. In the final quarter of 1987 the share of cash funding rose back to 50% and equity dropped to 46%. By the first quarter of 1988 cash jumped to a peak of 71% and equity financing collapsed to only 24%. Thus, after the most rapid post-war slump in equity prices, shareholders in acquired companies were only too relieved to be able to dispose of their shares at a premium to the heavily depressed market values. But they were no longer interested in receiving yet more shares in exchange; they wanted cash! In any case, the buying companies for the most part were now replete with cash from the steep increase in corporate profits of the previous two years. The opportunity cost of running down bank deposits and other liquid assets to finance acquisitions had dropped with the fall in interest rates following the equity crash. Combined with the increased cost of equity finance companies now had a strong incentive to use their spare cash to buy what they now perceived as the undervalued assets of their target companies.

Managing Risk

The financial manager's central goal is (or should be) the provision of finance for the firm's operations at the lowest overall cost consistent with maintaining access to sources of funds. But one elusive element in the cost of capital is the degree of risk involved to lenders and investors. As we have seen, an increase in gearing can raise the cost of both debt and equity finance because of the enhanced risks for both types of investor. Companies need to seek the optimum capital structure by evaluating the impact on the relative cost of different forms of finance of changes in risk levels. In practice, of course, the problem is a complex one because of the enormous variety of financial instruments available. The choice is not just the theoretical stylised one between equity and long-term fixed-interest debt but among a bewildering array of debt instruments — short-term and long-term, fixed and floating rate securities, secured and unsecured loans, leasing, borrowing from the banks, from the domestic money markets or overseas, or in the Eurocurrency markets.

In turn, the prices of all these financial assets are continually changing in response to fluctuations in supply and demand. Even if the financial manager can approximate an optimum capital structure today it is likely to be sub-optimal tomorrow. For example, the stock market crash of 1987 can be explained by a downward revision by investors of expected equity earnings. A company committed in the weeks before the crash to take over another with finance from a rights issue would have lost heavily through having to pay an excessive post-crash price for the acquired company's assets while its underwriters might have had to absorb large quantities of unsold stock (as with the BP share issue which straddled the crash). Similarly, companies which took on substantial floating-rate debt in 1987 and early 1988 in the expectation that interest rates would hold at or even fall from their relatively low levels were faced with steep increases in their interest payments by the summer of 1988 as governments generally, and in the UK in particular, tightened their monetary policy and forced up interest rates to deal with incipient inflation or, in some cases like the UK, with a balance of payments deterioration.

Companies, therefore, must continually cope with uncertainty about the future prices of financial assets and the risk that prices change adversely to reduce profits and the value of the company to its shareholders. For the Financial Director, concerned with long term capital decisions, this means determining gearing not just in the light of the current cost of debt and equity but also of expected changes. This is a matter of assessing and ultimately forming a judgment about the future direction of equity prices and long-term interest rates. Getting the long-term capital structure of the business right is obviously of central importance but the problem of risk management can assume almost nightmarish proportions in the handling of short-term finance by the corporate treasurer.

The Corporate Treasurer

The establishment of separate 'treasury' departments in corporations, particularly multinationals, is a relatively recent innovation, dating back to the 1970s when the major countries abandoned fixed exchange rates and allowed their currencies to float. Suddenly, companies were faced with an extra dimension of financial risk from fluctuation in the values of currencies. Moreover, it was soon realised that the risks to cash flows and profits could be severe as exchange rates became highly volatile with daily movements of as much as 5% and swings over longer periods of 100% and more. Profit margins on exports could be wiped out and the home currency value of payments abroad could rise steeply and quickly. The 'cashier's' departments of corporations therefore had to take on a new function of handling exchange risks on top of their basic traditional role of cash management. This expanded sphere of activity has become generally known as the 'treasury function', recognised in the UK in 1979 with the formation of the Association of Corporate Treasurers. The Corporate Treasurer's functions are discussed more fully in Chapter 7.

Interest rates

The Corporate Treasurer's role has expanded well beyond the relatively simple task of maintaining liquidity. The increased volatility of interest rates and especially of exchange rates since the early 1970s has added enormously to the potential for losses from adverse changes and made risk management of prime importance.

Interest-rate instability has been aggravated by the shift of governments and central banks towards active monetary policy as their principal weapon for controlling inflation and influencing the balance of payments and the exchange rate. An example is the forcing up of bank base rates by the Bank of England from 7.5 to 13% during 1988 in order to curb an inflationary expansion of credit-financed spending. The adverse impact on profits of companies with high levels of floating-rate borrowing was correspondingly severe.

Treasurers, in both their lending and borrowing decisions, must therefore form a view about the future direction of interest rates. How the market as a whole expects interest rates to move can be gleaned from the term structure of interest rates — the pattern of interest rates on loans with different maturities. If the general level of rates has been stable and is not expected to change significantly, the term structure is likely to be expressed in a gradually rising yield curve (the interest yield on fixed-interest bonds plotted against the period to maturity). In other words, long-term rates are likely to be higher than short-term ones because long-term lenders will demand a larger premium against the risk of an adverse rise in rates. If the expectation is of higher rates in the future, the yield curve will become steeper. Conversely, when rates are expected to fall, the curve will flatten out and may even become downward-sloping — short rates will exceed long rates.

While the yield curve indicates the market view it is still up to the Treasurer to form his or her own expectations. If the Treasurer expects rates to rise (relative to what the market thinks) in the relevant time horizon then there is an incentive to borrow at fixed rather than floating rates. The reverse obviously applies if rates look set to fall — the Treasurer can borrow short or take on longer-term debt with interest linked to market rates such as base rate or the London Inter-Bank Offered Rate (LIBOR).

But the risk remains that the Treasurer might be wrong. If variable-rate borrowing has been contracted in the expectation that rates will fall but, in the event, rates rise, the mistake may cost the company dear in a higher interest bill for months or even years ahead. Fortunately, Treasurers now have a wide range of methods to enable them to hedge interest rate risk or to insure against adverse changes (the instruments available are dealt with in detail in Chapter 16). For example, financial futures enable Treasurers to take offsetting positions so that losses made from, say, a rise in interest rates are matched by a gain on the futures contract. Futures enable the Treasurer to lock into a particular interest rate so that, while the risk of loss is eliminated, so is the possibility of a gain from a favourable change in rates. Interest rate options (usually linked to futures contracts), on the other hand, give the Treasurer insurance against adverse interest movements but leave open the opportunity to benefit if rates go in the company's favour. The snag is that the option premium can look expensive and has to be paid up front with the result that boards of directors often mistakenly bar their Treasurers from using a highly-effective method of covering interest rate risk.

Another development is the growing use of swaps in which companies exchange debt with different interest rate profiles. Thus, one company may be able to borrow cheaply through fixed-rate debt issues which it can swap for floating-rate debt with another company.

This allows each to achieve its desired debt structure at a lower cost although it is not strictly a means of dealing with risk in the case of the company which raises fixed-rate debt and swaps it for floating-rate finance.

Exchange rates

Means of dealing with exchange risks are covered in detail in Chapters 14 and 15. As noted, currency changes can have a large impact on a corporation's balance sheet and profits. Exposure to exchange risk means that changes in exchange rates will alter the value of assets and liabilities denominated in foreign currency or the value of future income. It is usual to distinguish three types of risk, which are also discussed in Chapter 14.

(a) Translation risk
(b) Transaction risk
(c) Economic or competitive risk.

Translation risk

This arises because foreign currency assets and liabilities have to be 'translated' into domestic currency for tax and reporting purposes. Thus, for a UK-based multinational a fall in the pound against the dollar will increase the sterling value of its US subsidiary's dollar assets and liabilities. The effect on the consolidated balance sheet depends obviously on whether there were net dollar assets or liabilities, but exchange rate changes can clearly produce distortions in the company's accounts. Thus, an increase in the sterling value of dollar-denominated debt may show up as a rise in gearing which could reduce the corporation's credit rating even though the servicing of the debt is adequately covered by the US subsidiary's potential dollar earnings. However, the increased sterling value of the stream of dollar earnings (and therefore of the assets producing those earnings) will not immediately show up in the balance sheet.

Translation risk can be covered by ensuring a matching of foreign currency assets and liabilities though some would claim that, since exchange-rate changes affect only the measurement of items in the balance sheet, this should be recognised by investors and that the 'risk' need not be hedged. Indeed, it may be argued that investors have invested because of the translation exposure and that companies therefore should not hedge it.

Transaction risk

This is the risk of actual or realised losses when foreign currency assets are sold or liabilities repaid. Thus, the corporation will have 'payables' and 'receivables' in foreign currency as a result of trade and investment transactions. A UK importer from the USA, for example, may have dollar payables in a month's time. The risk is that the dollar appreciates in the interim to increase the liability in sterling. An exporter with dollar receivables is of course exposed to the opposite risk of a dollar depreciation. Borrowing and lending in foreign currency gives similar exposure both on the interest payments and on the repayments of the loan.

Transaction losses are potentially very serious. Given the wide volatility of exchange rates there is a high probability of an adverse change turning profit margins into losses. Treasurers conventionally therefore tend to cover net exposure, most commonly in the forward-exchange market. Receivables are sold forward at an exchange rate fixed in advance; payables are purchased forward. Alternatively, the Treasurer can buy offsetting currency futures — contracts to buy or sell currency for future delivery. Use of forwards and futures, however, has the same disadvantage as futures have with interest rate hedging. The company is locked into a specific exchange rate so that, although risk of loss is avoided, so too is the chance of gain. Again, as in the case of interest rates, Treasurers are making increasing use of options which can partially or wholly eliminate 'downside' currency risks but keep the possibility of gains from a favourable currency movement.

Economic or competitive risk

The risk here is that an exchange rate change brings a deterioration in a company's competitive position in both home and foreign markets. For example, the appreciation of sterling in the early 1980s led to a severe loss of competitiveness for British manufacturing industry both in exporting and against imports in the domestic market. Companies like Jaguar suffered lost sales and reduced profit margins in the USA through the steep decline of the dollar from its peak in early 1985. In principle, economic risk can be hedged. Many Japanese corporations, for instance, sold large volumes of prospective foreign currency earnings forward in 1985 and 1986 in anticipation of a yen appreciation. When the yen did rise in value they were able to hold down their prices and maintain their profit margins and sales volume.

Currency options can be used in the same way with the advantage
again that the company can improve its competitive position if the
exchange rate moves in the opposite direction.

But scope for covering economic risk is limited because, even when
forward, futures and option contacts are available, Treasurers may be
reluctant to hedge positions for longer than, say, a year ahead.
Currency swings often persist much longer than that; the dollar, for
instance, has been in decline since 1985 and by the summer of 1989
showed little sign of recovery to anything like its peak values of more
than four years before.

The role of the Treasurer
Finally, it is a matter of debate among Corporate Treasurers
themselves as to how far they should adopt a passive or active role in
risk management. At one extreme, the conservative school would argue
that the Treasurer's responsibility is simply to avoid risk, implying that
all interest and currency exposure should be fully hedged. The activist
school says that is nonsense because there are many situations where
exposure should clearly not be covered. For example, if a currency
realignment in the European Monetary System is imminent it would not
make sense to hedge, say, Deutschmark receivables into Italian lire
because it is certain that the German unit will be upvalued against the
lira. Or, if interest rates are clearly sky high the Treasurer can be safe in
not hedging against a further rise. Treasurers who hedge every risk in
sight with forwards or futures stand as much chance of making losses
(foregoing profits) as those who hedge nothing. The activist often goes
further and argues that the treasury should be treated as a profit
centre. The Treasurer should be given wide discretion in deciding
which assets and liabilities to hedge and which hedging instruments
(options in particular) to use to generate income for the company.
There are clearly sound arguments on both sides and the 'right'
approach is inevitably some compromise between extreme risk-
aversion and outright speculation.

Summary

This chapter has reviewed the broad determinants of corporate
financial behaviour. The Financial Manager's task can be thought of in
terms of achieving an optimal capital structure or gearing with a mix of
debt and equity which minimises the cost of financing the company's
assets. The optimum will vary from company to company depending in

particular on the degree of risk perceived by investors in the firm's business. It will also be influenced by external factors such as the taxation of corporate profits, inflation, interest rates and the state of the equity market. Corporations in turn must manage the financial risks arising from uncertainty about these external variables. The Corporate Treasurer has a key role to play in risk management, particularly in hedging the risks from interest rate and currency fluctuations.

CHAPTER 3

Multinational Corporations

Nigel Jump

Editor's Notes

Against the background outlined in the first two chapters, the concept of the most complicated type of corporate is introduced and its development and behaviour described in relation to particular environmental influences, including those of governments which recently have become more neutral rather than antagonistic to MNCs as a genre. To understand the way in which MNCs operate is essential for a proper understanding of corporate finance, after all they represent in broad concept the ultimate among corporates.

Introduction

Multinational corporations (MNCs) constitute a major force for change in the global economy, contributing significantly to the rate and course of economic and social development in both market-orientated and centrally-planned economies throughout the world. The need for producers of most high-volume products to compete in a market which seldom respects political boundaries means that a wide range of economic actors play on an international stage. Even the broad definition of an MNC as *any company which produces goods or services in more than one country*, which would exclude companies such as Jaguar, which are highly dependent on export sales, fails to capture the full extent of economic integration and interdependence in the contemporary world. It is useful to have a definition, and this one is probably the most widely accepted, but the variety of organisational structures possible is almost coincident with the number of MNCs, the number of activities in which they are involved, and/or the number of geographical markets in which they operate.

The scale of MNC operations and their impact on overall economic progress make them a major influence on the markets for international finance and payments. If they are to meet, profitably, the MNCs' demands for an increasingly sophisticated range of international financial services, bankers must be aware of the motivations and strategies of MNC management. To this end, this chapter provides an overview of the development, structure and strategy of the modern MNC, the influences on decision-making within it and the current trends inducing change in MNC organisation and behaviour.

MNC Development

Historical context
The history of the modern MNC begins in the early years of the current century when the pace of economic development accelerated under the twin stimuli of technological change and the emergence of the mass consumer market, particularly in the USA. Epitomised by Henry Ford's innovation of the production line in the motor industry, many of the first, largely American, MNCs expanded into overseas markets because of a cost advantage based on improved production techniques.

In the European context, early MNCs tended to develop along colonial lines but, after the Second World War, the pace of development quickened. Higher standards of living created larger markets, allowing companies to derive the benefits of economies of scale and, as expertise in international affairs increased, MNCs spread their operations more widely, resulting in greater industrial concentration. By the late-1980s, many manufacturing and service sectors had become more global. Even the Japanese conglomerates and some companies in the emerging Asian industrialised countries, such as South Korea, long proponents of export-led growth, were turning to MNC status as the most efficient means of gaining access to the world's large and/or growing markets and, thereby, ensuring continued corporate development.

Relationship with hosts
Some of the advantages and disadvantages to the local economy of direct MNC investment are listed below.

Advantages:

(a)   An influx of capital, skills, management techniques and technology.
(b)   Direct and indirect increases in employment, output and economic growth.
(c)   Improved balance of payments and/or foreign exchange earnings, either through reduced imports or increased exports, or both.

(d) Raised quality of labour and technology and, thereby, productivity in general, resulting from imitation of the standards set by the MNC for its own subsidiaries, its suppliers, competitors and neighbours.

(e) Better allocation of resources and productive efficiency promoted by increased competition in the local economy.

(f) Higher central and local government revenues through taxation of profits, employees' incomes and sales.

Disadvantages:

(a) Global planning or 'home' political pressures may dominate MNC decision-making and have detrimental effects on local, 'host' environmental and/or social structures.

(b) The MNC's economic power may restrict local authorities' freedom of action with respect to economic and social development and political policies. For example, large movements of funds by MNCs can affect the exchange rate of the host country with serious implications for broader economic policy.

(c) If research, development and design are centred overseas, reducing local facilities to mere assembly operations, there may be little dissemination of technology and techniques.

(d) Environmentally damaging activities or obsolescent technologies may be placed overseas, away from the political pressures at the MNC's home base, causing adverse local problems or maintaining local economic disadvantage.

(e) Isolated centres of growth may be established with little or no impact on the wider community. This is particularly a feature of MNCs concerned with the exploitation of natural resources.

(f) Lack of competition in a MNC-dominated market may induce inefficiency.

Attempts to quantify the net benefit or disbenefit of inward investment are fraught with difficulty. About one in seven of British employees work for foreign companies, and the UK, accounting for around 10% of the world's stock of foreign direct investments, is the third most popular venue for overseas expansion (behind the United States and Canada). Is the UK economy more efficient because of its high MNC content or have the foreign MNCs displaced domestic enterprise? Is the UK economy in danger of becoming a branch economy, subject to the strategic planning of overseas residents whose decisions will seldom be motivated by 'what's best' for the UK? Is the UK economy letting in Japanese companies which will destroy indigenous competitors or will the transfer of Japanese technology and management style be diffused through the economic fabric of the country to the long-term benefit of the UK's industrial productivity?

Whatever the net benefit, it is clear that the existence of a significant MNC element in domestic economic life has, and will have, a profound effect on the continued development of the UK economy. The 'demonstration effect' of MNCs is potentially enormous.

Although West German and Japanese companies are steadily eroding its position as the second largest source of MNCs, behind the United States, Britain has many MNCs of its own. Over time, there has been a shift away from manufacturing and links with former empire towards services, such as banking and leisure, and investment in North America. Moreover, since British accession to the Treaty of Rome in 1973, the rest of the EEC has attracted greater British investment. Do UK MNCs replace employment at home with employment overseas? Is the deindustrialisation of the UK economy a direct result of UK industrialists' disregard for the domestic effect of their strategies to develop elsewhere? Are UK MNCs providing a lifeblood of earnings, technology and management practices back to the UK economy? Such questions must remain unanswered, since there is no way we can compare 'what is' with 'what might have' been.

Such issues may be more pressing in the developing nations where the balance between internal and external requirements is more precarious. The relationship between Third World countries and the MNCs has changed dramatically, from a period of MNC domination, particularly in the colonial era, through a period of great distrust, to the current tentative balance of power. Developing countries now recognise the advantages of inward investment by MNCs but are mindful of the need for some control of MNC operations to avoid any abuse of economic power. Indeed, several less-developed countries encourage their own companies to achieve MNC status within the Third World and/or request the MNCs inside their countries to convert local subsidiaries to minority interests controlled by indigenous capital and management.

Theory of large-scale operation
Most of the reasons for the development of MNCs derive from the fundamental concepts of economies of scale and oligopolistic industrial structure.

In many sectors of economic activity, greater efficiency relates both to the quality and quantity of output, and efficiency is a function of size. By spreading available resources over higher volumes of production, costs per unit of output can be reduced. Increased scale of operation implies that the costs of fixed resources, such as buildings, plant and machinery and an element of labour, are spread over greater production volumes, leading to lower unit costs. As the following list shows, economies of scale occur in several areas of economic enterprise and, for the MNC supplying large international markets, the benefits to short-term costs and long-term growth and investment can be substantial.

Potential economies of scale

Real:	Pecuniary:
(a) Production	—Bulk buying
—Labour	—Cost of finance
—Capital/technology	—Cost of advertising
—Inventory	—Transport costs
(b) Marketing	—Labour
—Selling	
—Customer service	
—Model changes	
(c) Managerial	
—Specialisation	
—Decentralisation	
—Mechanisation	
(d) Distribution	
—Storage	
—Transport	

Consider the high volume car producer in an industry where the MNC is dominant. On the production line, robots theoretically allow 24-hour use of the factory; labour can be specialised to repeat short routines at higher speed; and stock holding can be orientated towards 'just-in-time' rather than 'just-in-case' purchasing. Advertising and promotion can be targeted at a broad spectrum of the community across international borders; service can be channelled through an extensive dealer network; and model changes can occur more frequently because the volumes required to break even are reached earlier. Management can specialise; routine operations can be standardised and, possibly, mechanised; and decentralisation of decision-making can permit senior management to address strategic rather than operational issues. Also, warehousing and transport distribution can be centralised and co-ordinated with production levels and the needs of dealers. Moreover, the immense size of the automotive MNC gives it financial as well as physical benefits. Its economic power in the market-place allows it to get keener prices from its suppliers, lower interest charges from its bankers, highly-competitive advertising rates, discounts on high-volume transport contracts and, through its importance in the local labour market, may allow it to influence the level and pattern of wage and other labour agreements.

The ability of MNCs to achieve all these benefits varies over time but, in many industries, economies of scale have been a major motivating force behind the continuing trend to greater industrial concentration over the last half century.

The result of this concentration is an oligopolistic industrial structure. Under oligopoly, a relatively small number of producers supply the vast majority of the sector's output. Consequently, each company has a high degree of market power and all recognise their mutual interdependence, learning, reacting and influencing each other profoundly. This interdependence creates uncertainty in the market and encourages participants to compete in areas other than price. Thus, forms of non-price competition, such as product development and promotion, growth by acquisition and other tools to defend an increased market share, become very important.

Indeed, because price changes are a very visible competitive sign to which consumers and competitors can react very quickly, a tendency to favour non-price competition may develop. However, when market growth is weak or disappears altogether, price discounting is widely used to defend market share and, once one oligopolistic MNC takes this step and customers react, it is difficult for competitors not to follow. Moreover, the longer price discounting persists, the more consumers come to expect it and discounting becomes the norm rather than the exception. During the early 1980s, this phenomenon developed in a number of MNC-dominated markets, such as cars and consumer electronics. In the years of recession (1981/82), many MNCs used price incentives to protect market share in depressed markets but subsequently found it difficult to remove them when markets recovered.

The large scale of operation and the virtual divorce of ownership (shareholders) from control (senior management) — although the rise of institutional share ownership is blurring the edges of this 'textbook' dichotomy — mean a range of strategic goals play an important role in corporate development in the MNC-dominated oligopoly. An improving profit performance remains fundamental, but growth of sales and asset base is also vital and, unless clear strategic control is engineered from the top, an oligopolistic MNC can become an uneasy coalition of competing groups.

This discussion of economies of scale and oligopoly, and the corporate behaviour that stems from them, leads to an important conclusion. A prime motivation of companies in large-scale industries is access to markets. This allows cost efficiency, higher sales, increased prestige and growth of assets and profitability. For the MNC, access to markets, and, in particular, growing markets, is a major determinant of decisions about location. Although MNC-dominated industries are increasingly global in outlook, it is no accident that most MNC activity is concentrated in the high-volume markets of the developed countries or in those developing countries with most potential for market growth.

Foreign direct investment
Penetration of foreign markets takes various forms and occurs at various stages over the product life-cycle. First, companies may explore the possibilities for profitable international activity through direct exports. This may be followed or augmented by licensing agreements whereby local producers are permitted to make, assemble and sell an overseas company's products in local markets. Both these stages are less risky, but also potentially less profitable, than foreign direct investment (FDI), which involves the establishment of local production facilities and true MNC status. In essence, MNCs are often no more than oligopolistic companies transmitting their technical, financial or managerial advantages to other markets as a natural extension of competition with rivals at home.

FDI takes three broad forms. *Vertical FDI* involves the acquisition or establishment of overseas facilities at a different stage in the production process. For example, oil exploration and extraction occur at a different stage in the production process from product refinement and sale, and often in different countries. Many MNCs involved in natural resource extraction process materials and sell final products in countries away from the origin of the resource.

By contrast, *horizontal FDI* involves the production of the same products in overseas markets. For example, the various forms of the Ford Escort car are produced in Germany, the UK, the United States and Brazil. Similarly, the production and sale of the ubiquitous Coca Cola soft drinks occur throughout the world. More recently, service sector companies, such as those in advertising (Saatchi and Saatchi), transport (TNT) and the media and leisure industries (News International), have adopted global expansion policies along horizontal FDI lines.

With the emergence of the conglomerate MNC, a third form of FDI has developed. Often by merger or acquisition, a growing number of MNCs produce a range of, perhaps, unrelated product lines in different countries. Holding companies, such as Lonrho, are examples of *conglomerate FDI*. (Amongst other things, Lonrho sells Volkswagen cars in the UK, grows soft commodities in Africa and runs hotels in Mexico.)

Of course, many MNCs exhibit the three forms of FDI to different degrees. BAT is a company which trades tobacco from more than one country for processing and selling as cigarettes in many other countries (vertical FDI), operates retailing outlets in more than one country (horizontal FDI), and is involved in a number of other activities, such as financial services (conglomerate FDI).

Figures 3.1 to 3.3 show organisational charts for GKN, Hanson and Unilever, indicating the possible diversity of MNC structure but also some key similarities. First, each of these companies has a range of primary resource, manufacturing and service activities. To a greater or lesser extent, they are all vertically integrated. (For example, Unilever (Brooke Bond) grows tea in Africa which is sold as a branded manufactured product in Europe.) Secondly, they all manufacture the same or similar goods and services in facilities in more than one country and supply those goods and services to both commercial and final consumers. (For example, GKN manufactures automotive components in several European countries and the United States. In those markets, the products are sold direct to the vehicle manufacturers as original equipment and supplied, sometimes through GKN's own retail/wholesale distribution chains, to the after-market for replacement parts. GKN is, therefore, a horizontally-integrated conglomerate MNC.) Finally, GKN, Hanson and Unilever are all diversified conglomerate MNCs. (In particular, Hanson has built itself into a major commercial force through the acquisition of other companies, the divestment of 'unsuitable' subsidiaries within those

MNC Structure 1988

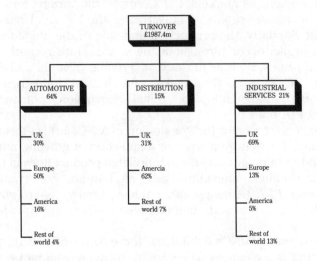

Figure 3.1   GKN plc organisational chart

MNC Structure 1988

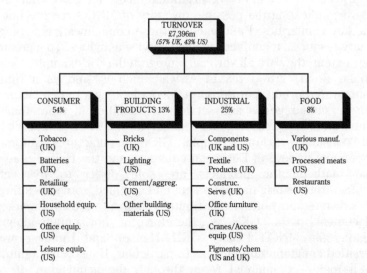

Figure 3.2   Hanson plc organisational chart

MNC Structure 1988

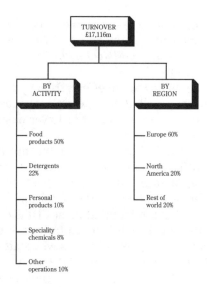

Figure 3.3 Unilever plc organisational chart

companies and the building up of the elements retained. The purchase of the Imperial Group in 1986; the subsequent sale of the Courage brewing arm; and the retention of the food and tobacco interests is only one example of this strategy.)

Influences on MNC location

Whatever form FDI takes, it usually relates to a company's strategic desire for growth through wider access to markets. However, beyond this, there are a number of factors which influence the choice of location. These are:

(a) *Specific advantage* — this may relate to technology (a patented or differentiated product or production technique which is easy to transfer but not easy to imitate), research and development expertise, or management skills and systems.

(b) *Capital abundance* — equity, loan facilities and/or surplus funds.

(c) *Entry barriers* — the company may invest overseas to circumvent import barriers (quotas or tariffs) in large/growing markets or to dominate the local market sufficiently to restrict access to it by other MNCs.

(d)   *Production costs* — access to cheap land, labour and/or raw materials.
(e)   *Marketing advantages* — to take account of a consumer preference for locally produced or serviced goods.
(f)   *State inducements and political stability* — grants, tax shelters, preferential credit.
(g)   *Fashion* — the 'bandwagon' effect, following oligopolistic rivals for fear that they will dominate an overseas market or even import back to the home market at lower costs.

Many of the factors listed above are 'nice' but not always 'necessary' and certainly not 'sufficient' conditions in the MNC's choice of location for FDI. Subjective factors, such as political similarity, language, customs and prestige, influence the decision too. This 'spatial preference' is reflected in the fact that most FDI is conducted between OECD countries with similar political institutions or between countries with close ex-colonial ties. It also explains why state incentives do not always attract MNCs as expected and MNCs have not all moved to countries with low production costs. Nevertheless, subjective factors remain subservient to the fundamental goal of wider economic power through access to large and/or growing markets.

MNC Structure

Central integration
Many MNCs organise themselves to achieve a high degree of integration within the company. The degree of integration reflects the freedom of trade, the potential for economies of scale, the nature of the product and the level of product differentiation in a particular industry. It also depends on the local and international environmental influences on the MNC, particularly political climate.

Although there is always an element of compromise with local conditions, central integration offers significant advantages in terms of co-ordinated planning and optimal productivity. It usually allows economies in research and development, although there are some advantages in having an element of internal competition between major centres of operation (e.g. between European and American design centres). Uniform marketing can be adopted (soft drinks) but there may be a need to orientate products differently in some markets (the larger Volvo cars are mainstream products in Sweden yet fill a luxury niche elsewhere).

Central integration also affects the MNC's relationships with host governments and labour organisations. Some MNCs attempt to imprint a global corporate culture on their employees; others operate as distinct satellites of the central organisation; and some develop close relationships with local government agencies. In recent years, there has been a shift away from localised bargaining with government, trade unions or suppliers towards co-determination and the achievement of closer integration across national borders through the promotion of a clear corporate identity. The Japanese companies, intent on incorporating their own working practices in their overseas plants, led this development but many other MNCs, wishing to copy Japanese best practice, are also adopting the strategy.

To achieve a degree of internal harmony, the centrally-integrated MNC requires clear paths of communication and movement between its centre and its subsidiaries. Centralised and common practices of accounting, measurement, evaluation and recording of performance are essential but the flow of information must run both ways to avoid loss of touch with local conditions. Communication should be co-ordinated at three levels: the *functional* level, relating to product development, manufacture and marketing; the *access* level, allowing local staff direct links with central senior management; and the *bargain* level, developing mechanisms to resolve internal conflict. The trend towards the creation of corporate cultures is one manifestation of the process by which communication can be improved and central integration achieved within an MNC. The management of *localism versus globalism* is a vital function of head office in the contemporary MNC.

Local orientation

At the other extreme, MNCs may adopt a disaggregated structure, more responsive to local conditions. This often reflects the greater involvement of political authorities in a country's economic life, including wide variation in labour laws, investment or tax regimes, local content and ownership rules, and accounting practices. It also frequently reflects geographical necessity. The locally-orientated MNC still needs a fair degree of uniformity in its control systems to ensure that, while local management may have considerable freedom of action to determine the process of local development, translation of performance to head office is both accurately and efficiently achieved. There is a trade-off between pleasing regional hosts and assuring the innate advantages, which allowed the company to achieve MNC status in the first place, are fully utilised by local representatives. Usually, this requires a central strategy implemented and co-ordinated by subsidiaries in a fashion suitable for the local conditions.

In practice, of course, most MNCs will lie along the spectrum between central integration and local orientation and the three main tasks of the centre are to ensure a free flow of relevant data so that decisions are taken on the best information available; to create a consensus on key strategies; and to manage the distribution of power and resources between the company's operational centres. In this way, strategic control and market penetration can be achieved wherever the MNC operates.

In terms of its impact on the local economic structure, the MNC usually produces a short-term reduction in industrial concentration as it competes 'head on' with indigenous producers but, in the longer term, since competition creates casualties, industrial concentration increases. The historical development of the UK car industry shows this clearly. Over a period of time, the entry of Ford and GM forced the amalgamation of a range of UK companies into the British Leyland Group (1968). Also, since the local subsidiaries of MNCs tend to be larger than their indigenous rivals, their power in the market is significant and threatens the independent future of local companies. The difficulties of ICL in competing with IBM and the former's eventual takeover by STC is an example of the pressures that can develop. Moreover, as the flood of motor manufacturers into Spain during the late 1970s shows, the presence of one MNC in a market encourages others to follow and, in time, competition takes on a 'global' or, at least, 'continental' aspect.

The creation of such widespread MNC competition forms barriers to entry because new companies find it difficult to achieve the scale necessary to compete with established MNCs. It also engenders excess profits, in terms of higher earnings than would be earned in a truly competitive market. Furthermore, price competition is weakened because, since the MNCs have the resources to survive a price war, it makes no sense for them or local companies to start one. However, in all economic activity, the seeds of decline are sown at the moment of greatest success. Excess profits, supported by non-price methods of competition, such as advertising and product differentation, permit inefficiencies and suboptimal behaviour to emerge, eventually allowing a fresh wave of 'hungry' companies to penetrate the market. Thus, the world dominance of the United States motor MNCs, built-up over the first 25 years of the post-war era, proved incapable of countering the new competitive threat from Japan in the 1970s and 1980s such that the United States MNCs, whilst remaining among the largest manufacturing companies in the world, had to concede market share and power to the Japanese companies. The latter are now reaching for full MNC status themselves, building plants in North America and Europe.

Apart from the removal of effective barriers to entry, other events can eliminate, even if only temporarily, the competitive advantage built up by MNCs operating in well-structured oligopolies. First, a fundamental shift in demand or severe recession can undermine an established company. Secondly, technological change can make successful products obsolete and can require the major readjustment of an industry's productive capacity. Thirdly, deregulation or privatisation can alter the 'rules of engagement' sufficiently to disrupt a stable market. Finally, the emergence of strong buyers (oligopsonists such as major retailers) can limit MNC power. These occurrences or shocks seldom happen overnight but they do, and will, occur and are an important element in the risk analysis of particular companies or industries.

MNC Decision-Making

Historically, decision-making in large corporations often appeared to be preoccupied with *operating decisions*, that is management objectives with respect to stocks, prices and output levels, the production and marketing process, research and development and day-to-day control. In this environment, crisis management was common with companies throwing resources at a problem when it developed to a significant level, only to find another problem emerging as the current one was resolved.

As the complexity of MNC operations increased, more attention was focused on *administrative decision-making*. The traditional hierarchical structure was re-examined in an attempt to create efficient delegation of authority and flow of information affecting the structure of production (flow and organisation), selling (distribution and organisation), and procurement (finance, personnel and raw materials). However, the crisis of the 1981/82 recession produced a further shift in decision-making towards more *strategic planning*. MNCs examined more closely their longer-term objectives and, thereby, the method, direction and timing of their product and growth strategies and the financial and administrative structures necessary to pursue these goals efficiently.

MNCs have been moving away from defensive strategies, based on imitation and remedial policies, to become more proactive, anticipating future trends and initiating change. Some companies have even examined their whole range of activities and emerged, in the second half of the 1980s, as very different companies from those that entered the decade. For example, Smiths Industries, a major UK supplier of electrical components to the auto industry in the 1970s, took the strategic decision to leave what it saw as a 'no' or 'low' growth sector and is now largely an aerospace and medical equipment manufacturer. Conversely, GKN, formerly a leading force in UK steel products, has virtually left this sector to concentrate on its motor component businesses. Similarly, seeing the decline of UK shipping, Ocean Transport and Trading has cut back its deep-sea activities considerably and now derives almost all of its sales and profits from land-based services. There are many more cases of MNCs concentrating on core activities, diversifying into new areas or divesting operations perceived to have weak growth prospects.

MNC Strategies

Product-related policies
With MNCs concentrating more on strategic planning and non-price competition, product development and marketing acquire even greater importance and have come to encompass a wider range of activities. As the pace of technological change accelerates, technical and quality standards with respect to design, production and after-sales service have increased. Companies seeking to defend or build on market share strive to cement brand loyalty by greater differentiation of their products and emphasis on customer satisfaction, whether those customers are individuals, other companies, retailers and wholesalers, service companies, state authorities or other institutions. Since all purchase decisions are based on incomplete information, firms recognise their ability to influence those decisions by real or apparent product changes and the product/market decisions as to what to make, where to make it and to whom to sell it are crucial to any MNC's long-term growth.

Product development in many MNCs evolves from a balance between internal and external pressures (see below). It involves the resolution of conflicts between expanding existing product lines and markets, developing new areas internally or by acquisition, and divesting mature product lines. Product variation reflects demand for the product, the technology of production, the MNC's internal characteristics with respect to structure and decision-making and the external influences of competition, technological progress and general business conditions.

Pressures on product development

Internal:

(a)   Management attitude to change/risk.
(b)   Skills available — design, R. & D.
(c)   Resources available — material, financial.
(d)   Synergy with existing operations.
(e)   Past experience and future ambitions.

External:

(a)   Rate of technical change — electronics.
(b)   Degree of competitive rivalry — cars.
(c)   Consumer demands — foods.
(d)   Social perception — tobacco.
(e)   Company status — financial institutions.

The success or failure of MNC product development is strongly influenced by product promotion. Advertising and other forms of marketing play a vital role in oligopolies because they are the main vehicle for getting product information to customers. Critics argue that advertising is persuasive rather than informative and, in many sectors, competitors' promotions cancel each other out, defending market share rather than increasing it. Product promotion may become excessive from time to time but it is not inherently wasteful and can be an important part of an MNC's corporate strategy. Interestingly, in the last few years, advertising has shifted somewhat away from brand advertising towards promotion of corporate identity, reinforcing the delineation of distinct corporate cultures within specific MNCs.

Growth-related policies
Internally, long-term corporate growth is achieved organically, by the extension of existing products and practices to new markets, and/or through integration and diversification. Externally, it is achieved by merger, takeover or collaboration. In each case, the MNC growth

decision is closely linked to decisions about financing (equity, loan capital or internally-generated funds). Internal growth, through replacement or new investment, can be organic, developing out of existing operations, or innovative, arising from the research and development of new ideas. In contrast, mergers and takeovers often reflect external financial market conditions as well as industrial logic. The historical 'waves' of merger activity have generally coincided with the emergence of bull stock markets when expectations are optimistic and surplus funds are available. For example, following the 1981/82 recession, a discrepancy developed between market and real asset values, allowing the purchase of weakened companies with good recovery prospects at cheap prices and culminating in successive record levels of acquisitions and mergers, in value terms, in each year from 1984 to 1988 (see Table 3.1).

Table 3.1
UK acquisitions and mergers

	Total value (£m)	Number acquiring	Number acquired
1972	2,532	928	1,210
1975	291	276	315
1979	1,656	447	534
1981	1,144	389	452
1984	5,474	508	568
1985	7,090	383	474
1986	14,935	529	696
1987	15,363	850	1,125
1988	22,123	902	1,224

The increase in the value of acquisitions and mergers during the mid-1980s was achieved by a smaller proportionate number of deals with a higher average value. It was an era of large conglomerate merger, reflecting a shift in strategic planning. Even after the stock market collapse of October 1987, the pace of merger activity did not slacken. Indeed, some MNCs used the opportunity to acquire targets at lower cost.

Another factor favouring the merger trend in the mid-1980s was the less intrusive attitude of the Monopolies and Mergers Commission and similar bodies in other countries. To a large extent, this influence reflects the political outlook of the government of the day. Certainly, in some developing countries, such as Malaysia, policies of national ownership have restricted the ability of MNCs to pursue organic or acquisitive growth. In some cases, such governments have made MNCs reduce their holding in local subsidiaries below 50% by forced selling to local interests.

When the senior management of large corporations are asked what motivated a particular acquisition, they usually reply in terms of synergy between the companies, the ability of their management to develop the full potential of the acquired assets, and a need to attain a scale making them fully competitive internationally. Ultimately, this translates into increased market power by buying control of inputs or eliminating a competitor, increased real or pecuniary economies of scale, and faster growth in sales and market share, leading to improved profitability. Alternatively, an acquisition strategy may be geared to reducing the company's vulnerability to the economic cycle through the purchase of companies making products less affected by cyclical fluctuations than existing product lines or peaking at different points in time. Finally, of course, acquisitions may be engendered by a 'me too' approach, copying competitors' strategies and satisfying senior management's desire for personal prestige.

Whatever the motivation, there is no doubt that mergers and acquisitions are an important element in MNC growth strategies. Nevertheless, few are an undoubted success: bull markets are usually followed by bear markets when the value of the acquired assets may fall considerably; the acquirer may encounter 'indigestion' problems producing managerial diseconomies because executives are paying less attention to existing activities; and there are high costs of winning as well as costs of losing contested bids.

Broad strategic policies

Although effective demand recovered strongly in the developed economies after the recession of the 1980–82 period, many of the individual markets for non-durable consumer products in these economies, having already attained a considerable degree of maturity, grew only sluggishly. This encouraged *product proliferation* in three forms: new products involving genuine innovation, new brands involving imitation of competitors' products or line extensions, and new items involving the repositioning or reformulation of existing products.

At the same time, there was an increase in *conglomerate growth:* this too taking three forms. First, cross-market entry in consumer non-durables allowed companies to extend their production/marketing expertise at 'making what sells' into similar markets, achieving growth by a widening of the MNC's brand portfolio. Secondly, successful manufacturers of more durable products applied technological advantages in 'selling what they make' to new but related product areas. Thirdly, the holding companies, whose competitive edge lies in a management style distinct from any specific product characteristics, acquired companies with perceived growth potential but in need of better management direction. The corollary of this 'portfolio' approach to management was the divestment of unsuccessful or less synergistic activities, spawning an increase in management buy-outs.

MNCs involved in relatively mature markets for non-durable consumer goods, such as food or drink brands, and cosmetics, toiletries and other household products, have moved into related areas, increasing industrial concentration in stable sectors. They have also divested unsuccessful activities and adopted portfolio management styles. In the short term, market maturity encourages product proliferation and promotion to defend or build market share. In the longer term, the MNC's desire for growth is satisfied by conglomerate diversification.

Conversely, in industries where technology is more important, (especially consumer durables such as cars and electronic consumer goods), increased costs of research and development and more rapid rates of technical change have imposed different requirements on MNC strategy. Primarily, companies have rationalised product lines, concentrating on core items, because of the need to spread higher development costs over higher output volumes. In a world of rapid technical advance, new product launches become even more crucial than usual. Therefore, more investment is made to get the new product right and a higher level of sales is necessary to cover the higher investment.

However, technological excellence is no guarantee of success. There is continuous conflict between the need to 'get it out' and the need to 'get it right'. For example, the Lockheed L10–11 was a fine piece of high-tech aircraft engineering but, by the time it was available, the bulk of its market had been claimed by the Boeing 747. Lockheed no longer makes civil airliners. On the other hand, as a number of post-war UK car manufacturers found, getting a new product out before technical quality is assured can be even more disastrous.

Thus, as lead times and the fixed costs of product development increase, MNCs attempt to reduce product differences, depending on niche developments of basic designs to satisfy consumers' desire for variety. Component ranges are rationalised and, in order to spread the high costs of development, federal links with suppliers, customers and even competitors are forged. The paradox of market maturity accompanied by technological innovation is that industrial concentration and competition intensify yet this leads to greater collaboration within an industry. Increased competition in the market produces internal consolidation and external co-operation amongst rivals on (i) product development through joint ventures, (ii) component standardisation and local assembly from internationally-sourced parts, and (iii) closer equity ties and market access agreements.

A number of examples from the aerospace and motor industries illustrate these strategic developments:

(a) Rolls Royce collaborates with Pratt and Whitney and others to spread the development costs of a new generation of aeroengines.

(b) Peugeot and Fiat collaborate on the development of a new small car engine yet compete aggressively in the showrooms.

(c) Rover and Honda assemble each other's models in each other's markets for sale locally and co-operate on the development of new models.

(d) Chrysler (USA) has a minority shareholding (20%) in Mitsubishi Motors (Japan) which has a small equity holding (15%) in Hyundai (South Korea).

Summarising this discussion of contemporary corporate strategy, in pursuit of market share and long-term growth, MNCs adopt a range of policies aimed at increasing their power and influence in their industries. For MNCs producing and selling non-durable products with relatively low technical content, knowledge can be acquired by external mergers and takeovers while, for the durable goods manufacturer, knowledge can be acquired by collaboration on research and development with competitors. In both cases, the end structure is remarkably similar with a small number of MNCs dominating the industry, recognising their interdependence and the need for close federal links throughout the economic chain. These MNCs are highly competitive on the market-place yet co-operate intermittently on technical development. In the modern world of oligopolistic multinational business, as in politics, a balance between competitive, yet peaceful, co-existence needs to be struck.

MNC Environment

Success in international competition is now determined by the efficiency with which MNCs turn technological leadership into dominant market share. Advances in information technology and deregulation of markets within, and sometimes between, major trading blocs increasingly allow companies to be 'footloose' or, more importantly, to integrate operations across international boundaries more effectively. Nevertheless, there is a third leg of the environmental stool affecting MNC strategy: governmental involvement in, and restrictions on, MNC behaviour. (The whole process of market harmonisation in Europe under the EC92-banner will be a very important external influence on MNC behaviour in the 1990s.) At any one time, the MNC has to balance its own plans against the boundaries set by technology, market conditions and government interference.

To identify ways in which these three factors influence MNCs, consider a number of major international industries, analysing the relative importance of each of these three variables in the particular circumstances of each industrial sector.

Civil aerospace — technology, government, market
Industrial concentration has progressed to the point where there are just three major airliner manufacturers (Boeing, McDonnell-Douglas and Airbus) and three major aeroengine makers (Pratt and Whitney, General Electric and Rolls Royce) in the western world, supplying a global market of internationally competitive airlines. Thus, sources of supply and demand in the civil aerospace industry are fairly clearly prescribed and, while the airlines' requirements are an important element in product development, the leads and lags in design, development and production of these high-tech products mean that technological factors play the crucial role in industrial strategy. Aeroengine manufacturers are currently developing engines that will be fitted to airframes 10 to 15 years from now. Since the actual market for airliners that far ahead can only be estimated from forecasts of air traffic growth and the age distribution and, therefore, likely replacement of existing aircraft, technology is the dominant environmental influence on the industry.

In addition, the strategic importance of the industry means that government involvement, through front-end loans, grants or subsidies and back-end procurement policies for state-controlled airlines, is significant. As the controversy between the United States and European governments over support for Airbus indicates, the civil aerospace market is one in which companies take considerable heed of political interference. Thus, while technological development is the prime influence on the industry, government policy is also important and both may be more important constraints on companies' strategic planning than fluctuations in the market.

Soft drinks/fast foods — market, technology, government

In many ways, the MNCs operating in the world's markets for soft drinks (such as Coca Cola and Pepsi Cola) and fast foods (such as McDonalds and Burger King) are at opposite extremes to the civil aerospace industry. Technology is important to the costs and quality of production but the industry is driven by the changing tastes of consumers. Creation and maintenance of a growing market is all important. Similarly, as long as fundamental requirements of hygiene, ingredients and planning rules are satisfied, state interference is usually minimal. Thus, soft drinks and fast foods constitute the typical non-durable consumer product for which marketing is the prime tool of strategic planning. Product development involves incremental changes in product range (or reformulations) and matching the initiatives of competitors.

Banks — government, market, technology

As with non-durable consumer products, technology in banking allows the MNC to provide its services more efficiently but seldom leads to the creation of completely new products. The banks argue that information technology and the plastic card allow them to extend the range of products offered to customers but, more accurately, they improve the quality and convenience of the payment and other systems offered, without constituting wholly new products. Thus, technology is, or should be, an enabling rather than leading influence on banking and is, itself, driven by the demands of the consumer for improved service in an increasingly competitive market.

With the removal of barriers of demarcation between domestic banks, foreign banks and other financial institutions, the importance of competition for market share in the provision of financial services has increased in recent years. This has resulted largely from a relaxation of state control. Despite this, government policies with respect to the monetary sectors of the economy remain a major environmental influence on the behaviour of banking MNCs. Through a wide range of economic policies and legislative procedures, governments impinge on the financial sector and, even in these market-orientated times, the prime importance of state interference in banking should not be overlooked.

Media — technology, market, government
Although, in many countries, media services (TV, radio and newspapers) are state controlled, for the emerging MNCs in this industry, state regulation is the backdrop against which to operate. At present, technological advance in production, transmission and receival and globalisation of the market are leading the regulators. Moreover, with the advent of satellite broadcasting, it is inevitable that consumer demand (whether it be the viewers, listeners or readers of the service or those promoting the advertising which pays for it) will play an increasingly important role. However, this industry shows how the relative significance of environmental factors on the MNC can change. At present, technological change is leading the market and government regulation but this situation could change quickly. To a greater or lesser extent, this applies to all sectors.

Conclusions and Outlook

In discussing the behaviour of MNCs in the contemporary world, the structural differences between the centrally-integrated and locally-orientated companies have been stressed. Also, the growing importance of strategic planning with respect to product development and the long-term growth of the organisation has been documented. Finally, it has been emphasised that MNCs operate within an environment in which changes in technology, market demand and state regulation/interference can profoundly affect MNC strategy and behaviour. Thus, a picture has been built up of MNCs becoming increasingly forward looking, willing to adjust administrative and operating procedures to the requirements of their evolving long-term strategies and responding to a changing external environment.

Global trends towards the harmonisation of markets, infrastructure, distribution and marketing, together with the integration of capital markets, the lowering of tariff barriers and policies of deregulation and privatisation, are all encouraging the integration of MNC operations.

The development of the single European market (EC92) will only serve to accelerate these MNC behavioural patterns. Meanwhile, microelectronic-based information systems and the advent of new materials are allowing faster dissemination of technology and the rapid development of global industries. Paradoxically, customisation and market segmentation of products through advanced CAD/CAM techniques (computer-aided design/computer-aided manufacturing) promote technical and market collaboration between MNCs wishing to spread development costs, and comparative advantage, across increasingly mature markets. Moreover, fears of protectionism between the major economic blocs encourage such international co-operation.

In this volatile environment, two broad types of MNC are emerging:

(a)   the truly integrated, global MNCs, such as IBM, with a unique organisational/psychological structure and high degree of internal co-ordination; and
(b)   the portfolio 'multidomestic' companies, such as Inchcape, with more geographically dispersed activities and locally-orientated product development and marketing.

The complexities of a world market affected by a variety of socio-economic and political factors ensure that uniformity of structure and action amongst MNCs is a mirage. Nevertheless, the trend towards globalism is clear and the banker wishing to monitor the performance of existing, and target, MNC clients needs to be aware of the strategic outlook which is likely to be the basis of his or her customers' negotiating positions. To satisfy the demands of the globally-orientated MNC for financial services, the banker needs to be able to analyse the structures and strategies of, and environmental constraints on, contemporary MNC management, as well as the financial, industrial and political risks of lending.

Further Reading

1   A. Altshuler et al., *Future of the Automobile*, Allen and Unwin, 1984.
2   R. Ballance and S. W. Sinclair, *Collapse and Survival: Industries In a Changing World*, Allen and Unwin, 1983.
3   A. Baruffi, 'The Battle for Corporate Control', *Business Week*, 18 May 1987.
4   J. Boranson, *Technology and the Multinationals*, Lexington, 1978 (out of print).

5   P. Cecchini, *The European Challenge — 1992*, Wildwood House, 1988.
6   R. Clarke, *Industrial Economics*, Basil Blackwell, 1985.
7   J. M. Connor, 'Food Product Proliferation — A Market Structure Analysis', *American Journal of Agriculture*, November 1981.
8   B. Curry and K. D. George, 'Industrial Concentration — A Survey', *Journal of Industrial Economics*, March 1983.
9   Y. L. Doz, *Strategic Management in Multinational Companies*, Pergamon, 1986.
10 B. D. Henderson, *Henderson on Corporate Strategy*, Abt Books, 1979.
11 N. F. Jump, 'Corporate Strategy in Mature Markets', *Barclays Review*, November 1982.
12 N. F. Jump, 'Competition and Cooperation in Consumer Durable Industries', *Barclays Review*, May 1983.
13 A. Koutsoyiannis, *Non-Price Decisions: The Firm in a Modern Context*, Macmillan, 1982.
14 M. E. Porter (ed.), *Competition in Global Industries*, Harvard Business School, 1987.
15 J. D. Richardson, 'On "Going Abroad" — The Firm's Initial Foreign Investment Decision', *Quarterly Review of Economics and Business*, 1971.
16 J. B. Schnapp, *Corporate Strategies of the Automotive Manufacturers*, Lexington Books, 1980.
17 F. Stephen (ed.), *The Firm: Its Activities and Evolution*, MCB University Press, 1984.
18 J. M. Stopford and L. Turner, *Britain and the Multinationals*, Wiley, 1985.
19 A. A. Thompson, 'The Implications of Corporate Strategy for Competition and Market Analysis — An Expanded Role for the Business Economist', *Business Economics*, September 1982.
20 Various OECD and UNIDO publications on MNCs.

CHAPTER 4

The Development of Specialist Corporate and International Banking Activity

Gillian McGrattan and Jan Toporowski

Editor's Notes

As a parallel to the development of the large corporate and MNC, so financial markets have developed to meet their needs and banks as the corner-stone of financial activity have been forced to adapt to the change in demands of the market. This has been demonstrated in the trend towards merger in order to create institutions large enough to service the needs of the largest corporates, and by the geographical expansion by the largest banks seeking to provide worldwide service for their multinational customers, particularly in the most important financial centres. Chapter 4 describes the background of this development which has changed the face of banking, particularly in the last two decades, whilst Chapter 5 outlines the present situation and the response to it, spawning a variety of new financial instruments.

Introduction

Multinational corporate and international banking dates back to as long ago as the 16th century, when bankers such as the Fuggers of Augsburg financed the wars of princes and great colonial and trading enterprises. More recently, during the almost one hundred years of relative stability in Europe that followed the defeat of Napoleon in 1815, banking played an important part in the economic link up of the great empires that were carved out in Africa and Asia. The First World War seemed to put an end to an era in which comparatively free trade between large empires provided plenty of scope for the development of international banking. Certainly it did not recover its former eminence during the two decades of economic and financial turbulence that followed the Armistice of 1919. The Wall Street Crash of 1929 sent many banks into liquidation and was followed by smaller financial crashes in Europe, economic protectionism, and wholesale defaults on their external debt by the many smaller countries that were economically crippled by all this.

Contemporary international banking therefore dates back mainly to the political and economic settlements that were made after the Second World War, between 1945 and 1947. These settlements, known for short as the Bretton Woods System, created an environment of unprecedented stability (until the 1970s) in which international banking could develop. They also brought to it entirely new opportunities to meet challenges (such as decolonisation and development) that went far beyond encouraging bankers to look after their assets prudently, as the previous decades had done.

In this chapter we shall look at the system of international trade and payments that was established in 1945–47 and the limited role that it gave to private international banking and finance. We shall see how developments in international trade and economic relations eventually gave rise to a new kind of unregulated banking in the so-called Euromarkets. It was in these markets that the most exciting developments in international banking took place so that, by the mid-1970s, the official government and inter-governmental banking institutions had been squeezed into a seemingly supportive role in international lending. But the financial imbalances and opportunities in new markets gave rise to a need for new kinds of banking operations, liability management, and institutions such as consortium and specialist banks.

The pressures that gave rise to these developments eventually changed in the early 1980s, leaving banks with no easy and economic way out of the sizeable commitments that they had so recently taken upon themselves. The pace of financial innovation (i.e. the rate at which new financial instruments and services are developed and come into use) accelerated with the new opportunities of the 1970s, but responded even more rapidly to the difficulties that emerged in the 1980s. We shall therefore conclude this chapter with an outline of the constraints facing international banking at present, namely the growth of bad debt, the challenge of new markets, and the underpricing of banking risks. The origins of these difficulties in economic developments and in the structure and organisation of international banking activity will be discussed.

It is convenient and useful to divide the post-war years into four periods, corresponding roughly to the relative importance of private international banking since the Second World War. From 1944 to 1971, official (i.e. government and inter-governmental) institutions dominated international banking. However, that period also saw the emergence and development of important private banking markets. This was followed by the period 1971 to 1973 when the official arrangements governing international payments and capital flows broke down in confusion. This disorder, exacerbated by the economic and financial consequences of the quadrupling of the price of oil at the end of 1973, gave way to a period when private commercial banking set the pace for developments in international banking and finance, while official institutions remained largely passive participants in it. This period came to an end in 1982 with the maturing of the sovereign debt crisis, when Mexico, followed by other major borrowers in the Third World, announced that it could not service its external debt as agreed. The resultant crisis in international banking has brought official institutions back to the forefront in facilitating the management of the crisis and developing new arrangements for the preservation of the banking system.

This division into periods implies the existence of certain cyclical patterns in the development of international banking arrangements. The official international payments and credit system founded at the Bretton Woods Conference in 1944 and developed afterwards, was in disarray in 1971–73, after the emergence of the institutions that took over the role of creating a new international banking and credit system in the 1970s. International order broke down again in the early 1980s, giving rise to a prolonged period of reorganisation and adjustment. Each of these periods threw up new challenges, opportunities and dangers which, with the development of banking technology, induced successively different kinds of financial innovation. The view that banking and financial markets are engaged on a smooth long-term course as a result of innovation and changing regulation needs to be heavily qualified if applied to international banking.

The Bretton Woods Ascendancy

The foundation of the present international banking system was laid down at a conference of the Finance Ministers of the western allies in July 1944 in Bretton Woods, a country resort in New Hampshire, USA. The purpose of the meeting was to determine the conventions and institutions that would govern international trade, payments and credit after the war. The chief consideration of the participants in doing this was to avoid the accumulation of tariffs and quotas on foreign trade and competitive devaluation of exchange rates by countries desperate to secure balance of payments equilibrium, which had dampened international trade in the inter-war years. The major political and financial factors determining the outcome of their considerations was the fact that the war effort had drained the public finances of all the allies, with the exception of the United States, with the result that all were heavily indebted to the United States.

It was proposed that all countries should commit themselves as far as possible to free trade and the eventual convertibility of their currencies. Convertibility was to be against gold, but the war effort had stripped nearly all the allies of the bulk of their gold reserves, which had gone to the United States in payment for arms and equipment. The formula then devised was one of eventual convertibility at fixed exchange rates against the US dollar, which the American authorities committed themselves to exchange on demand for gold at a rate of $35 per ounce. The International Monetary Fund was set up with capital subscribed by the member countries. This was intended to be lent to member countries unable to finance temporary balance of payments deficits. The International Bank of Reconstruction and Development (the World Bank) was also set up at the same time to provide development finance for the reconstruction of Europe and the economic improvement of the developing countries.

In this international order, private commercial international banking was not so much severely circumscribed, but given very little scope for operation. The main function for commercial banks engaged in international financial flows was trade finance, i.e. handling bills of exchange and letters of credit to finance the shipment of goods worldwide. Thanks in large part to rapid growth of the world economy (albeit unevenly over time and in different countries), this has proved to be an exceptionally dynamic market in aggregate (see Table 4.1).

In the years immediately after the Bretton Woods settlement, international trade and finance was nevertheless inhibited by the absence of full multilateral convertibility. In 1948 the main industrialised countries in North America and Western Europe formed the Organisation for European Economic Co-operation (OEEC) to administer the huge infusion of Marshall Aid into Western Europe. With the addition of, among others, Japan, Australia and New Zealand this became the Organisation for Economic Co-operation and Development (OECD), in 1961.

In the early years when the OEEC was still administering Marshall Aid, member countries made some brave but ultimately unsuccessful attempts to achieve full currency convertibility, notably the UK in 1947.

Table 4.1
The foreign trade of IMF
member countries, 1950–85 (US$bn)

	1950		1960		1970		1980		1985	
	Imports	Exports	Imports	Exports	Imports	Exports	Imports	Exports	Imports	Exports
Industrial countries	39.8	36.4	85.5	83.9	227.0	220.0	1,369.4	1,239.5	1,361.8	1,258.5
of which:										
the US	9.6	10.3	16.4	20.6	42.7	43.2	257.0	220.8	361.6	213.1
Developing countries	20.2	22.0	38.3	34.2	72.0	64.9	539.4	623.7	497.1	493.8
of which:										
Africa	3.7	4.0	7.6	6.9	13.6	12.9	83.1	95.5	55.2	66.0est.
Asia	6.3	7.1	12.6	10.4	20.3	15.6	160.8	144.3	201.2	177.0
Europe[1]	2.0	n/a	4.1	2.9	11.8	7.6	68.4	42.8	60.0	49.6
Middle East	2.0	n/a	3.9	4.4	9.0	12.8	113.3	237.4	101.5	104.6
Latin America[2]	5.9	6.6	9.6	9.3	17.3	15.9	113.8	103.7	72.3	98.4
World total[3]	60.1	58.4	124.1	118.2	300.4	286.4	1,928.6	1,883.0	1,879.0	1,782.9

Notes:
1. i.e. Developing countries in Europe, which are listed by the IMF as Cyprus, the Faeroe Islands, Greece, Hungary, Malta, Portugal, Romania, Turkey, Yugoslavia.
2. i.e. The Americas, excluding the United States and Canada, but includin excluding the United States and Canada, but including Greenland.
3. Unallocated trade flows have not been incorporated in the Table.

Source: IMF

The result was that, while the individual currencies of member states were convertible in respect of foreign trade transactions against the US dollar, the European currencies were not convertible directly against each other, and the exchange of capital into other currencies for transfer abroad was severely limited. It was only in 1958 that the main Western European countries agreed to introduce multilateral convertibility, i.e. allowed their currencies to be exchanged for each others' currencies as well as the US dollar. These arrangements, in addition to the predominant size of United States foreign trade, are largely responsible for the widespread use of the US dollar as an international currency.

This not only tended to inhibit trade finance and the development of international banking, but also inclined to reinforce the division of the world economy into currency areas. The two main areas were the dollar area, comprising mainly the Americas and the Pacific Basin where the US dollar was used in settlement of international trade, and the sterling area, comprising the British Commonwealth and a large part of the Middle East, where sterling was the main international currency. There was a French franc zone, comprising the French empire, but the French franc was a much weaker currency then than it is now. China, the Soviet Union and the Socialist economies of Eastern Europe opted out of any of these currency zones, carrying out their trade by a series of bilateral arrangements or, where unavoidable, via the US dollar. In Western Europe, certain banks kept reserves of both US dollars and sterling to finance intra-European trade and the investment that was funded by Marshall Aid.

Exchange controls severely limited transfers of funds between the currency areas. True there were some inter-area private capital flows as opposed to public ones like Marshall Aid. But these were largely remnants of flows established much earlier, such as the London Stock Exchange quotations of Latin American railways, or the Latin American subsidiaries of UK insurance companies.

Thus, international banking in the 1950s consisted largely of trade finance, and the provision of credit facilities for multinational corporations, mainly within these currency zones. Within and across currency zones, there were multinational banks, mainly the British banks, like the Chartered Bank, or the French banks, like Banque de Paris et de Pays Bas, which had extensive branch networks outside the countries where they were based and where their capital was raised. Although these banks engaged in a small way in project finance in developing countries, they played only a minor role in lending to governments and then mainly in the few developing countries that were sufficiently independent politically to be able to borrow in their own right. Official financial flows between central banks, from Marshall Aid, and from the IMF and the World Bank dominated international development finance and external lending to governments.

The limited size and range of private banking activity at this time is apparent from Table 4.2, which shows the distribution of banks' main foreign assets and liabilities from 1950 to 1975. It also shows the very rapid increase in foreign borrowing and lending by banks in London and Luxembourg, and subsequently also in the offshore centres of the Bahamas and Singapore. In 1950, for example, non-American banks took merely US$5.2bn in deposits in the United States. Twenty-five years later this had increased by a factor of ten to US$52.9bn. However, in Luxembourg where a new market in international banking was emerging, borrowing by foreign banks rose from US$6m in 1950 to US$26.6bn in 1975. These trends were apparent also in lending abroad.

Table 4.2
Deposit money banks' foreign assets
and liabilities (US$m), 1950–75

	1950	1960	1965	1970	1975
Liabilities in the					
United States	5,200	8,300	15,100	26,700	52,900
UK	n/a	n/a	10,887	40,368	135,965
Luxembourg	6	32	123	2,468	26,576
Bahamas	–	n/a	n/a	4,725	65,600
Singapore	–	n/a	207	171	1,191
Assets in the					
United States	n/a	3,200	7,500	7,700	46,000
UK	n/a	3,055	7,663	37,433	124,694
Luxembourg	22	105	369	3,613	29,005
Bahamas	–	n/a	n/a	4,756	44,269
Singapore	–	n/a	232	214	956

Source: IMF

There were two main factors responsible for this rapid growth. One was the rapid expansion of foreign trade, as evidenced in the figures on non-Communist countries' exports and imports in Table 4.1. The second was a genuine growth in capital flows moving around the world, as the industrialised economies in the world experienced a rapid investment boom during the first post-war decade. These two provided the ultimate demand for international banking and corporate finance in a new kind of market that emerged in the 1950s and the 1960s. This was the Euromarket.

The original Euromarket was a market for the lending and borrowing of currencies that circulate outside their country of issue. It has developed to include markets in all sorts of money and capital market instruments denominated in most of the major currencies, for example Eurobonds, floating rate notes, and Euro-commercial paper. Because it is outside its country of issue, the market in which these currencies are exchanged is largely unregulated by the credit, liquidity and capital rules of central banks.

In the immediate post-war years the chief and most widely used Eurocurrency was the US dollar, which circulated around Europe as virtually the only hard currency. The onset of the Cold War in 1958 caused the Soviet Union to withdraw its dollar deposits from New York and place them with banks in London and Paris. There was a ready market for these funds in financing trade and other transactions in which, as we saw, the use of European currencies was limited.

A second source of funds was Marshall Aid. This contributed just over US$13bn to the recovery of the European countries after the war. But although these were official funds which largely found their way back to the United States in orders for equipment, materials, etc., they were largely in the form of concessionary lending, much of which was never effectively repaid. It ensured the continuing existence of an unofficial market in US dollars in Europe.

The introduction of multilateral convertibility in 1958 gave a big boost to the Euromarkets since it lifted certain exchange controls and also obliged central banks to be much more active in the management of their foreign exchange reserves against currencies other than the US dollar. By then the Bank of International Settlements (through which the central banks place their funds for short-term lending to each other and into financial markets) was an active participant in the Euromarkets, so that American dollars found their way from central bank reserves into the Euromarkets and vice versa, even when officially the central banks were only dealing directly with their own regulated currency markets.

The main centre for the Eurocurrency markets was London, where the Bank of England was happy to allow British and overseas banks to borrow and lend foreign currency freely as long as it was not on behalf of residents within the sterling area. As Table 4.3 shows, the advantage of London was that interest rates on dollar deposits were higher than in New York. There was also no formal capital or liquidity requirements for Eurocurrency operations. Banks, and American banks in particular, therefore had every incentive to borrow dollars in the United States, where interest rates were held down by Regulation Q, and lend them on in London. Where exchange controls made it illegal for funds to be transferred directly from New York to London, American and international banks found ways of accumulating foreign payments in dollars in London, which were then used to service the Eurodollar markets, while payments of interest and settlements were made in New York with funds from money markets there. Foreign payments in dollars accumulated rapidly, as from the 1950s onwards the United States ran large balance of payments' deficits that rarely fell below US$2.5bn a year. Arguably, it was in everyone's interests — those of international banks, their customers and even the European central banks — for the Eurodollar markets to flourish.

Table 4.3
Money markets interest rates
1964–76 (% per annum at year end)

	1964	1966	1968	1970	1972	1974	1976
New York (US$)	3.55	4.88	5.35	6.44	4.07	7.87	4.99
London (£)	4.61	6.10	7.09	7.01	5.54	11.37	11.12
Tokyo (yen)	10.03	5.84	7.88	8.29	4.72	12.54	6.98
London, 3-month LIBOR (US$)	4.32	6.12	6.36	8.52	5.46	11.01	5.58

Source: IMF

The next major Eurocurrency to emerge was the Deutschmark. During the 1950s the West German economy was reconstructed and emerged in the subsequent decade as a major force in European trade. Nevertheless, West German banks remained under strict controls to prevent the capital outflows that, it was feared, would undermine continuing domestic investment. There were stringent capital ratio requirements on overseas lending. This made it profitable for the West German banks to accumulate foreign payments in Deutschmarks in their branches in Luxembourg, where capital and reserve requirements on the lending of these Deutschmarks were minimal by comparison with those of West Germany. The progress of Luxembourg as a Eurocurrency source is shown in Table 4.2. It has only been during the 1980s that the Euro-Deutschmark business moved over to London in any significant way.

The Euromarkets developed quickly but somewhat unobtrusively (except when politicians denounced foreign currency speculators) during the 1960s, fed by continuing American balance of payments' deficits. This effectively forced countries that had payments surpluses to take large quantities of American dollars into their foreign exchange reserves, from which they could only be lent in the Euromarkets, if they were not to be sold and thereby threaten the fixed exchange rate structure by driving down the US dollar.

After Bretton Woods

The central bank-controlled international monetary system went through a period of disarray between 1971 and 1973. The issue of huge quantities of dollars by the United States in order to finance the war in Vietnam and chronic payments deficits depleted the American gold reserves to the point where a cornerstone of the Bretton Woods system, the convertibility of the US dollar into gold, was no longer feasible. Expanding world trade (see Table 4.1) also required considerably more liquidity to facilitate its transactions than could be provided by a gold-based system. The latter problem was tackled by the IMF's introduction in 1969 of a new composite currency called the Special Drawing Right (SDR). An attempt was made at a conference in the Smithsonian Building in Washington in December 1971 to rearrange exchange rates and devalue the US dollar to US$38 per ounce of gold. However, by the following June the new exchange rates were themselves in disarray, and in March 1973, the Finance Ministers of the Group of Ten countries (plus Switzerland) abandoned any attempt to keep their currencies pegged to the US dollar.

By the mid-1970s the confusion also blew away what was left of the old sterling zone (although UK exchange controls remained in place until 1979). This left the French franc, now pegged within the European Monetary System's 'snake' or system of fixed exchange rates, as the only currency having a separate international currency zone (although Belgium and Luxembourg have had a currency union since the war). The French franc zone covered mainly France and some of its former African territories, and convertibility in it against other currencies was guaranteed. For most purposes, Europe and North America was an area wherein international banking currencies competed, with the US dollar no longer a standard but a numeraire.

The disarray of the foreign currency markets coincided with another development which had a decisive influence on the expansion of international banking. At the end of 1973, the member states of the Organisation of Petroleum Exporting Countries (OPEC) decided effectively to quadruple the dollar price of oil. At a time when exchange rates were being destabilised, the oil price hike imposed serious balance of payments deficits on most oil-importing countries, which corresponded with vast balance of payments surpluses in the oil-exporting countries. The official institutions, mandated at Bretton Woods to cope with these kinds of imbalances, were unable to cope with their scale, but financing the adjustment was taken up by international commercial banks with enthusiasm. This enthusiasm was understandable. Some of the largest of the oil producers, notably Kuwait and Saudi Arabia, have tiny populations (relative to their size) and relatively few opportunities for domestic investment. Among their customers were countries desperate to finance the payments deficits inflicted on them by the high oil price. Bankers quickly realised that they could take in all the deposits that they could by offering higher interest rates which, together with a good margin could be on-lent to countries anxious for loans. Thus in 1975 some 40% of the total cash surpluses of oil–exporting countries (amounting to £360.9bn) was deposited with international commercial banks.

Lending at this time was mostly in the form of Eurocurrency credits offered by syndicates of international banks at rates of interest that simply specified a margin over the London Interbank Offered Rate (LIBOR), thereby avoiding the interest rate risk inherent in fixed interest lending. Syndicated lending was for medium and long terms, but the maturity mismatch with the short-term deposits which financed these loans has proved to be unproblematical, with the rapid growth of liquidity in the Euromarkets (see Table 4.4). Thus traditional liability management gave way to the now fashionable asset management as the common practice in commercial banking.

Table 4.4
The Eurocurrencies markets
(US$bn), 1970–82

	1970	1973	1976	1979	1982
Gross assets	110	315	595	1235	2015
Net assets	60	160	320	590	940
Eurodollars as % of all Eurocurrencies	81	74	80	72	81

Source: Morgan Guaranty

International bond markets also expanded rapidly. From the 1060s onwards, multinational companies found it increasingly convenient to set up subsidiaries in less regulated financial centres such as the Netherlands Antilles, and the Bahamas, which issued bonds and loans on behalf of their parent companies. The advantage of these bonds was that interest could be paid without deduction of withholding tax. This made them more attractive to investors and thus enabled companies (mainly large corporations with good credit ratings) to raise money at lower rates of interest than in their domestic markets, where interest was paid net of tax. International bond issues have flourished since then, albeit with some hiccups.

With strong growth of these markets, offshore financial centres in the Netherlands Antilles, the Bahamas, Singapore and Hong Kong expanded rapidly (see Table 4.5). Other countries, such as Bahrain, tried to establish their own offshore financial centres. There was a revival in the 1970s of consortium banking, mainly in the Euromarket centres of London and Luxembourg, which brought together smaller banks seeking an international presence. These consortia provided little challenge to the traditional correspondent banking business of banks and may even have complemented it.

At this time too, technological innovation greatly speeded up international banking transactions. By 1978 SWIFT (the Society for World Wide Interbank Financial Telecommunication) was transmitting a wide range of messages and credits between nearly 600 banks throughout Europe, North America and Japan. CEDEL and Euroclear, the two Eurobond clearing systems in Luxembourg and Brussels, respectively, were 'bridged' in 1971, greatly increasing the efficiency of these markets.

However, the 1970s also brought greater dangers to international banking. The instability of exchange rates made foreign currency business more risky, effectively causing banks to gamble more on movements in particular exchange rates. In 1974, Bankhaus Herstatt in West Germany collapsed due to massive foreign exchange losses causing knock-on losses in many institutions outside Germany which had placed interbank deposits. Lloyds Bank International, Westdeutsche Landesbank, and Union Bank of Switzerland also suffered badly from exchange losses due to unmatched positions. The trouble was that dealers broke their own internal rules, and gambled to recover their loss situations.

Nowadays, currency futures markets offer some protection against the often substantial changes in exchange rates that occur in the post-Bretton Woods regime. In the United States, in particular, new kinds of financial options and futures markets became active fairly early on, although it was not until the 1980s that European centres established such markets.

Towards the end of the 1970s and in the early 1980s, it was becoming clear that this expansionary phase of international banking was

Table 4.5
Deposit banks' foreign assets
and liabilities (US$bn), 1971–85

	1971	1975	1980	1985
Liabilities				
United States	26.91	62.72	151.45	381.06
Luxembourg	5.78	28.39	97.26	116.80
United Kingdom	51.07	135.62	375.29	610.13
Total industrial countries	194.80	456.50	1,340.00	2,158.40
Singapore	1.28	10.60	43.50	129.71
Hong Kong	0.58	6.62	32.68	83.33
Bahamas	n/a	n/a	n/a	141.45
Cayman Islands	n/a	n/a	107.92	170.47
Developing countries	28.53	132.81	516.66	825.55
of which: major off-				
shore banking centres	17.67	94.88	367.02	611.83
Total liabilities	223.40	589.30	1,856.70	2,984.00
Assets				
United States	13.61	54.70	203.98	449.01
Luxembourg	6.25	30.15	104.76	131.48
United Kingdom	45.49	125.74	356.32	587.24
Total industrial countries	183.70	457.20	1,360.20	2,212.90
Singapore	1.20	10.55	44.62	120.36
Hong Kong	1.76	9.04	38.06	101.17
Bahamas	n/a	n/a	n/a	143.06
Cayman Islands	n/a	n/a	84.53	173.85
Developing countries	24.77	121.98	461.99	758.76
of which: major off-				
shore banking centres	17.62	96.75	375.38	628.86
Total assets	208.50	579.20	1,822.60	2,971.70

Source: IMF

creating its own problems. Competitive lending and borrowing, the ascendancy of monetarist doctrines in governments' monetary policies, and falling inflation in the 1980s pushed real interest rates up quite sharply to levels from which they have never really fallen in any substantial way (see Table 4.6). This has caused enormous problems for countries that are having to pay floating rate interest on huge external borrowing.

Table 4.6
London Interbank Offered Rate on 3-month deposits
1981–86 (% per annum, annual averages)

	1981	1982	1983	1984	1985	1986	1987	1988
French franc	18.16	19.45	16.53	12.77	10.76	9.46	8.64	8.09
Deutschmark	11.89	8.62	5.60	5.83	5.37	4.64	4.06	4.33
Japanese yen	7.73	6.99	6.57	6.43	6.68	5.12	4.26	4.51
Swiss franc	9.29	5.19	4.19	4.45	5.03	4.33	3.91	3.20
Pound sterling	14.28	12.60	10.26	10.11	11.99	10.82	9.80	10.36
(Relates to Paris market)								

Source: IMF

During the 1970s, private banks began to lend substantial sums to foreign governments. But intense competition among these same banks caused many developing countries to become overborrowed (see Table 4.7). These were mainly oil-importing countries with large under-employed populations, like Brazil and the Philippines, which gained and sometimes wasted easy credit at times when prices for their commodity exports were high (as they generally were in the mid-1970s) as a way of financing investments to develop productive capacity. Some were even oil-producing countries (like Indonesia and Mexico) seeking to diversify away from their dependence on oil exports.

It was the announcement by Mexico at the end of 1982 that it was unable to service debts (of which $80bn was owed to no less than 1,400 individual banks around the world) that confirmed that the debt servicing problems experienced by countries like Brazil, Argentina, Zaire, North Korea, Chile, and Poland in 1981 and 1982 really were so serious that commercial banks could not cope with them on their own. This event may be said to mark the relinquishment by commercial banks of the leading intermediary role in international banking that they had held since the early 1970s. It was accompanied by a rash of

Table 4.7
External debt of major sovereign borrowers
(US$bn) 1975–84 (year end)

	1975[1]	1980	1982	1984	1987
Brazil	23.5	70.0	91.0	104.4	123.9
Mexico	15.6	57.1	85.8	97.3	107.9
Argentina	6.9	27.3	43.6	45.8	56.8
Korea	6.4	29.3	38.3	43.1	40.6
Venezuela	1.5	29.6	31.8	34.2	36.5
Indonesia	10.4	20.9	26.5	32.5	52.6
India	13.3	19.2	24.9	30.7	46.4
Israel	7.1	13.8	22.6	23.8	26.3
Poland	8.0	25.1	25.2	26.8	42.1
Philippines	3.0	17.4	24.2	24.4	30.0
Egypt	4.9	17.3	20.1	30.5	40.3
Turkey	3.5	19.3	20.0	22.3	40.8
Chile	4.9	12.1	17.3	20.0	21.2
Yugoslavia	6.0	18.5	20.0	19.8	23.5
Nigeria	1.2	9.0	19.7	19.7	28.7
Thailand	1.4	8.3	12.2	15.3	20.7
Portugal	1.2	9.2	13.3	15.0	18.2

Note
1. Excludes short-term debt.

Source: World Bank

bank failures in the United States, culminating with the virtual collapse of the Continental Illinois Bank in 1984.

After the Debt Crisis

The Third World debt crisis, and the realisation that assets many times greater in nominal value than the capital of the banks holding them, whilst possibly not worthless, were definitely worth much less, brought on a change in direction and nature of innovation in international banking. First of all there was a realisation that the debt crisis could only be managed (it is now clearly too great to be resolved on its original terms) with the co-operation of official central bank and inter-central bank institutions. This was needed, both as a source of additional lending to ease the cash flow of indebted countries, but also in what became known as 'hand-holding operations' whereby the IMF and the World Bank joined commercial banks in negotiating new debt packages, working out economic adjustment programmes for the debtor nations and providing reassurance to the private banks that they had the sympathy and understanding of central banks. This also implied that the latter would not stand idly by if sovereign debt default got the major commercial banks into difficulties. The Paris Club and the London Club of commercial and official lenders respectively emerged at the start of the 1980s to co-ordinate the creditors' approaches to different sovereign borrowers.

Third World countries, which had welcomed commercial banks in the 1970s as an alternative source of finance to the official institutions which often attached stringent conditions to loans, now found themselves forced to go back to the IMF and the World Bank. The IMF and the central banks, aware of the problems that commercial banks were having, were galvanised by these difficulties and the scandal of the collapse of Banco Ambrosiano in 1982 into reasserting their control over the international monetary and banking systems. The Basle Concordat concluded between the main central banks in 1975, which was supposed to provide comprehensive supervision of banks, was shown to be inadequate to prevent insolvency and unsound banking. Proposals were put forward for more stringent capital requirements and a detailed critique of many of the most fashionable banking practices was published by the 11 main central banks of Europe and North America in 1986. This focused on what the central banks saw as the underpricing of risks by banks, driven to such lengths by fierce competition.

But even in these difficult circumstances new opportunities were found by international bankers. The chief one was the opening up of domestic banking and financial markets in some of the OECD countries to foreign banks, most notably in Britain but also to a limited extent in the United States and Scandinavia. This coincided with a credit boom in Britain and the United States (in the latter case primed by a huge government budget deficit) which meant that there appeared, temporarily at least, to be plenty of business for allcomers in securities markets and mortgage lending. Thus commercial banks which seemed to have been badly affected by the Third World debt crisis simply diversified into lending to 'sounder' economies. As Table 4.5 shows, the proportion of United States assets in the foreign portfolios of banks rose from 11.2 to 15.1% between 1980 and 1985.

However, greater competition in all market segments took its toll on banking margins which have been progressively squeezed as banks compete more intensively for the small amount of sound international lending opportunities available in the mid-1980s. For example, syndicated international bank lending went into a sharp decline after 1982 (see Table 4.8). At the same time the mechanisation of banking transactions effectively stripped away the mystique and some of the specialist skills of banking. Large corporates such as British Petroleum and General Motors found it easier to set up their own corporate banking subsidiaries and avoid having to pay more traditional banks for the execution of treasury transactions. American banks such as Citibank and Chemical Bank readily supplied the technology to these corporate subsidiaries, advising them on hardware, software and their use, and effectively teaching their largest clients to do their own

Table 4.8
International bond and loan issues
(US$bn), 1981–85

	1981	1982	1983	1984	1985
International bonds and notes	44.0	71.7	72.1	108.1	162.8
of which: floating rate notes	7.8	12.6	15.3	34.1	55.4
Convertible bonds	4.1	2.7	6.8	8.5	7.3
Syndicated international bank loans[1]	96.5	100.5	51.8	36.6	21.6
of which: managed loans[2]	–	11.2	13.7	6.5	2.4
Note issuance facilities[3]	1.0	2.3	3.3	18.9	49.4
Total	141.5	174.5	127.2	163.6	233.8

Notes:
1. Excludes United States takeover related standbys.
2. New money element of rescue packages.
3. Includes revolving underwriting facilities, multiple-component facilities (if these include a note issuance option) and other Euronote facilities.

Source: Bank of England

banking. In turn these banks themselves concentrated more on the booming corporate banking business, as takeover booms developed in the United States and Britain.

Faced with this squeeze on their business, international banks had to seek new opportunities. International banks now sought fee income to replace income from margins. These were mainly from two thriving activities which were new to many banks, namely securitisation, or the issue and trading of securities, and off-balance sheet lending. The growth in note issuance facilities, for example, was particularly striking in the mid-1980s (see Table 4.8). It was also relatively easy to make money by the issue and trading of securities when securities markets around the world were booming as was the case from 1980 to the autumn of 1987. However, the collapse of large parts of the floating rate note market in early 1987 indicated that liquidity in such markets can be ephemeral. At the same time, central banks have targeted off-balance sheet lending as requiring much stricter regulation.

Other innovations of the mid-1980s have been a growing array of currency futures and options, of which international banks have been major suppliers as well as users. The London International Financial Futures Exchange opened in 1982 and now has liquid markets in a wide range of futures instruments. Other such exchanges have been mooted in Paris and Zurich. Continuing exchange rate instability has renewed interest in composite currencies such as the ECU (the European Currency Unit, a currency made up of the weighted currencies of the EEC countries) and attempts are being made to develop banking instruments in this unit. It is interesting to note that the last time when composite currencies caught the interest of international bankers in the second half of the 1970s, was also a time when the US dollar was volatile on foreign exchanges. This perhaps shows how little we have actually moved away from a US dollar standard since it was formally abolished in most countries at the start of the 1970s.

In conclusion we may venture the judgement that most businesses are cyclical, and international banking as a business is no exception, despite its superficial appearance of rapid expansion and development since the war. What progress has been made has not been linear (except perhaps in the technology used where progress has probably accelerated over time). Different circumstances have given rise to different opportunities, however much the immediate past has weighed heavily upon corporate international banking at any one time. In summary we may say that international banking increasingly requires specialist attention, but the capital required for it can only be provided by large banks, and specialist attention has to switch its focus as circumstances and profitable opportunities change. Hence the attempt of consortium banks in the 1970s to get into international banking failed in the 1980s because they proved to be insufficiently flexible for the changing opportunities that they faced. By contrast, financial conglomerates with subsidiaries operating across a wide range of markets have become more common in the 1980s precisely because they have the greater flexibility and can afford the large capital necessary to operate in the new markets in off-balance sheet lending, forfaiting and so on.

CHAPTER 5

The Current Environment of Corporate and International Banking

Gillian McGrattan and Jan Toporowski

Introduction

Chapter 4 described how the 1970s was marked by a sharp increase in demand for funds from the international capital markets. Developed and developing countries alike faced yawning gaps in their balance of payments following the 1973/74 oil crisis. In an era of relatively low real borrowing costs and a seemingly unlimited supply of funds channelled through the international banks, many developing countries chose to supplement the finance they received through official channels in order to sustain development. The problems caused by world recession, high real interest rates and low non-oil commodity prices in the early 1980s are well documented and the years of the 'world debt crisis' have been marked by retrenchment on the part of both borrowers and lenders. The recycling of private international capital has essentially become a redistribution among the industrialised countries and, until very recently, was falling increasingly outside the sphere of the international commercial banks. The supply of private capital to developing countries has not recovered and the developing world as a whole has assumed the unnatural role of a supplier of funds to the international banking system.

The changing pattern of international borrowing and lending causes concern for a number of reasons. First, borrowers and lenders have become more remote, given the generally diminished role played by banks as direct providers of funds. Second, the LDCs, even the most heavily indebted, cannot postpone necessary investment and, therefore, growth indefinitely and, as real inflows of official finance are unlikely to accelerate, a voluntary inflow of private capital will be needed to ensure future development. In turn, this will depend upon private markets being assured that the LDCs are pursuing policies which will not result in another overcommitment of debt.

Most importantly, it is becoming widely recognised that the vigorous process of liberalisation and financial innovation in recent years may, unless adequately regulated, have undermined the stability of the international financial system. There is certainly some evidence that it has increased the volatility of asset prices, whether it be of equities, currencies or bonds. As a result, strenuous efforts are being made by central bank regulators to control the growth of certain types of instruments and to ensure that the major players on the international financial markets are adequately capitalised. The fact that rules about capital adequacy may be enforced internationally to provide a 'level playing field' for banks demonstrates the strength of this commitment.

This chapter describes the recent evolution of international financial instruments in the context of the economic and institutional developments, and attempts to forecast how the demand for and supply of international banking products will change over the next few years. Given the variety of products available, it is not possible to describe in detail the structure of each and every available instrument, but some will be dealt with in succeeding chapters.

The Process of Securitisation

The process of securitisation of both domestic and international financial markets in the 1980s has been well documented. Briefly, securitisation describes the shift away from bank-intermediated credit and loans to the use of tradeable instruments which can be bought or sold in a recognised financial market-place. The most commonly-traded securities are clearly fixed rate bonds and equities, but financial innovation has thrown up a myriad of other means of lending and borrowing, including commercial paper (both domestic and Euro), multi-option facilities, floating rate bonds (sometimes with interest rate caps and floors) and innumerable rather exotic and shortlived versions of each of these. In a number of instances, particularly in the United States market, straightforward asset-backed mortgage and consumer loans are often repackaged and traded widely in the secondary market. Some of these instruments are hybrid (i.e. involve some element of direct credit provision by a bank), but essentially all of them rely upon an active, liquid secondary market. Straightforward loans have in some cases been repackaged and sold off to streamline banks' balance sheets and this has given rise, for example, to trade between banks in Third World debt.

A related but not identical phenomenon to securitisation has been disintermediation, the erosion of the traditional relationship between lender and borrower through the aegis of the commercial bank. Clearly it is impossible for a borrower to gauge to whom he is beholden if the initial arranger of finance sells his bond or note on in the secondary market. To begin with, the shift towards the use of capital market instruments was largely confined to blue chip names, whether sovereign or corporate, since end-investors would normally only be willing to hold the debt of a good name with a superior credit rating. However, by the mid-1980s second-tier international borrowers were finding it increasingly easy to acquire funds through the issue of notes or bonds. Similar trends were also evident in domestic financial markets, one example being the popularity of the American 'junk' bond. 'Junk' bonds are high-yielding second-tier debt issues often used for highly leveraged takeovers.

Table 5.1 summarises the trend towards securitisation at the international level, tracing the pattern of borrowing back to the immediate aftermath of the world debt crisis. Quite apart from

Table 5.1
Funds raised in international financial markets
($bn)

	1981	1982	1983	1984	1985	1986	1987	1988
Syndicated loans	95	98	67	62	60	53	89	127
Underwritten note facilities	14	6	10	29	46	29	30	13
Euro-commercial paper	–	–	–	–	22	68	70	77
Total credit-like facilities	109	104	77	91	128	150	189	217
FRNs	7	15	20	38	58	51	11	22
Other bonds	42	60	57	74	110	177	166	203
Total	158	179	154	203	296	378	366	442
of which: Securitised borrowing (%)	39.9	45.2	65.4	69.4	79.7	86.0	75.7	71.3

Source: OECD

demonstrating the turnaround in investor and borrower tastes, the figures also highlight the rapid rate of growth in total borrowing demand in the middle 1980s following an initial period of retrenchment in 1982 and 1983.

The Economic Influences

The economic background to developments on the international financial markets can be summarised as follows. The 1980s were ushered in with a second oil price shock which — unlike the 1973/74 episode — was met by a general policy of retrenchment in the industrial countries. The governments of the major economies generally pursued harsh anti-inflationary policies which, almost overnight, produced a massive hike in worldwide nominal interest rates. This phenomenon was exacerbated by a rather schizophrenic situation in the United States where a very tight monetary policy was accompanied by an extremely lax fiscal policy. As inflationary pressures began to weaken, interest rates became startingly positive in real terms, a sharp contrast with the 1970s when nominal interest rates were generally lower than the rate of inflation. The resumption of worldwide economic growth from 1982 onwards did nothing to reverse this process, and for the period 1983 onwards we have seen modest but sustained global expansion, accompanied by lower inflation and high real interest rates.

Potentially, the most destabilising influences have been the gyration of exchange rates and a build-up of substantial global trading imbalances. The value of the US dollar rose by almost 50% (see Figures 5.1 and 5.2) between 1980 and February 1985, as massive amounts of foreign capital, attracted by high interest rates, flowed into the United States. In turn, foreign capital helped to finance a growing United States budget deficit and offset a substantial current account shortfall occasioned in part by the dollar's over-valuation.

Substantial capital flows from countries in current account surplus (in particular Japan) to the United States domestic capital markets were another factor supporting the securitisation process. Japanese institutional investors bought heavily into US dollar-denominated bonds and notes, a situation which contrasts sharply with the behaviour of the OPEC surplus countries in the 1970s which chose to place their deposits with the international banks. To some extent, therefore, the international commercial banks were excluded from the recycling process in the 1980s, losing heavily to investment banking intermediaries.

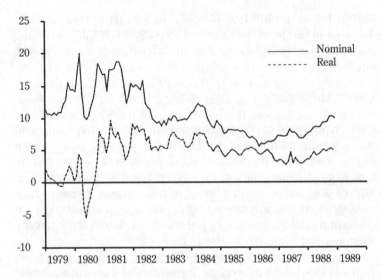

Figure 5.1   US nominal and real interest rates

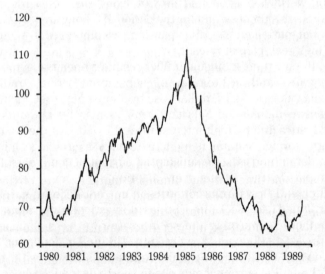

High: 113.1, 26 February 1985
Low: 63.1, 29 December 1987
Last: 72.2, 29 May 1989

Figure 5.2   Bank of England US dollar index (1985=100)

In the period following the dollar's peak in February 1985 private investors became much more wary of the exchange risk posed by the United States currency, and voluntary inflows of private foreign capital to the United States began to dwindle. This encouraged a greater degree of currency diversification in the international capital market, illustrated in Table 5.2. By 1987 the dollar's share of international transactions had fallen to less than 60% compared with 88% in 1982. Financing the United States current account deficit that year fell almost entirely into the domain of the official institutions, and central bank purchases of United States debt amounted to more than $100 billion. Confidence in the dollar was partially restored in 1988 and 1989. By mid-1989 the dollar had appreciated by almost 20% from its end-1987 trough against the other major currencies. However, policy makers were still highly concerned about the dollar's volatility and by continued imbalances in the United States economy.

Several more specific economic factors encouraged the securitisation of international credit flows in the 1980s. The reappearance of positive real interest rates and, more importantly, the emergence of positively-sloped yield curves enhanced the appeal of longer-term bonds to investors, and made it more attractive for the market-makers to hold and trade inventories of such bonds. It is interesting to note that the first signs of vulnerability in the international bond markets emerged during 1989, a year in which the yield curves in the United States, UK, Japan and West Germany flattened out or became downward sloping.

Institutional Influences

Deregulation

During the course of the 1980s there has been widespread deregulation of both domestic and international financial markets. One obvious example of the former is London's 'Big Bang' but there are numerous others, including massive revisions to the Japanese financial system which included the removal of interest rate controls on large-scale deposits and loans and the setting up of an offshore banking market. In many contros, controls over nationality of ownership of financial firms have been lessened or removed, and foreign firms have been allowed to participate in a wider sphere of activities, such as underwriting government bond issues and being eligible for Stock Exchange membership. International transactions have also largely been freed from exchange controls, and withholding tax on the interest payments made to overseas holders of domestic bonds has been abolished in the United States, Japan, Germany, France and a number of smaller centres.

The net result of deregulation has been to globalise financial markets, by breaking down many of the barriers between domestic financial markets. It has thus blurred the distinction between international and domestic transactions, although perhaps surprisingly this has not signalled the demise of the Euromarkets which initially came into being to circumvent national regulations.

Table 5.2
Currency composition of international bank lending (%)

	1982	1984	1986	1987	1988
US Dollar	88.2	73.3	67.0	65.1	70.7
Yen	3.7	11.6	16.1	10.8	5.4
Sterling	2.8	4.6	6.4	14.7	14.0
ECU	0.3	2.7	2.2	2.4	2.7
Deutschmark	1.5	2.0	3.0	2.4	2.2
Swiss franc	0.1	1.6	2.1	0.7	0.2
Others	3.4	4.2	3.2	3.9	4.8
	100.0	100.0	100.0	100.0	100.0

Source: IMF

There has also been an erosion of the traditional barriers between credit markets and capital markets and between the institutions operating in each of these. Regulatory boundaries (such as those imposed between 'banks' and 'securities firms' by the United States Glass-Steagall Act) have also diminished and may well disappear altogether within the next few years in the major economies.

Financial innovation
The 1980s has undoubtedly been marked by a once-and-for-all increase in the pace of financial innovation, and this has been a major factor behind the rapid increase in total borrowing and lending activity in the period 1984–87.

The forces driving the process of financial innovation have both a supply and a demand aspect. On the supply side, financial institutions have been encouraged to innovate by a combination of business circumstances, one of which is clearly much greater competition. In domestic markets, banks and non-banks have increasingly been competing against one another in the same product markets. In the international markets there are far more participants, and well-established United States and European commercial banks have had to face new challenges from both Japanese commercial banks and from investment banks entering the international arena. Japanese institutions have been particularly competitive and have shown a considerable appetite for asset growth in the 1980s. Partly as a result of the revaluation of the yen, they now predominate the league table of the world's largest banks. Japanese banks have an advantage of being able to raise equity capital relatively cheaply in the Tokyo stock market. The net result has been that financial institutions have become more willing to make markets in new instruments where they feel that they have at least a temporary comparative advantage, normally at highly favourable terms. Not only has competition for business increased the range of borrowing vehicles, but it has created a general reduction in the cost to borrowers.

Other influences have been equally important. Chief of these is the role of new technology, particularly developments in tele-communications, information and computer systems. The Bank for International Settlements (BIS) concluded that technology has had three major effects on financial innovation. First, it has simultaneously reduced costs and allowed the development of a genuine global financial market. As a result, no borrower or lender is now stranded in an isolated market without full access to information. Moreover, this has helped to enhance liquidity by building up a broader market in particular instruments. Second, technology has enabled participants to calculate the price of increasingly complex instruments on a continuous basis, enabling exposures to be monitored and hedges put in place. Finally, a better flow of information has encouraged more competitive pricing by reducing search costs, particularly in traditional business areas. Enhanced transaction speed also means that price differentials between markets can only be shortlived. In turn, this has encouraged market-makers to construct more complex products with initially higher margins.

Aside from enhanced competition and advances in technology, the other major force driving the process of financial innovation during the 1980s has been the regulatory pressure for increased capitalisation. Essentially, banks have been required to reduce their gearing and simultaneously improve asset quality. Given both the cost and frequent difficulty of raising new capital, this has encouraged banks to diversify into off-balance sheet fee-earning business. This has often made them arrangers rather than direct providers of finance, and the most important instruments examined in this chapter are major examples of the off-balance sheet activities of commercial as well as investment banks. To the regulators these instruments have posed something of a conundrum; while they do not appear as direct balance sheet loans with attendant capital requirements, in many cases they represent contingent liabilities. Much of the work done recently on new international regulations concerns the growth of these instruments.

Demands for financial innovation

Financial innovation has also been driven by the need, in increasingly sophisticated financial markets, for products which, *inter alia*, enhance liquidity and help to transfer or cover risk. The globalisation of financial markets and the removal of controls on interest and exchange rates means that borrowers and investors have been faced with much greater volatility in asset prices than was previously the case. Minimising risk exposure has therefore become of extreme importance. A BIS study group set up in 1986 under the Chairmanship of Mr Sam Cross of the New York Federal Reserve Bank categorised the demand for financial innovation under five broad headings. These are:

(a) Innovations which transfer price risk;
(b) Innovations which help to transfer credit risk;
(c) Innovations which tend to increase liquidity;
(d) Innovations which encourage the generation of credit;
(e) Innovations which generate equity, such as equity warrants attached to bond issues.

The most prevalent category has been innovations which transfer price risk, principally because of the volatility of exchange and interest rates in the 1980s. The most obvious examples of instruments which transfer price risk are financial futures, forward exchange contracts, options and swaps. Another is floating rate debt which enables borrowers to match assets and liabilities, particularly popular with institutions which have found their cost of funds being decontrolled while the return on assets remains fixed. One example is provided by the experience of American Savings and Loans institutions, which are now required to pay a floating rate of interest on their deposits whilst a significant proportion of their mortgage assets have been advanced at fixed rates.

Innovations which try to generate liquidity arise from the persistence of high real interest rates, since these have significantly increased the opportunity cost of holding liquid assets. Another factor has been a worldwide increase in debt/income ratios (particularly for the household sectors in the UK and the United States), which is of widespread concern and demands a degree of supporting liquidity in the event of the real debt burden becoming too large. Such concerns provide some, but not all, of the explanation for the increasing securitisation of mortgage and consumer lending.

New Financial Instruments

As a result of the accelerated pace of financial innovation, both borrowers and lenders are currently faced with a plethora of potential financial instruments. Some of the instruments of the 1980s have been 'nine-day wonders', falling from grace when it has become obvious that they have too liquid or too narrow an underlying market for survival. On occasions this has been because the arranger, in his quest for business in an over-competitive market, has made it uneconomical for other institutions to participate. In most cases it is because there is no supporting secondary market in which investors can sell on their asset.

In this section we shall analyse the main characteristics of some of the more durable instruments of the 1980s, including Euronotes, Euro-commercial paper, forward-rate agreements and Swaps.

The Euronote

The Euronote has a number of definitions. For the sake of clarity, we shall use it to mean a tradeable short- or medium-term instrument for which a commercial bank provides a guarantee to advance a loan in the event that the note cannot be placed with final investors. The Euronote came into being in 1981/82 and for a number of years was an important off-balance sheet instrument which enabled both sovereign and corporate borrowers to obtain cheap finance, largely as a replacement for traditional syndicated bank credit (see Table 5.3).

The most common form of Euronote is the note issuance facility (NIF) which, in 1983 and 1984, was the most popular low-cost substitute for the syndicated loan for sovereign borrowers. Banks became major underwriters in this market, and by late 1984 the average size of an issue stood at almost $500m, double the average size of the previous two years. By 1985 corporate borrowers had entered the market, often using the Euronote as a substitute for more expensive long-term sources of finance such as variable rate bonds. Until 1986 Euronotes attracted a zero balance sheet weighting for capital adequacy unless banks actually had to take the paper on to their own books.

The reason for the popularity of the NIF in the mid-1980s was therefore its cheapness. Because this was off-balance sheet business, banks were not obliged to provide a capital commitment and could thus underwrite the paper more cheaply than a direct loan, and their income from this activity was largely in the form of arrangement fees.

Table 5.3
The Euronote market ($bn)

	1982	1983	1984	1985	1986	1987	1988
Underwritten Euronotes	2.5	3.9	28.8	42.9	29.3	29.9	13.2
of which:							
Multiple component							
facilities	–	–	8.0	15.0	13.2	17.1	7.9
Non-underwritten							
facilities (e.g. ECP)	2.9	5.6	18.9	23.2	67.6	72.3	76.8
Total note programmes	5.4	9.5	47.7	66.1	96.9	102.2	90.0
of which:							
Underwritten (%)	46.3	41.0	60.4	64.9	30.2	29.2	14.7

Source: OECD

The popularity of the NIF-like underwritten Euronote reached a peak in 1985, when it accounted for almost 15% of all international borrowing. Thereafter, its popularity began to wane, although the concept of an underwritten note by no means disappeared. The reason for the relative decline of the NIF was twofold.

First, central banks became very concerned that the underlying market for NIFs was illiquid and, in the event of the notes becoming unplaceable, underwriting banks could be faced with a sudden large demand for loans for which they had set aside no capital. As a consequence, led by the Bank of England, central banks began to impose capital requirements on the underwriting and holding of NIFs whether or not the facility was actually drawn down. This made it uneconomical for many banks to participate without a rise in costs to the borrower.

By late 1985, meanwhile, prime borrowers were beginning to tap a growing market for Euronotes which were not backed up by a bank guarantee. The most common form of non-underwritten Euronote is Euro-commercial paper, the main characteristics of which are described below.

As a direct result of regulatory pressure on NIFs and similar Euronotes such as revolving underwritten facilities (RUFs), the share of underwritten facilities in the total issue of short-term Euro-securities fell from a peak of more than 60% in 1985 to less than 15% in 1988. The only underwritten facility which has grown in popularity is the multi-option facility (MOF). This is a highly-flexible instrument underwritten by commercial banks which, as its name suggests, allows a borrower to tap a number of different markets (e.g. commercial paper, NIFs and direct loans), often in a combination of currencies.

Euro-commercial paper

Euro-commercial paper (ECP) has much in common with domestic commercial paper. As with the underwritten Euronote, ECP is basically a promissory note, but one where the issuance of paper is separate from any standby credit arrangement. ECP also tends to be distributed by dealers rather than by bank tender panels and there is a broader investor base. Because the issuing bank provides no commitment to provide funds, the cost of borrowing through ECP programmes is less than that of underwritten Euronotes. However, it is a market which largely excludes second-grade borrowers and to date the most active participants have been 'blue-chip' corporates in the industrialised countries.

Since its inception in 1985, the ECP market has expanded rapidly (see Table 5.4). Initially, the primary currency for ECP programmes was the US dollar but more recently paper has been issued in ECU, yen, and both Australian and New Zealand dollars. The range of maturities has also expanded; at first, ECP borrowing was normally for short time-spans but in the last 18 months there has been rapid growth in medium-term note programmes. These have begun to attract large-scale sovereign borrowers, such as Belgium.

Unlike other Euro-securities, the ECP market appeared fairly resilient to the effects of the stock market crash in October 1987, and issuing activity has remained brisk ever since. This has much to do with the perception that ECP has a broad investor base, and ECP has remained immune from a post-crash shift back to traditional forms of financing.

Table 5.4
Euro-commercial paper borrowing (US$bn)

	1985	1986	1987	1988
ECP	12.6	59.0	55.3	57.3
Other non-underwritten Euronotes	10.6	8.6	14.3	19.5
Total	23.2	67.6	69.6	76.8
of which:				
medium-term programmes	–	1.7	7.9	12.4

Source: OECD

Forward-rate agreements (FRAs)

A forward-rate agreement is one good example of an instrument designed to cope with interest rate volatility. The market has grown rapidly since its inception in late-1984 and trading activity is currently estimated to be well in excess of $100 billion per annum. An FRA is basically an interest rate future, in which two parties agree on the interest rate to be paid on a notional deposit of a specified maturity at a settlement date. The buyer of an FRA is normally looking to protect himself from a future rise in interest rates and the seller from an interest rate fall. Because no principal is exchanged and buyers and sellers merely settle in cash at the end of the contract period, FRAs enable banks to adjust their interest rate exposure without any need for extra liquidity; at settlement date the amount paid to either party depends only on the difference between the actual interest rate and the interest rate agreed in the contract.

The market in FRAs is predominantly in US dollars, although currencies where interest rates are perceived to be volatile have also attracted attention. The biggest centre is London, closely followed by New York. It is mainly an interbank market, although corporates occasionally use FRAs to cover future borrowing rates or, if cash rich, to protect deposit rates. Banks are prepared to provide tailormade FRAs which means that their customers do not have to enter the futures market or trade in pre-set periods. This is a very good example of innovation. By reducing a bank's recourse to the normal interbank market (which of course entails a balance sheet commitment), FRAs have been widely used to preserve capital at a time when regulators have been anxious to improve capital adequacy. The popularity of FRAs, as with many other 'new' financial instruments, is closely linked to interest rate volatility which, as we have seen earlier, has been one of the dominant economic features of the 1980s. Further details are provided in Chapter 16.

Swaps

A swap transaction is essentially one which enables the two parties involved to exploit each other's comparative advantage in the financial markets. The swap may be a currency or an interest rate transaction, in which two counterparties agree to exchange streams of payments over time. A swap can give a borrower access to a segment of the market from which he is either excluded or can only obtain funds at a higher cost.

Both currency and interest rate swaps have earlier origins than the 1980s, but the market in its present form began to evolve in 1982/83. Activity accelerated sharply in 1984 and 1985 in both domestic and international markets and since then has continued to grow in size and sophistication. Today, outstanding swaps are estimated to stand between $300 and $400 billion, and swap activity supports demand in many other sectors of the international capital market. The largest intermediaries are the United States, UK, Japanese, Swiss and German banks (both commercial and investment) which act both as arrangers and as principals in swap transactions.

The currency swap, covered in detail in Chapter 15, is very much like the old-fashioned back-to-back loan when two parties in different countries make loans to one another, of equal value, denominated in the currencies of each lender and maturing on the same date. In the 1970s, UK borrowers often used the back to back loan to circumvent exchange controls. The major difference between the back-to-back loan and the currency swap is that the former incurred a balance sheet commitment by each party; in the latter no exchange of principal is made until the swap matures and in the interim only different streams of interest payments are exchanged. By swapping currencies a borrower may gain access to currency markets where he has no 'name', where there is little active trading, or where there are still residual exchange controls. Swaps have underpinned the international market in bonds and notes denominated in relatively minor currencies, such as Australian and New Zealand dollars and the Scandinavian currencies.

The interest rate swap, which is examined in greater detail in Chapter 16, was a natural progression from the simple exchange of currencies, and swapping of debt has been a rapidly expanding market over recent years. Again, counterparties exploit each other's comparative advantage so as to obtain funds more cheaply than would otherwise be the case. The simplest example is where one borrower who desires fixed rate debt but can only raise floating rate funds, swaps with a counterparty able to raise fixed rate finance but who would prefer floating rate funds in the belief that they would be cheaper. In this example the first party might be a corporate with a reasonably good name in the short-term market but with no track record of raising long-term finance, who wants to know precisely what its funding costs will be throughout. The variations on this theme are endless and can be extremely complex.

Prospects

Throughout this chapter we have examined the advantages and disadvantages of financial innovation, the major feature of international capital markets in the 1980s. The process can generally be regarded as desirable, since it increases the efficiency of financial markets. The potential drawback is the fact that highly-developed financial links can be destabilising, as witnessed by the events of both October 1987 and, on a smaller scale, October 1989. 'Black Monday' has sparked many moves to limit the volatility of securities transactions, particularly in the United States, but problem areas still remain. The main risk lies in a downturn in the world economy after many years of sustained growth. This would expose the vulnerability of the build up of debt/income ratios, particularly in the United States and UK. This was one factor behind recent concern about the accumulation of leveraged debt (used to finance takeovers) in the United States market, which occasioned the mini Wall Street crash in October 1989. The major conclusion is that a less favourable world economic climate, if accompanied by even more volatile asset prices, may spark a period of retrenchment in financial markets and a partial return to more traditional forms of international finance.

CHAPTER 6

Prudential Banking

Peter Davies

Editor's Notes

Having described the position of banks in the current financial markets, the need to consider the limitations of the financial institutions to the provision of finance is outlined. The harmonisation of rules about capital adequacy and risk weighting among banks in the OECD countries has now been achieved and will have, as a result, an increase in the cost of providing finance in some areas of activity. For example, the effect of regulations currently may increase the cost to a bank of adding its confirmation to letter of credit to the equivalent of over $\frac{1}{8}$% per annum.

Students will recognise that securitisation as mentioned in the previous chapter owes its development at least in part to some of the concepts covered in this chapter.

Introduction

The aim of this chapter is to crystallise the reader's understanding of the factors which constrain the ability or willingness of the financial markets to finance the operations of corporates. Such finance can be direct or indirect, which latter would include not only lending to customers of the corporate with or without recourse to it, but also such mechanisms as leasing and forfaiting.

The factors which affect the financial markets' ability or willingness to provide finance fall into three broad categories:

(a)   Those connected with the risk that borrowers may not repay the lending when required to do so (or deliver currency in conformity with the terms of their contract with the bank or other financial institution).

(b)   Those arising directly from intrinsic characteristics of the individual operators in the market.

(c)   Those arising from the activities of regulatory authorities (these usually have the force of law).

The Risk That Borrowers May Not Repay or Deliver

It is outside the scope of this chapter to discuss the basic canons of lending which must be a component of any risk-taking decision on the part of the banker. Suffice to say that corporate risk assessment in most financial institutions is characterised by the consideration of lending propositions from the viewpoint of a corporate's past track record as disclosed in its published accounts and the availability of assets chargeable as security, rather than from an analysis of cash flow, other future projections and confidence in the ability of management. This is not necessarily unreasonable when so many major companies are really conglomerates operating in several different countries and industries with the added risks of currency and parity changes, and political interference.

Within most financial institutions the assessment of sovereign risk is now characterised by the use of matrices which take into account financial, structural and economic, and political and strategic factors. Typical of these is the matrix set out below which gives the relative weightings of an assessment of the short to medium term.

Financial factors		50
of which:		
Current account deficit/GNP ratio	10	
Import coverage	10	
*Liquidity gap ratio (% of exports)	10	
Outstanding debt/GNP ratio	10	
Total debt service ratio (% of exports)	10	
Political/strategic factors		30
Structural/economic factors		20
of which:		
Commodity reliance (% of exports)	5	
Economic structure and management	15	
		100

* an indicator of a country's foreign currency cash flow strength (or weakness)

Using such categorisations as these, an institution may quite arbitrarily decide whether it regards a particular country as being a good or less satisfactory risk. Different institutions lay greater or lesser stress on individual components but they are all in broad agreement and the classification of countries as between the various banks' methods show relatively few major divergencies.

Some institutions also have a different categorisation for longer term, e.g. investment projects involving terms of 20 years and more. In this the table would typically be as follows:

Economic structure and management	15
Financial indicators	25
Political/strategic	45
Resources vulnerability	15
	100

If one compares the two different tables above, one will notice how the political/strategic component of the calculation is increased from 30% to 45% in the longer term, whilst that of the financial factors is halved from 50% to 25%.

Taking the case of a long-term capital project it is apparent that such a major project, which when completed may improve the various poor ratings under these headings, will nevertheless often be subject to critical appraisal using short-term criteria which will make it an unacceptable risk to commercial banks. It is in this context that the co-financing activities of the World Bank and other such institutions come very much more into focus. Although commercial banks cannot be expected always to look at a repayment horizon of 20 years, even in support of the exports of their most important corporate customers, they do indeed take on such lengthy commitments from time to time, for example in the energy project field. However, there is an ongoing need for very long-term finance which in many cases can only be met by State and supranational institutions.

In extending facilities to overseas banks, most financial institutions take the sovereign risk aspect very much into account because they judge that the authorities in any country will tend to stand by major commercial banks and would not wish to see them collapse. The ability of some countries (mostly LDCs) to support their indigenous commercial banks by supplying the necessary foreign currency is questionable and thus an adverse factor in determining the level of facilities which should be made available to those banks. This is particularly the case if the external debt situation of the country itself is serious since the application of criteria like those in the tables above leads inevitably to an unfavourable assessment of risk. This is important from a corporate's point of view if it is offered an unconfirmed letter of credit from a foreign buyer of its products. A distinct unwillingness on the part of London banks generally to add their confirmation to such transactions is characterised not so much by their assessment of the bank involved but very much more from the situation involved in the economic life of that country. This is not necessarily the wisest course in the long run, and indeed banks have, with some justification, been criticised for their attitude towards the financing of short-term trade lines. However, the banks' argument is that they are looking at the worst possible situation and wish to limit precisely the amount at which they are at risk if the worst comes to the worst, and they can point to situations where short-term trade finance loans have been included willy-nilly in the rescheduling of some longer-term sovereign indebtedness.

Similarly, some financial institutions take into consideration the sovereign risk aspect if they are asked to lend to the overseas subsidiaries of major corporates, unless the parent itself is willing to give a full guarantee. Clearly, if a bank has less security than the formal guarantee of the parent then it is likely to seek a higher rate of interest in order to reward itself for the slightly higher risk or alternatively, may decline altogether.

In foreign exchange contracts (especially forward ones) the risks are twofold, first that the other party may not be able to deliver, in which case the bank will have to close out the deal, perhaps at an irrecoverable loss (or possibly at a profit which, dependent on the wording of the contract, may or may not be due to the defaulting party). This loss can usually be limited to that resulting from parity changes provided some forewarning is received, but if none is received, the bank then runs a second risk that it might have made an irrecoverable delivery of funds. Thus whilst the first risk is essentially marginal the second can represent a potential 100% loss.

In Swaps activity the scale of risk is different as between interest rate, and currency swaps. The failure of one party in an interest rate swap gives rise only to a small figure of risk in relation to the loan amounts, whilst in a currency swap the risk can be the whole of the parity rate divergence as between the two sums involved. Needless to say the bank will seek to limit the costs by the substitution of a new counterparty if the contract still has some time to run before full maturity.

Intrinsic Characteristics of the Organisation

There is a wide variety of difference between the varying operators in financial markets as to their ability or willingness to provide finance.

Size must be the first factor to be considered and clearly a relatively small bank is in no position to make loans of very large amounts in relation to its existing capital. A number of banks have internal rules that they will not lend more than a certain percentage or multiplier of their capital base to any one country, or companies and banks operating within a country, or to all the companies in a particular industry, or for a certain length of time. Such rules are often more severe and restrictive than those imposed by the regulatory authorities.

Incidentally, it was partly the scale of the credit requirements of large corporates in relation to the lending capacities of all but the largest banks which originally led to the syndication of major borrowing opportunities since no bank wants to be too greatly extended in any one sector of its lending and the satisfactory spread of risks is one of the principal canons of successful banking.

Major banks in many countries regard themselves as having social responsibilities over and above those forced on them by regulatory authorities and in addition they wish to avoid adverse criticism in the financial press or from their shareholders, for example certain major banks will never knowingly lend money to finance the supply of arms, or for political reasons will not lend to certain countries. Corporates active in such markets are usually well aware of which banks are particularly restrictive in their attitudes.

Traditionally, merchant banks which do not have the capacity to make loans in large amounts carved a niche in the 1960s for themselves in financial advice and as syndicate leaders in raising large amounts of money. Their dominance of this latter activity has since been successfully challenged by commercial banks. They gain their income via the commission for arranging the deal and are less concerned about the return to the banks which they manage to persuade to join in any particular deal. This is particularly noticeable in respect of certain deals which have been done at a few basis points where there are numerous recent examples of the major banks being unwilling to join in such financings even though they are principal bankers to the borrower.

Certain other banks have set out to develop different niches in the market, specialising in a narrow range of services where they consider that they have a genuine competitive advantage. In addition there are banks which specialise in individual types of finance or, alternatively, finance for specific areas of the world. There are, for example, specialist banks for ship mortgage, energy projects, and Latin America and Middle East lending.

Common to many banks is the practice of imposing a limit on their unbalanced positions, for example the extent to which they will fund long-term lending with short-term deposits, or fund a swaps book. For example: a typical rule requires that 75% of long-term assets must be matched by similarly long-term deposits. Since banks can usually fund more cheaply from shorter-term deposits such rules restrict their opportunities for profit but also limit the potential danger if short-term deposits become scarce or prohibitively expensive.

Similarly, some major banks decline as a matter of principle to provide standby lines (except as a component of a MOF) because they believe that in a 'holocaust' situation every corporate and financial institution will call on these lines at the same time creating a catastrophic domino effect.

Finally, and perhaps most crucial of all, some banks impose specific conditions as to the profit that they expect to make out of individual deals. They insist that all proposals to lend must give minimum returns on capital employed. Those banks which have highly-developed costing systems are more prone to impose higher margins or minimum rates of interest below which they will not lend.

Regulatory Requirements

Central banks and other regulatory authorities usually have specific social, economic and political objectives in framing the rules, for example:

(a) *The maintenance of confidence in the banking or other financial system.* This confidence is not only to assure the man in the street that his savings are safe but also to ensure that no operators in the market are allowed to take unfair advantage of their privileged position and that there are seen to be effective means to ensure the stability and orderly development of financial markets. Methods employed to cover the former include deposit protection and insurance, restriction in expansion (licensing of new branches or banks) rules as regards minimum capital (varying as to type of operation), the maintenance of specific financial ratios and in the case of non-resident controlled banks a guarantee of the controlling shareholders.

In order to ensure the probity of operators in the market, restrictions on the transfer of information between different parts of an organisation (the Chinese Wall concept), and more particularly the recent appointment of compliance officers in many London institutions, reflect the vastly increased legally-backed directives of central agencies set up to control the markets.

Most jurisdictions have regulations which require permission before a bank is established. Banks are usually categorised and certain operations are not allowed to certain types of bank licence holders, and in some cases specific approval of the appointment of top executives is required.

It is, however, the requirement to maintain specified balance sheet and other ratios which impacts most upon the ability of banks to expand their operations. Whilst in London the Bank of England was flexible in its requirements, other jurisdictions had more rigid rules which for example (typically) precluded a bank from lending more than 18 times its defined capital base. Another required that the defined capital base shall comprise at least 4% of the balance sheet total. Similar regulations may specify a proportion of each category of deposit which may be lent. For example, in Germany, where only 10% of short-term interbank deposits were available for commercial lending, the effect was to make wholesale lending to corporates totally unprofitable with the result that German banks established Luxembourg subsidiaries in order to circumvent the effects of this regulation. Similarly, where only 70% of other deposits taken from non-banks were available for lending this meant that the liquidity requirements affecting the 30% not available made it impossible for banks to take wholesale deposits from non-banking sources and lend them both profitably and competitively. The result was inevitably disintermediation and the spawning of numerous money brokers who have stepped in to meet the resultant commercial needs.

Whilst such directives may in fact protect the interests of depositors and other participants there can be little doubt that these restrictions slow down the speed with which financial institutions can act to assist their corporate clients. In addition, these directives must inevitably put up the price of services which the banks offer.

No comment on banking regulations would be complete without mentioning the activities of the 'group of ten' countries to achieve common capital adequacy requirements for banks. In the summer of 1988 the central bank governors of these nations agreed on a set of rules for the amount of capital banks must maintain relative to the volume and perceived risk of their assets and exposure off-balance sheet. These rules which are to be introduced by the end of 1992, include the requirement that banks with significant international business must maintain capital equivalent to at least 8% of assets weighted according to risk, and that not less than 50% of the defined capital must comprise equity, disclosed reserves and non-cumulative participating preference stock (core capital). The balance (supplementary capital) may comprise revaluation reserves, general provisions, various hybrid debt instruments, some subordinated debt, etc. Whether this will spawn 'tax haven' type activities by institutions attempting to circumvent the agreement remains to be seen. However, in some of the existing tax havens, e.g. Cayman Islands, a banking inspectorate exercises strict control.

(b) *Control of credit.* Whilst control of credit by the government Treasury and central banks is the most widely acknowledged method of harnessing the markets to meet the economic and political objectives of the State, most jurisdictions give the central bank or finance minister sweeping powers to direct almost all of the groups of operators in the financial markets. This control may be:

(i) quantitative, i.e. total volume of credit;

(ii) qualitative, i.e. direction of lending to specific types of activity;

(iii) by price, i.e. usually across the board by an increase in the official discount rate or equivalent.

Any forms of credit control which may be introduced can have a significant serious impact on the investment decisions of a corporate. If a project is calculated to be profitable provided the interest rate remains below a certain level then any increase close to that level or above it is likely to erode significantly or even totally the operating profits. Nowhere is the effect of this better demonstrated than in the major investment project where due to a change of interest rate a project becomes uneconomic, and because of long lead times the ultimate deficit reaches catastrophic proportions. The importance of obtaining fixed-rate funding cannot in such cases therefore be ignored.

(c)   *Exchange control.* Many countries have restrictions, the object of which is much more to prevent capital outflows than to restrict trade or current account items. Similarly, in some countries foreign currencies may only be used for foreign trade transactions and special and indeed exceptional permission has to be sought to use foreign currencies for any other purposes.

The effect of exchange control in many instances is to prevent corporates from taking relatively speedy advantage of market opportunities for investment. In some cases the delay in obtaining permission, caused partly by their own internal problems of building a convincing case for the authorities and partly by the delay which the authorities inevitably impose while they consider the matter, can lead to useful opportunities being missed.

At the time of writing there is no exchange control for UK residents but it should not be overlooked that in some cases UK incorporated companies controlled by non-residents are also limited by exchange control regulations in the countries of their parents. For example, United States legislation impacts upon the investment decision of subsidiaries of United States corporates based overseas and is usually regarded by them as entirely binding on what they do.

The Reaction of Corporates

The Corporate Treasurer has prudential banking objectives parallel to those of the banks themselves. First and foremost he will only deposit his liquid reserves with first-class institutions. Obviously it is far better to receive a $\frac{1}{16}\%$ per annum less interest on your short-term money than to risk losing it due to failure of a less than adequately capitalised bank. As a direct result of this the leading banks in London which are well capitalised receive deposits at well below market rates placed by Treasurers and others who are more concerned with the safety of their deposit than the maximum interest return. This flight to quality gives the larger banks the opportunity to decline to take deposits at market rates thus giving them a competitive advantage as regards the price at which they lend.

As a corollary, the Corporate Treasurer is also concerned to ensure that his sources of funds are secure and hence prefers to foster active banking relationships with a number of quality banks rather than to borrow only from the cheapest source.

Similarly, a corporate with extensive overseas operations may well decline to place funds overnight or for short periods in London with the branch or associate of the same bank in the overseas territory with which it does business. If the situation in the overseas territory deteriorates then the parent bank might well wish to claim or freeze deposits in London in respect of lendings to the overseas subsidiary of the corporate.

The individual characteristics of banks operating in the market leads corporates to identify which banks have particular interests in certain areas. A company exporting capital goods to Latin America is likely to foster relationships with banks which are established in or with specialist financing banks for those areas. Similarly, a capital goods exporter wishing to export to other difficult territories will be concerned to find out which banks, including its major clearers, have an appetite for more business in those countries. It is by no means unusual for Treasurers to telephone round all the banks with which they deal to establish their potential interest before they advise their colleagues on the manufacturing or selling side that there is likely to be some difficulty or otherwise in obtaining credit support for the buyers of their products. Many major deals have been lost by companies which have not been able to find banks willing to lend money or give other forms of credit to the potential buyers of their projects and products. This situation impacts far less on a company which, for example, only exports consumer products to OECD markets.

Where there is a shortage of credit available for a particular country or for the buyers established in it, the price is likely to rise. A direct result of this has been much higher fees charged by banks for the confirmation of letters of credit for certain countries and in some cases the exporters have been happy to pay these additional fees in order to obtain confirmation.

The Corporate Treasurer must keep a close track therefore on the economies and trading conditions in all those countries with which his company regularly does business. Political and economic problems in a country can cause the availability of credit to disappear overnight and the Treasurer can only protect his organisation against such sudden withdrawal of credit by prior arrangement and, usually, the payment of commitment fees in one form or another. These include specific higher charges for confirmation of documentary credits, performance bonds, repayment guarantees, etc.

In conclusion, it should be recognised that Corporate Treasurers are usually fully conversant with the ability of the financial markets to meet their needs. This is essential not only to help them forecast their own expected future situation in relation to market trends and their expectations, but also to enable them to take advantage of any favourable opportunities which may develop within their overall remit to ensure that the company always has access to available funds from the market-place.

Further Reading

The Treasurer: July/August 1988, 'Capital Adequacy Ratio'.

PART B

Editor's Notes

A study of the finance function within the large corporate introduces a series of chapters commencing with considerations of capital both as to its inherent characteristics and its acquisition, and followed by a similar analysis of medium- and longer-term borrowing with some practical examples of the instruments available and their application in given situations.

Shorter-term borrowing is introduced by a chapter on the management of a corporate's liquidity followed by one on the instruments available for providing short-term funds.

Chapters 14, 15 and 16 on currency and interest rate exposure are introduced with an outline of the considerations applicable in the management of these risks before a description of the relative instruments available and their practical application.

Chapter 17 stresses the importance to the corporate of effective and rapid transmission of funds as it is a vital component in managing its liquidity. The need to take into consideration the effect of differences in taxation rules, both in their own right and in relation to investment overseas (as well as other factors), is outlined in Chapter 18.

The various instruments utilised in financing foreign trade are described in Chapter 19 and their application discussed as an introduction to the final chapters which cover financial packages and project finance, concepts which draw together many of the techniques described earlier.

CHAPTER 7

The Finance Function

*Jennifer Hopper**

Editor's Notes

*Having introduced the reader in the first six chapters to the
background against which the large corporates have developed and
the environment in which they operate, Chapter 7 outlines the
finance function. It is based on an example of a major UK group
which is typical of many enterprises broadly similar in size and in
many different sectors of activity. The level of autonomy granted to
subsidiaries and other group companies will vary widely, but central
to all such groups are the carefully thought out policies on all aspects
of finance with specific directives and authority being given to
designated officials or committees and with defined procedures to
cover the action required in exceptional circumstances.*

*Contrary to what is sometimes said, an essential task of the
Treasurer is to ensure that funds are always available to the
corporate rather than always to obtain funds at the lowest possible
cost.*

Introduction: The Position of the Finance Function in a Corporate

A primary objective of any corporate activity is the maximisation of
proprietors' wealth. This objective is achieved through commercial
activities, the success of which is measured and controlled mainly in
financial terms. Responsibility for financial measurement and control
within the company falls to the finance function. Its role therefore is to
establish a financial framework within which the commercial activities
of the company can be undertaken. Within this framework the finance
function has three main objectives:

(a)   planning the business's financial requirements and controlling its
      finances in line with stated objectives;

*Jennifer Hopper's chapter was prepared with the help of Stephen Crompton, formerly
Group Treasurer, Unigate plc, and now Director of Treasury at Beecham plc.

(b)   funding the commercial activities;
(c)   allocating capital to the various business activities and marshalling internal and external capital resources to ensure the business can carry on its activities at a profit.

The position of the finance function relative to other functions within a large organisation can best be illustrated by way of a group organisation chart. It must be made clear at this stage however that not all corporates will have a structure comprising an independent finance function. The existence of a finance function depends entirely on the administrative structure of the corporate itself and the complexity of its financial requirements.

For example, in a small-scale enterprise, the managing director will be responsible for all commercial and financial activities. As the company grows, through expansion, acquisition or diversification, it is likely to establish separate commercial units or profit centres, which in turn may become subsidiary companies. As the 'group' of companies expands further, the decision may be taken (on administrative or legal grounds) to bring together a number of operating companies into divisions, based on the types of service offered or products sold.

During this expansion, the commercial and financial needs of the group will become too complex for the group and operating company directors to manage. Centralised staff functions therefore develop, in the form of finance, personnel, company secretarial, planning, etc. to provide administrative aid for the operating companies, which, whilst they will often have their own sub-structure of support functions, are nevertheless primarily concerned with line activities — that is the manufacture, production and sale at a profit of the company's goods and services. A suggested organisation chart in Figure 7.1, shows a typical structure for a large corporate, in which the centralised staff functions are each headed by a director who reports to the chief executive. At the same time each operating company or Divisional Managing Director reports directly to the Chief Executive.

Within each operating company, the heads of the staff functions will report to their own Managing Director; they will however have another reporting line to the head of the centralised staff function as illustrated in Figure 7.2. This 'dotted line' responsibility to the head of the central staff function does not interfere with the company Managing Director's control, but deals only with the specialist function concerned. For example, the company Finance Director's responsibility to the group Finance Director will be in terms of group-imposed standards of financial management, reporting and regulations rather than in the specific utilisation or control of the company's own resources.

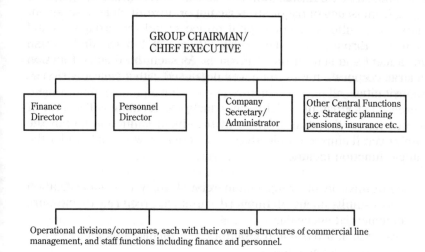

Figure 7.1   Example of an organisation chart (1)

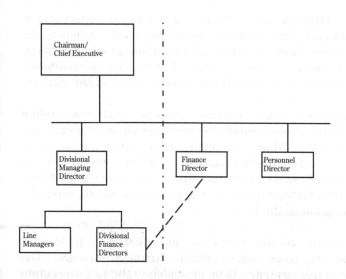

Figure 7.2   Example of an organisation chart (2)

Activities of the Finance Function

The operation of the finance function covers a vast number of activities ranging from issues of major strategic importance, such as assessment of large acquisitions, major capital projects, and the group's capital structure, through to day-to-day tasks including daily cash management and settlement of invoices. As such the finance function in a large corporate needs to be well organised with a clear division of responsibilities.

Three main areas of activity can usually be identified. The first of these concerns the strategic role of the finance function within the group's overall aims and objectives. The activities which fall under the strategic function include:

(a)   co-ordination of group commercial strategy (the identification and establishment of financial yardsticks required to measure commercial success);

(b)   resource allocation and monitoring of financial targets;

(c)   corporate finance policy;

(d)   acquisition and divestment (i.e. establishing the criteria for purchase or sale of businesses and reviewing all proposals);

(e)   dividend policy.

Any one of these strategic issues can have a significant impact on the company's profitability and therefore its ultimate aim, which is the maximisation of shareholders' wealth. It is therefore proper that these decisions are the remit of the board of directors (or a committee nominated by and reporting to it) through the medium of the Finance Director.

In many companies, the Finance Director will take initial responsibility for the above matters by co-ordinating information and papers on the relevant topics for presentation either direct to the board, or to a board-nominated committee which may consist of himself, divisional Managing Directors and other senior executives. This committee would then consider the proposals before making a final recommendation to the board.

Financial strategy is the result of the finance department's appreciation of its roles within group business strategy. The implementation of this strategy will be delegated to the various section heads, i.e. the Financial Controller, the Group Treasurer and the Tax

Manager, but full authority will rest with the head of the function, the Finance Director.

Points which should be covered under the financial strategy are:

(a)   corporate finance policy — i.e. the establishment of a capital structure and optimum debt capacity;
(b)   funding management;
(c)   currency strategy;
(d)   tax strategy.

The third sphere of activity lies in the control of the routine tasks of the function itself. The finance function is responsible for establishing the rules and procedures covering its regular activities, which both the central function and the individual finance functions of the subsidiaries are to follow. In most cases, the rules and regulations established here form part of a manual or formal set of instructions.

Day-to-day management will include the role of the company Management Accountants in preparing and monitoring the financial accounts, and budgeting and forecasting; the activities of the treasury departments, both centrally and locally, in terms of funding, cash and currency management, forecasting future requirements and bank negotiations, etc. The Tax Manager will also have a role to play here in ensuring that both the group as a whole and individual companies comply with the basic tax regulations, for example completion of VAT returns and payment of corporation taxes on the due date.

The above summarises briefly the activities of the finance function; the remainder of this chapter will examine in more detail the respective roles of the finance function personnel as a means of illustrating the strategic, functional and day-to-day decision-making required.

The Finance Function — Reporting Structure and Responsibilities

Figure 7.3 indicates a typical reporting structure and responsibilities of the finance function personnel. It is worth pointing out that the degree of responsibility and levels of delegation shown would probably be found only in the most highly-organised finance departments. This would not be so in smaller organisations, or indeed those with different structures. In younger companies, for example, the strategic planning process may not be so developed and therefore the Finance Director will be responsible for the day-to-day matters, with little or no time to consider strategic issues. Similarly, groups of companies with a relatively simple structure, and which are neither in a tax paying position nor have an international division (which usually brings with it additional tax complexities) may not have a Tax Manager. Nevertheless, in a large well-organised group, the division of responsibility along the lines indicated in Figure 7.3 is usually essential to ensure that the strategic overview is given the priority it deserves, with sufficient authority at the functional level to ensure sound financial management.

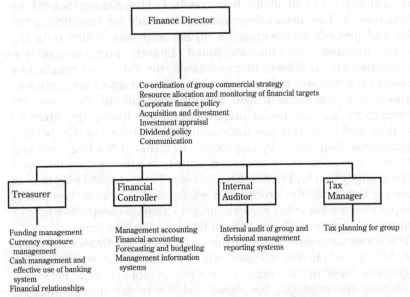

Figure 7.3 The finance function – reporting structure and responsibilities

Finance Director

If we were to look at the boards of directors of the top UK multinational groups, we would find, with very few exceptions, that the Finance Director was a member of the board. One might be tempted to describe him as the Chief Executive's 'right-hand man'. This description is not intended to denigrate the heads of other central staff functions, whose roles are also of great significance.

But let us consider the Finance Director's position more closely: His fellow executive directors will have operations of their own to run (either divisions or operating companies), and they will often be located away from the group's head office or administrative headquarters. The Finance Director is however usually located at head office with the Chief Executive. He does have his department to run, but once he has formulated his own strategy, he has capable subordinates to implement it. The Finance Director is therefore able to fulfil a key role — that of a senior executive, free from divisional responsibilities, with whom the Chief Executive can freely discuss any new commercial ideas, and receive feedback from his senior financial adviser on the viability of these ideas in financial terms.

The benefits of such a relationship are enormous for a group in a dynamic, changing environment, where the ability to react quickly to changing market conditions will be a key factor in commercial success.

Whilst the above illustrates one view of the Finance Director's role, let us turn to his more defined responsibilities, which, following the format of Figure 7.3, can be analysed as follows.

Co-ordination of group commercial strategy

For most large corporates a statement of strategic objectives will be under two headings: commercial and financial. The commercial objectives will cover a variety of subjects depending on the nature of the company, and might include improved product quality, improved market share, the aim to be No. 1 in a particular field, etc. The prime purpose of the financial objectives is to support and complement commercial objectives.

The strategic task of the Finance Director lies in defining and establishing financial targets which can be used to measure and control the achievement of the group's strategic commercial objectives. The financial targets must also be consistent with the attainment of the group's ultimate aim — that is the maximisation of shareholders' wealth.

The targets are likely to state specific objectives covering the following financial criteria:

(a)   Return on trading capital employed. (Trading capital employed means net working capital (excluding short-term debt) plus fixed assets.)

(b)   Cash flow generation.

(c)   Profit growth.
(d)   Quality of earnings (e.g. a group's possible preference for cash flow and profit from a business in a stable or growing market rather than in a declining one).
(e)   Growth in earnings per share.
(f)   A maximum and optimum level of debt.
(g)   Interest cover.

In some groups, however, the statement of financial targets may not cover all of the above points, since different companies will have different financial priorities, depending both on their own position and requirements, and on general economic conditions. For example, young high-technology companies will look on a positive cash flow as a key target and may have to sacrifice some potential growth in order to achieve this. More mature companies, or those with healthy cash balances, may be able, if they wish, to opt for some other key target, for example profit growth, with cash flow as a secondary target.

The Finance Director is ideally placed to assess the group-wide commercial position and hence establish financial targets which should be rigorous but attainable, and should, if they are achieved, give the group the commercial success to satisfy all claims on the company and to improve shareholders' wealth.

Resource allocation and monitoring of financial targets

Resources, both internal and external, are limited, and allocation of these resources for capital projects, expansion and continued business growth must be rationed for use in those businesses and divisions which have the best prospects of achieving the commercial and financial targets laid down by the group.

There are limits to the capacity of shareholders and other outside investors to provide more cash as and when the group requires. Moreover, these externally-generated funds can only be raised infrequently without damaging the group's share price and its overall market prospects. The group should therefore aim to maximise internally-generated resources.

The large corporate needs a rigorous means of identifying and allocating group resources, firstly to those businesses which best match the group's commercial and financial objectives, and secondly to those new acquisitions or capital projects which also appear to have the capacity to match the group criteria.

The process of resource allocation involves three stages:

(a)   To establish what the resources are or are likely to be.
(b)   To establish the balance between the various criteria against which each unit's claims on the resources will be judged.
(c)   To establish an order of preference/priority as to which should be recommended to the board for approval.

A suggested procedure for resource allocation (which would be at least annual, with monthly or three-monthly review) would be to involve it as part of the annual budgeting process. Completion of a preliminary budget covering one year and a longer-term plan (3/5 years) by the individual business units will show each unit's projected performance, together with its claims on group resources by way of capital expenditure, working capital requirements, acquisition requirements, etc. The individual budgets will then be consolidated to give a group overall view of the likely resources available together with the total claims on those resources. The group finance function will then assess carefully all claims on the resources, from individual projects to major group projects or rationalisation plans.

In order to finance those projects which meet the group's established criteria, both commercial and financial, each division and operating company is then allocated financial targets which aim to ensure that sufficient resources are generated to match overall demand.

Regular assessment of divisional and group performance against targets is a vital part of the resource allocation process. Although the figure work will be collated and analysed by the Financial Controller's staff, full reviews will be undertaken at the highest level, usually involving the group Chief Executive, Finance Director and the divisional Managing Director. These reviews will analyse actual results against targets, overall trading performance, capital expenditure and acquisitions, together with a thorough review of those companies or operating units which do not match group criteria. The purpose of these reviews is to assess those factors which have a significant impact not only on the division or operating company's results, but also on the group budget as a whole, such that both the division and the group forecasts will need to be revised,

These reviews should not interfere with the autonomy of the divisions, but at the same time they should ensure that the group as a whole acts as a cohesive business unit, aiming at a common goal.

Corporate finance policy

The Finance Director has a strategic responsibility for the co-ordination and implementation of a corporate finance policy throughout the group. This policy will incorporate a statement as to how the business is to be funded, and will cover in particular the group's capital structure and its debt capacity.

The major sources of funding for any business are equity (shareholders' funds and retentions) and debt. In financing the company's assets from these sources, it is the duty of the Finance Director to achieve a balanced structure. It must be said that there is no such thing as an ideal capital structure, since this will vary from company to company dependent on the different activities of each operation, and hence the capital requirements, the availability and cost of debt and equity, and the attitudes of the management towards the levels of risk involved.

The ideal capital structure for an individual company can be established in a number of ways, the most important of which is to assess the company's debt capacity, that is the level of debt that the company can comfortably adopt without placing the business itself and ultimately the shareholders' investment at risk. The Finance Director will judge the debt capacity by assessing the company's present and future likely cash flows and hence its ability to service any debt. At the same time, he has to assess the claims on capital which will be achieved through the resource allocation exercise. In establishing the debt capacity, the Finance Director should also stipulate that the type of debt available is appropriate to the asset being financed. Long-term assets should be financed by long-term debt, leaving short-term borrowings available for peak requirements and contingencies. It would be a major error for any corporation to rely on short-term borrowings to finance permanent requirements, since in the event of emergency, the buffer of short-term finance which a company would normally have at its disposal, would not be available.

Based on the group's debt capacity, and taking into account the views of lenders who may wish to impose capital and interest gearing restrictions within loan agreements, the Finance Director will then be able to establish a maximum level of borrowings which the company can finance, and also an optimum level which will represent the group's strategic target.

Once the group's capital structure and debt capacity have thus been defined, the implementation of the strategy falls to the treasurer and will be discussed later on p. 127.

Acquisitions and divestments

Both acquisitions and divestments are of major strategic importance, since both can have a significant impact on the corporate's health, and consequently on the wealth of the proprietors.

Just as the group's commercial objectives must be supported by financial objectives, so all commercial criteria for aquisitions must also be supported by financial ones. The role of the finance function is therefore to define and apply appropriate financial yardsticks in judgment of acquisitions and divestments.

On the commercial side, the group's strategy should be clearly stated, together with further points to be considered for any new acquisition to match the group's aims. (Such points might include the quality of management to be acquired and whether it will meet group requirements, or the potential purchase of a business in a recovery situation.) The financial criteria should ensure that any new acquisition is able to meet either now or within some pre-determined time-scale the group's own financial targets.

Where acquisitions are considered to be of major strategic importance, some of the stated financial criteria may be flexible, but the board, on the recommendation of the Finance Director, should define the limits of flexibility to ensure that all acquisitions are assessed on a similar basis.

Divestment is a drastic, but often necessary, step to take to ensure that there are no unnecessary drains on the corporate's resources. The monitoring of financial targets on a regular basis at the highest level can be considered a strategic task in as much as it will highlight those businesses which do not meet the group criteria. Similarly, it gives senior executives the opportunity to review constantly the activities of the corporate; if an individual company's activities are inconsistent with the group strategy, divestment can be considered.

A large corporate will also undertake at the highest level a review of under-performing assets, with a view either to improve the performance of the business unit if possible, or alternatively to restrict capital to that unit and ultimately to divest if appropriate.

One of the features of a large corporate is that it has a clear strategy by which to judge potential acquisitions and divestments. In the medium and smaller company, which may well be run through the persuasion and influence of a key individual, the drive for acquisitions may be derived from that individual rather than from an objective assessment within previously agreed guidelines and objectives.

Investment appraisal

The actual process of investment appraisal (which can be defined as a commercial and financial assessment of all major capital expenditure and new acquisitions) is routine; it involves a mathematical and accounting assessment of the project or investment, with the return on the investment being adjusted for risk; a meticulous sensitivity analysis is also required, testing all the key assumptions and the effect any variability in these assumptions will have on the overall return. The guidelines nevertheless need to be laid down at the highest level to ensure a standard approach.

The group board, through the Finance Director, will define the overall criteria, both commercial and financial, for investment appraisal which should normally be the same as for acquisition strategy. A standard format for assessment will be laid down, which will include identification of levels of authority at which decisions on capital expenditure will be made. The largest capital expenditure projects will generally be agreed and reviewed by the board of directors.

An important feature of investment appraisal has to be the review of the expenditure at appropriate and regular intervals, at the same level of authority at which the decision was first taken. It is only through this review of all acquisitions and capital expenditure that the corporation will be able to judge the quality of its investment appraisal and forecasting techniques and to monitor its progress.

Dividend policy

A decision on dividend policy is usually made at board level, since this decision represents a direct statement of the company's objective of providing a return for its shareholders. The decision will have regard not only to the requirements of the shareholders, but also to the needs of the company itself.

In assessing the needs of the shareholders, the Finance Director will consider:

(a)   the need for a steady smooth stream of earnings (particularly if the shareholder requires income rather than capital growth from his investment);
(b)   the need for an increase in the real level of return for shareholders;
(c)   the need to maximise the share price.

This last factor is important for a number of reasons. The declaration of an increased dividend can be seen as communication to the market of the board's optimistic view of the company's future. As such, this could attract shareholders to maintain their holdings, particularly if the share price is at its maximum, given the increased earnings per share. It also has the added benefit of making the holding more attractive should the company need to raise more funds by way of a rights issue. Finally, it can help to avoid takeover predators, who are normally looking for companies, whose assets may not be used to the full, and hence the share price of which may be rather deflated.

As far as the needs of the company are concerned, the following factors will be taken into account:

(a)   The cash cost of the dividend and the company's ability to pay it, which will depend both on cash flow and the level of distributable reserves.

(b)   The company's future financing requirements, i.e. should the company distribute its earnings now or retain them to finance future developments.

(c)   The level of wage increases, together with some consideration of possible closures or redundancies within the group as a whole — a large dividend increase could give ammunition to union pay negotiators, whilst the cost of rationalisation, closures and redundancies may well reduce the cash available for payment of dividends.

The Finance Director will research the various options and present his findings to the board of directors with his recommendation for a final decision. In practice his recommendation will usually be based on the previous year's dividend duly adjusted, to ensure market satisfaction and a smooth stream of earnings. The final decision should, however, provide the company with sufficient retained earnings to finance growth in its core activities and the shareholders with a reasonable dividend yield.

Communication and information

Whilst communication itself may not be considered of strategic importance, the Finance Director does have a responsibility to ensure that communication channels are efficient so that:

(a)   he has enough information available on which to base his strategic decisions, and

(b)   he can inform his subordinates on the implementation of his or the board's policy decisions.

The Finance Director controls communication on four main levels. It must be stressed, however, that communication at all levels must be two-way. Not only must the Finance Director issue information, but he must also ensure that the lines of communication are sufficiently open to allow him to be kept fully informed by all parties, from the board of directors, his own subordinates, through to outside investors and institutions.

The first main level of communication is with the board of directors. Here, as a member of the board, the Finance Director presents his information through written reports, for example on dividend policy, finance strategy, or through management accounting and treasury reports. Each report is likely to bear his interpretation and recommendation for action.

Secondly, the Finance Director is responsible for all financial communication downwards through the divisions and operating companies. This communication may be on strategic or policy matters, the latter perhaps by way of a policy manual approved by the Finance Director. Operating company or divisional Managing Directors have their performance assessed on their company's targets which are a part of the overall group budget, and they therefore need to have the basis of these targets clearly communicated to enable the operation to run as cohesively as possible. They must also have the opportunity to respond and to discuss the budgets.

External communication is a third important area of the Finance Director's responsibility. This may take the form of press releases or interviews concerning acquisitions, disposals or group results, or statements and responses to shareholders at annual general meetings.

Fourthly, communication is a key factor in any corporate defence policy where dissemination of group results and information to all parties concerned on a timely basis is essential. This will involve a well-co-ordinated policy of internal and external communication. Some companies will have a corporate defence committee, which will ensure that the following key information is always available:

(a)   Updated budget statement.
(b)   Regular statistics on company performance in comparison with others in the same industry including R. & D. etc. to counteract shorter termism on the part of investment managers.

(c)   Regular information on shareholding changes on the company's share register.

The Finance Director is usually a key member of the corporate defence committee and as such, he will hold overall responsibility for co-ordinating internal and external communication in this case.

Corporate Treasurer

The role of the Corporate Treasurer is to define and organise the financial strategy of the department, i.e. implementing the financial elements of the group's overall plan. His role can be subdivided into four major sections, each of which is described below; the first three of these will however be discussed in greater detail in later chapters.

Funding management

Whereas the Finance Director has to define the parameters of the debt capacity and capital structure for the group, the Treasurer now has to formulate a working strategy within the group's overall debt and investment policies, in order to control its internal capital structure and to manage external funding.

At the outset, in defining a suitable debt strategy, the Treasurer needs to ensure that sufficient debt is available to finance the company's assets. His preliminary action will include an assessment of the overall funding requirements, both present and future, including the permanent requirements for long-term assets, and the peak short-term requirements which will best be financed by way of short-term lines, including overdrafts, acceptance credits, commercial paper, etc. An allowance should also be made for present and future contingencies.

Once the funding requirements have been identified, the following features of the potential debt portfolio need to be considered:

(a)   *Maturity* — maturities should be spread on as even a basis as possible. If all debts mature at the same time, the company could well suffer a liquidity crisis, unless provision has been made in good time either to meet the repayments, or to refinance the debt.

(b)   *Fixed or floating rate* — if a corporate has its entire loan portfolio at variable rates, any rise in interest rates could have a devastating effect on profits. It is therefore prudent to aim for a

certain percentage of debt at fixed rates, the appropriate
percentage being defined by the Finance Director and
implemented by the Treasurer in accordance with the group's
needs, the type of industry the group operates in, and general
interest forecasts.

(c)   *Currency* — the choice of currency for a loan should be
considered in the light of the location of the asset being
purchased and the corporate's likely income flow in that
currency. (Currency risks can however be limited through other
hedging techniques — see Chapter 15.)

(d)   *Costs* — interest rates, fees and the cash cost of the debt (after
tax adjustments) all require consideration and comparison.

(e)   *Covenants* — the lender may require either direct security over
the company's assets or restrictions on the company's financial
performance through covenants. (See Chapter 10 for a more
detailed discussion of these factors.)

Some companies are fortunate enough to have surplus liquidity. Others
will have surplus liquid investments concentrated in certain areas or
geographic locations. In any event, investments, like debt, need to be
managed and an investment strategy for a company will bear many of
the same considerations as debt strategy.

The assessment of surplus liquidity, i.e. whether it is permanent or
temporary, should be followed by consideration of the likely maturity
of the investment (short or long term), the liquidity (is it easily
realisable), the cash value at maturity and the risk element involved.

An important element of overall funding management is the
construction and maintenance of a suitable internal capital structure
for the various divisions or operating companies in the group. The
Finance Director will establish the overall group capital structure, but
in order to ensure that all divisions have an equal chance of achieving
financial targets set by the group, they ought to have the benefit of
starting with the same capital structure or debt/equity ratio. (The actual
amount of debt or equity involved will differ in each division, however,
depending on its size and its capital requirements.) Therefore in
deriving the group debt strategy, the Group Treasurer needs also to
consider the internal capital structures of the divisions to allow himself
sufficient leeway and liquidity in group resources to give subsidiary
companies the correct debt/equity relationship. This will often be
achieved by means of inter-company loans, either with funding from
the parent company or alternatively with loans from subsidiaries to the

parent company. These internal capital structures will be reviewed and adjusted periodically.

Currency exposure management

Another of the Treasurer's duties is to identify and manage the foreign currency exposure of the group.

The first requirement here is to identify the nature of the exposure. Transaction exposure arises through normal payments for imports or exports, when receivables or payables in one currency need to be converted into another. Translation exposure arises in terms of foreign assets or liabilities, denominated in a different currency from that used by the group for accounting purposes. The exposure would occur following a change in exchange rates between one year-end and the next, when the value of these assets or liabilities is converted to the group or holding company currency.

Finally, economic exposure can be defined as the risk that long-term movements in relative exchange rates will cause structural changes which undermine the basic profitability of a company.

The Treasurer has to establish criteria for managing or hedging the exposure, and the policies derived will be dependent on the type and duration of the exposures concerned. In addition, due regard will be taken of the group's overall philosophy towards risk. The guidelines are laid down, often by way of a policy manual, and will then be applied by the group-treasury department on a day-to-day basis.

By way of example, a group may choose to allow all transaction exposures under £10,000 sterling to be unhedged, but forward contracts need to be taken out for all exposure above that amount.

Depending on the complexity of the group's foreign exchange turnover and requirements, more sophisticated hedging techniques may well be used, taking into account options, futures and currency swaps.

This subject is covered in more depth in Chapters 14 and 15.

Cash management

The Treasurer is usually responsible for co-ordinating a strategy to cover the external and internal elements of cash management.

By external elements is meant the management of working capital or credit control. In some groups, the types of business are so diverse that strict rules regarding credit control cannot be applied systematically across the group. In such cases, the group treasury may choose to operate a 'cash limits' system, giving each division or operating company a separate cash limit so that it can manage its own working capital requirements (within general guidelines). This has the benefit of delegating cash management to a certain extent, but always retaining ultimate control within the group treasury department.

As far as internal elements are concerned, this basically concerns how the group as a whole manages its cash resources in order to optimise the use of the banking system. Cost is a prime consideration here and listed below are some methods of keeping the costs resulting from the obligatory use of the banking systems to a minimum:

(a)   Reducing the number of inter-company transactions by aggregation and netting, for example through an internal inter-company clearing system so that only necessary transfers are made between group companies' banking accounts.

(b)   Arranging banking activity through a minimum number of accounts, for example through concentration accounts. The benefits are:

(i)   maximum control for the Treasurer on the overall group cash flow (provided that the operating company's reporting system is accurate);

(ii)   surplus credit balances where appropriate through the netting arrangements.

(iii) economies of scale, in that once the group cash is centralised, the treasury is able to obtain better rates for investment of surplus liquidity, or to borrow to cover group requirements at very fine rates.

(c)   Optimising 'float'. In an ideal world, a corporate would aim to maximise disbursement float — the delay between issuing a cheque to a creditor and having the cheque debited to the bank accounts — and minimise collection float — the time taken in receiving value for funds from debtors. In practice, the former can be difficult to achieve, so a corporate will often concentrate on minimising collection float and ensuring that its banks give it the best possible 'value-dating' arrangements.

For all corporates operating in the international field, the above considerations will be complicated by different countries' banking systems. Whilst advantages should be taken where possible, after taking account of tax and currency complexities, the most important feature of any cash management strategy must be that it should be simple and efficient to operate.

A further important feature regarding the use of the banking system is the negotiation and monitoring of interest rates and bank charges. This is a prime responsibility of the Treasurer and requires a rigorous and standard approach, to ensure that the group is being given good value for money from its banks.

The smaller corporate has the option of transferring business to another bank if the costs are unattractive. A larger corporate will however often limit its own exposure to one particular bank, so the Treasurer should carefully compare the arrangements offered by all existing bankers to ensure competitive prices both on interest and commission charges.

At the same time however, he should also watch the market for cost-saving developments, either in new lending and investment products or in money transmission and payment systems.

Financial relationships

No company can survive without financial backing, firstly in the form of investors' funds and secondly in terms of debt provided by financial institutions.

It is therefore of paramount importance that the group maintains good and honest relationships with both sources of finance. Traditionally, the Finance Director had the task of liaising with press, shareholders and financial institutions. However, following the integration of investment and commercial banking, stockbroking and fund management, there is a strong argument for one person alone to be responsible for all financial relationships, so that a coherent picture of the group can be given to commercial bankers, investment bankers, stockbroker analysts and credit rating agencies. The Treasurer usually has responsibility for bank relationships, and in some groups he may come to assume overall responsibility for all external financial communication, leaving the Finance Director free to deal with strategic matters.

The Treasurer has a duty to his investment and commercial bankers (and the credit rating agencies, where appropriate), to keep them adequately informed as to the changes in the group's financing structure, since any such changes could have a direct impact either on the company's credit rating, or on loan agreements. He will require a professional service from them in terms of sound and profitable investment advice, or attractive lending products (or a good credit rating), hence the need for channels of communication which are as free as commercial practice permits.

Similarly, any financial presentations to stockbrokers and fund management analysts should also be frank, giving the analyst sufficient background as to the structure and prospects of the company without of course divulging any price sensitive information.

In establishing general principles for bank relationships, the Treasurer will be looking at all times for efficiency and competitive pricing. No bank is perfect and it is well known that individual banks have their strengths and weaknesses, which can be fully exploited by Treasurers. As such, the banks come to realise that they cannot always service a group's full requirements, but the Treasurer himself probably owes each bank the courtesy of letting it know the internal pecking order, and at the same time allowing the true relationship banks the opportunity to quote for potential business. Not all Treasurers are perfect and errors and misinterpretations can occur in banking matters. Openness and flexibility from both parties will ensure that a good relationship is maintained.

It goes without saying that good manners on both sides will enhance a true banking relationship, and such manners include the necessity to be honest about the real likelihood of business, to be straightforward when asking for quotes, and to ensure that the small print of agreements is adhered to. Such honesty will often ensure that whilst banks are more than willing to help out in the good times, the true relationship banks will also be willing to help out over difficult periods.

Financial Controller

Whereas the Treasurer normally controls the flow of funds resulting from the Finance Director's commercial and financial strategy, the Financial Controller has overall responsibility for the correct recording of the group's financial results in a manner which both reflects accurately its progress and conforms with accepted accounting principles.

Management accounting

One of the aims in this area is to establish a standard format for all management accounting information. This is essential to ensure that those financial controls established at a strategic level are converted accurately into an accounting basis and then communicated reliably through the divisions so that the group is able to rely on the financial information on which major decisions are based. The primary requirement is that accurate information is available in a format which is readily usable by the group. The format will differ from group to group depending on individual requirements, but in the most well-developed finance functions, regular reports on a monthly basis will usually include a balance sheet, profit and loss account and funds flow statement for each operating company, which will then be consolidated on a divisional and group basis.

Financial accounting

The Financial Controller has to ensure that statutory accounting policies are adhered to throughout the group for the purposes of interim and year-end accounts. All relationships with the external auditors will be through the Financial Controller and the Finance Director, although the task of co-ordinating a full audit usually falls to the former.

Budgeting and forecasting

The budgeting procedure is usually undertaken at least on an annual basis, as far as setting original targets is concerned, but again within well-developed finance functions, monthly revised forecasts are a vital part of management information. All types of financial forecasts will be provided, depending on the group's needs, ranging from daily and weekly cash and foreign exchange exposure positions (which more correctly fall to the treasury function) to five- or ten-year financial plans.

Whilst individual operating companies and divisions will produce their own budgets, the Financial Controller has the responsibility of summarising the group's position by way of financial figure work and narrative, and he will be responsible for updating the position and reporting via the Finance Director to the main board on a regular basis.

Management information systems

In the largest groups, much of the management accounting and financial information is computerised on a management information system, sometimes designed in-house to meet the corporate's unique needs. Responsibility for the system usually falls on the Financial Controller. A computer co-ordinator will take technical decisions, but the Financial Controller remains accountable for the accuracy and reliability of the information provided.

Internal auditor

In many young and developing companies, the position of an internal auditor will not be available, such a function more often than not being fulfilled by the company's external auditors. However, in a fully fledged finance function, the position of an internal auditor is extremely valuable, and should be distinctly separated from the role of the Financial Controller, so that he can independently assure the board of directors that the systems of internal control are effective and that management and financial information is accurate. The internal auditor will have the responsibility of inspecting all aspects of the company's financial procedures, including management accounting, management information systems (for example, security checks and access arrangements) and treasury procedures.

The head of an internal audit section will normally report directly to the Finance Director and may in some cases have senior functional responsibility, either to an audit committee of the board, the Chairman or the Chief Executive.

Tax Manager

The Tax Manager has two key functions within an organisation:

(a)   To set a formal tax strategy.
(b)   To ensure compliance with tax regulations.

Through skilful management of its financial affairs, every group whatever its size will strive to reduce as far as possible the impact of tax on its profits. The Tax Manager is therefore obliged to keep fully abreast with local and international taxation legislation to ensure that he sets specific tax objectives concerned with the financial strategy of the company, within which day-to-day financial management can be carried out without adverse tax consequences.

In many groups, the Tax Manager will report directly to the Finance Director. In an international group, however, there is an argument for integrating the treasury/tax function below the level of the Finance Director. Many international financing decisions are based more specifically on the requirements and stipulations of a local and an international tax regime, rather than purely on treasury guidelines; there is, therefore, merit in considering a reporting line from the Tax

Manager to the Treasurer, since many of the greatest tax problems and opportunities arise in the international treasury field, both in terms of internal capital structures and external financing.

The role of the Tax Manager and the importance of taxation within the treasury field will be discussed in more detail in Chapter 18.

Summary

In describing the role of the finance function we have attempted in this chapter to outline:

(a) The position of the finance function relative to other functions in the organisation.
(b) The activities of the function, covering commercial strategy, finance strategy and day-to-day administration.
(c) The respective roles of the finance function staff.

Our aim has been to include the core elements of finance function activities. We must however stress again that the reporting structures and organisation charts illustrated here are not necessarily ideal. Since finance is a crucial part of any corporate's existence, each group should plan and develop its finance function specifically to meet its own requirements.

Further Reading

1   J. Argenti, *Practical Corporate Planning*, Unwin, 1989.
2   H. Bierman, *Strategic Financial Planning*, Free Press, Macmillan, 1981.
3   D. K. Eitman and A. I. Stonehill, *Multinational Business Finance*, 4th ed., Addison Wesley, 1986.
4   J. R. Franks, J., E. Broyles and W. T. Carleton, *Corporate Finance — Concepts and Applications*, Kent Publishing, 1985.
5   ICMA and Society for Long Range Planning, *Corporate Planning in Practice*, ICMA, 1985.
6   P. A. Vale, *The Role of the Finance Director, Financial Management Handbook*, 3rd ed., Gower Press, 1987.
7   J. M. Samuels and F. M. Wilkes, *Management and Company Finance*, 4th ed., Van Nostrand, 1986.

CHAPTER 8

Capital

Rachel Sopp

Editor's Notes

Chapters 8 and 9 cover the bedrock of corporate finance, i.e. capital. The first examines what capital is, identifying its characteristics and factors which influence the choice which the company makes between the two components of capital (equity and long-term debt). The risk which the company faces when its share price declines is the threat that it will be a cheap buy for a takeover predator (but as a corollary the company can purchase its own shares more cheaply as a defence). Similarly, if the share price rises the company can raise capital more cheaply. These two factors demonstrate just how critical are the decisions of the directors and their investor relations activities. Chapter 9 covers the various sources of capital available to the corporate.

Introduction

This chapter investigates equity financing and examines the following topics:

(a)   The characteristics of share capital
(b)   Factors affecting the level of share capital versus debt
(c)   Types of share capital available
(d)   Factors influencing a company's choice of share capital.

Characteristics of Share Capital

The memorandum of association states the authorised share capital and the number and nominal value of the shares. However, for practical purposes, share capital is usually considered to be the issued share capital, that is, the value of shares issued and paid up.

The shareholders carry the main risk of failure of the company and expect correspondingly higher rewards in the event of success. The extent of risk and potential reward varies according to the type of share, the detailed rights and obligations of which are defined in detail in the articles of association.

An important feature of share capital is its permanency. Shares are almost invariably issued in non-redeemable form and, as such, provide a permanent source of finance which offers many advantages in comparison with debt finance. For example, the company is not required to generate sufficient funds to meet a fixed repayment schedule or, alternatively, to take the risk that the market is prepared to supply new loans. Nor is there a risk that the finance may unexpectedly be withdrawn as is possible in the case of overdrafts or on the breach of a ratio covenant or other default clause included in a loan agreement.

For example, consider a company that is generating significant positive cash flow in excess of suitable reinvestment or acquisition opportunities. The company has a dilemma over how to use the surplus cash. On the one hand, it could invest the cash on, say, the money market. However, this will probably not be acceptable to shareholders who have already demonstrated their preference for the higher potential returns of shares by choosing to buy shares rather than themselves investing on the money market. Another option for the company is to repay borrowings. However, this would have the effect of increasing the cost of capital and hence reducing returns to shareholders because of the higher proportion of more expensive equity funding. The best option open to such a company may therefore be to repurchase some of its own shares — a complicated exercise in overcoming the permanency of share capital. A third course is to make an exceptionally large dividend payment, but this distorts the dividend pattern and could create tax and financial planning problems for investors.

A second important characteristic of share capital is the capital base it provides which can be used to raise other forms of finance. Providers of debt finance such as banks can be more confident of the security of their lending in the knowledge that any losses suffered by the company will first be borne by the shareholders.

A consequence of the risk taken on by shareholders is the generally higher return demanded on share capital. As the reserves of a company increase, shareholders expect growth in both dividend and share price in line with the growth in earnings of the company. Dividends on shares may be low in the first few years following a share issue, but may prove very costly after a period of profit-driven expansion. Figure 8.1 illustrates this growth characteristic. The opposite is true in years where profits are low. In this case, lower dividends can be paid or, if necessary, the dividend can be 'passed' altogether. This provides a vital buffer to assist recovery.

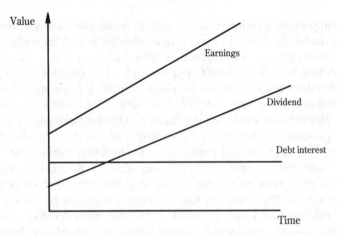

Figure 8.1   Effect of a profit-driven expansion on the cost of capital

Another characteristic of share capital is the vulnerability of the share price to the fortunes of the company. The importance of maintaining investor confidence brings additional responsibilities to the management of the company. These include long-term planning of dividend levels and the provision of carefully prepared information on the activities of the company to the financial markets and the shareholders.

The final feature of share capital that we should consider is its tax position. At first glance, debt has an advantage from a tax point of view since interest on debt is deductible for tax purposes whereas dividends are paid out of post-tax profits. However, in Britain this preferential treatment is partly eliminated by the imputation system for dividends and the present relatively low rate of corporation tax.

When a dividend is paid by a company in the UK, the company is required to retain income tax at basic rate on the gross dividend payment. This tax is called advanced corporation tax (ACT) and must be paid over to the Inland Revenue. However, it can then be deducted from the company's corporation tax liability up to certain limits. The end result is that the company may only suffer tax on dividends equal to the difference between the corporation tax rate and the basic rate of income tax. With basic rate at 25% and corporation tax at 35% in 1989/90, the difference is 10% as shown in the following example where company A pays 10% less tax (31.5) than company B (35.0).

Company A pays gross interest of 10.

Company B pays gross dividends of 21.

Company A		Company B		
Operating profit	100.0	Operating profit		100.0
Interest paid	(10.0)	Corporation tax		
		(35%)	(35.0)	
Profit before tax	90.0	ACT offset	2.5	
Corporation tax (35%)	(31.5)	Corporation tax paid		(32.5)
Profit after tax	58.5	Profit after tax		67.5
		Dividend paid (net)	7.5	
		ACT paid on		
		dividend	2.5	
				(10.0)
Retained profit	58.5	Retained profit		57.5

The limit to the set-off of ACT is the value of basic rate income tax calculated on the UK profits before tax. Any ACT that cannot be used may be carried forward or back but if it cannot be used in the short term, this has the effect of increasing further the relative cost of dividends in comparison with debt finance.

Factors Affecting the Level of Share Capital Versus Debt

Cost
At first glance, debt appears to be cheaper than share capital, both because of the preferential tax treatment discussed above and because of the lower risk and hence lower compensation carried by debt.

The logical application of such a conclusion would be to increase the proportion of debt finance indefinitely in order to reduce the average cost of capital. This argument is only valid, however, if the relationship between the cost of debt and the cost of equity remains constant as the proportion of debt financing increases.

An important question therefore is: Is there an optimal gearing level for a company? There are two sets of theories that seek to answer that question, the first being those developed by Modigliani and Miller which, for simplicity, we will refer to as Theory A. Secondly, there are the so-called 'traditional' ones which we will refer to as Theory B. Numerous variations and different stages of development of these theories exist and·the graphs shown in Figure 8.2 illustrate a typical result from each approach. Theory A indicates that no optimal capital structure exists, whereas Theory B shows that such an optimal capital structure does, in fact, exist.

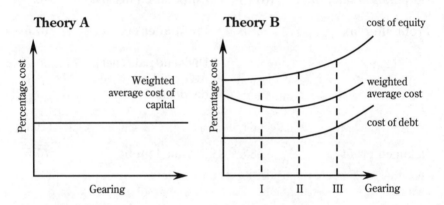

Figure 8.2   Effect of the level of gearing on the cost of capital

Theory A argues that an investor has no preference between two identical funding schemes in different companies as long as the companies have the same earnings capability, risk and size. The value of those companies, and hence their cost of capital, are therefore the same, regardless of their different capital structures. The theory assumes perfect market conditions (costless information, rational investors, no dealing costs, etc.), constant future profit streams, no taxation and no bankruptcy costs. However, the conclusions are broadly similar if the last two assumptions are relaxed.

Theory B is a more qualitative approach based on the likely reaction of shareholders to increases in gearing. Three stages of reaction can be identified as follows:

I   When debt is first introduced into a balance sheet, it is likely that the shareholders will not perceive any increase in risk because the proportion of debt is so small. The cost of equity will therefore remain constant and may even fall temporarily in expectation of improved profits as a result of cheaper debt financing.

II   However, when a significant proportion of debt has been introduced, investors in both debt and equity will perceive risk to their income and capital as a result of the larger fixed servicing commitment on the debt financing. However, the increase in interest and dividends demanded may be more than offset by the reduction in the average cost of capital as a result of the continued drift towards the cheaper debt financing.

III   Finally, when the gearing level rises from, say, 50 to 80%, the risk to both shareholders and debt investors takes on a new importance to these investors and they demand significantly higher returns as compensation. This will cause the cost of equity and debt curves to rise more steeply and thereby increase the average cost of capital.

The question of which result is more valid is still being debated as further development work is carried out and the underlying assumptions are relaxed. There is therefore presently no clear conclusion as to whether or not cost considerations should influence the level of share capital versus debt financing. Each company should consider its own experience of debt and equity financing costs to determine at what level of gearing, if any, its cost of capital may be minimised.

Debt capacity
An important upper limit on the gearing level of a company is given by its debt capacity. That is, the maximum proportion of debt that a company can service comfortably without risking its survival.

The concept of debt capacity is based on the assumption that the cost of debt performs in the manner shown in Figure 8.3. The cost of debt increases with increased debt financing because of the greater element of risk to income and capital invested. This increased risk is also illustrated by the interest cover ratio which will fall as the level of debt increases, both as a result of the higher amount of debt and because of the higher rates of interest being charged. At a certain level of gearing, however, few banks or other investors are willing to invest in the company because they consider that the company cannot safely support any additional debt. At this point, the cost of debt rises steeply and soon reaches an unacceptably high level.

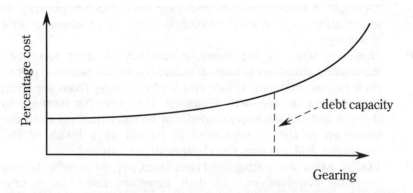

Figure 8.3   Relationship between the cost of debt and the level gearing

The strength of a company's cash flow and liquidity are the key to its ability to support a high level of debt financing and ultimately to its cost. A cash flow forecast incorporating differing levels of debt is therefore the best tool for determining the debt capacity of a company, and it should include pessimistic forecasts of likely operational and market conditions in order to ensure that the company would not fail should these deteriorate in the future.

Other factors
Other factors that influence the optimal level of share capital versus debt include:

(a)   The rate of growth
(b)   The vulnerability of earnings
(c)   Ownership and control.

First, the rate of growth. A company that can demonstrate strong growth is usually able to support higher levels of debt. This is similar to the belief that a 'crippling' mortgage can be taken up to purchase a home in the expectation of future salary increases. For the company, cash flow is critical to its debt service ability and will strengthen with growth in profits.

Secondly, vulnerability of earnings. High gearing has the effect of improving shareholders' returns in good years but also increases their losses in bad years. This feature is illustrated in Figure 8.4. Large

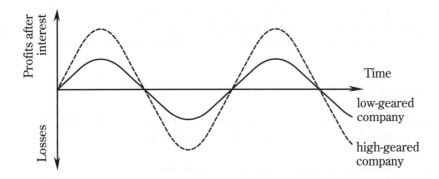

Figure 8.4   Impact on the vulnerability of earnings of different levels of gearing

fluctuations in profit can be serious in poor years if they lead to a lack of confidence in the company. They are particularly serious if a company experiences a downturn in profits for a number of consecutive years. A company that tends to show large fluctuations in earnings, such as those in the fashion industry, may therefore prefer a high proportion of equity financing.

Finally, the type of ownership and control of a company can also affect the optimal gearing level. In particular, private companies may prefer to issue new debt rather than equity so that the existing shareholders can retain control of the company, although this may make it vulnerable to a downturn in the market.

Types of Share Capital Available

Shares can be issued in a variety of forms. The main types are ordinary and preference shares, but within these broad categories shares can be structured with a variety of rights and obligations to meet specific requirements, the most common form being the ordinary share. Ordinary shareholders enjoy many of the privileges of ownership, such as participation in capital growth, at the same time as bearing the main risk of loss.

In contrast, preference shares carry many of the characteristics of debt. They usually earn a fixed return and carry less risk of loss of capital than ordinary shares.

Both ordinary and preference capital can be raised directly via a new issue or a rights issue, or alternatively as a result of a debt issue structured in the form of convertible loan stock or with warrants attached. Warrants can also be issued independently.

The characteristics of each of these main types of share are as follows.

Ordinary Shares

Ordinary shares, which usually comprise the greatest proportion of share capital, generally carry the following rights:

(a)   To receive dividends, when and if declared.
(b)   To vote at general meetings of the company and thereby to elect and remove directors.
(c)   In the event of the company being wound up, to receive an allocation of the assets of the company in proportion to the number of shares held, after all other claims have been settled.

The dividend to ordinary shareholders is paid out of retained profits, once interest on debt, corporation tax on profits and dividend on preference shares have been paid.

Many other rights and obligations can be added to this list to suit a company's individual requirements. For example, in the British Gas share issue, discounts were provided to new shareholders on gas bills. Regarding discounts, it should be noted that the qualification period for any discount can have a significant impact on the movement of the share price, which may not be acceptable to the company.

Shares can also be segregated into groups, for example as 'A' and 'B' shares. Different rights and obligations regarding votes, dividends or share of assets on liquidation can be applied to each class. Clearly this is useful in areas such as voting rights, since new shares can be issued with less voting power thereby protecting the original shareholders' control of the company. In a takeover battle, the predator company can acquire a large proportion of the total shares and still not gain control of the takeover candidate if it has not acquired a sufficient proportion of the voting shares. This element featured prominently in the failure of the Trusthouse Forte bid for the Savoy Hotel Group. This example also helps to explain why shares with low or no voting rights are generally not so popular with investors.

Ordinary shares are not usually redeemable except on the winding up of the company, although redeemable ordinary shares can be issued if the company has already issued some non-redeemable shares. There are also some provisions in the Companies Acts for the purchase by a company of its own shares. This procedure appears to be gaining popularity.

Preference shares

Preference shares provide an alternative form of share capital. They carry at least one preferential right over ordinary shares, namely the prior right to dividends and to the repayment of capital on liquidation.

Typical characteristics of preference shares are as follows:

(a)   Fixed rate dividend based on the nominal value of the shares.
(b)   Cumulative, that is the dividend may be 'passed' but no dividend can then be paid on ordinary shares in the current year or in any future year until all arrears of preference dividends have been paid.
(c)   No voting rights unless the dividend is in arrears.
(d)   Right to repayment of capital on liquidation before any assets are distributed to the ordinary shareholders, but after all other claims have been settled.

The dividend to preference shareholders is paid out of retained profits after interest on debt and corporation tax on profits but before any dividend to ordinary shareholders.

Several alternative types of preference shares are possible, including:

(a)   *Non-cumulative preference shares.* Any dividend that is 'passed' in a year is not carried over into the next year. Therefore, only the current year's dividend need be paid in future years.
(b)   *Redeemable preference shares.* The nominal value of these shares is repayable at a specified future date or in a specified future period, usually at the discretion of the company. Redeemable shares may normally only be redeemed if sufficient reserves are available to form the necessary capital redemption account or from a fresh issue of shares.
(c)   *Participating preference shares.* In this case, the preference dividend includes a variable element in addition to the fixed dividend. This additional component is frequently defined as a proportion of the ordinary dividend.
(d)   *Convertible preference shares.* The shares can be converted to ordinary shares, usually at the discretion of the shareholders and at a specified date or during a specified period of time.

Convertible loan stock

Convertible loan stock is a 'hybrid' in that it is a combination of debt and equity. The holder has the option of converting the loan stock into shares and has the right to choose whether or not to exercise. For example, if the future share price is not attractive, the investor can choose to retain the loan stock.

Normal characteristics of convertible loan stock are as follows:

(a)   It is based on unsecured loan stock rather than debentures.
(b)   Conversion is to ordinary shares, although it is also possible to issue convertibles which convert to preference shares.
(c)   The option is only valid at a specified date or during a specified period of time.

Conditions can also state that the loan is automatically converted to shares if the company is taken over by another company, and rules relating to pre-emption rights apply to the potential equity equivalent of the convertible loan stock in the same manner as any share issue.

Warrants

A warrant is an option to acquire shares at a specified price, called the exercise price, during a specified period of time. They may be issued as part of a loan issue (usual in UK) or issued separately. Warrants can be detached from the loan stock and traded separately from the loan stock.

Factors Influencing a Company's Choice of Share Capital

Ordinary shares

Ordinary shares provide an important source of finance that is attractive to a wide range of investors.

They provide the greatest buffer for a company since low dividends or none at all can be paid in years when results are poor, although this will depress the share price and may attract takeover predators. However, they can also be a relatively expensive form of equity finance if profits are high since a corresponding high dividend is expected.

Preference shares

Preference shares can be used to segregate shareholders, as an alternative to classifying ordinary shares into 'A' and 'B' shares with different rights and obligations. In particular, the lack of voting power makes preference shares attractive to family-controlled companies, since new equity capital can be raised in the form of preference shares without diluting their voting power.

Special rights such as customer discounts can be offered on preference shares. The resulting distortions to the preference share price during the period of eligibility for the discount, such as reduced ferry crossings, are less serious than similar distortions to the price of ordinary shares.

Different types of investors may be attracted to preference shares. The shares provide a less risky form of equity investment than ordinary shares, and offer a regular, predictable income.

Before issuing preference shares, however, the company should be aware of the greater obligations relating to them and the effective reduction in the buffer provided by ordinary shares. A fixed level of dividend is required each year, regardless of the level of profits, and although it is possible to 'pass' on the preference dividend, this should only be regarded as a last resort. The company should include preference dividends together with interest on debt in calculations such as interest cover in order to ensure that the preference shares can be comfortably serviced.

Indeed, to the company, the preference shares have many of the characteristics of debt, but are effectively more expensive than debt. This arises from the higher risk perceived by the investor in preference shares and also because of the preferential tax treatment of interest on debt.

Convertible loan stock

Convertible loan stock can be a cheap form of fixed rate finance up to the conversion date. The investor is willing to accept a lower coupon than for straight debt or preference shares in the expectation of making a capital gain on conversion to shares.

The low coupon is, however, a misleading indication of the effective cost of the convertible loan stock to the company because of the hidden benefit to the investor in the conversion to equity below the market rate. Indeed, it may prove to be cheaper to raise debt at full coupon and issue equity at a later date. Other forms of finance may therefore be more suitable in cases where the company is confident that the growth in its share price will exceed market expectations.

Convertible loan stocks are particularly useful in attracting investors who require a relatively secure income as well as some participation in any capital growth, for example, pension funds.

The same attribute is also useful in takeover situations since shareholders of the takeover candidate can be offered a guaranteed initial income without relinquishing their share of capital growth if the new group performs well.

The hybrid nature of convertible loan stocks is an advantage in the circumstance mentioned above but can also create new problems. For example, investors may have a preference for debt or for equity and be unwilling to invest in a combination of the two. In addition, the uncertainty regarding the timing of conversion creates planning problems for the company.

Convertible loan stocks could be considered as an alternative to preference shares because of their preferential tax treatment, as interest on the debt is tax deductible whereas preference dividends are paid from post-tax profits. However, they are not as tax efficient as other forms of debt because the hidden cost of the equity conversion is not tax deductible.

Finally, convertible loan stocks also provide a useful method of access to the international equity market. The recent popularity of convertible Eurobonds is indicative of the finer rates usually attainable on a larger market, but this avenue is restricted to all but the largest companies.

Warrants

Warrants are usually attached to a debt issue to increase its attractiveness and in this way the issuer may obtain a lower coupon on the debt. As in the case of convertible loan stock, the total effective cost calculation should include the cost of the share option as well as the coupon.

Warrants attached to loan stock share many characteristics with convertible loan stocks. They are a useful instrument in many of the situations already described for convertible loan stock. Such as:

(a) For investors requiring a more secure income plus participation in capital growth.
(b) In takeover situations.
(c) As a tax-efficient alternative to preference shares.

Indeed, in takeover situations, warrants attached to debt may prove to be more flexible than convertible loan stock because of the possibility of varying the number of warrants attached to a predetermined level of debt, whereas for convertible loan stock, the number of ordinary shares obtained at conversion is largely determined by the exercise price implied by such a conversion. The exercise share price is, in turn, determined by market opinion and the current share price.

In addition, debt with attached warrants may be designed to be more tax efficient than convertible loan stock if deep discount bonds are used. With a deep discount bond, that is a bond with a low coupon issued at a large discount, the investor is able to defer his tax liability on the capital gain represented by the discount until the bond matures or is sold. Part of this tax benefit can be retained by the issuer when structuring the bond.

An effect of the detachability of warrants is that the detached warrants can be attractive to speculators. Speculation usually has the undesired effect of increasing fluctuation in the share price of the company. It also means that the options are likely to be taken up near the end of the option period. This can delay the receipt of new equity capital to an unacceptable extent especially in a volatile market.

To summarise the main differences between convertible loan stock and warrants are:

(a)   the warrants can be detached and traded separately from the loan stock;
(b)   convertible loan stock is, in effect, a form of deferred equity whereas warrants attached to debt result in both debt and equity for the company.

The differences affect the choice between the instruments in particular circumstances.

Further Reading

The Treasurer: May 1988, 'Capital Structure and Cost of Capital'.

CHAPTER 9

The Market for Capital

Richard Taylor

Introduction

The market for capital may be considered as a very general term referring collectively to the various, more tightly defined, individual markets catering for corporate capital requirements in the short, medium and long term. This chapter concentrates on equity rather than loan capital, and deals exclusively with the medium- and long-term markets which include public quotations, venture capital funds, the financing of management buy-outs and private sources, such as the Business Expansion Scheme.

Firstly, though, we need to know exactly what we mean by equity. Equity is the permanent risk capital of a business and represents the proprietors' funds invested in a company. It is most usually comprised of ordinary shares, preference shares and accumulated reserves, but convertible securities and debt securities with options or warrants attached may have similar characteristics. Every company needs an adequate equity base to demonstrate the commitment of its owners to the business, and thus equity is always required when a company initially starts trading. Additions to equity during the lifetime of a company most commonly occur when a major expansion of business through either organic growth or takeover is planned, or upon a restructuring of the balance sheet.

Ordinary shares are the basic equity investment and, except in very specific circumstances, are non-redeemable. In return for their investment, ordinary shareholders receive voting rights, dividends according to the company's ability to pay and, in the final event, the surplus upon liquidation.

Lenders, on the other hand, must be paid interest on their loans regardless of profits and, in a liquidation, receive repayment before equity holders. Shareholders, therefore, carry additional risks and will inevitably seek to achieve a return on their investment in excess of that received by lenders. It is thus generally found that equity is more expensive than debt to a company, especially as interest is also a tax-deductible expense.

It is for this reason that the Finance Director or Treasurer will tend to favour a higher ratio of debt when assessing an appropriate debt:equity structure for a business. However, other factors affect this decision. The providers of debt look to the shareholders' equity as the permanent foundation of the business, and provide finance in a prudent relationship to this, having taken account of debt servicing and repayment capabilities. Also, if debt is disproportionately high in relation to equity, the share price might be adversely affected or the cost of capital rise, as shareholders either sell or demand higher returns to compensate for their increased risk exposure. The Treasurer will also give considerable thought to the effect his debt:equity structure will have upon earnings per share. Obviously, the more equity there is in issue, the proportionately lower will be the earnings per share. However, when considering an issue of further equity, the Treasurer may well give thought to the issue of a convertible stock. Here, by initially issuing debt, earnings per share can possibly be enhanced in the short term, and allow the full benefits of the planned growth or acquisition to come on stream and enhance profitability before the capital base is enlarged at conversion.

Another consideration could be the issue of preference shares. These will have the effect of reducing gearing, but at a lower cost than an issue of ordinary shares. This is because preference shares usually have a dividend stated as a fixed annual percentage and, in a liquidation, the holders are repaid before ordinary shareholders. Thus, working again on the rewards for risk basis, preference shares should be more expensive than debt to the Treasurer, but cheaper than ordinary shares.

Thus, a company must discover its ideal balance between debt and equity, as this will ensure the share price and disposable income are optimised. Once calculated, it is not uncommon for the optimal debt: equity ratio to be ratified by the board of directors and incorporated into the company's overall strategic financial policy as a target level. Having said this, only on rare occasions will the debt:equity ratio exactly match the target figure, for debt and equity are usually raised in occasional, large tranches rather than small, regular amounts. Therefore, whilst at any one time apparent divergences will be seen, it must be acknowledged that the Treasurer's long-term plans and policy will always be aimed ultimately at achieving the target ratio.

Public Quotations

Before we discuss how a public quotation may be achieved, we will firstly consider the relative advantages and disadvantages of obtaining a public quotation.

The principal advantages to a company of a public quotation are:

(a)   It will provide access to additional share capital which can be used to fund expansion or be retained to improve the balance between debt and equity.

(b)   Shares having a public quotation may be used as consideration for further acquisitions instead of, or in addition to, cash, provided the market is stable.

(c)   A public quotation can increase general awareness of the company and its products. Its creditworthiness, in the eyes of suppliers, may become substantially enhanced.

(d)   Employees who benefit from share option and/or share related profit-sharing schemes can more exactly value their package and have a wider market into which shares can be sold.

The original shareholders may also benefit from a public quotation as:

(e)   The wider market for the shares of original shareholders can increase their potential value and all or some of the original shareholders' interests may be realised by sale to the public when the quote is obtained.

(f)   Where a UK company is quoted on the Official List and has a public shareholding that exceeds 35% of the voting power, it generally ceases to be a 'close' company for tax purposes. Thus, shareholders will no longer be taxed on a notional distribution of all corporate profits and their personal tax burden could be considerably reduced.

Against these advantages must be balanced inevitable disadvantages, namely:

(a)   A public quotation is costly and the costs of continuing obligations to meet reporting requirements, shareholder communications, documentation and annual general meeting requirements, must be assessed and taken into account.

(b)   The company must be run for the benefit of a wider shareholding who will wish to see optimal dividends and possible restrictions in directors' benefits to those considered suitable for a publicly-quoted company. Pressures of reporting requirements, public accountability and media comment could also make possible the loss of some commercial secrecy.

(c)   Increased vulnerability to an unwanted takeover bid due to the more diverse shareholding and open marketability of the shares.

(d)   All major decisions will need to be considered from the view of a wider shareholding and their investment objectives.

The original shareholders also have a disadvantage:

(e)   Shares of original shareholders sold as part of the initial flotation will attract capital gains taxation and the possible increased value of retained shares could also have implications on any existing capital transfer tax planning arrangements.

Both the short- and long-term implications of the advantages and disadvantages will need careful consideration in the light of each individual company's particular circumstances. In many cases it is the opportunities for further expansion by organic growth or acquisition which become the deciding factors.

However, a public flotation is not the only source of equity capital available, therefore making it essential that all possible avenues are explored before the most suitable option is selected.

A Full Stock Exchange Listing

The Stock Exchange

Both companies and investors need a fair, efficient and orderly market to facilitate the transfer of shares, and the Stock Exchange exists to satisfy these objectives. It is, therefore, concerned to see that all investors deal:

(a)   on the same terms;

(b)   at the same price;

(c)   with all current and relevant information.

The Bank of England oversees general control of the London financial markets, but there are also minimum statutory requirements for the market of listed securities and these are contained in the Stock Exchange (Listing) Regulations Act of 1984 and the Financial Services

Act of 1986. The council of the Stock Exchange is appointed the 'competent authority' under the Acts, and the council incorporates the statutory regulations within its own rules and regulations for the listing of securities. Where issues of £3 million or more were contemplated prior to the Finance Act 1989, the Control of Borrowing Act 1958 applied and the government broker controlled the timing of issues to avoid bunching and ensure an orderly stream of issues to the market. As part of the trend to free the capital markets which occurred during the 1980s, the 1958 Act was repealed by the Finance Act 1989 and a period in which there was complete freedom to issue at any time followed.

Issuers found this new freedom problematical and worrying, for the prospect of bunching or, even worse, two major issues coming to the market on the same day, considerably reduced the certainty of a full take-up and trouble-free launch. After only a few months of this freedom the issuers asked the Bank of England to keep a record of proposed issues. From 25 September 1989, the Senior Manager of the Sterling Capital Markets section at the Bank of England, agreed to maintain a calendar of all rights issues, placings and offers advised to him on a voluntary basis, and to give a warning if two issues were planned for the same day.

At present, the stock market provides a three-tier market structure consisting of:

(a)   The Official List
(b)   The Unlisted Securities Market
(c)   The Third Market.

The official list
The listing requirements of the council are detailed in a publication entitled 'Admission of Securities to Listing' (commonly referred to as 'the yellow book' on account of its bright yellow binder). This sets out the basic requirements and mechanics of an issue as well as the continuing obligations and requirements necessary after listing.

It is not relevant to list all the various requirements here, but the major criteria for entry to full listing are:

(a)   five-year trading record;
(b)   £700,000 minimum market value of shares (£200,000 for debt);
(c)   25% or more of shares to be held by the public.

Points (b) and (c) are to ensure a sufficient depth of market after flotation. The quotations department of the Exchange deals with all applications for listing and is approached only through the company's sponsoring broker. Section 3 of the 'yellow book' lists the information required.

There are five alternative methods of obtaining a quotation.

(a) *Offer for sale.* This is the most frequently used method and involves an issuing house subscribing for all the shares which are to be marketed, and selling them to the public by way of a prospectus at a slightly higher price.

The company's objective is to obtain the widest possible shareholding as it is unlikely to wish to find itself with a very large tranche of shares with one investor, and thus a possible takeover target just a few days after listing.

(b) *Offer for sale by tender.* In a tender issue the shares are not sold to an issuing house, but offered directly to the public using broadly the same mechanics as an offer for sale. However, the potential investors are required to bid for the number of shares they require at a price equal to or more than a declared minimum known as the tender price. Formerly, it was common for all shares to be sold at one price, i.e. the striking price, that being the highest price at which all the shares could be sold. Recently, however, there have been issues where the striking price has been omitted and, in fact, bidders have paid the price they bid, right down to a minimum level. However, again, the company might be concerned at a small shareholder base and may lower the price by scaling down larger applications to achieve a wider spread. The tender method has the advantage of avoiding the opportunity cost of a large premium on the first day of issue, but the price uncertainty confronting potential investors could reduce the issue's attraction and make under-subscription more likely.

(c) *Introduction.* Where the shares of a company are already widely held they may, subject to approval, be introduced to the Official List. An introduction is unlikely to involve the marketing and issue of new shares, and other than formal notice and the issue of a prospectus, the normal advertising requirements of the Stock Exchange prior to admission can be waived.

An introduction is used where:

(i) the securities are listed outside the UK;
(ii) the securities are already sufficiently widely held to ensure marketability;

(iii) a holding company is formed and its shares are issued in exchange for those of one or more listed companies.

(d) *Placing.* A placing may be used where the value of the securities to be issued is less than £3 million and is particularly suitable for smaller issues as advertising costs are lower. In a placing, the shares are purchased at a fixed price by an issuing house or broker and 'placed' with their clients. However, at least 25% of the issued securities must be made available to the general public to ensure good market ability. As well as for very small issues, this method is also suitable for issues of limited public interest such as loan stocks and debentures.

(e) *Offer for public subscription.* Offers for public subscription had been relatively infrequent until the privatisation issues of the 1980s. They involve the issue of a prospectus direct to potential investors by the company concerned, inviting offers to subscribe for the securities at a fixed price. The method may only be used for the issue of new shares and, because of the uncertainty of subscription, usually requires underwriting to ensure success. As this almost inevitably involves an issuing house, it can often become more cost-effective to leave all arrangements to the issuing house and use the offer for sale method.

Pricing

A major consideration, immediately prior to the offer, will be the price at which each share will be sold. The sponsoring broker and issuing house will advise on how to price the issue, but the main considerations will be:

(a) The level at which any existing shares have recently changed hands.

(b) The underlying asset value of the group.

(c) The dividend yield and price/earnings ratio of comparable groups in the same industrial sector.

A well-priced offer for sale could normally be expected to open for trading on the stock market at between 10 to 15% above the price of the original offer. Any higher opening price would amount to a considerable opportunity cost to the company and provide a killing for the stags.

Timing of the issue will also impact upon pricing and this is where a Treasurer's skill at reading the capital markets will come to the forefront as, to maximise pricing, the issue of new shares will ideally be made when the market is high. Despite timing being so critical, it is not entirely in the hands of the company or its advisers as to precisely when the issue will come to the market. Flotation must occur within six months of the company's latest audited accounts where a full listing is being sought and, if the £3 million level is reached, notification of the proposed issue to the Bank of England might be considered advisable to ensure there is no direct clash with another major issue or cash raising exercise.

Raising additional capital

The main source of additional equity capital for quoted companies in the UK is by way of a rights issue. UK company law and Stock Exchange rules give shareholders pre-emption rights and, as a general rule, they must be offered new issues of shares on a pro-rata basis to their existing holding. This system has two main advantages to the shareholders. Firstly, the price of the new shares is struck at a discount to the existing market price and, secondly, the shares are purchased free of stamp duty and brokerage.

However, there are disadvantages to the company:

(a) Most rights issues are discounted by between 15 to 20% on the market share price, meaning the company is not theoretically achieving the maximum possible proceeds.

(b) Underwriting is usually necessary so as to ensure any drop in the share price below the rights discount level does not leave a large part of the issue unaccepted, and the company short of the cash it expected.

(c) Costs of the issue can be high, typically between 3 to 7.5%, depending on the size of the issue.

As mentioned in (a) above, not all rights issues are discounted at the 15 to 20% level. Some companies have used deeply discounted rights issues to raise additional capital. A good example of this is the NatWest Bank issue of May 1986, where a one-for-one issue at £2.00 per share was made when the market price stood at £8.55. An issue like this has a large scrip factor, making it very attractive to shareholders and thus making underwriting unnecessary. NatWest reckoned to have saved £15 million to £18 million in underwriting fees by using the deeply discounted issue. Where a company wishes to see a reduction in its share price and to raise funds, the deeply discounted rights issue enables both operations to be achieved in one issue. There are few disadvantages of a deeply discounted issue to shareholders, but those selling their rights do have a possibly unexpected cost. The 1979 Capital Gains Tax Act only excludes the sale of rights from capital gains tax where the sale involves less than 5% of the original investment. With a deeply discounted issue there is far more chance of this ceiling being breached.

During the mid-1980s, some companies attempted to eschew shareholders' pre-emptive rights by use of vendor placings and issuance of debt securities with equity warrants attached, aimed at overseas investors. This was because, in their view:

(a)   The UK equity market represents less than 10% of the total worldwide funds available for equity investment and British companies wish to tap the overseas pool of investment funds.

(b)   A broader and more international shareholder base could be invaluable to a company should the UK investors' willingness to support industry evaporate in the future. It is felt the wider shareholder base gives more long-term stability to the share price and gives greater freedom to the company in the issuance of new or further shares.

(c)   A presence in investor markets outside the UK could increase name recognition and lower the costs, especially in Europe, of other funding such as commercial paper and Eurobonds.

(d)   Using equity to fund international acquisitions is more difficult and frequently impossible when pre-emption issue timetables and rights must be recognised.

(e)   Sales of equity at the current market price do little harm to existing shareholders.

(f)   Amongst the larger financial markets, only the UK retains pre-emption rights.

At the same time, a trend towards the raising of additional equity through the use of vendor placings was taking place. Here shares were placed with prospective vendors contingently upon and in conjunction with an 'open offer' to existing shareholders to 'claw back', if they so wished, a number of shares in direct proportion to their existing holding. This compromise enabled shareholders to increase their holding without dealing costs, but did not give them 'rights' which could be sold at a possible premium, as in the case of a traditional pre-emptive rights issue.

With the advent and wider use of the overseas issues and vendor placing with 'claw back' agreements, the institutions took exception to the gradual erosion of pre-emptive rights, especially where the new securities were issued at a discount to the market price and an effective transfer of value from existing shareholders to the new subscribers was taking place. As a general rule, the London institutional investors do not take an active interest in the running of companies, but do keep a keen eye on anything which might cause a dilution of equity. In these particular cases though, the major institutional associations, the Association of British Insurers (ABI) and National Association of Pension Funds (NAPF), decided to give guidance to their members as to what was considered acceptable. Pressure was brought to bear on companies and the Stock Exchange, and a working party was formed to find mutually acceptable guidelines. These were issued in October 1987 and, very briefly, the major constituents were:

(a)   shareholder approval for a special resolution to disapply pre-emption rights would continue;
(b)   the ABI and NAPF would recommend their members to accept such resolutions provided they were restricted to 5% of issued ordinary share capital shown in the latest published annual accounts;
(c)   a cumulative limit of 7.5% would be expected in any three-year rolling period;
(d)   companies should seek to limit any discount on new shares issued for cash, other than to shareholders, to a maximum of 5% of the middle of the best bid and offer prices immediately prior to announcement of a proposed issue.

For Treasurers, these guidelines will probably have the effect of limiting entry to the equity-linked Eurobond market to all but the largest companies, as only they will be able to issue the proportionately larger amounts of capital necessary to make the exercise worthwhile and justify the costs involved.

American depository receipts

American depository receipts (ADRs) can be used as a method of gaining access to the far larger United States investor market and spreading the shareholder base. It is necessary to follow the ADR route as UK company law presently prohibits the holding of a share register outside the Commonwealth, effectively precluding a direct United States listing. An issue is commenced by the deposit of a stated number of shares with a custodian bank in the UK. A United States depository bank, sponsored by the company, will then issue United States registered, dollar denominated, securities which can be traded on the New York, American and over-the-counter markets. As United States investors have historically shown a preference for higher value shares, it must be remembered that one ADR does not necessarily equal one share in the company. It has become quite typical for one ADR to represent five shares in the UK company.

ADR programmes are popular because:

(a) Capital can be raised on the world's largest market.
(b) Investor interest from the United States in successful companies can be satisfied (e.g. Jaguar and ICI).
(c) The listing and trading of the ADRs can give greater international awareness of the company name and its products.
(d) This gives employees in United States subsidiaries a ready market for the sale of registered shares received in profit-sharing or share option schemes.

However, certain other considerations need to be taken into account:

(a) The pre-emptive rights of existing shareholders will need to be waived prior to the issue of any new shares for placement with a custodian bank.
(b) The SEC registration, accounting principles and disclosure requirements can be time-consuming and more comprehensive.
(c) The Company Secretary may have more difficulty in ascertaining who owns ADRs, although Securities and Exchange Commission (SEC) rules oblige anyone holding 5% of a registered security to disclose their interest. Whilst perhaps a little more difficult to discover quickly the identity of a potential predator purchasing ADRs, it is interesting to note that Plessey was assisted in its initial takeover defence against GEC by its ADR listing, as GEC was unable to offer its UK shares to holders of United States registered ADRs (shares offered to United States residents must be fully registered with SEC).
(d) If there is a continued net selling of ADRs in the United States contemporaneously occurring with purchasing on the UK

market, a flowback of shares could occur as shares previously held by the custodian bank are released. This can be a particular problem where new shares are issued purely to back an ADR capital-raising exercise.

To launch a successful ADR programme, most companies will need to arrange an investor communications programme in the United States which might include (what have become known as 'road shows') presentations to market makers, analysts and potential investors in a number of cities. Most companies who run an ADR programme do so to obtain a listing on a second major Stock Exchange and thus have the ability to raise capital in an alternative market should the domestic market become illiquid. For these same reasons, and as a natural continuation of their wish to have a wider investor base, many larger UK multinational companies have not stopped at just a second or ADR listing, but sought quotations on other major exchanges around the globe such as those in Frankfurt and Tokyo.

Shareholder relations

As we have seen in the British Gas and other privatisation issues, whilst expensive, good public relations and advertising can go a long way to achieving successful, oversubscribed flotations. However, this aspect does not disappear once the furore of flotation has passed. A company must win and keep the hearts and minds of its shareholders to ensure their expectations are in line with potential achievements. If they are not, the share price will stagnate or fall, and this could lead to an unwelcome takeover attempt by a predator company. It is fruitless to have ambitious plans and strategies which will provide vastly-improved future results if existing and potential investors are unaware of them. Companies must establish and maintain excellent lines of communications with major shareholders, financial analysts, stockbrokers and the financial press to keep them abreast of topics such as long-term investments, brand strength and depth of market coverage.

In more recent times, these lines of communication have become more important to companies as they seek to counter the increasingly short-term views which appear to have grown enormously throughout the markets. It is of great importance to ensure shareholders, especially the institutions, are aware of the underlying reasons for particular investment decisions and the impact they will have over the longer term. Frequent checks of the share register will reveal not only potential stake-building but also large institutional investors who might be conspicuous by their absence, and worthy of a special briefing.

The Unlisted Securities Market

Launched in November 1980 by the Stock Exchange, the Unlisted Securities Market (USM) provides a formal, regulated market to meet the needs of smaller, less mature companies which would be unlikely to apply or qualify for a full listing.

As such, entry requirements are less rigorous, but do require:

(a) A three-year trading history (but exceptions can be made).
(b) At least 10% of the equity must be held by the public.
(c) Only one newspaper advertisement is required and the audited figures quoted can be up to nine months old.

With reduced advertising costs and less complex procedures to follow, the expenses of a USM flotation will, in most cases, be considerably lower than a full listing. The advent of this new market has given smaller, growing companies the opportunity to make their shares marketable in a regulated capital market at an earlier stage than has hitherto been possible. The market greatly encourages would-be investors to take a stake in growing companies, whilst the lower minimum percentage of shares which must be publicly owned gives the original shareholders less concern about unwelcome takeover bids, or ceding more equity than they would wish to outside investors.

Shares must be made available by way of an offer for sale where £3 million or more is to be raised, but below this level either an offer for sale or a placing may be used.

In exactly the same manner as a full listing, a company considering a USM flotation must have clearly established objectives for going public. For instance, if a shareholder purely wished to realise his investment, perhaps a sale to a larger company would raise more money, cost less, and be more sensible. An ideal candidate for the USM must have good growth prospects, good stable management and an excellent product. This will help assure the shares' appeal to outside investors and give adequate liquidity in the market for the shares after flotation. This is important as it may be found that lowly-rated shares can only be sold if there is an interested buyer, i.e. there is no jobber available in this market.

The advantages to the company of a USM flotation are:

(a)   Retention of management control.
(b)   Shares may be used as consideration for future acquisitions.
(c)   Increased public awareness of the company.
(d)   The future ability to raise more easily further share capital to fund expansion or repay debt.

The disadvantages are:

(a)   The costs and imposition on senior management's time, of flotation.
(b)   Restrictions placed on directors by outside shareholders' investment objectives and the continuing obligations to the Stock Exchange as set out in the General Undertaking signed immediately prior to flotation.
(c)   Greater adverse publicity if results slip.
(d)   The possible tax liabilities of original shareholders.

The USM provides an important equity market for growing companies and, as they have expanded, some groups have already made the transition to a full listing on the Stock Exchange.

The Third Market
Following a number of problems in the unregulated Over-the-Counter Market, the Third Market was launched by the Stock Exchange in January 1987 to provide a disciplined market with a suitable standard of investor protection for companies unable to qualify for USM listing.
It is aimed at young, growing companies which need to raise capital at reasonable costs provided they:

(a)   are incorporated in the UK;
(b)   have at least three directors;
(c)   are able to submit one year's audited accounts;
(d)   can demonstrate commercial viability.

There are no restrictions as to minimum size or specific percentage of issued share capital to be offered, but the sponsoring broker must ensure sufficient shares are offered for reasonable expectation of a liquid market after flotation.
The Third Market enables new or young companies to tap the market for capital at a much earlier stage in their development than has ever before been possible in the UK. Disclosure, costs and continuing

obligations have deliberately been made less onerous than the USM, but these very concessions to ease companies' administration automatically make the shares a more risky investment to outside investors. However, unlike the USM this can, to some extent, be ameliorated, as the Board of Inland Revenue has agreed that the trading of shares in Business Expansion Scheme companies on the Third Market will not, under present regulations, prejudice the eligibility of investors for tax relief.

The Over-The-Counter Market

The Over-The-Counter Market (OTC) is not regulated by the Stock Exchange, but companies with shares quoted must, of course, comply in full with the Companies Acts. The OTC is not a single market-place as the USM or any Stock Exchange. Each market maker involved, who must be a licensed dealer, will trade stocks on a 'matched' or two-way price basis, dependent on the market maker's policy or the depth of market for individual companies. The market was originally established in the early 1970s by Granville & Co. Ltd, to provide a more ready market for shares in closely-held, often family-run companies. The market offers companies the preservation of independence, but with the long-term shareholder support of financial institutions.

Whilst each market maker's criteria differ, the agreed criteria for quotation are:

(a)   The company should be raising at least £500,000.
(b)   The largest proportion of funds raised should be for the company.
(c)   There should be at least a one-year track record.
(d)   Profits should normally be in excess of £100,000 p.a.
(e)   The company should have an experienced and dynamic management team.

However, in recent years a number of licensed dealers have, under the generalist umbrella of the OTC Market, started selling shares in newly-formed, speculative and smaller companies, sometimes to unsophisticated private investors. The smaller the company, the more vulnerable it is to even minor setbacks and thus, the risk to investors is increased. Some have failed quickly (both dealers and companies), and created considerable adverse publicity for the market as a whole. However, utilised in the manner for which it was originally created, the

OTC Market operates as an important bridge between investing financial institutions and the closely-held company. This market trades shares in a number of highly respectable and substantial companies although, with the advent of the Third Market, many could now be suitable candidates for this more closely-regulated market.

The Venture Capital Market

Venture capital can be described as an equity stake taken in an unquoted company which is either established or in a start-up situation, and requiring new or additional equity capital to expand or restructure.

The UK venture capital market is not a new innovation. In 1945 the government formed Investors in Industry (3i) to provide finance for smaller businesses, but it is only in recent years that it has expanded at a rapid pace. There are now over 200 venture capital providers in the UK ranging from government bodies such as the Welsh Development Agency and CoSIRA to investment trusts, bank development capital companies and private investors, who usually take advantage of the Business Expansion Scheme tax incentives.

Venture capital is normally sought when a company finds it cannot raise all the funds it needs to finance its planned growth from the commercial banking market. For a successful application, it will need to demonstrate good prospects for long-term, rapid growth and usually operate in a sector of industry less susceptible to technological changes. The overriding factor though, will be the strength, experience and resilience of the management team, who must be considered capable of developing with the company through growth cycles and maintaining, at all times, good product quality, a good reputation and continuing success.

These conditions are considered necessary by investors so as to protect their funds. They are, after all, providing medium-term capital which is only usually repaid when the company obtains a public quotation or is sold to a larger company. The investors purchase a minority but, usually, significant shareholding in the company, and may well not seek dividends initially, as they will be looking for the increased capital value of their shares to provide their profit upon eventual sale, usually in a five-year time-scale. The risks can be high, but so are the potential returns.

The company benefits from additional capital on which to grow, and also from the advice and guidance of a non-executive director, who is normally nominated by the venture capital organisation. Against these advantages, the original shareholders must be willing to cede a portion of the share capital and be committed to an eventual sale or flotation to release the venture capitalists' investment.

Management Buy-Outs (MBOs)

These are sometimes also known as leveraged buy-outs due to the high gearing usually associated with their financing. They occur when some or all of the management and employees of a business raise the finance to acquire the business from its shareholders. Typically, the business involved is long-established and its success may be heavily associated with the management team. Particular features of companies suitable for a management buy-out are:

(a)   experienced, good quality and proven management team;
(b)   strong and predictable cash flows;
(c)   low 'market' value, perhaps due to low growth prospects,
(d)   strong asset backing to secure the debt.

These companies are, therefore, far removed from the usual candidates for start-up or development capital.

The finance raised for an MBO will normally be packaged in a complex manner, but will basically consist of three main elements:

(a)   bank secured, or senior, debt;
(b)   preference shares subscribed by specialist institutional investors which increase the gearing further;
(c)   equity, subscribed by management and the institutional investors.

The mix between debt and equity will be established by calculating the maximum amount of bank secured debt the predicted cash flow and assets will support. It is important from the potential investors' point of view that bank debt is maximised as it carries no equity dilution and the interest is tax-deductible. Typically, banks might look to cash flow to repay 30 to 40% of debt by the end of year three, 50 to 60% by the end of year five, and effect complete repayment by the end of the seventh or eighth year.

Management buy-outs can be advantageous in situations where the board of directors of a company has decided to divest a subsidiary or division which is no longer part of the group's mainstream business, or where a way is needed to raise cash to reduce overburdening debts. Sale by MBO saves searching for a possible buyer which could be a competitor, can save fees, and often leaves the employees feeling more comfortable than being transferred to another group. A particularly good example of a successful management buy-out is that of the National Freight Consortium. This was sold by the UK government to its management and employees in 1982. Here two different types of equity, 'A' and 'B' shares, were issued; the 'A' shares issued to employees and the 'B' shares to a syndicate of banks who also provided the debt element. Both sets of shares carried identical voting and dividend rights, but no market was available for sale, except to other employees on four stipulated dealing days per year. Since 1982 the Consortium has very successfully grown and in February 1989 the company successfully achieved a full Stock Exchange listing.

In the United States, MBOs have also been used by managements to purchase their companies while the share price has been well below net asset value. Managers take considerable personal risks when participating in MBOs as heavy borrowing supported by personal assets is usually necessary to facilitate purchase of their shares. Against these risks are the potentially high rewards emanating from a rising share price and the personal income tax relief obtainable against the interest paid on funds borrowed to buy shares. Buy-out companies will have relatively higher levels of debt than their competitors and tight financial controls will be necessary to manage cash and ensure covenants in loan agreements are not breached.

In general, after a buy-out the management's aim will be to reduce the gearing as rapidly as possible through operating cash flow and disposal of under-utilised assets.

The Business Expansion Scheme

The Business Expansion Scheme was introduced in the 1983 Finance Act as an incentive for individual investment in new and smaller companies operating in specified industrial sectors. It provides private individuals with relief from income tax at their highest rates when the investment is made and exemption from capital gains tax on the first disposal of the shares. The maximum amount for which relief may be obtained in any one year is £40,000, although the investment may be spread amongst a number of companies. The minimum investment in any company is £500. There are detailed and complex rules for both investor and company which will not be covered here, but it is important to note that companies listed or quoted on the USM do not qualify, although those quoted on the Third Market can be eligible. The scheme has undoubtedly provided a tremendous boost to private investment in the UK, and many smaller unquoted companies which would have been the most unlikely to have reached the Third Market quickly or perhaps ever reached the USM have been able to raise outside capital. This capital does come at a price, though, as investors will eventually require dividends and a market into which to sell their shares. This could occur through sale of the company or by its launch on the Third Market or USM, but to ensure that the tax advantages are not lost, this can only take place after the shares have been held for five years.

Further Reading

1   *Directors' Guide to Sources of Business Finance*, 1986.
2   *Banks and Specialised Financial Intermediaries in Development*, OECD, 1986.
3   *Venture Capital — Context, Development and Policies*, OECD, 1986.
4   *Money for Business*, The Bank of England.
5   *Admission of Securities to Listing*, The Stock Exchange.
6   *Unlisted Securities Market*, The Stock Exchange.
7   *The Third Market*, The Stock Exchange.
8   *Corporate Finance Textbook*, The Association of Corporate Treasurers.
9   *The Treasurer*: January 1986, 'External Relations'; March 1986, 'Arranging an ADR Programme'; June 1986, 'Debt: Equity Ratios — Finding the Right Gear'; December 1986, 'The USM and Small Companies'; May 1987, 'Pre-emption — Whose Rights?'; November 1987, 'Development Capital'; March 1988, 'Capital Market Instruments'; April 1989, 'Innovative Equity Instruments'; June 1989, 'Fixed Interest Debt'.

CHAPTER 10

Medium- and Long-term Borrowing

Philippa Back

Editor's Notes

Chapters 10 and 11 are concerned primarily with medium- and long-term borrowing with the subject being introduced and examples being given of the choices likely to be made by different types of company in different circumstances. Students should note that it is the type of business (i.e. is it cash generative or capital intensive) and the purpose of funding (i.e. specific project, liquidity, etc.) which usually determine the period and method of funding.

Chapter 11 discusses the various medium- and long-term debt instruments utilised by three differing companies with varying financial needs.

Introduction

Companies require access to funds in order to finance growth, which may result from increased productivity due to the introduction of automation, or by modernisation of manufacturing processes, i.e. as a result of investment. Companies can also grow by merger or acquisition, or by increased profitability through disposals of unprofitable operations or rationalisation. Such growth is planned over a period of time, which will allow an organisation to negotiate the necessary financing. However, at other times funds may be required 'at a moment's notice' and the company should be able to cope with such demands. The overriding need is therefore for the company to have a flexible portfolio of facilities on which it can draw.

There are certain factors that will affect the 'why and how' a company finances itself.

The Company

The nature of the company, its size, its structure, its profitability, whether it is private or public, will to some degree affect how it can finance itself.

A privately-owned company with a patchy track record of profitability will find it more difficult, and of course more expensive, to raise medium-term finance in the bond or private placement market, than say a public company with a healthier profitability record. Larger companies generally have many more bank relationships to turn to for sources of finance than smaller companies.

A company, however, may be constrained in what finance it can raise by its present structure, or by pre-existing covenants it has in place in its loan agreements with other lenders. The ratios typically monitored in this context are the gearing and interest cover, and other governing conditions might include current asset ratio, tangible net worth covenant and a negative pledge covenant.

Gearing measures the proportion of the company's borrowing relative to either the total capital employed or to shareholders' funds. For example:

	Company A	*Company B*
Total borrowings	50	25
Shareholders' funds	100	125
Capital employed	150	150

Gearing calculations:

(a) $\dfrac{\text{Borrowings}}{\text{Shareholder's funds}}$ 50%   20%

(b) $\dfrac{\text{Borrowings}}{\text{Capital employed}}$ 33%   17%

In both methods of calculating gearing Company B is the stronger. It could more readily raise funds by borrowing, prior to calling on its shareholders, than Company A.

Interest cover gives a differing type of indication in that it measures the number of times that the company's interest expense is covered by the company's annual profit, before interest, tax and dividend payments. The higher the cover the less vulnerable the company is to setbacks in profits or rises in interest rates. For example:

	Company A	Company B
Profit before interest tax and dividends	100	60
Interest expense	35	15
Interest cover: $\dfrac{\text{Profit}}{\text{Interest}}$	2.86 times	4 times

Again Company B would be viewed as more resilient to changes as an interest cover ratio of 2.86, as in the case of Company A, is low by market standards. In all these instances the ratios cannot be looked at in isolation, but understood against the background of the company's historical development, and those of the industry in which it competes.

The Financial Requirement

A company will seek different types of facility to fund differing requirements. Typically a company will have an overall financial plan, or strategy. This plan will be updated at least annually as part of the budget process, but will also be reviewed if a major acquisition or disposal occurs. In setting the plan the Treasurer will seek to establish a level of facilities, of different types, to give a cushion over and above known requirements to allow for unforeseen circumstances. Usually the worst time for a company to negotiate facilities is when funds are required urgently.

The plan will take into account the maturity mix of loans and loan facilities. Revolving term facilities tend to have a fixed maturity date, unless they are 'evergreen' facilities, whereby they are renewed/ extended automatically for a further period unless they have been cancelled under the provisions of the facility agreement. A Treasurer should be conscious of this maturity profile and should graph the facilities available and their run off, that is taking into account any amortisation schedules and bullet maturities. This is important in the context of reviewing and revising facilities, to be sure that the company has an adequate balance of facilities to meet its needs

A further perception in the mind of the Treasurer is that loans will be rolled over and that the company will always be in a position to facilitate this. This belief continues until the Treasurer becomes aware of factors which could mean that the company would not be able to meet its liabilities. In the absence of plans to raise further capital it would be prudent in such circumstances for the company to approach its close relationship bankers in order to pre-empt any possible default.

Facilities

These facilities will encompass short-term uncommitted lines, under which the bankers will make funds available on a best efforts basis; medium-term, typically five to seven years, committed facilities, under which the company pays a commitment fee in order to ensure the banks will lend to that company, when called upon to do so, provided of course no event of default has taken place. Long-term facilities, those in excess of, say, seven years are usually entered into on an *ad-hoc* basis, as and when required, or when market circumstances allow such funds to be raised. Facilities will typically include a number of options, so the company can choose how funds will be drawn. Whether or not long-, medium- or short-term facilities are negotiated will be determined by the company's need, but as mentioned above, a balance should be maintained. The documentation requirements will vary to a certain extent as in theory a short-term loan bears less risk than a long-term loan. In reality the credit risk view taken on a company is broadly similar whether the view is short or long term. A Treasurer should take as much care in negotiating documentation irrespective of the maturity of the facility. However, the Treasurer will more readily accept covenants for a long-term loan than a short-term one, due to the perception of the relative risk weighting between long- and short-term loans.

Alternatives

The various possibilities offered may overlap between the type of facilities, that is whether they are short or long. The most common are:

(a)   *Periods of drawdown.* These may be typically one, two, three or six months or as mutually agreed with the lender. This allows the company to choose whether to 'roll' the borrowing on a short-term basis (floating rate) or to 'fix' the borrowing rate for a longer period. The decision as to which will depend on the view taken on the yield curve.

   Essentially whatever period is chosen the loan is then 'fixed', but in general the term 'fixed rate' implies a longer maturity period, in excess of one year.

(b) *Multicurrency.* This allows the Treasurer to choose which currency to utilise in funding the requirement. Commonly, the same currency will be borrowed as is required. However, opportunities do exist which allow the Treasurer to fund a requirement more cheaply by using an alternative currency. This should only be done on a fully covered basis, in order to negate any currency risk attached to the borrowing. This is known as short-term swapping, although the length of maturity is flexible. The formula below explains how a cheaper borrowing may be achieved:

$$\frac{365}{\text{no. of days}} \times \left[\frac{\text{spot rate}}{\text{forward rate}} \left(1+ \frac{\text{borrowing rate} \times \text{number of currency of days}}{360} \right) - 1 \right] \times 100$$

Example:

Number of days	180
spot rate	1.75
forward rate	1.7625
borrowing rate	6.5% (i.e. 0.065)

$$\frac{365}{180} \times \left[\frac{1.75}{1.7625} \left(1 + \frac{0.065 \times 180}{360} \right) - 1 \right] \times 100$$

$$= 2.03 \left[(0.9929 \times 1.0325) - 1 \right] \times 100$$
$$= 2.03 \times 0.0251692 \times 100$$
$$= 5.11\%$$

This implies that by borrowing US dollars on a fully hedged basis (selling forward sterling to match the total of US dollars required to meet the principal and interest repayment then due) the company will borrow sterling at an effective rate of 5.11%. This method of borrowing uses arbitrage, which is not always achievable due to the nature of the market, as discrepancies between markets are negated by the arbitrageurs. However, this method is useful if a company has access to a cheaper source of funds in one particular market, which can be used to its advantage in another through the swap mechanism.

(c) *Straight loans.* Funds are typically drawn down by way of straight loans, for instance when the company states a requirement for an amount of sterling for a set period. Most facilities are utilised in this manner, however a borrower may seek within a facility the opportunity to be allowed to draw down funds using other methods.

(i) *Acceptance credits.* These may also be referred to as banker's acceptances. These are bills of exchange drawn by a customer on a bank, which are 'accepted' by that bank, that is endorsed on the back, and subsequently discounted in the market. The discounted proceeds are paid to the customer. The accepted bill may be held by that bank to maturity or sold on, as the credit (bill) once accepted becomes a negotiable instrument. This is attractive to corporates where the bill is 'eligible', that is eligible for rediscount at the Bank of England and therefore qualifies for the finest discount rate.

(ii) *Notes.* These evidence the company's promise to pay on maturity of the loan. Like acceptance credits they are negotiable instruments and are traded in the market. However, to date, notes have typically been issued only in the Euromarket. These notes are for a medium maturity, three or six months, and only a small secondary market exists.

(iii) *Commercial paper.* This is a form of 'securitised' borrowing, whereby the borrower (the issuer) issues 'paper' that is bought by an investor. The investor may be a bank, institution or corporate. It is a professional market, rather than a retail market. The paper is sold via a dealer, typically an investment bank.

Many countries now have commercial paper markets in operation. Each domestic market is governed by its own rules, but a Eurocommercial paper market also exists. The latter tends to be governed by market practice and perception by the investors of the issuers, i.e. quality, and consequently liquidity.

In the United States commercial paper market, issuers must be rated by two recognised rating agencies. As yet this is not a requirement in the UK.

Although the above in accounting terms are regarded as short-term instruments, they actually can take on the guise in money management terms of being medium to long term if they are continually rolled over. However, these facilities may not necessarily be of a committed nature.

The company being prudent would ensure adequate committed facilities existed in parallel in order to meet all maturities. This will cover the situation that the company is unable to 'roll over', or sell its paper in the market. Obviously there is a cost to this, but commitment fees are viewed as 'insurance'.

Where a company has in place committed facilities, such as a multiple option facility (MOF), it will be rolling over a series of short-term borrowings, under the umbrella of the facility. The committed element ensures that the company has access to funds at all times, during the life of that facility.

The structure of a MOF combines a committed syndicated facility, and a tender panel arrangement under which each tender panellist (a bank) will bid to lend funds to the company. The latter equates to a money market borrowing under an uncommitted facility.

(d) *Long-term funds.* These are typically drawn down under separate facilities, tapping the capital markets as opposed to the money markets. In these instances an investment or merchant bank would advise the company regarding the processes and timing of an issue. The issue may be public or private, domestic or Euro.

The types of issue that a company might consider in order to raise long-term funds could involve a borrowing (debt) or a share issue (equity) or a combination of the two. The latter is typically known as a loan stock, convertible or issue with warrants, depending on its structure.

(i) *Debt issues.* The usual form of straight debt issue is a bond, either domestically placed, domestically placed abroad, for example a UK company raising US dollars in the United States domestic market (a yankee issue), or a Eurobond issue, for example a UK company raising US dollars in the London market.

The company would appoint a lead manager, to arrange the issue, who would invite other banks, a syndicate, to participate in (underwrite) it. In turn the syndicate members would sell the bonds on to end investors, being other institutions, or in some instances private individuals.

(ii) *Equity issues.* Raising funds in the form of equity is typically via a rights issue, whereby the company's existing shareholders are approached to buy further shares, in proportion to their current shareholding, at a discounted price from the present market share price. Equity may be issued in connection with an acquisition, known as a vendor placing.

All equity issues of UK companies are governed by the London Stock Exchange, which monitors issues.

(iii) *Debt/equity issues.* A convertible bond or loan stock is one where initially a bond or stock is issued by the company, but under its terms, the holder, or company, or both have the option to convert that holding into shares of the company. At the original time of issue all the terms detailing the right of conversion are stipulated. An issue with warrants is similar to a convertible except that the warrant element, being the option to buy shares in the company, can be traded separately from the underlying debt issue.

As alluded to earlier there is a range of debt instruments available to a corporate borrower, depending on its strength, and the reason for the borrowing. In essence there is no absolutely right or wrong way for a company to structure its finances. However, obviously some methods are more apt for a requirement than others. By way of example there follows a description of three companies, representing different industry types, at different stages of growth, and the funding issues that they may face.

Example 1
Smallco is a private family run company in the service sector. It is a printer specialising in printing news-sheets and catalogues. Its financial record has become mixed as outside management was introduced. It began to increase profit margins by cost reduction, but then expanded the company by purchasing new assets, funded by debt.

£000s Year	1	2	3	4	5
Profit and loss					
Sales	750	800	875	1,750	1,350
Profit before					
interest and tax	37.5	80	105	43.75	40.5
Interest	0.5	0.5	5.5	10	25
Tax (40%)	14.8	31.8	39.8	13.5	6.2
Profit after tax	22.2	47.7	59.7	20.25	9.3
Balance sheet					
Fixed assets	75	75	175	275	455
Current assets	50	55	65	70	50
less Current					
liabilities	45	27.8	40.1	40.4	30.15
Total assets	80	102.2	199.9	304.6	474.85
Long-term debt	5	5	55	100	250
Equity	15	15	15	15	15
Reserves	60	82.2	129.9	189.6	209.85
Total liabilities	80	102.2	199.9	304.6	474.85
Ratios					
Profit margin	5%	10%	12%	2.5%	3%
Gearing	6.7%	5.1%	38%	48.9%	111.2%
Interest cover	75x	160x	19x	4.4x	1.6x

The change in the company is most readily viewed by reference to the ratios, to the extent that sales have peaked, and profit margins tailed off to below previous levels. Gearing has been increased sharply to over 100%, whilst most concerning is the reduction in interest cover to 1.6 times. The company is now vulnerable to interest rate rises. The company though is still in its modernisation phase, and wishes to continue by purchasing another machine at a cost of £100,000. To do so would strain its ratios further, particularly if the sales level remains static or deteriorates again.

The company's position is made difficult because it has only limited resources to tap for the extra funds, the family or its bankers. It is likely there is only one bank involved with the company. That bank has probably been lending on secured terms, with a charge over the fixed assets.

How should the company fund its next phase of expansion?

(a)   It would have to justify to the board that it should go ahead now rather than be delayed, based on the anticipated benefits of the new machine. The board would want to know for example what would happen if interest rates were to increase by, say, 5%. Similarly, they might ask what would be the result if the sales were to fall back to levels approaching those in year 3.

(b)   Alternative methods of funding should be reviewed. In this case the alternatives would be:

  (i) *Purchase.* This could be funded by a rights issue to the shareholders, but is reliant on the family putting up the cash; or increasing bank debt, which is unlikely to be approved as the gearing level would worsen to around 150%.

  (ii) *Lease.* This would be a viable option to the company, as a medium-term lease of say five to seven years could be entered into, which would match the expected life of the machine. Under SSAP21 the depreciated assets, although leased and in law owned by the lessor not the company, would be shown on the balance sheet. The contra entry is the liability of the future lease rental payments. The two sides will net, with the current rental being charged to the profit and loss statement, although the gearing of the company will be affected nevertheless.

Leasing is merely an alternative method of borrowing, and should be appraised as such. If in this instance leasing would be cheaper, then the company might consider selling and leasing back other assets previously purchased. This would enable the company to reduce its level of borrowing.

In assessing the lease versus buy equation, the present value of discounted future rental payments is compared with that of purchasing outright, both being post tax. The method of financing producing the lower net present value will be chosen.

To decide which is the best alternative, the company would review the relative cash flows on an after-tax basis. This would allow some sensitivity analysis to be done, such as improved credit terms from the supplier, or initial purchase and subsequent lease through a sale and lease-back arrangement to take advantage of improved rates at another period of the year.

Example 2

Multico is a multinational, multi-product company. Its name is well respected in its markets, being in a traditional capital intensive industry. However, on the stock market the share price has not been highly rated, which has meant that the company relies heavily on its bankers for funds.

The company is now in a phase of further overseas expansion, by acquisition. This, in combination with the company's previous borrowing situation, will create various funding issues.

£m Year	1	2	3
Profit and loss			
Sales	750	800	900
Profit before interest			
and tax	19	40	54
Interest (average 12%)	10	11.8	12.3
Tax (40%)	3.6	11.3	16.7
Profit after tax	5.4	16.9	25
Dividends	5	5	7
Retained profits	0.4	11.9	18
Balance sheet			
Fixed assets	200	210	215
Current assets	50	62	74.6
less Current liabilities	26	33.3	34.6
Total assets	224	238.7	255
Long-term debt	84	98.3	102.7
Equity	80	80	80
Reserves	60	60.4	72.3
Total liabilities	224	238.7	255
Ratios			
Profit margin	2.5%	5%	6%
Gearing	60%	70%	67.4%
Interest cover	1.9×	3.4×	4.4×

As previously stated, gearing and interest cover are key ratios. In this instance, both are weak, and below market acceptable levels. Prior to arranging finance for the new acquisition the company could redress its balance sheet:

(a) In a lower interest rate environment it could reduce its cost of borrowing from 12%. This could be done by entering into a series of swaps. The long-term debt may be either at fixed rates for the term of the loans or be on a roll-over basis, with rates being revised every six months. A swap is an agreement between two parties to exchange the interest flows on a notional principal amount. By this method a company presently paying 'floating rate' interest can lock-in and pay 'fixed rate' interest, without having to repay or renegotiate the underlying original borrowing.

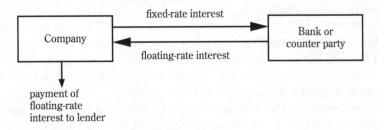

Note: that the receipt of floating-rate interest will match that owed to the original lender. There may be a slight 'loss' as funds received are at LIBOR, whereas funds paid to the lender would be at LIBOR plus margin over LIBOR.

The benefit is in the lower cost of fixed-rate funds.
This mechanism is extremely flexible and can be used for cross-currency exposures too.

(b) The company could consider leasing its purchases of capital equipment, or selling and leasing back existing equipment. The funds released could be used to reduce third party borrowings.

(c) The company could make a rights issue to inject new funds, in order to reduce borrowings.

In assessing how the new acquisition will be financed, again there are a number of options. Firstly though the decision regarding the currency exposure should be taken. When purchasing a company abroad there are two issues to be addressed.

(a)   The balance sheet exposure, when the assets are revalued at each year-end. Any changes, from one year to the next, due to exchange differences, are charged through reserves.
(b)   The profit and loss exposure, arising on consolidation of the overseas company. A good profit performance overseas might be 'negated' if the exchange rate in translation is weaker, compared with base currency. (Translation exposure is covered in more detail in Chapter 14.)

Typically, most companies will 'match' the balance sheet exposure and leave the profit and loss exposure. The medium- and long-term balance sheet hedge is most readily accomplished by borrowing in the currency required to purchase the asset. In this way any revaluation of the asset is matched by a revaluation of the liability (the loan). The profit and loss exposure will be managed via the foreign exchange market, normally by entering into forward exchange contracts to 'lock-in' the base currency receipt of a foreign dividend, or cover in interest and trade currency flows in foreign currencies.

In terms of the actual method of borrowing, the company may choose a fixed-rate loan, or a loan fixed on a six monthly (or other period) roll-over basis. The latter allows the company to 'fix' at a later stage, either with the lender or through the swap mechanism. The actual borrowing might be through the public, or private debt market, or from a bank, on a straight or syndicated basis.

(a)   For a company to tap the public markets, it will need to be a good 'name'. This is more important in the Euromarkets, than domestic markets. The size of an issue is also an important factor.
       In this instance the company could issue a convertible bond, which would serve to increase its equity base, rather than add the total amount to borrowings.
(b)   A viable alternative for a company in this position would be a private placement. The size of issue tends to be smaller, and it is a useful way of introducing the company name to a new range of investors. The costs of issue are cheaper than a public issue.
(c)   Straight bank or syndicated bank credit is the most obvious for this company, although the level of gearing would cause the

banks to negotiate hard on the covenants they would expect to see in the loan document. This would also affect the cost of raising debt in this way.

All of the options have to be carefully considered and evaluated. Usually the least expensive option will be chosen, but occasionally it is more beneficial to the company in the long run to raise funds by way of a Euromarket issue, rather than rely on bank debt. The former has the potential of widening investor awareness of the company, but the choice depends on what the company's management wishes to achieve strategically.

One consideration not mentioned, which is very important when assessing acquisitions and funding, is the tax implication of what is being done. A company should discuss the issues at an early stage with its tax advisers.

Example 3

Bankco is a long established wholesale bank, with loans to supranationals, sovereign states and corporates. It has no retail business, or private clients. It has a proportion of bad debts, which have been provisioned, though not written off. As the bank is involved in issuing letters of credit and so forth it has some contingent liabilities. It is of course regulated by the central bank, and as such needs to keep its ratios within the guidelines set, the key one being the capital adequacy test.

A bank has to react to its customers' needs in terms of setting up facilities, and provide funds as required. The bank's financing needs will centre on being able to meet demands, at a lower cost, and to be able to reduce the market risk of so providing funds to its customers.

The commercial risk of lending is taken by the bank's officers and credit committees, but the market risks are run by the bank's treasury department.

These latter risks are those associated with interest and currency rate movements, which cannot be recouped from the bank's customers. So the funding problems that it has to contemplate are in reality similar to those of any other large corporate.

The bank will seek to have a balanced portfolio of medium- and long-term loans to its customers, matched by liabilities to third parties. To do this banks use the swap markets and other risk management tools extensively, utilising options, futures, future rate agreements, swaptions (an option to enter into a swap at a future date), and so forth.

The balance that is sought is in terms of matching maturities and currencies. This may not be directly achieved, in other words in order to lend US$, a bank may choose to borrow sterling and arrange a currency swap, and lend US$ to the customer. Like a corporate, though, the bank will probably do this on a fully-hedged basis, in order to minimise risk.

The funding problem facing most banks is that of meeting the capital adequacy ratio requirements of central banks. How can a bank ease the pressure on such ratios?

(a)   It can have a rights issue to raise more capital and reduce third-party obligations.

(b)   It could issue perpetual floating rate notes, which some central banks accept as being quasi equity in the ratio calculation. However, in reality they are not.

(c)   It can reduce its loan portfolio, and change the nature of its business, to provide advice rather than money. For the advice given it can charge a fee, and as no funds are being lent, such services are outside the scope of capital adequacy. In order to achieve this the bank needs to persuade its customers to issue paper or notes, as evidence of debt, which other corporates will purchase, thereby lessening the role of banks as providers of funds.

(d)   It can sell off its assets to third parties, or sub-participate its portfolio. In both instances the customer's agreement should be sought.

(e)   It can increase the marginal cost of borrowing to its customers, like implementing a price rise. This may take time to show through as increased profits, and its effectiveness will be dictated by the competitive situation.

(f)   It can reduce the extent of the bank's contingent liabilities, by increasing the cost to customers to prudent levels to cover the bank's service costs, or it can discontinue that service.

Whatever course the bank chooses to follow, may and will be dictated by market conditions. At times the equities markets reach saturation, and the rights issue option would not be prudent, or the perpetual market may be effectively closed due to investors' attitudes against buying such paper.

Summary

The options open to a company in raising medium- or long-term funds are varied, and cannot be differentiated on cost alone. A company will have to choose between that most applicable at the time of requirement, bearing in mind other factors such as maturity, currency, size of requirement, where funds are required and so forth. Once the choice has been made the company will then have to document it with the lender. This stage can be more tiresome than making the initial choice. If a company is of sufficient size, it may be best to have its 'standard' terms and conditions, such as covenants, representations and warranties, and events of default. This makes it easier for the company to police, than if there is a range of each under differing agreements. In most instances the onus is on the company to inform the bank of a default or breach, so banks are willing to consider a company's standard documentation.

In financing a company, essentially there is no right or wrong way, only one that is most appropriate at the time. This should be chosen, but an open mind retained if opportunities subsequently exist to change the facility or debt portfolio mix.

Further Reading

The Treasurer: July/August 1989, 'The Corporate Debt Market'.

Medium-term Debt Instruments

Alan Colley

Introduction

A British company seeking medium-term debt 30 years ago may have looked no further than its clearing bank and may even have relied on overdraft facilities rather than formalising a separate loan facility with defined repayment arrangements. If it qualified, it may have issued loan stock, in sterling, through the Stock Exchange where maturities of up to 30 years were available. However, this market failed to survive into the 1970s due to high interest rates and being crowded out by the borrowing requirement of the government.

The Eurocurrency market, conceived in the 1960s, rapidly developed as an avenue for borrowing during the 1970s, either in the form of floating-rate loan facilities provided by banks at margins over interbank 'offered' rates, via syndicated loans for larger amounts, or, for companies with the highest credit rating, at fixed rates by issues of Eurobonds. The fact that UK companies were constrained by exchange control regulations from using sterling abroad was a further impetus to borrowing in Eurocurrencies, but this frequently left companies with currency exposures as well as interest rate risks.

The 1980s have witnessed further developments in the type of medium-term funding instruments available from commercial and investment banks. Floating-rate loans have retained a role for one-to-one (single lender and single borrower) and syndicated facilities. However, at the beginning of the decade, major companies realised that they could raise finance more cheaply in the securities markets through the issue of both short- and medium-term paper, rather than continue to use commercial banks as intermediaries. In addition, when short-term Euronotes were issued, under note-issuance facilities (NIFs), revolving underwriting facilities (RUFs) were often arranged with commercial banks to guarantee the availability of funds in the medium term. It was a short step to combine all the short-term funding options available to the company and the committed standby lines into multiple option facilities (MOFs). Banks and dealers now bid against each other on tender panels to provide companies' short-term funding requirements. Committed 'standby' lines are made available by banks with the interest rates based on interbank 'offered' rates, plus margins, as part of the package.

The Eurobond market is principally a source of fixed-rate funds and the volume of new bonds issued in this market has increased greatly in the 1980s. However, of the US$187 billion of new issues in 1986, only around 25% of these in value were by companies. The task of the investment banks is to ensure that the bonds are sold to end investors, whether retail or institutional. They will advise which market should be tapped and on the use of 'swaps' to obtain the desired currency or interest rate basis. They will advise whether the issue should be 'straight' or whether features to encourage investors to buy should be added, for example convertible options or warrants.

New financial instruments have been devised which allow companies to structure their medium-term debt portfolios in line with specific objectives and policies, thereby hedging perceived or accepting measured risks, and they may be used in conjunction with new debt or arranged separately as hedging mechanisms. They include interest rate and currency swaps (details of which are often the unpublicised elements of bond issues) and interest rate caps.

What is appropriate to a company as medium-term funding is dependent on a combination of factors, including the perceived creditworthiness of the borrowing company and its relative size in relation to the amounts, maturities and currencies required and the ability of the financial markets to match these needs.

In order to demonstrate the range of medium-term instruments available to companies, the remainder of the chapter will encompass four case studies — four companies of different size and with differing requirements. The companies have net worth of £15 million, £250 million, £1,500 million, and £15,000 million. The debt instruments which meet each company's needs are outlined by means of a letter to the company, an application to the credit committee within one of the company's banks, a presentation to the company and a memorandum of interview with the company, respectively, used here as media for explaining the basic issues.

Company A

Company A is a private limited company in the services industry. Its net worth is £15 million, capital gearing 12%, turnover £25 million and pre-tax profits £1 million. It anticipates additional debt requirements of a maximum of £4 million on a fluctuating basis over the next four years to cover some capital outlay and for trading purposes, particularly for its operations in Europe.

Letter to the company from its bank

When I saw you yesterday, you explained that you will have a fluctuating requirement for funds up to £4 million over the next four years. You asked me to explain 'floating-rate' loan facilities (so that you may prepare a full briefing for the board) and asked whether fixed-rate funds are available to finance the capital outlays. You intimated that you wished to borrow in currency to fund your European operations.

I believe we can arrange a suitably flexible package for you. A 'revolving' facility is appropriate, that is, the full amount of the credit will be available for drawing throughout the term, so when you repay a fixture, that is, a loan for an agreed period, you retain the right to redraw at a later date.

Within the facility of £4 million, you would be able to make drawings in multiples of £50,000 or the currency equivalent, subject to minimum drawings of £250,000 or equivalent. We set this as the minimum drawing even though amounts usually dealt in the interbank markets, where our dealers obtain their deposits, are in multiples of £1 million. You will be contacting our 'corporate' dealers rather than the interbank dealers and we should be able to agree other amounts with you outside the parameters outlined. The standard fixture periods in the interbank markets are one, three, six and twelve months. Again, we should be able to agree maturities of your choice for each drawing.

We can normally fund you in currencies for periods up to twelve months, particularly in the European currencies you have requested. Even if our dealers cannot borrow the funds to on-lend to you, they can buy the currency for you, and sell forward the funds you are due to repay at maturity of the fixture. However, we always add the proviso that currencies will be 'subject to availability'.

We can build into the agreement the ability for you to borrow fixed-rate funds, again 'subject to availability'. Although our dealers can normally meet your exact needs, the markets become 'thin' in the longer dates, and consequently more expensive, particularly in other than the major currencies.

You asked me to explain the basis of the interest payments and the other costs you will incur. The interest rate charged is based on the London interbank 'offered' rate (LIBOR) to which we will add our margin of $0.xx\%$ per annum. I propose the same margin throughout the life of the loan. If the facility were for longer than four years, I would expect to see an increased margin for the later years.

For drawings in sterling, you will also be asked to cover our 'reserve costs'. These reflect the opportunity costs to the bank of maintaining lower-yielding liquid assets on our balance sheet in accordance with the Bank of England's requirements. We calculate this cost weekly and will invoice you on the basis of the average of the weekly rates at each interest payment date. You asked whether we could fix these costs in advance, particularly on longer-term fixtures. It is fairer, and will be cheaper for you, if we don't. This would be only a minor proportion of the costs of the loan to you and the only way the bank could protect itself against subsequent higher reserves costs is to load the up-front calculation against you.

Since we will be committed to provide funds on a revolving basis, we will charge you a commitment fee, payable every six months, on the undrawn portion of the facility at a rate of 0. xx% per annum. If you should want the amount available under the loan to be reduced in the last year(s) please let me know and this will be written into the loan agreement.

You must also bear in mind the following points when calculating the overall cost of funds to the company:

(a)　You will be asked to pay interest every six months on fixtures in excess of six months. The interest cost on an annualised basis will therefore be higher.

(b)　Care must be taken with value dates when fixtures are arranged. Sterling is for 'same-day value' whereas Eurocurrencies are 'spot' deals, that is, for value in two business days' time.

(c)　Interest on Eurocurrencies is based on a 360-day year, with some exceptions, e.g. Belgium and Luxemburg francs and Irish punts which, like sterling, are based on a 365-day year.

(d)　You must also take into account the arrangement fee of £$xxxx$ which was agreed.

You asked whether it is possible to repay drawings before the maturity date of the fixture. We cannot prohibit this, but if interest rates have fallen in the meantime, you must expect to pay compensation to the bank, since we will not necessarily be able to replace the funds in the market and earn the same yield as you were paying, although we are still committed to pay the original higher rate to our depositor(s).

You are aware that we have branches in the European centres where you are represented and we could structure an 'umbrella' facility for you, permitting drawings out of any of these branches, subject to satisfactory control procedures as to the overall level of utilisation under the line.

I am making an application to the bank's credit committee for a four-year revolving credit including all the options outlined. Once approval is received, I shall send a copy of the draft loan agreement for your approval. We will of course require copies of the usual board resolutions, up-to-date memorandum and articles of association and specimen signatures, together with a copy of the executed loan agreement in due course, before the first drawdown can be made.

In summary, the *benefits* of the facility we can offer you are that:

(a)   You will obtain funds based on short-term interbank rates of interest which are generally lower than medium-term rates.

(b)   This is a 'committed' facility whereby the bank guarantees to provide sterling (the currency in which the loan is denominated) for periods up to twelve months.

(c)   You can draw in sterling when you want for as long as you want for fixtures up to and beyond twelve months.

(d)   You can draw in most currencies for periods up to twelve months and we will endeavour to provide fixed-rate funds in the European currencies you require.

(e)   We can include other lending centres of the bank within the facility.

Overall, the facility can be tailormade to meet your funding requirements.

You must bear in mind that there are some *limitations:*

(a)   Interest rates may have increased significantly at times when you are obliged to borrow.

(b)   Currencies, and fixture periods over twelve months, are 'subject to availability'.

(c)   We may wish to restrict the number of currencies borrowed at any one time. Also, if you wish to renew a currency drawing and the sterling equivalent is higher due to exchange-rate fluctuations, we will ask you to repay any excess (of the overall facility) at the time of the roll-over, if the excess is more than 5% of the facility amount.

(d)   As a service company, we do not believe that you can meet the criteria laid down by the Bank of England to allow you to include sterling bankers acceptances within the options available to you, even though this is generally a cheaper method of raising finance.

(e)   You will need to confirm subsequently with the tax authorities that all interest payments and expenses relating to the facility are tax deductible. There is, in our experience, rarely a problem in this regard.

I will be in touch with you again once I have heard from our credit committee.

Company B

Company B is a publicly-quoted company producing industrial goods. Shareholders' funds total £250 million, capital gearing is 50%, turnover £350 million and pre-tax profits are £10 million. It wishes to rationalise its medium-term funding.

Extract from a report to the bank's credit committee

(A synopsis of the company's activities, supporting data for the rationalisation of the company's debt structure and financial analysis, including the need for financial covenants in the documentation, have already been covered. A summary and recommendation to make the facilities available on the terms set out would follow.)

Proposition

The company has requested terms for a seven-year £100 million facility including currencies, subject to availability. We wish to offer a MOF on a syndicated basis with this bank retaining £20 million for its own book. We are confident that we will be able to achieve selldown to this level. We anticipate approaching six banks to join the syndicate as underwriters and tender panel members. The terms we propose are as follows:

(a)   *Committed loans/sterling acceptance credits*

   (i)   Rates:

1, 3, 6 and 12-month fixtures	— LIBOR plus 0.*xx*% per annum plus reserve costs for sterling drawings
Acceptances (maximum 187 days)	Acceptance commission — 0.*xx*% per annum — Discount at eligible bill rates

   (ii)   Commitment fee, payable on undrawn balances — 0. *xx*% per annum. Up to 0. *xx*% of the facility may be designated 'unavailable', becoming 'available' for drawing after an agreed period of notice. The commitment fee will be at the lower level of 0. *xx*% per annum on the 'unavailable' portion.

(b)   *Uncommitted loans/sterling acceptance credits*

   Rates:

1, 3 and 6 months acceptances	— LIBOR/market rates — Acceptance commission, minimum 0. *xx*% per annum — Discount at eligible bill rates

(c)   *Front-end/management fees*

— Participation fee, depending on the final level of commitment by the bank	0. *xx*% flat
— *Praecipium* (payable to the lead manager bank(s) only)	0. *xx*% flat
— Agency fees	$*xxxx* p.a.

Overall cost to the customer 0. *xx*% p.a. fully drawn and 0. *xx*% p.a. undrawn
Overall yield to this bank 0. *xx*% p.a. fully drawn and 0. *xx*% p.a. undrawn.

Commentary on the proposition

(a)   It should be noted that any combination of pricing and fee structure is possible and the above is intended to demonstrate the range of fees currently seen.

(b)   Other variations could be: to have, say, only 50% of the facility on a committed basis, with the balance available under the tender panel arrangements on a 'best efforts' basis; a facility fee, at a lower level, could be paid instead of the commitment fee, but this would be payable on the whole amount of the facility whether drawn or not.

(c)   Options to issue sterling and Eurocommercial paper could also be included.

(d)   The considerations regarding semi-annual interest payments, value dates, 360/365-day years, documentation and tax need to be borne in mind by the company's Treasurer.

(e)   The objectives of the company are, of course, to reduce the overall cost of borrowing, and of the Bank to maximise its own yield.

(f)   Not every bank in the syndicate of banks would necessarily be able or willing to bid on tender panels even on the skeleton terms outlined above.

The *benefits* of a MOF to Company B are that when it requires funds, the company can tap the cheapest source of money available to it under the tender panel mechanism.

(a)   Drawings can be made for periods to match the fluctuating borrowing requirements of the company.

(b)   The committed 'standby' element of the package provides a guarantee of availability of funds if the securities/capital markets are closed and banks are unwilling to bid for cash advances.

(c)   The optimum combination of fees can be negotiated to reduce borrowing and associated costs.

(d)   It is possible to bring all the main funding requirements of the company into one facility, thereby simplifying negotiations for the borrowing and making administration of drawings, through the agent bank, less complicated.

(e)   At the same time, the company can ensure that its sources of funds are diversified by including all its relationship banks in the syndicate and by tapping outside investors in the capital markets.

(f)   It is possible to arrange such facilities purely as revolving standby credits.

MOFs are a logical development of traditional syndicated loan facilities, enabling banks to provide substantial lines to companies and spread the credit risks.

The *limitations* of MOFs are that:

(a)   They have developed during a decade which has not seen credit squeezes or prolonged bear markets. There is always the possibility that banks and dealers may not be able or willing to quote under tender panels at some date in the future. The company will therefore need to be satisfied with the soundness of the banks providing the committed lines.

(b)   It is difficult to introduce elements which a bank could provide on a one-to-one basis, for example a wider range of currencies (under MOFs, the company may only get bids in sterling, US dollars, Deutschmark and ECUs), alternative lending centres and fixtures in excess of twelve months. For these reasons large panels of banks should be avoided.

(c)   The competition between banks in this market has driven fees down to such an extent that UK clearing banks will, and have, declined to participate in MOFs for UK companies.

Company C

Company C are high-street retailers, principally in the UK. A public quoted company, it has net worth of £1,500 million, minimal term debt, turnover of £4,000 million and pre-tax profits of £200 million. It has established a credit card operation which, along with other expansion plans, particularly in the USA, will involve expenditure of £200 million this year. It is seeking information from investment houses on making a bond issue.

An explanation of Company C's medium-term debt requirement and a presentation to the company by an investment bank
Company: You are already aware of our credit card activities and the expansion plans we have, particularly in the USA, for which we will need to find £200 million this year, only a portion of which we can finance from cash flow. In view of the nature of our credit card operations, we wish to raise finance on a floating-rate basis, in sterling.

We already have floating-rate facilities totalling £100 million available, including a tender panel option, from which we obtain funds at around LIMEAN. We are interested to hear your proposals regarding more permanent financing of around £100 million for a five-year period.

Bank: Thank you for the explanation of your requirement. You have not made an issue in the Eurobond market before, nor have you had the need to! However, the amount and period you indicated, together with your credit standing, provide the right ingredients for a successful issue on that market.

Our presentation will cover, first, the terms of a bond issue, that is, the currency, interest rate basis, amount and maturity. Secondly, we shall look at other aspects you will have to bear in mind as regards investors, including whether a formal credit rating is required. Third, we shall examine the procedures for syndication of an issue and, finally, the level of fees and expenses you are likely to incur, after which we will answer any questions you may have. Your requirement is too large for a private placement with financial institutions, so it is a public issue we are considering.

The terms of a bond issue

You require sterling and you are no doubt aware that at the moment there is no satisfactory market for domestic sterling corporate bonds and debentures. The Eurosterling bond market could be used and would require a roadshow, visiting major European centres in order to make your name known to the investment community. However, windows for making sterling issues tend to occur only occasionally and the market may be closed, for example due to concern over the level of sterling interest rates or when large privatisation issues cause the Bank of England to delay issues in sterling. We can, however, make an issue in another currency and swap the proceeds into sterling. In order to gain wide distribution of your paper, we recommend that your first issue is in US dollars. We could tap the Deutschmark or yen markets for you, but the range of investors is not as wide as for US dollars and you have no natural inclination to, or connection with, these currencies.

You require floating-rate funds, but issues for companies on the Eurobond market are usually at fixed rates. Floating rates, when available, are more usual for banks and sovereign borrowers. We will be able to arrange an interest rate swap in conjunction with the currency swap, but the timing of the issue becomes more critical because of the swap — there may be only one or two days in a month when the swap can be effected.

Bond issues for companies are frequently in the range of US$50–200 million. If the issue is too small, it will not generate demand because investors will be worried about liquidity in the secondary market, that is, their ability to sell their holding before maturity. If the issue is too large for your name, there may also be difficulties in finding sufficient investors. We recommend an issue of the US dollar equivalent of £100m as being a reasonable amount for the market and for your requirement. The period you want the funds for, five years, is an accepted maturity in the market, as would be seven years. It would be less usual, for a first issue, to issue a two- or three-year bond or a ten-year bond. Investors' preferences at the time have to be taken into account if you make issues outside the 'norm'.

Investors' considerations

The success of an issue also depends on the credit rating of the issuer. Companies can be rated informally, that is, on the basis of being 'household names', and we believe we could issue a bond for you on this basis. However, you have plans for expansion in the USA and if at a later date you wish to tap the large United States domestic market, then you will need a credit rating from one of the agencies, 'Standard and Poors' or 'Moodys', so it is worth obtaining a rating now. On the basis of your accounts, we believe you should obtain the best bond rating — AAA or Aaa respectively, which will enhance your chances of a successful issue.

We will also arrange for your issue to be listed on the London and Luxemburg Stock Exchanges. Investors like to have ready access to a current price for their holdings and it will satisfy them that you have complied with the Stock Exchanges' formalities for issues.

Procedures for syndication of an issue

Once you have decided to proceed with the issue, you will give a mandate to an investment house to syndicate the bond. He will appoint co-lead managers whom in this instance we would expect to have the capability to join in the 'swap'. The lead manager will also assemble an underwriting group who provide a guarantee that you will receive the funds up to the time that the bonds are sold. The management group of banks will contact other investment houses to form a selling group with a view to achieving as wide distribution of the bonds as possible. Were you making issues in two or more currencies simultaneously, it would be wise to get different co-management groups together for each currency.

You will also need to appoint lawyers, auditors, trustees, printers, paying agents and a clearing house for various aspects of the prospectus, documentation, printing and custody of the bonds, and for a first issue, a signing ceremony and dinner will be expected.

We will indicate the fixed interest rate payable when the bond issue is announced. There is a risk that, before the bonds are finally sold, market conditions may change adversely, but for what we call 'bought' deals, which are normal nowadays, we will bear (and possibly hedge) that risk.

The interest rate for the bond will be set in relation to US Treasury bond yields at the time (a comparable index would be used for issues in other currencies) and you can expect to pay xx basis points above the Treasury yield for the equivalent maturity.

Fees and expenses

The fees you will incur for the issue will cover the lead managers', underwriters' and co-managers' fees and selling agents' commissions. The latter is the largest part — typically 1.5%, although the selling agents will quite likely use part of it to provide a discount to purchasers of the bonds. After paying all the other parties involved, you can expect the issue to cost around 2% of the principal amount of the bond.

In summary, the *benefits* of a Eurobond issue to your company are that:

(a)   It will allow you to tap the cheapest and possibly the only source of fixed-rate funds, and allows you through swaps to convert the benefit you have of raising funds on favourable terms in one market into another currency and interest rate basis — your real requirement.

(b)   It allows you to diversify your sources of funds and establish an investor base which can be used to advantage when making issues in the future.

(c)   It allows you to obtain medium-term funds on an unsecured basis, other than for the provision of a 'negative pledge' covenant.

You should nevertheless be aware of the following *negative factors*:

(a) This is a public issue and the interests of the bondholders must be taken into account in the same way that you maintain your relations with shareholders.

(b) Once you have locked into a maturity structure for the bond, you cannot amend it or pre-pay if this is not within the terms announced at the time of issue.

(c) Bond issues are more expensive to arrange than commercial bank syndicated floating-rate loans, although they are not as expensive to arrange as issues of equity.

(d) As with equity issues, the timing is critical and an issue can only be made when the market is receptive, so you must have other sources of funds available to 'bridge' the issue proceeds if needed.

Have you any questions?

Company: What are the main differences between domestic and Euro issues?

Bank: The main differences are as follows:

(a) Domestic bonds are usually registered, whereas Eurobonds are bearer securities and investors will accept a slightly lower yield in return for this anonymity.

(b) Longer-term maturities may be available in the domestic markets, since domestic and Euro issues are targeted at different investors who have different criteria for buying bonds.

(c) Interest is payable annually on fixed-rate Eurobonds and semi-annually for domestic issues.

(d) Withholding tax is usually applied to domestic issues but not to Eurobonds.

(e) Issuing procedures are easier and quicker for Eurobonds.

Company: We have heard much about Eurobonds being an unregulated market, are there any restrictions?

Bank: The market for US dollar bonds issued in London is unrestricted, provided bonds are not sold to United States residents for a period of 90 days from their issue date, otherwise the bonds are treated as domestic issues by the Securities and Exchange Commission.

The authorities in the country of the currency may have some say in how and when issues in their currencies are made. For instance, until 1989 the Bank of England operated a queuing system for both domestic and international securities in sterling in excess of £3 million, in order to ensure a steady flow of new instruments.

Company: What are the usual features that can be added to corporate bonds?
Bank: These features or sweeteners are added in order to make the bonds more attractive to investors. I will explain call and put options, convertibles and issues with warrants.

(a)   *A call option* allows you, as issuer, to redeem the bond at or between advised dates, usually at a premium if it is still in the earlier years of the life of the bond. Call options have not been acceptable for UK domestic bond issues. Your reason for issuing the bonds means that this is not appropriate for you.

(b)   *A put option* gives the investor the right to redeem his holding at or between specified dates before maturity. Again, as you have an on-going requirement for the full five-year term, this is not appropriate.

These options are really only appropriate for companies which tap a variety of markets and can be flexible in the flow of funds they obtain and repay by way of bonds. In addition, the 'swap' proposed could not be unwound so easily. You require all parts of the deal to go to full maturity.

(c)   *A convertible issue* allows the investor to swap the bonds for shares in your company at a fixed conversion price which will be higher than the market price of your shares at the time of issue. The benefits of convertibles are that you can pay a lower coupon on the bonds, which you may never have to redeem. They are a way of broadening your shareholder base, if that is one of your objectives. Also, when sentiment is against the bond market, but equity markets are favourable, an equity-linked issue such as a convertible is more likely to be well received.

However, you may find that existing shareholders are less happy with the arrangement. If your share price performs well, the new shareholders will be seen to be acquiring shares cheaply and earnings per share will be affected when bonds are converted. You will also be converting debt into equity at a time when you have more capacity for debt. Convertible issues are usually only well received when both the stock market and your own shares are strong. In the UK, there is a limit on the amount of shares which can be issued each year other than to existing shareholders who retain 'pre-emption rights' — the right of first refusal of any new shares on offer. You should not 'swap' the proceeds of a convertible issue if you expect the bond to be converted into equity before maturity.

(d)   *Warrants* attached to bonds give the holders the right to purchase, usually, equity in your company, but may as one alternative, for example, allow the holder to take up more bonds on pre-set terms. The benefits to you would be that you could charge a purchase price for the warrant, which brings you cash up-front, and you pay a lower coupon on the bond. In addition, you can choose how much equity is to be issued when the warrants are exercised. You could choose, say, 50% warrant coverage, whereas a convertible entails 100% coverage. You also retain the debt on your balance sheet until its final maturity and so you can 'swap' the bond proceeds for the full term.

You are, however, getting involved in a market which allows the warrants to be traded separately and speculatively. The purchasers of warrants are less likely to be committed, long-term investors. Also, a guaranteed rate on a 'debt' warrant may be expensive in future years if interest rates fall.

We have by no means covered all the possible features which can be added to Eurobonds. This is a continuously innovative market and sometimes new features are fashionable for only a short time. You should ask what the benefit is to you as issuer and to the investor of any 'features' which are proposed on bond issues for your company. For instance, zero coupon and deep-discounted bonds are useful for projects with no cash flows in the early years and for investors requiring capital gains — but not for you. We recommend that your first issue is a 'plain vanilla' deal, with no complicated variations.

Company: If we return to you for advice on a bond issue in twelve months time, would you give us the same advice as now?
Bank: That would be most unlikely since market conditions may well be different. We would expect to be able to meet your needs, but not necessarily by means of a straight fixed-rate US dollar issue. With access to a number of capital markets, you can choose the one which offers the best terms at the time to achieve your target currency and interest rate. An issue on the domestic market in another country might be an appropriate channel at the time.

Company D

Company D is an international energy company with surplus resources of £15,000 million and capital gearing of 40%. Turnover is £19,000 million, and pre-tax profits £1,200 million. It has submitted a bid for US$2,400 million for a North American oil company and has sought tenders from its main relationship banks for bids to provide finance, both on a 'bridging' and longer-term basis, for the acquisition.

Memorandum of interview by an accounts executive in a commercial bank

We visited the Treasurer following the request to submit bids in respect of financing of the acquisition of OilCo, a United States Corporation, at a price of US$2,400 million. Initially, a bridging loan commitment is required to confirm the company's ability to meet the purchase costs. The company expects this commitment to be provided by a syndicate of four of its major relationship banks, including this bank, each undertaking to provide US$600 million for up to twelve months on one- and three-month fixtures. However, the company expects that major portions of the acquisition cost will be met initially from its liquid resources, its US commercial paper programme, and from the MOF which was put in place last year. In the longer term, refinancing of the line will be from cash flow and from bond issues in New York and London.

The initial borrowing line we are asked to provide is large but we have confirmed with the bank's Treasury Manager that if drawdown in one amount is required, it could be funded in one tranche with no additional notice being required. We have contacted our investment bank which is advising on current prospects for issues in the capital markets.

Action: Prepare an application to credit committee with a recommendation that we provide US$600 million for the bridging finance out of our London and New York offices.

Commentary

The above demonstrates one of the areas where the 'traditional' syndicated loan retains a role in modern financing — as bridging facilities in respect of acquisition finance. The *benefits* are summarised as follows:

(a)   Very large sums can be mobilised which cannot be accommodated by other markets.
(b)   They can be arranged at very short notice, within a matter of days of the need for funds being advised.
(c)   The short-term roll-overs provide natural break points when funds raised from other cheaper sources can be deployed.

The *limitations* of this market are that:

(a)   The largest amounts can only be raised in one or two major currencies — principally US dollars.
(b)   Fixed-rate finance cannot be arranged. The only exceptions are 'club' deals between two or three banks when an average of rates quoted, rounded upwards, could be taken.
(c)   With pricing over LIBOR, this method of finance is perceived as relatively expensive by many major companies.

Syndicated loans are, in addition, appropriate for borrowers with limited access to capital markets, for project and asset financings where sophisticated risk assessments are required and for 'standby' credit insurance facilities — the 'committed' element of a MOF.

Summary

Whilst the 1980s have been characterised by the trend to securitisation of debt, the case studies have demonstrated that there is a role for most medium-term debt instruments which have become complementary to each other. A company's objectives should include diversifying its sources of medium-term funds and utilising the different sources of funds to meet its particular requirements. In such a competitive and dynamic market-place, the Corporate Treasurer must evaluate the alternatives proposed to him with great care in the light of his funding objectives and strategies.

Further reading

1   J. A. Donaldson, *Corporate Funding*, *Financial Times* Business Information, 1983.
2   J. A. Donaldson and T. H. Donaldson, *The Medium Term Loan Market*, Macmillan, 1982.

3   D. Hodson (ed.), *Corporate Finance in Treasury Management*, Gee, 1984.

4   A. J. W. Watson and R. Altringham, *Treasury Management: International Banking Operations*, The Chartered Institute of Bankers, 1986 (Sections five and six).

5   *Financial Times* — International Capital Markets Section (particularly Monday editions).

CHAPTER 12

Liquidity Management

Sarah Laws

Editor's Notes

Chapters 12 and 13 cover short-term finance with the general concepts being introduced under the heading of liquidity management. The Corporate Treasurer usually defines working capital as the cash invested in trading activity, a definition which excludes cash and bank balances (or overdrafts) and which is at variance with that usually accepted by bankers. Chapter 13 discusses the way in which the various short-term finance mechanisms meet the needs of the corporate.

Introduction

Liquidity management involves the management of short-term borrowings and the investment of short-term cash surpluses. Short-term is defined as relating to periods of up to 12 months.

In order to carry out this function, the Treasurer or other financial manager must have available a forecast of the cash requirements and surpluses of the business. This chapter will therefore be concerned with the methods of forecasting and controlling the cash flows of the business together with the methods and objectives of the management of the cash positions arising from these flows.

The Objectives of Liquidity Management

The objectives of liquidity management may be summarised as follows:

(a) *Liquidity*. The management of the short-term cash position will involve ensuring that the business will have funds available to meet its liabilities as they fall due.

(b) *Safety*. Short-term investments should not be made where there is an unacceptable level of credit risk. To this end companies may draw up lists of banks with which they are prepared to invest cash surpluses. Similarly, where investments are made in the paper or other securities of fellow corporates, a company should draw up a list of those in which it is prepared to invest. Risk may be further reduced by setting a limit on the amount which may be invested with any one bank or company. Less obvious is the risk attached to borrowings but this should not be overlooked. This may arise if funds are not forthcoming when a call is made on a facility available at the lender's option. The failure of a lender to assist will at the least give rise to some uncertainty and may lead to borrowings from that source having to be repaid unexpectedly and at short notice. The Treasurer is therefore faced with the dilemma of having to pay the bank some form of commitment fee in order to secure his source of funds and so increase his cost of borrowing by a known amount, or to risk the possibility of having to borrow at a high and unknown cost in difficult market conditions.

(c) *Profitability.* After taking into account the problems of liquidity and safety outlined above, the aim should be to minimise the costs of borrowing and/or to maximise the profit from depositing. This will involve consideration of not only interest rates and the potential for capital gains or losses but also transaction costs, including minimisation of transmission delays, foreign exchange exposure and the amount of administrative time and effort involved.

(d) *Flexibility.* Liquidity management should be carried out in such a way as to allow response to changing market conditions such as changes in interest or exchange rates. Although it may be claimed to be part of the Treasurer's function to anticipate such changes and to act in accordance with these expectations, there should also be sufficient flexibility to cope with unforeseen circumstances such as a sudden large cash requirement or a change in trading conditions altering the liquid position of the business.

There may be some conflict between these objectives. For example, an investment bearing a high return may well be more risky than an investment with a lower return so that high profitability is only achieved by sacrificing some of the safety of the investment. The Treasurer will have to decide the relative importance of each of the objectives bearing in mind the nature and requirements of the business and of its shareholders. The attitude of companies to risk varies, some companies being highly risk averse whereas others are willing to take risks which are compensated for by high returns.

Factors Affecting Liquidity Management

As indicated above, the relative importance of the four principal objectives of liquidity management will vary between different companies. Whilst this arises in part from the differing risk attitudes of companies, the nature of the business also will determine the factors which are important in decision-making.

There is a general principle that the assets of a business should be matched by liabilities of similar maturities. For example, a capital-intensive manufacturing company will have a high proportion of fixed assets amongst the assets on its balance sheet. These assets should be financed by long-term debt or equity. The assets of a computer software company, however, are likely to consist largely of debtors and work in progress; fixed assets will probably be limited to computer equipment and a few cars. Such a company will have a relatively high proportion of current assets to fixed assets. If these are financed with debt of a similar maturity profile then the company will also have a relatively high proportion of short-term debt. However, to the extent that a proportion of working capital may be considered as fixed, part may be financed by longer-term capital.

But which of these businesses is likely to be the most liquid? It may seem at first glance that it will obviously be the computer software company as it does not have so much of its capital tied up in fixed assets. This is not necessarily the case. The manufacturing company may be involved in a small number of long-term projects, for example building oil rigs or chemical plants. Alternatively, it may be involved in some kind of continuous process such as the manufacture of small items such as nuts, bolts and screws supplied to industry, builders merchants and retail outlets. The first company is likely to have a few projects of long duration for which it may receive progress payments from time to time from its customers and it will therefore experience a somewhat 'lumpy' cash flow (see Figure 12.1). The second company is likely to have a number of small sales to a large number of customers and is therefore likely to experience a more even cash flow. The time it takes for cash paid out for purchases to be realised as cash received for sales is likely to be a great deal shorter than for the first company.

However, a computer software house working on tailormade programs for a small number of customers will in fact experience cash flows more like those of the first manufacturing company; it too will experience a 'lumpy' cash flow as progress payments against contracts are received.

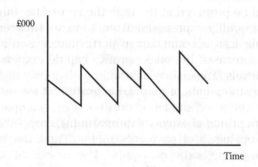

Figure 12.1   Cash flow of a company with a small number of large contracts

The varying nature of these cash flows will affect the view that the Treasurer takes of the relative importance of the objectives of liquidity management. For example, a company that knows it can rely on a reasonably even cash inflow may be less concerned about the liquidity of its investments. Conversely, a company which is relying on the receipt of one large contract payment to provide it with the liquid funds to meet its liabilities over, for example, the next month may also wish to keep some of its investments relatively liquid so that it has access to funds should the payment be delayed.

The relative importance of the objectives of liquidity management may also vary for the same company at different times. A company may become more risk averse and therefore more concerned with the safety of its investments at times when profitability is low as it cannot risk diminishing profits further. Conversely, at times of high profitability it will feel more able to take a risk that is compensated for by a high return. Also, a company not usually concerned to maintain a portfolio of highly liquid investments may nevertheless wish to do so at a time when a proposal which will involve a high level of capital expenditure is being considered.

Cash Flow Forecasting and Budgeting

In order to determine the amount of funds available for investment and the length of time for which those funds are available, or conversely to determine the amount and period of short-term borrowings, a company will need to prepare a cash-flow forecast. In general a budgeted cash-flow forecast will be prepared at the time the rest of the budget is set. Revised forecasts will be prepared from time to time as the year progresses, taking into account actual performance and adjusted to reflect revised forecasts of sales, profit, capital expenditure and working capital levels. These forecasts should obviously tie in with the other accounting statements prepared, i.e. profit and loss account and balance sheet.

There are two principal ways of preparing a cash-flow forecast. These are the receipts and payments method and the source and application of funds method.

Receipts and payments method

A cash-flow forecast will be presented as a series of rows and columns of data. The columns represent units of time, for example one week or one month. The rows represent different categories of receipts and payments. Conventionally, the total for receipts and for payments is shown. The difference between the two is the movement or net change in the cash position for the period represented by the column. This is added to the balance at the beginning of the period to give the balance at the end of the period. An example of a cash-flow forecast prepared under the receipts and payments method is given in Figure 12.2.

	January £000	February £000	March £000	April £000	Total £000
Debtors	397	337	279	300	1,313
Sundry income	10	15	10	10	45
	407	352	289	310	1,358
Suppliers	162	130	153	172	617
Salaries	75	75	75	75	300
Tax	100	—	—	—	100
Dividend	—	45	—	—	45
Capital expenditure	—	—	—	200	200
	337	250	228	447	1,262
Opening balance	25	95	197	258	25
Net cash flow	70	102	61	(137)	96
Closing balance	95	197	258	121	121

Figure 12.2 Burg and Dee cash-flow forecast

The preparation of a cash-flow forecast of this type will involve a number of assumptions regarding the timing of receipts and payments. For example, the forecast for receipts from debtors may assume that 65% of sales are paid for after one month, 25% after two months and 10% after three months.

A further assumption may be made to obtain the phasing of supplier payments. If purchases are 50% of sales, goods are held in stock for an average of one month and 80% of supplier payments are made one month after receipt of the goods, the remaining 20% being paid for after two months, then supplier payments for a particular month will be made up as follows:

> Sales for the month × 50% × 80%
> plus   Sales for the previous month × 50% × 20%

Figure 12.3 shows the way in which the debtor receipts and supplier payments were calculated for the Burg and Dee Ltd cash-flow forecast.

The payment dates for certain other items, in particular tax and dividends, will be known in advance.

	Oct £000	Nov £000	Dec £000	Jan £000	Feb £000	Mar £000	Apr £000
Sales	320	370	420	300	250	320	350
Debtor receipts							
(month − 1) × 65%				273	195	162	208
(month − 2) × 25%				92	105	75	62
(month − 3) × 10%				32	37	42	30
				397	337	279	300
Supplier payments							
Current month sales × 50% × 80%				120	100	128	140
(month − 1) sales × 50% × 20%				42	30	25	32
				162	130	153	172

Figure 12.3 Calculation of debtor receipts and supplier payments for Burg and Dee Ltd

The source and application of funds method
This may be used to predict the cash balance at the end of a period. Essentially a statement of source and application of funds explains the movement from the balance sheet at the beginning of a period to that at the end of the period. Working through the sections of a balance sheet, a forecast source and application of funds will be prepared as follows:

(a)   The movement in fixed assets is explained by additions less depreciation less book value of fixed asset disposals.
(b)   There will be a movement in each of the components of working capital, i.e. stock debtors and creditors.
(c)   Movements in long-term creditors which result from a flow of funds will need to be included. This will arise where a loan has been repaid or fresh funds advanced.

(d)　Movements in share capital, reserves and provisions need to be identified. These will include cash received on the issue of new shares giving rise to movements in share capital and share premium, payments of dividends or tax, and of course funds generated from operations (cash profits).

Figure 12.4 shows how the financial statements of Burg and Dee Ltd may be used to prepare a cash-flow forecast under the source and application of funds method.

Profit and loss account

for year ended
31.12.90

	£000
Profit before tax	600
Tax at 35%	(210)
Profit after tax	390
Dividend	(50)
Retained profit	340

Balance sheets

	Forecast as at 31.12.89 £000	Budget as at 31.12.90 £000
Fixed assets	100	275
Stocks	320	350
Debtors	420	450
Cash	25	265
	765	1,065
Taxation	(100)	(210)
Dividend	(45)	(50)
Other short-term creditors	(200)	(220)
Net current assets	420	585
Long-term creditors	(250)	(100)
Net assests	270	760
Shareholder's funds	270	760

Figure 12.4(a) Burgh and Dee Ltd — synopsis from budgeted profit and loss account and balance sheets

	£000
Fixed assets	
At 31.12.89	100
Additions	200
Depreciation	(25)
At 31.12.90	275
Taxation	
At 31.12.89	(100)
Charge for year to 31.12.90	(210)
Paid during year to 31.12.90	100
At 31.12.90	(210)
Dividend	
At 31.12.89	(45)
Dividend for year to 31.12.90	(50)
Paid during year to 31.12.90	45
At 31.12.90	(50)
Shareholders' funds	
At 31.12.89	270
Retained profit for year to 31.12.90	340
Issue of shares	150
At 31.12.90	760

Figure 12.4(b) Detail of budgeted balance sheet movements

	for year ended 31.12.90	
	£000	£000
Sources of funds		
Profit before tax	600	
Depreciation (see Note 1)	25	
	625	
Issue of shares	150	
		775
Application of funds		
Repayment of long-term loan	150	
Purchase of fixed assets	200	
Taxation paid	100	
Dividend paid	45	
		(495)
Movements in working capital		
Increase in stocks	(30)	
Increase in debtors	(30)	
Increase in creditors	20	
		(40)
Net increase in cash		240

Note 1: Profit must be adjusted for items which do not involve the flow of funds.

Figure 12.4(c) Budgeted source and application of funds

The receipts and payments cash-flow forecast is a simple concept and is reasonably straightforward to prepare. If it is prepared on a week-by-week or month-by-month basis as part of the budgeting process it gives an indication not only of the cash position at the beginning and end of the year but also at intermediate points throughout the year. It may therefore form the basis of the calculation of the interest budget. It does however have the disadvantage that although receipts and payments and their timing may be predicted with some accuracy in the short term the method becomes more and more prone to inaccuracy the further into the future the forecast is taken.

The source and application of funds forecast has the advantage of integrating cash forecasting with the forecasting of other financial statements. It ensures that the cash-flow forecast is consistent with forecasts of profits and with the forecast balance sheet. It is also a useful tool for determining the way in which various factors are affecting the cash position of the business and can be valuable in demonstrating the effect that controlling certain items can have. For example, reducing capital expenditure or stocks from the planned level will reduce borrowings or increase cash at the year-end.

Working Capital Management

Working capital is generally defined as current assets less current liabilities. However, for the purposes of managing a business, a useful definition, and that adopted by Treasurers, is stocks plus receivables less payables. Only those receivables and payables relating to the trading activities of the company are included and cash and bank balances and overdrafts are excluded. Using this definition working capital may be viewed as the cash invested in trading activity and each item included is linked to the level of sales. The stocks held by the company will eventually be sold giving rise to trade debtors. Cash is not however realised from trading until the end of the credit period extended to customers. The cash invested in stocks and debtors is offset to the extent that finance is effectively provided by the trade creditors of the company up until the time they are paid in cash.

A key ratio in monitoring the performance of a company is the working capital to sales (WC/S) ratio. This ratio will vary as between companies, particularly between companies operating in different industries. For example, the manufacturer of nuts, bolts and screws mentioned above should have a considerably lower WC/S ratio than the company involved in heavy engineering projects. A typical example of a company likely to have a high WC/S ratio would be the manufacturer of oil rigs which will have a very high level of work in progress within its stock figure. Companies operating in the same business are likely to have similar WC/S ratios. The WC/S ratio for a particular company is unlikely to fluctuate over a period of years by more than a few per cent.

The WC/S ratio has several limitations. The first of these is that all the components of working capital are related to past sales in the calculation even though it is only trade receivables which are derived from the past level of activity. Trade creditors relate to past purchases and not to past sales, and stocks may vary for reasons other than the past level of trading, for example if the company is building up stocks for a new contract or has been able to obtain raw materials at particularly advantageous prices.

Another problem with the WC/S ratio is that it relates the components of working capital to annual sales. Trade receivables are likely to relate to, at the most, three months of past sales, and stocks and creditors will also relate to periods of considerably less than one year ahead.

It may be difficult to separate trade payables or receivables from other debtors and creditors, for example the accounts of a company may include as accruals both unpaid expenses such as legal or audit fees and amounts in respect of goods received but not yet invoiced. The latter form part of trade creditors but cannot be separately identified. Finally, the WC/S ratio assumes that the sales mix of the company will not alter in such a way as to alter the ratio.

It is important to look not only at the trend of the WC/S ratio but also to look at the trend in the components of working capital. For example, a constant WC/S ratio may mask the fact that overstocking has been financed by taking extended credit periods from suppliers.

An essential part of managing the cash position of the business is the management of working capital. Efficient working capital management may improve the cash position and hence profitability through reduced interest charges.

(a) There may be scope to reduce stock levels by holding lower stocks of raw materials and finished goods, by more balanced stock levels of components used in manufacture, by selling off parts no longer required or by reducing the level of work in progress by the introduction of network analysis. All of these will reduce the amount of cash invested in working capital. Care should however be taken not to impair the efficient running of the business; an out-of-stock position in either raw materials or finished goods could have disastrous results.

(b)   Improved credit control may reduce the level of debtors by ensuring that customers adhere closely to the credit period granted. Discounts for early payment may be offered either to ensure customers remain within overall credit limits or to reduce credit control costs. Time and expense spent chasing old debts may be justified but the company will have to consider the likelihood of recovery and the costs involved in order to determine whether to proceed. Again as in the case of stock control it is necessary to take a commercial view. Credit management should not be pursued to the detriment of the business and lost sales resulting from impaired customer relations must be taken into account. Rarely will the business of a worthwhile customer be lost by a professional approach to the collection of debtors.

Another way in which receivables may be managed is to ensure that the payment method used is efficient. For example, if payment is by means of a bank transfer the customer should be given the bank and routing details necessary to minimise bank float time.

(c)   The level of working capital may be reduced and that of cash balances increased by taking extended credit periods from suppliers. The company must ensure that suppliers are not alienated by such a policy. In addition, particularly in the case of smaller suppliers, the extension of the credit period could put suppliers under undue financial pressure and in some instances even lead to bankruptcy. This might give the company considerable difficulties as an alternative supply may not be readily available and disruption in production may result.

Money Transmission Management

This subject is covered in more detail in Chapter 17 on electronic banking and cash management services.

It is important to note that the efficient transmission of funds is an essential part of liquidity management. Value should be received for cash receipts at the earliest possible date and float time in the banking system minimised wherever possible. This will involve *inter alia* providing customers with clear instructions. Optimal payment methods should be used, trading off the cost of the method against the interest benefit and any other factors, for example the effect on supplier relations.

Managing the Short-term Liquid Position

In order to manage the short-term liquid position the company's Treasurer will need to determine the surplus funds available to the company or the extent of funds required. A forecast of the position over the next few days and weeks will also be required in order to determine the period for which investments or borrowings may be undertaken. The information is generally assembled as follows:

(a)   The previous day's cleared balance is obtained from the bank, either by means of a telephone call to the branch or through an electronic balance reporting service.

(b)   The bank will also be able to provide some details of cheques and credits which will be cleared on the current day.

(c)   Using the information from (a) and (b), together with any other relevant details such as same day transfers to be notified to the bank, the Treasurer can estimate the cleared balance at the close of business on the current day.

(d)   A forecast for the next four or five days can be prepared from details of cheques sent out and amounts banked.

(e)   This may be combined with a week-by-week forecast for the next, for example, three months.

(f)   The compilation of this information should enable the Treasurer to make his investment/borrowing decisions. For example, the forecasts may reveal that, although it will be necessary to borrow overnight, value should be received for a large credit on the following day which will mean that the company will be in a position to invest, say, £5 million for three months. The Treasurer may, however, decide that he wishes to maintain flexibility by investing only £4 million for three months restricting £1 million to shorter dates so that funds are readily available.

The above assumes that only one bank account is being managed. However, the principle remains the same for a group of companies. The management of the group's liquid position becomes rather more complex when each company within the group has a number of accounts with different banks. The central treasury department will receive details of the cleared position at each bank and will incorporate forecasts from the major trading companies in order to reach investment and borrowing decisions.

As part of the management of the group's liquid position the treasury department may choose either to pool all the balances with a particular bank or to clear down the funds from every account into one central account each night. A pooling system would generally mean that credit balances offset debit balances so that interest is paid on the group's net position with the particular bank. Where funds are cleared into a central account on a daily basis, surplus funds in certain companies would also offset debit balances elsewhere in the group. Both these arrangements facilitate the management of the group's liquid position.

Short-term Borrowing

The methods which a company may use to borrow in the short term and the instruments available are described more fully in Chapter 13. They include the use of overdraft facilities, money market borrowings, the issue of acceptance credits, the issue of commercial paper or the use of currency borrowings.

The decision taken will depend on the factors described above; that is on liquidity, safety (i.e. reliability of source of finance), profitability (i.e. minimisation of cost) and flexibility, and on the relative importance ascribed by the company to these considerations. The company must ensure that it has adequate facilities to cover its liabilities over, for example, the next 12 months as they fall due. The company must also be sure that funds will be available when facilities are called upon and that funds will not have to be repaid at short notice and in advance of maturity due to the failure of the lender. The borrowing methods undertaken must give the company sufficient flexibility to deal with unforeseen circumstances. Finally, subject to the preceding requirements a company will aim to borrow at the lowest all-in cost after taking account of tax and of the administrative costs involved.

In order to minimise borrowing costs the Treasurer will have to make several decisions about the nature of the borrowings. The first of these will be the choice between borrowing at fixed or variable interest rates. If expectations are that interest rates are likely to fall then the Treasurer may choose to use the company's overdraft facility or to borrow for very short maturities, for example overnight, until interest rates do fall. If however it is likely that interest rates will rise then the

Treasurer may choose to fix the interest rate on a known requirement by borrowing for the whole of the period for which the funds will be required, for example for six months. It may even be worthwhile borrowing in advance of the funds being required and depositing the proceeds in the very short term. This of course depends on the extent to which interest rates are likely to rise. Interest rate exposure may also be dealt with by using specific hedging products such as forward rate agreements, swaps and options (see Chapter 16), and its management is covered in more detail in Chapter 14.

The second decision that will have to be made concerns the maturity of the borrowing. This will mainly be derived from determining the length of time for which the funds are required as demonstrated in the above section. Other factors may however also be involved, for example interest rate expectations as discussed in the previous paragraph. The Treasurer may also wish to borrow for a shorter period than otherwise indicated in order to ensure that the interest payment made on maturity will fall within a particular tax year as, in general, interest is deductible for tax purposes on a paid and not on an accruals basis.

The timing of interest payments must be taken into consideration. If the company obtains funds by issuing acceptance credits the issue proceeds less discount are received on day one and the principal amount is repaid at maturity. This means that 'interest' is effectively paid at the beginning and the rate must be converted to a yield basis in order to compare it with the interest rates quoted for borrowings of a similar maturity where interest is paid at the end. The formula for calculating the yield is:

$$\frac{\text{Discount} \times 365 \times 100}{\text{Proceeds} \times \text{Number of days}}$$

where

$$\text{Discount} = \text{Principal} \times \frac{\text{rate}}{100} \times \frac{\text{number of days}}{365}$$

The discount on a 90-day acceptance credit for £500,000 at a discount rate of 15% will be

$$£500,000 \times \frac{15}{100} \times \frac{90}{365} = £18,493.15$$

This implies that the proceeds will be

£500,000 − £18,493.15 = £481,506.85

and the yield will be

$$\frac{18,493.15 \times 365 \times 100}{481,506.85 \times 90} = 15.5761\%$$

(*Note:* these calculations relate to sterling for which interest is calculated on a 365-day basis. Interest for most other currencies is calculated on a 360-day basis.)

Detailed discount to yield tables are available which set out the equivalent yield for a given discount rate quoted for 30, 60, 90, 120 or 180 days to maturity. Alternatively, a program for this may be set up on a personal computer.

The Treasurer should also consider the timing of interest payments on borrowings in relation to the next date on which overdraft interest will be charged. For this the discount to yield tables will also be of use. For example, if overdraft interest is currently charged on a quarterly basis at 16% and the Treasurer has an overnight requirement for £1 million for which he has been quoted a money market rate of 15.875% then an immediate response would be to borrow on the money market as it appears cheaper to do so. If, however, the company is at the beginning of a new quarter for overdraft interest then the company will effectively have to pay interest on the money market interest for the next 90 days whereas the interest for borrowing by means of overdraft would not be payable until 90 days' time. This means that the actual cost of the money market borrowing is higher and using discount to yield tables or the formulae quoted above it may be seen that the money market borrowing will actually cost 16.5217% against the 16% payable on the overdraft. In addition there will be transfer costs to pay when the money market borrowing is repaid, where the bank from which the borrowing was obtained is not the same as the one where the account being funded is held.

On occasion there may be opportunities to use hedged currency borrowings to borrow at a lower cost than sterling sources of finance. Usually such opportunities will quickly be eliminated as the arbitrage opportunity is exploited. The potential for such borrowings is more likely to be available to large groups with access to a foreign domestic source of funds such as the United States commercial paper market where interest rates tend to be less volatile than those for Eurodollars.

The mechanics would be for the company to issue US commercial paper and use the proceeds to purchase sterling, simultaneously entering into a forward contract to purchase dollars at maturity. The forward contract means that there is no exchange risk and so such an arrangement would meet the requirement of safety.

Short-term Investments

When considering how to invest short-term surplus funds the Treasurer must again aim to make the optimal decision taking into account the four objectives of liquidity, profitability, safety and flexibility. Instruments available are set out below.

(a) *Bank deposit accounts.* Funds may generally be withdrawn from a bank deposit after seven days' notice. The credit risk is on the bank and there is no market risk but the comparative yield is low. (Market risk arises where the price of an instrument can change due to market fluctuations, such as changes in interest rates.)

(b) *Money market deposits.* Funds are not available until the maturity of the deposit. Again the credit risk is on the bank with which the deposit is made and there is no market risk. The yield will depend on the current level and profile of the yield curve.

(c) *Certificates of tax deposit.* These may be held until used to make a UK tax payment. There is a penalty in the form of a lower rate of interest if they are not to be used to pay UK tax. The credit risk is the government and there is no market risk.

(d) *Bank or building society certificates of deposit* (CDs). CDs are issued in the form of fully negotiable bearer certificates. They therefore have the advantage of liquidity as they may be sold. This does however mean that there is a market risk unless the securities are held to maturity. The credit risk will be on the bank or the building society.

(e) *Commercial paper.* A company may choose to invest in the commercial paper of another corporate. The paper is generally held to maturity. At the time of writing there are discussions regarding the desirability and feasibility of a formal secondary market for commercial paper. However, although there is currently no organised market for disposing of an investment in commercial paper prior to maturity, dealers acting on behalf of the issuers of paper will invariably buy back paper at market-related rates. In addition some discount houses will purchase commercial paper.

Investors will either rely on the rating given to a commercial paper issuer or, where no rating has been obtained, will need to rely on some form of credit analysis or knowledge of the issuing company.

(f) *Treasury bills.* These are issued with a maturity of three months. Shorter maturities may be bought in the secondary market and the investment may be liquidated by selling the treasury bill in the market. The investor is exposed to market risk unless the bills are held to maturity. The credit risk is the government.

(g) *Bank (or eligible) bills.* These are liquid investments as they may be disposed of on the secondary market. They are exposed to market risk unless held to maturity and the credit risk is on the bank.

(h) *Trade bills.* Again there is a secondary market where the bills may be disposed of prior to maturity. The credit risk is higher than for bank bills as they are drawn by one company on another without bank endorsement. If they are endorsed by a discount house and drawn on a first class name then risk is low.

(i) *Short-dated gilts.* These take the form of a registered security for which there is an active secondary market. Interest is paid net of basic rate tax half-yearly and maturities are for up to five years. The company is exposed to market risk unless the gilts are held to maturity. The credit risk is the government.

(j) *Floating rate notes/Euronotes.* These are a form of bond generally issued by very large banks and which bear a variable rate of interest. The credit risk is on the issuer and there is market risk unless held to maturity. They may be sold at seven days' notice. Alternatively, Euronotes which are short-term bearer notes, offer a LIBOR-linked return, with similar risks to floating rate notes.

In general, the return from a particular investment will be determined by a combination of the degree of risk attaching to the investment and to its maturity. The yield curve is used to describe the relationship between the level of interest rates and various maturities. For example, an upward sloping yield curve as shown in Figure 12.5 would imply a higher rate of interest would apply to a longer maturity. This might occur when interest rates are expected to rise as an investor will wish to be certain of gaining the benefit of the higher rates if he locks in a rate now. The market will be very liquid for short maturities as investors will be investing only for very short terms such as overnight until rates do rise.

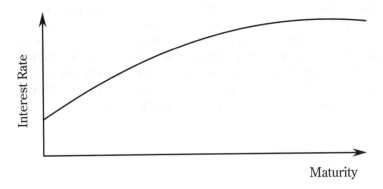

Figure 12.5 An upward-sloping yield curve

The credit risk for each of the above investment instruments has been given and the return will diminish the lower the risk of the investment. For example, investing in the UK government will be assumed to be less risky than investing in a medium-sized corporate.

Some examples of comparative interest rates as at 23 November 1989, are set out in Table 12.1 below:

Table 12.1
Comparative sterling interest rates as at
23 November 1989 for three-month maturities (%)

Certificate of tax deposit	13
Treasury bills	14.46875
Bank bills	14.5
Interbank bid rate	15
Certificates of deposit	15.0625
Trade bills	15.125

Summary

Liquidity management includes the management of borrowings and investments for periods of up to 12 months. The four objectives of liquidity management are liquidity, safety, profitability and flexibility, and the relative importance of these factors will vary according to the nature of the business. The decision-making process will require a forecast of the future cash position. Cash-flow forecasts may be prepared under either the receipts and payments or the source and application of funds methods. Both methods have certain advantages and disadvantages. Managing for liquidity requires efficient working-capital management which can improve the cash position. Combining information on the actual cash position with forecasts of the future position will enable borrowing or investment decisions to be made and the Treasurer will select between the instruments available, always bearing in mind the objectives of liquidity management.

CHAPTER 13

Debt Instruments — Short Term

Adrian Coats

Introduction

A company with a large amount of debt in its balance sheet is likely to use many different forms of borrowing facilities, each of which will satisfy a different need. Some borrowings will be long term in nature, perhaps matching in maturity the expected life of the company's assets, and certainly providing a core of funds which remains comparatively constant. Other borrowings will be of comparatively short duration, having been put in place to meet the requirements of what may be an annual business cycle, and bearing a life of perhaps a few months. Others still will vary day by day.

Figure 13.1 shows how a company's indebtedness may vary over time. The company illustrated has a mild net cash inflow over a year taken as a whole but this hides a minimum level after six months, at which point the trading cycle is at its most favourable, and at a peak in month 7, which may correspond to the payment of a dividend. At no point in the year do the borrowings drop below £50 million and this level could be regarded as core debt in this year. If each successive year follows the pattern of this one then the level of core debt itself will decline in response to the net cash inflow.

Borrowing techniques, then, are varied to match the liquidity requirements of the company. Where there are rapid swings in the level of borrowings a company must maintain a liquid stance; indeed some companies vary between surplus cash and substantial indebtedness and as a result must maintain maximum flexibility if they wish to avoid borrowing and depositing at the same time. The more stable a company's cash flow profile the less flexibility is required and the more likely that the core debt will form a high proportion of total debt.

Figure 13.1 is drawn to indicate four main elements in a company's cash usage:

(a) Daily fluctuations due to routine banking.
(b) Monthly fluctuations which may arise from salary payments or purchase ledger payment runs.

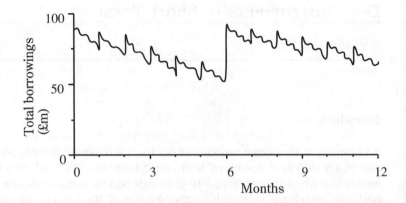

Figure 13.1 Annual cash flow

(c) Large one-off transactions. In this case a dividend is suggested although it might equally be a small acquisition for cash or a payment of tax.

(d) The annual business cycle such as may be experienced by any seasonal business as working capital (stock, trade debtors and trade creditors) requirements fluctuate.

It is to cope with all of these elements that short-term debt instruments are designed and they are best suited for this purpose. Many companies in fact use short-term debt instruments to finance core debt as well as their short-term needs. This is because there is often a slight interest rate advantage in borrowing for short periods as opposed to long ones. It must be recognised, however, that the financing of the longer-term aspects of a business by the use of short-term debt may leave the company exposed to a rise in interest rates as well as the risk that it will be forced to sell sections of its business in order to repay the short-term borrowings.

The question of comparative cost is an important one. In general, it costs more to borrow for long periods than for short ones and there is therefore a penalty to achieve a degree of certainty about the future. The cost is made up of two parts, namely the greater risk to the lender on the one hand (the lending bank will require a higher return for a long-term commitment) and the way that interest rates themselves rise for longer periods if market conditions follow a normal pattern.

Fortunately, since the advent of interest rate swaps, it is now possible for the borrowing company to separate the maturity of a loan from the fixing of interest rates and a Treasurer can now handle the two risks as different problems. It is common practice now to finance core debt by arranging committed borrowing facilities with a long maturity but by borrowing under that facility (or issuing negotiable instruments in association with that facility) for short periods. Flexibility is therefore increased without additional cost. The problem of interest rates and the risk that they might rise can be handled through the mechanism of interest rate swaps.

It should also be mentioned that currency swaps must be borne in mind when examining short-term debt instruments. Although currency swaps are dealt with elsewhere in this book the student should remember when considering any debt instrument that the borrower is not confined to the specific currency of that instrument. It may be cheaper, for example, to issue dollar commercial paper and swap into sterling rather than to issue sterling commercial paper. Indeed, it is frequently better to issue sterling acceptance credits and swap into dollars than to borrow dollars direct in any form.

Taking the various short-term instruments in turn, therefore, and progressing from the most flexible to the least flexible instruments we start with the overdraft.

Overdrafts

The overdraft, as it exists in the UK banking system, provides a highly-flexible borrowing tool for any business or, for that matter, individual. It provides the basis on which all companies undertake their day-to-day transactions, allowing both payments to be made and receipts to be banked. (Contrast this with the more rigid American system where overdrafts do not exist and where day-to-day outflows can only be financed from surplus funds.)

The main features of an overdraft are:

(a)   It is made available for a specified period after which it must be renewed but is technically repayable on demand. Although, in practice, most commercial lenders recognise that an overdraft facility has a rolling maturity of, say, 12 months while a company is in sound financial shape, the overdraft will provide the first signs of a company's deterioration. It can be the first act of a lending bank which is concerned about the ability of a company to meet its obligations to demand repayment of its overdraft.

(b)   It is subject to a limit below which the company is expected to keep.

(c)   Interest is calculated on a daily basis on the amount outstanding, usually at a margin over base rate with a specified minimum.

Other important points with regard to overdrafts:

(a)   *Security.* A bank may require security for its facility. This may be in the form of a floating charge over the company's assets, the assignment of marketable securities with sufficient value, or a guarantee from directors or a parent company.

(b)   *Groups of accounts.* Many groups of companies arrange for their individual overdrafts to be aggregated into a central pool in order to achieve offset of interest wherever there are credit balances present. Credit balances rarely earn interest and such a pooling scheme is an efficient use of any surplus funds that may be available since they automatically earn funds at the overdraft rate. The bank may or may not claim the right to set-off credit balances against overdrafts in the event that a company within the scheme exceeds its limit. Many banks now operate zero-balancing schemes in which the balance outstanding on all accounts is transferred at the close of business each day into a single central account. In this way a group of companies can maintain a set of different bank accounts for convenience while having only one real account with the bank.

(c)   *Interest.* This is calculated daily on the cleared (not ledger or statement) balance. The cleared balance is that which recognises the delay in obtaining value for cheque lodgements which have not yet been through the clearing system and have not been confirmed as paid by the banks on which the cheques are drawn. A prime borrower will pay interest at 1% over the relevant bank's base rate and interest will be debited to the account quarterly or in some cases half yearly.

(d)   *Bank charges.* The flexibility of an overdraft is obtained at a price. It is clear that the processing of cheques and cash is administratively demanding, and as a result it is normal for a bank to recoup its costs in a number of ways:

(i)   a fixed price per transaction;
(ii)   a charge based on a percentage of turnover;
(iii)   the maintenance of a minimum credit balance (although this is unusual in the UK).

The overdraft provides the most flexible borrowing tool available to a company and is used by any business for the processing of cash movements arising from its day-to-day transactions. It is not long since the overdraft provided the only source of short-term funds for companies other than the largest ones, but with the growing sophistication of the debt markets, a range of short-term instruments has been developed to fill the gap between overdraft and long-term finance.

The main advantage of these alternative sources of funds is price. It is clear that no company would wish to re-finance an overdraft at a greater cost unless forced to because it has exceeded its overdraft limit. Generally, however, funds are available at significantly below the cost of an overdraft and it is in the interest of any borrowing company to replace part of its overdraft by one of the other means available. As a rule, the borrowing company will have to sacrifice a degree of the flexibility available in an overdraft in order to achieve the cost-saving. This sacrifice will be given in the form of a stated maturity of the loan (an overdraft, as noted above, varies day by day).

Assume, for example, that a company's overdraft, which has been running at a level of around £500,000, is raised to £2½ million as a result of the purchase of a major item of capital equipment. Future cash flows indicate that the level of 22½ million will be reduced by £100,000 each month for the foreseeable future. Figure 13.2 illustrates what a graph of the company's cash requirements would look like.

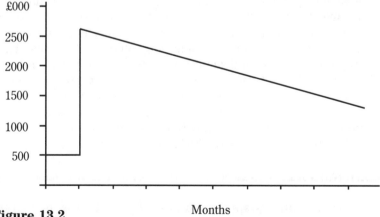

Figure 13.2   Months

The company is able to obtain alternative short-term finance more cheaply than its overdraft but likes to maintain an overdraft of about

£500,000 to avoid the risk of going into credit (credit balances earn no interest and are, therefore, very wasteful from the point of view of the company). There are several ways in which the company can approach the problem. For example:

(a)   It can borrow £2 million for one month, using the first inflow of £100,000 to reduce this debt to £1.9 million in the second month, and so on until the loan is reduced to nil. The overdraft will therefore remain at around £500,000 from the time the proceeds of the loan are paid into the bank account.

(b)   It can borrow £100,000 for each of one, two, three, four, five, six, etc. month periods, repaying each of the loans at maturity with the monthly cash inflow.

(c)   It can combine the two methods by borrowing, say, £500,000 for five months, 10 months, 15 months, etc. and allow the cash inflows to reduce the level of the overdraft which would then be drawn down to repay each of the £500,000 loans. This method, however, causes the overdraft level to vary significantly and may be unacceptable to the company.

The link between overdraft and other forms of finance is examined further in later sections of this chapter, particularly in the next section on money markets.

A final word about comparative cost is appropriate before we examine each of the alternative means of raising short-term finance.

A company generally pays overdraft interest quarterly in arrears. Comparison of the rate incurred with the cost of alternative sources of funds must not be carried out by comparing interest rates unless they are adjusted to show an equivalent time value. Interest paid today is more expensive than interest paid next week since it must be funded for the intervening days, and $9^{15}/_{16}$% p.a. overnight tomorrow is, therefore, *not* necessarily more attractive than 10% p.a. payable in 87 days' time. The overnight rate must be adjusted so that it can be compared correctly with the overdraft rate.

Money Market

Just as a person can buy apples and pears from a barrow in a street market, so can a company 'buy' money in the money market. This market grew from the needs of banks and other financial institutions which found that they had a cash surplus or deficit in the course of their normal business. It became common practice to borrow from each other on a short-term basis in order to satisfy requirements.

Large companies have now joined the market which is highly competitive and active and must be distinguished in the following ways:

(a)   The market does not operate in one location (like the stock or futures markets or for that matter Smithfield) but corresponds to the foreign exchange market to the extent that it is largely conducted by telephone.
(b)   Prices are conveyed electronically or by telephone and bargains are confirmed subsequently in writing.
(c)   Amounts dealt in are usually in multiples of £1 million.

Clearly this is a market for the large player.
Certain other important points are worth making.

Money brokers

Just as a person might ask a friend or agent to buy his apples for him so may a company request a broker to arrange for funds to be made available from a third party at the best possible rate. A money broker will ring round the various likely sources of cash and will arrange for the borrower to borrow from the most competitive of them. The broker's fee for his services will be $\frac{1}{16}\%$ per annum on the amount but this may be incorporated in the quoted rate.

It is clear that a company which employs a broker must expect the benefits in terms of lower interest cost achieved to outweigh the commission of $\frac{1}{16}\%$. This might be possible where:

(a)   the borrowing company cannot justify a well-developed dealing function of its own; or
(b)   the borrowing company has low or infrequent demand for funds.

The company is clearly employing the broker to provide an expert service and it is probably true to say that the largest borrowing companies in the UK do not employ brokers since they would not gain from doing so.

Direct dealing

Rather than use a broker, many companies apply direct to those banks which may have funds available. Such a process may be made formal by the establishment of an uncommitted facility whereby a bank will agree to make funds available to the company when it has them. Such an arrangement may be evidenced by a facility letter but since it is uncommitted (and the bank is not obliged to lend) documentation is little more than a simple letter outlining the administrative arrangements. Such a facility may be set up for a specified period or 'until further notice' on both parts. Drawings are not usually available for more than six months so there is not often any question of security; the bank will rely on its own knowledge of the borrower as comfort that the funds will be repaid.

The cost to the borrower
A company which wishes to borrow funds in the money market will generally seek quotes from more than one lender and will probably wish to have access to up-to-date data through the use of a Reuters screen or other suitable medium. Some lenders will wish to add a margin to quoted rates but, since the market is only open to larger companies, and since there is already a spread quoted in the market between borrowing and depositing prices, the range of margins is low and prime borrowers can expect to obtain funds at interbank rates.

Interest rates are normally quoted for periods of one day, one week and up to 12 months. Rates for periods other than those quoted can be obtained but may be fractionally more expensive than would be suggested by interpolation. Interest is calculated on the actual number of days to maturity and a year of 365 days in the case of sterling, Belgian francs, Irish pounds and Australian dollars. Other Eurocurrency interest costs are computed on the basis of a 360-day year.

Money market lines and overdrafts
For major companies the money market loan is often that borrowing instrument which falls closest in terms of flexibility to the overdraft. Funds can be obtained with minimal effort or documentation on a committed or, more often, an uncommitted basis and can be arranged in a matter of a few seconds on the telephone once a procedure has been established. As a result it is common for money market lines to be provided by a company's clearer (clearers) in conjunction with the overdraft facility. Although the market is highly competitive the borrower should not necessarily rely upon his clearer for the provision of money market funds but may be able to obtain funds much more cheaply from another bank. A prime borrower would expect to obtain funds at or near interbank rates.

Unlike overdraft rates which change infrequently in response to movements in base rates, overnight money market rates can fluctuate wildly within a day and from day-to-day in response to the demand for and supply of money. US dollar interest rates frequently reach very high levels on 31 December as many American businesses seek to achieve their desired year-end balance sheet position. Sterling rates, too, can fluctuate significantly and this fluctuation, when compared with the steady base rate of any overdraft, presents an opportunity for making what could be regarded as easy money.

Assume the overdraft rate is 10%. Sometimes overnight borrowing rates might reach 14% and the borrowing company will naturally wish to fund as much of its requirement as possible on the overdraft by drawing down to the limit. On another occasion, when the overnight rate falls to 6% the borrower will wish to repay the whole of his overdraft by drawing down on the money market. Naturally, as rates move all the time and since the wildest fluctuations are seen during the last few minutes of the trading day there is scope for the skilled practitioner, who can read the way the market is developing, to profit from his expertise.

The logical extension of this scenario is the practice of 'round tripping'. If overnight *deposit* rates rise above the overdraft rate it pays any company to draw down to the limit of its overdraft and reinvest the funds at a higher return. Needless to say banks do not welcome this practice which is regarded as abuse of the flexibility of the overdraft system, and the Association of Corporate Treasurers recognises that it is in the enlightened self-interest of its members not to follow this course of action and to do nothing that would threaten the existence of the overdraft system.

Commercial Paper

The term 'commercial paper' is one of those items of financial jargon which, when first encountered, conjures up all sorts of strange images. The term gives no assistance to the layman who wishes to identify the underlying meaning but it is in fact accurate to the extent that it refers to pieces of paper issued by a company. Commercial paper is a form of short-term, unsecured promissory note which is issued by a borrower, usually made payable to bearer, and sold to an investor. It therefore corresponds to longer-term debt instruments or bonds which are tradable certificates of the issuing company's indebtedness. Commercial paper comes in many different forms and currencies and is generally issued in notes of a specific nominal value which are sold at a discount. The discount suffered by the borrower is his cost of borrowing. Of the different types of commercial paper in existence it is worth examining the three most important.

Sterling commercial paper (£CP)

The market for £CP was opened in April 1986 and has developed gradually since that date. Until April 1986, UK companies were unable to issue short-dated sterling debt (of less than one year maturity) since to do so would have been regarded as deposit-taking and as such was prohibited under the Banking Act regulations. Moreover, even after April 1986 there were initial complications as a result of the requirement to issue a prospectus every time an issue was made, and some early issuers chose to issue through an overseas subsidiary as a result (thereby circumventing the then current prospectus requirement).

The birth of the £CP market represented a major development in the UK financial markets since it displayed further progress along the path of 'disintermediation', the process by which borrowers and lenders can form a direct link while cutting out the intermediary role of the banks.

Characteristics of the instrument

The notes are normally unsecured, unquoted, bearer notes with a term of 7–364 days and a denomination of £500,000 or £1,000,000.

Eligibility to issue

Issuing companies must have net assets of at least £25 million and must be listed on the London Stock Exchange. Wholly-owned subsidiaries of such companies can also issue £CP provided the notes are guaranteed by the listed parent company. Issues may also be guaranteed by a bank or licensed deposit taker in order to enhance the credit risk of the issuer.

Regulations

The Bank of England must be advised of the size of the programme and of amounts outstanding.

Method of issue and distribution

£CP is normally issued under a dealership programme using one or more dealers. The size of the programme as publicised is a measure of the upper limit of likely issues although some companies choose to have no limit. The only snag with this practice is that some investors like to restrict themselves to a specified proportion of the total programme and this, of course, is impossible if they cannot identify the size of the programme.

The dealers (who may be merchant, investment or other banks) act as intermediaries, matching investors with issuers and taking a margin in the middle. The issuing process can take several forms:

(a)   The issuer requests bids from the dealers.
(b)   The issuer requests the dealers to arrange for the placement of paper at agreed rates or within defined parameters.
(c)   The dealer contacts the issuer with direct bids.

The relationship that grows between issuer and dealers will depend on the issuer's flexibility and attitude. The issuer who pushes out large quantities of paper will pay more than the issuer who waits for investors to express their demand. A large borrower who can satisfy demand for odd maturities or amounts will find safe hands for his paper and perhaps a regular network of investors. The market for £CP is like any other with buyers and sellers. If a seller floods the market the price of the paper will fall and his cost of borrowing will rise; careful thought must be given on how to develop demand for a company's £CP.

Pricing

As with other forms of tradable debt the price will reflect the risk to the investor. Prime borrowers will be able to issue paper at well below LIBOR, in some cases even below LIBID, while others will pay over LIBOR. In these circumstances the cost of borrowing by issuing £CP must be compared with the cost of borrowing in other ways, particularly sterling acceptances. (A comparison of £CP with sterling acceptances is shown later in this chapter.)

Issuing and paying agent (IPA)

The issuing and paying agent is responsible for the settlement of payments between investor and issuer and his main duties are, therefore, at the time of issue and at maturity.

At issue the IPA:

(a) Authenticates notes.
(b) Releases notes in accordance with issuer's instructions.
(c) Holds notes for safekeeping if requested by purchaser.
(d) Pays proceeds of issue to issuer.
(e) Sends confirmation details to issuer and purchaser.

At maturity:

(a) Receives proceeds from issuer.
(b) Pays maturity proceeds against surrender of notes.
(c) Returns cancelled notes to issuer or destroys them as requested.

US dollar commercial paper ($CP)

The market in domestic US dollar commercial paper is similar in many respects to that in £CP (which followed $CP and was, therefore, based largely upon it). Similarities will be referred to in passing while differences will be emphasised. The main difference at present is the size of the market. While £CP has recently passed through £4 billion and is reckoned to reach perhaps £20 billion, the United States market is in the region of $300 billion. Maturities are up to 270 days — with 15 to 45 days being the most common — in order to gain exemption from registration under United States securities legislation, and there are rules governing the use of the proceeds of issue. These specify that the proceeds should be used to finance current operating transactions, a loose term which is understood to exclude money-market investments.

Investors are mainly insurance companies, pension funds, banks and some large commercial companies which can obtain a higher yield than bank deposits while investing in prime risk credit with the added bonus of good secondary market liquidity. There are estimated to be no more than 500 active investors.

Advantages for the UK issuer:

(a) Interest saving — at times there is a material difference in the yield on $CP as compared with other sources of funds denominated in US dollars.
(b) The market is large and stable.
(c) Flexibility — notes can be issued to precise maturity dates without any extra charge for 'broken dates' that may occur in the interbank markets.

(d)   Promotion of the company's name. This is seen as being increasingly important where a company has a material presence in the USA. Investors of all kinds (debt as well as equity) are now being cultivated.

Disadvantages for the UK issuer:

(a)   A rating is required (see below) as well as committed funds to support outstandings.
(b)   The production of additional financial information which many UK companies find burdensome.

Euro-commercial paper (ECP)
Euro-commercial paper is similar to both the domestic types described above but represents the trade in freely-transferable offshore US dollar funds in the Euromarket. Being in the Euromarket, the trade in ECP is not controlled by the regulatory frameworks which surround the domestic markets. As a result it has grown rapidly to its current level of about $68 billion and liquidity and secondary market trading are of paramount importance. As well as the substantial volumes of dollar paper, ECP can be issued in other Eurocurrencies, for example yen or even European currency units (ECUs). Maturities are usually up to one year.

Other matters

Tender panels

An alternative to the dealership process described above is the system known as a tender panel. In this case, instead of having a small number of dealers who trade a company's paper, a panel of a larger number of banks will be established and paper will be issued to them in response to formal tenders which are submitted at the issuer's request, via the tender panel agent. Successful banks may then sell the paper, just as a dealer might, or they might hold it until maturity. Under many tender panel systems the members of the panel are permitted to make direct bids to the issuer if, for example, they have a particularly favourable position. In this way a tender panel has the advantage of the highly-competitive environment of the tendering process as well as the flexibility of the dealership.

Tender panels for the issue of commercial paper are, however, becoming less popular. The main reasons for this are that:

(a)   Their administration is cumbersome, there being so many parties involved.
(b)   There is often a longer period of notice required to arrange an issue.
(c)   Many of the members of the tender panel fail to purchase paper and the successful bids tend to be dominated by a few banks, turning the process into a dealership programme anyway.

'Backstop' facilities

The issue of commercial paper is uncommitted to the extent that the issuer has no guarantee of his ability to raise the funds required. Just as with the money market, if market conditions make an issue impossible or highly unattractive the issuer could be left without funds. In order to avoid this problem it is common practice to link the issue of uncommitted commercial paper or sterling acceptances to a syndicated bank facility which underpins the issue of the commercial paper.

A group of banks commits funds to the issuer as if by means of an ordinary medium-term bank facility in the knowledge that the issuer will only draw upon those funds if it is unable to raise the amounts required by means of its dealership programme, tender panel or other method of issue. A typical example might be where a borrower sets up what is now called a multi-option facility (MOF) with the following constituent parts:

(a)   A tender panel for Euronotes up to $300 million.
(b)   A dealership programme for £CP up to $300 million equivalent.
(c)   A tender panel for sterling acceptances up to $300 million equivalent, all of which are supported by:
(d)   A syndicated bank credit for five years for $200 million.

The maximum amount outstanding under (a)–(c) would be $300 million but any excess over $200 million would be unsupported to the extent that the company cannot be sure that the funds will still be available at next maturity. This excess over $200 million would, therefore, be treated as uncommitted short-term debt in the company's balance sheet, while the $200 million could be treated as bank debt with the same maturity as the 'backstop' bank credit.

Ratings

An investor who purchases any form of negotiable debt instrument will be concerned about the repayment of his asset. As disintermediation increases and the direct relationship between investor and issuing company develops, the need for some common measurement of risk grows. Banks which lend to companies carry out their own credit research. It is less appropriate for small or even large investors who may not be prepared to devote valuable resources to research the creditworthiness of a wide range of companies.

The result is that there is a demand for independent credit-rating agencies and these have developed fully in the USA where commercial paper has been in existence for many years and where it is essential to have a rating. The use of such agencies has developed more slowly in the Euromarket and is in its infancy in the UK where investors have shown themselves more flexible than in the USA and where knowledge of a company and its 'name' in the market-place are still sufficient for investors' purposes. The development of credit ratings in the UK is, however, regarded (by most people) as inevitable.

There are several well-known United States rating agencies of which Moody's and Standard & Poors are the most famous, and there are several new European rivals who are competing for the European end of the market. All these agencies operate in the same way to the extent that they carry out detailed research into the company, its products, markets and management and they formulate an index of credit risk which an investor can use as a measure for his investment. Their methods of charging vary in that the Americans charge the issuers while some of the European rivals charge the investor. Either way the issuer who elects to have a rating must consider the following other advantages and disadvantages.

Advantages of a rating:

(a)   May assist in the development of demand for commercial paper and other debt instruments. (Essential for domestic dollar commercial paper.)
(b)   May help to develop recognition of the issuing company as a whole.
(c)   May reduce the cost of debt.

Disadvantages:

(a)   Cost — initial and annual reviews.
(b)   Risk of downgrading, particularly from investment to non-investment grade.

Issuing companies in the UK are proving reluctant to accept the rating process although once the majority have ratings it seems clear that all companies will have to have them. It is true that a company which has a rating calculated can refuse to have it published but once the process has been adopted a downgrading cannot be withheld without it being obvious to investors what the reason must be.

Trade Bills

A trade bill as defined in the Bills of Exchange Act 1882 is:

> An unconditional order in writing addressed by one person to another, signed by the person giving it, requiring the person to whom it is addressed to pay on demand or at a fixed or determinable future time a sum certain in money to or to the order of a specified person, or to bearer.

The issue of a bill is normally in connection with the supply of goods and usually drawn by the seller and forwarded to the buyer in respect of those goods. On the bill itself will be stated the amount and the due date of payment. The period between the date the goods are supplied and the maturity of the bill is known as the tenor of the bill and is often three months although other set periods in multiples of months are seen.

The logic behind the existence of trade bills is based on the periods of credit given by suppliers. Suppose A sells goods to B who works on them and then sells them to C. A requires payment from B after 30 days, it takes B 30 days to complete his work and B gives 30 days' credit to C. In these circumstances B must pay A for his goods 30 days before he receives any funds from C. B's requirement for funds is, of course, the working capital of his business but he can avoid the cash shortage by using bills. B will draw a bill on C and once C has signed the bill acknowledging his liability, B can sell the bill to a third party, usually a bank or discount house, thereby obtaining funds immediately. B will receive less than the face value of the bill in recognition of the time value of money. The difference between the amount received and the face value of the bill is known as the discount and represents the cost of finance. The bank which purchases the bill has recourse to B if C does not pay, provided the bill is properly accepted.

The advantages of trade bill finance are:

(a) The seller can receive immediate funds albeit at a discount.
(b) The purchaser does not have to accelerate payment.
(c) A bill can be renegotiated by any holder.
(d) The finance is off balance sheet for the seller.
(e) If the funds are not required immediately the bill can be held until maturity and the full face value obtained. When there is an interest clause in the bill this would increase the proceeds.

The disadvantages of trade bill finance are:

(a) A contingent liability remains with the seller until the bill has been paid by the purchaser.
(b) Bill finance can be relatively expensive.
(c) Bill finance is not appropriate if the purchaser is a poor credit risk.
(d) The bill must be linked specifically to the supply of goods.
(e) There is additional paperwork.

An alternative in some cases to a trade bill is an acceptance credit.

Sterling Acceptance Credits

An acceptance credit is a facility under which a bill of exchange is drawn on a bank which will accept the bill thereby lending the bank's own standing to it. Since the bank is placing itself at risk to the issuing company's credit it is usual for acceptance credits to be made available under a formal committed facility letter frequently as part of a revolving bank credit facility. The face value is normally in standard amounts of £250,000 or £1 million and maturities are usually of 30, 60 or 90 days. Although the acceptance credit is not linked to the supply of specific goods, like the trade bill, it must still finance working capital generally and will contain clausing which shows what sort of working capital it relates to. An example might be: 'group sales of wines & spirits'. This clausing is important since it is required for the bank to be able to re-discount the bill with the Bank of England. This procedure, which is available to those bills which are 'eligible' for such discounting means that the borrower is able to obtain finer terms than would be the case with a trade bill or an ineligible bill. Eligible bills are ones accepted by an eligible bank and which carry acceptance clausing. There are over 100 eligible banks including the accepting houses and the clearing banks.

Obtaining funds

Bills are typically in maximum amounts of £500,000 and if a large amount is required there is a significant amount of administration required in comparison with a straight money-market or other type of bank loan. Bills totalling the amount required must be completed, signed and forwarded to the bank by 11 a.m. and to avoid this problem it is common practice for bills to be pre-signed and kept by the bank, ready for use. The bank will then probably sell the bills at a discount and pay the proceeds to the borrower after deducting its acceptance commission which will vary depending on the credit standing of the borrower from a few basis points to perhaps ½% per annum of the face value.

Tender panels

It is common for the issue of bills to be included in a multi-option facility. Bills are typically distributed to a group of banks which are eligible and which have agreed to bid at the issuer's request. The issuer will state the maturity and the amount in which he is interested and the 'bidding group' or tender panel will submit their bids to a tender agent. The bids will be in the form of the number of basis points acceptance commission over the rate for eligible bills for the stated period and the issuer will accept the best bids that fall within the amount he wishes to borrow. Bids may total far more than the amount stated.

Pricing compared with alternative sources of funds

In recent years, acceptance credit finance by use of eligible bills has been one of the cheapest sources of funds available to a borrowing company. The reason for this can be explained as follows:

(a) The government finances its borrowings by the issue of government stock, usually with long maturities.
(b) It has tended to over-borrow.
(c) It has reinvested its short-term surpluses by the purchase of eligible bills through the Bank of England.

The eligible bill market has, therefore, enjoyed conditions which have benefited the borrower. Because of the distinct nature of the market it has not been possible for natural arbitrage to iron out the benefits of this market *vis-à-vis* other short-term markets and a price differential has been maintained.

When the sterling commercial paper market was being set up there was some doubt as to whether the bill market would maintain this advantage, thereby preventing the development of sterling commercial paper. In the event, however, there are periods when it is cheaper to issue £CP than acceptance credits.

The cost of borrowing under an acceptance credit is measured and published as the discount to face value rather than as true rate of interest. The decision to borrow in one form rather than another must always be made using comparable rates and this is best done by calculating the 'true' rate applied to the bill. To do this the discount must be divided by the discounted amount (i.e. the face value less the discount) to obtain the true rate of interest.

Other points

(a) An eligible bill can be re-discounted by a bank with the Bank of England as part of the bank's reserve assets. As a result the Bank of England uses bills to control the money supply (as well as invest short-term government cash surpluses).

(b) Since banks generally sell bills of this type rather than hold them to maturity they have no balance sheet exposure, only a contingent liability for bills accepted. In the current environment, where banks are carefully examining the use of their balance sheets, competition for this off-balance sheet business is aggressive.

Summary

A wide range of short-term debt instruments is available to borrowing companies. The foundation will always be the overdraft but a company can usually obtain cheaper funds by sacrificing flexibility to some extent and borrowing for a fixed term. The choice of which fixed-term debt instrument is appropriate will depend upon market conditions at the time of borrowing and the specific circumstances of the borrower.

Some companies will choose to fund long-term debt by the use of short-term instruments, particularly at a time of falling interest rates or where interest rates have been fixed for long periods through the use of interest rate swaps. The commitment by lenders of long-term funds has now been separated from the maturity of debt instruments by the growth of syndicated credits forming part of multi-option facilities.

CHAPTER 14

Currency and Interest Rate Exposure Management

Robert Hudson and Nicholas Tonkin

Editor's Notes

Having covered the various mechanisms for obtaining money for the business, Chapter 14 tackles the problem of currency and interest rate exposure management from a conceptual viewpoint, introducing separate chapters first on methods available to a corporate to protect itself from changes in currency parity, and second on changes in interest rate.

Introduction

At the start of the 1970s few Corporate Treasurers would have spent much time worrying about their company's exposure to exchange rate or interest rate movements. Exchange rates were pegged and moved either in large and predictable amounts or not at all, whilst interest rates were usually in single figures and their impact on total cost was small. In the years that have followed the economic environment has totally changed, interest rates can double in a few months and exchange rate movements can wipe out profits overnight with the result that problems generated in controlling budgets and cash flows are now of pressing importance for every company. The financial markets have, however, developed a number of products which can help in solving them and this chapter and Chapter 15 explain their structure and use. In this chapter we examine the nature of the problems and the strategies which can be adopted in tackling them.

Currency Exposures

Transaction exposure
The simplest and best understood type of foreign exchange exposure is that arising from payments or receipts of foreign currency which a company is required to enter into as part of an import or export

programme. A British company ordering its raw materials from France at an agreed price of 100,000 French francs to be paid 90 days after shipment will pay £10,000 if the exchange rate is FF10 = £1 but £12,500 if the exchange rate is FF8 = £1. Similarly, a company selling to West Germany at a price of DM60,000 will receive £20,000 if the exchange rate is DM3 = £1 but only £15,000 if the exchange rate is DM4 = £1. This type of exposure is referred to as transaction exposure as it arises from the company entering into individual *transactions* in foreign currency, each of which gives rise to a specific exposure.

Transaction exposure is of clear and immediate relevance to a company's profitability as profit is merely the difference between revenue and cost. A company making a 20% profit per item on its exports could lose half of its profit on a deal if the exchange rate moved against it by just 10%. Exporters with receipts in a foreign currency are exposed to an erosion of profit if the domestic currency strengthens whilst importers paying in foreign currency are exposed to a risk of loss on a weakening of the domestic currency.

The significance of these risks can be seen from Figure 14.1 which shows movements of the dollar/sterling exchange rate from 1971 to 1987. Movements of 10% in the rate over the course of a few months are not at all unusual and far greater movements can occur over a year, with the result that cash-flow budgets drawn up for a year ahead could be badly disrupted if foreign exchange transaction exposure is ignored.

Translation exposure

With the growing internationalisation of companies, a second type of exposure to exchange rate movements has come to be acknowledged. Companies whose assets and liabilities are spread across several countries are likely to have those assets and liabilities denominated in several different currencies. Movements in the exchange rates of these currencies will therefore cause movements in the values of the company's assets and liabilities when *translated* into the domestic currency. This is translation exposure.

The following simple example illustrates the problem. Consider a company which operates in the USA and the UK. Its assets and liabilities are as shown in the balance sheet below.

	Liabilities	Assets
Dollar denominated	$200	$400
Sterling denominated	£200	£100
Total: At $2 = 1	£300	£300
At $2.5 =1	£280	£260

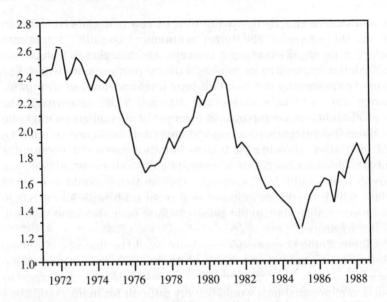

Figure 14.1   Dollar/sterling exchange rate, 1971–88

With an exchange rate of $2 = £1, total assets equal total liabilities at
£300. If, however, the exchange rate rises to $2.5 = £1, the revaluation
of the dollar assets and liabilities in sterling terms leads to an excess of
liabilities over assets of £20. In order to balance its accounts the
company will need to transfer £20 out of its reserves.

Multinational companies clearly face far more complex problems
than that shown here. Each currency of operation needs to be
examined separately and consolidated exposures for any subsidiary
companies constructed. Only in the unlikely event of assets and
liabilities being exactly equal in every currency can a company
consider itself to be free of translation exposure.

Whilst translation exposure does not immediately impact on cash
flow it can affect the structure of the balance sheet adversely,
particularly the gearing if, for example, some long-term loans have
been taken in currencies other than the domestic one of the company.
Since the company may have to abide by certain covenants regarding
its gearing, parity changes can have a serious effect.

Economic exposure
Economic exposure is the most difficult type of exchange rate
exposure to identify and to counter, but it is no less real than other

types and can be equally damaging to a company if ignored. Authors differ on the scope of the term 'economic exposure', sometimes regarding it as an all-embracing concept which includes transaction and translation exposures as subsets. For our purposes, we will define economic exposure as the risk that long-term movements in relative exchange rates will cause structural changes which undermine the basic profitability of a company. An example of such changes might be if the domestic currency of a major competitor weakened to such an extent that, after adjusting for relative inflation rates, the competitor was able to produce his goods at a significantly lower cost, in common currency, than could our company. This situation could present a company which has never engaged in foreign trade with an exchange rate exposure! A good example is the clothing manufacturing industry in Western Europe.

Another example of economic exposure would be that of a company which imported a major proportion of its raw materials from a single overseas country. Current contracts would clearly give rise to transaction exposure but it would be very difficult for many companies to predict just how much they would need to import in, say, five years' time and to cover the potential cost on a *transaction* basis. If the company does nothing, however, and exchange rates move so as to increase greatly the domestic currency cost of its imports, it may be forced to change its sourcing procedures completely or find itself uncompetitive.

Table 14.1 gives an illustration of the effects of exchange-rate movements on the profitability of a long-term project. The table shows two discounted cash-flow analyses of the viability of a project, one conducted in advance using forecast profits and exchange rates and one conducted with the benefit of hindsight at actual rates. The project will cost FF50 million today, and expected profits, in francs, are shown in the table. The company requires a return of at least 10% p.a. in sterling (its domestic currency) in order to make the investment worthwhile. Converting the forecast profits to sterling at a budgeted exchange rate of FF10 = £1 gives the cash flows shown in the '£m' column of the top half of the table. At a 10% discount rate, this cash-flow stream has a positive net present value of £0.10m thus making the project worthwhile.

Table 14.1

Economic exposure

(a)   Budget at FF10 = £1

	£m	FFm
Investment	(5.00)	(50.0)
Forecast profits:		
Year 1	0.50	5.0
Year 2	1.50	15.0
Year 3	2.00	20.0
Year 4	2.00	20.0
Year 5	1.50	15.0
Net present value at 10%	0.49	

(b)   Outturn

	£m	FFm	Actual exchange rate
Investment	(5.00)	(50.0)	10.00
Actual profits:			
Year 1	0.47	5.0	10.64
Year 2	1.39	15.0	10.79
Year 3	1.82	20.0	10.99
Year 4	1.77	20.0	11.30
Year 5	1.29	15.0	11.63
Net present value at 10%	(0.05)		

The company therefore decides to undertake the investment. As the profits stream is uncertain, it cannot regard future exchange requirements as a transaction exposure and does not take out foreign exchange cover. The second part of the table shows the position five years later when it is able to look back with perfect hindsight and assess whether it was indeed the right decision. It finds that its profits forecast was perfectly correct but it had underestimated the strength of sterling when making the initial calculations.

Converting the French franc profits into sterling at the actual rates gives the cash flows in the £m column of the second part of the table.

The net present value of this stream discounted at 10% is negative. Had the company been able to foresee this, it would not have undertaken the project. The project proved to be a mistake, not because it was intrinsically unsound (indeed, the profits forecast was accurate) but because exchange rates moved adversely.

Deciding how, or indeed whether, to cover uncertain exposures such as this is no simple matter and will be returned to below and in the next chapter. Ignoring economic exposures can, however, be equally damaging as ignoring the more obvious transaction exposures which companies face.

Managing exchange rate exposure

Given the experiences of recent years, no one doubts the importance of controlling exchange rate exposures. The international banking community has developed an array of products which can be used by Corporate Treasurers, and Chapter 15 is devoted to a description of the instruments currently available, although there are, however, a number of opportunities available to the Corporate Treasurer which can be exploited without the need to use the services of foreign exchange specialists.

The first action is to structure the company's own affairs in such a way as to minimise the foreign exchange exposure incurred. The currency in which prices are fixed should be considered carefully. Competitive pressures are likely to force companies into invoicing in a variety of currencies in order to accommodate the wishes of the customer but, where possible pricing in your own local currency is a fully-effective solution to transaction risk: it avoids it entirely. If the customer's currency is expected to strengthen against sterling then it might pay a British exporter to set his price in terms of the customer's currency, but to price in sterling if the customer's currency was expected to weaken. A British importer would wish to set the price in sterling for imports from strong currency countries but in the foreign currency where it was expected to be weak.

This procedure does not eliminate the risk, of course, since no one can be certain of the direction of future exchange rate movements. An active currency manager may however sometimes fool it is a risk worth taking.

An extension of this idea is the practice of 'leading' and 'lagging' payments. With a payment to make in a weak currency, a company will delay (i.e. 'lag') payment as long as possible before settling a debt. If it were expecting a receipt in a weak currency it would, of course, press for rapid payment! Conversely, with a payment to make in a strong currency, the company should settle immediately (i.e. 'lead') but would not be averse to an extension of the credit period if it were expecting a receipt. In deciding whether to lead or lag, a company must consider not only whether it expects a currency to strengthen or weaken but also the interest cost of its decision to vary its credit period. Borrowing sterling for three months in order to settle a Deutschmark bill at a rate of DM3 = £1 rather than at the rate of DM2.9 = £1 which the company expects to prevail in the future will make sense if sterling can be borrowed at an interest rate of 10% but not if the interest rate is 20%. In the latter case the interest cost will exceed the exchange gain.

Companies with a two-way cash flow in particular currencies may find it advantageous to run bank accounts in each separate currency so as to match receivables against payables directly rather than using a multiplicity of foreign exchange deals. The negotiation of borrowing facilities in a variety of currencies would permit temporary imbalances to be incurred although, again, interest cost must be considered. Situations may arise where the customer is happy to accept invoicing in your currency in order to match an opposite cash flow which he has incurred in a different deal. It could also be the case that invoicing in a third currency is mutually beneficial. Use of the dollar as an invoicing currency is common and a sale in dollars between, say, a British and a Dutch company may conveniently balance both companies' exposures on other dollar transactions. The ECU is also growing in importance for trade as its composition reflects the relative economic size of the member countries of the European Community and hence mirrors their relative shares in the trading portfolios of many other countries and companies. ECU denominated deals can therefore be useful for balancing a number of separate currency accounts.

The most important internal structures to set up are those which defend a company against economic risk. They are important because it is difficult to counter that risk using the simple tools of the foreign exchange markets and also because the evolution of these risks takes place over a long period and can often only be corrected over a similarly long period, but companies can respond by diversifying the currency composition of their sources of supply, their sales and their balance sheet. If the company fears that an overseas competitor may achieve a competitive edge as a result of exchange rate movements then it may be wise to establish a subsidiary in the competitor's country so as to obtain the same benefit for themselves.

Composite currencies such as the ECU may in certain circumstances be useful in guarding against economic exposure. With its composition reflecting the relative size of western European economies, using the ECU is regarded (particularly by American companies and the Soviet Union) as a more stable and reliable alternative then dealing in a single constituent currency, thus reducing long-term uncertainty. However, if the threat of economic exposure is United States- or Japanese-based, the ECU will of course provide only marginal protection.

Finally, diversified multicurrency balance sheets must guard against problems of translation exposure, particularly as they impact on the company's capital base. UK companies are now permitted to denominate their equity capital in currencies other than sterling if they so wish. Whilst this is only likely to be valuable to the most internationally-oriented companies (and especially banks which are subject to constant capital adequacy monitoring), the flexibility which this offers to companies operating in several different countries is useful in managing their longer-term exposures.

Interest Rate Exposures

The need for interest rate risk management
Undoubtedly there has been a tendency for companies to concentrate their attentions on the monitoring and control of currency exposure, perhaps because there is a widely-held belief that profits are harder hit by currency movements than by interest rate fluctuations. As demonstrated above, losses incurred by a failure to hedge foreign exchange exposures can be very large and traditionally such losses have been highlighted in company annual reports and press commentaries. Accounts are, of course, drawn up in a single currency and foreign exchange exposures are immediately apparent, so their failures to hedge such exposures are also readily identified, whereas failures to hedge against adverse interest rate movements are less obvious but can have equally disastrous consequences. The prevalent inclination has until recently been to view such losses as opportunities foregone rather than tangible costs.

There can be no doubt that the climate of opinion has changed dramatically during the 1980s. Over this period, companies in the UK have experienced severe financial pressure which has been accompanied by both a high real (after taking account of inflation) cost of finance and an unprecedented volatility in interest rates. These phenomena can be traced to an increased emphasis on monetary control by UK and other western governments and moves to deregulate financial markets.

The end result is that governments are now more willing to alter interest rates to influence the economy, and financial markets respond much more quickly to changes in demand and supply. The impact on borrowing costs of high and variable interest rates had a major, sometimes terminal, effect on many UK companies and survivors have developed a healthy appreciation of the need to identify and control interest rate exposures.

By way of illustration, consider a company manufacturing items at a total cost of £100 per item and selling them at £120. This is based on the assumption that the machinery used in the manufacture of the product and the working capital required to finance stocks of raw materials and finished goods are financed by means of short-term bank loans at 10% per annum. Let us assume that interest costs were originally budgeted at 25% of total costs. A 2% rise in interest rates — perhaps at a loan roll-over after acquiring the raw materials to produce the items concerned — would give rise to an increase in interest costs from £25 to £30 per item and the profit margin would be eroded by a quarter.

The section on economic exposure above provided an example of how currency exposure could affect the profitability of a French franc investment (Table 14.1). It can also be demonstrated that, even if the budgeted exchange rate were achieved, the profitability of the investment could be dramatically affected by the financing decision and resulting interest rate exposure (Table 14.2).

Before discussing the sensitivity of the project to interest rates, it should be noted that the rate of discount used to evaluate this project is 10%. This is the company's average cost of capital and for ease of exposition, is also the cost of fixed-rate finance. Although most companies use an average cost of capital, some companies use a marginal cost of capital thereby reflecting the decision as to how the project will be financed. The key point in the example below is that, *before* embarking on the project the actual cost of financing it will only be known with certainty if the fixed-rate financing route is selected.

Turning to Table 14.2 itself, this shows the sensitivity of the net present value of the project to a range of modest variations in interest rates. As before, assume that the budgeted exchange rate was FF 10 = £1 and that this assumption proved to be correct. Further assume that the project could have been financed at a fixed rate of 10% over the five-year life of the investment.

Table 14.2

Investment at time 0 (FFm)	**(50)**

(a)   Fixed rate finance at 10%

	Revenue	Finance costs	Profit
Year 1	10	5	5
Year 2	20	5	15
Year 3	25	5	20
Year 4	25	5	20
Year 5	20	5	15
Net present value at 10%	4.9		

(b)   Floating rate finance

		Rates fall			Rates rise		
	Revenue	Rate for year (%)	Finance cost	Profit	Rate for year (%)	Finance cost	Profit
Year 1	10	8	4.0	6.0	12	6.0	4.0
Year 2	20	7	3.5	16.5	13	6.5	13.5
Year 3	25	6	3.0	22.0	14	7.0	18.0
Year 4	25	5	2.5	22.5	15	7.5	17.5
Year 5	20	5	2.5	17.5	15	7.5	12.5
Net present value at 10%				11.9			

At the budgeted interest rate of 10%, the project has a positive net present value of FF 4.9 million. If the company chooses to borrow at floating rates, the funding cost of the project will vary with interest rates. If interest rates rise according to the pattern shown, the funding cost will rise sufficiently to make the net present value of the project a negative FF 1.35 million.

The profit stream is sensitive to both interest and exchange rates and the viability of the project will depend to a large extent upon the steps taken either to remove these exposures or to accept the risks and trust to judgment about the future course of rates. The effect of interest exposure in this example is as great as that of the currency exposure analysed earlier. This need not always be the case. Currency exposure applies to the entire transaction while the interest exposure only pertains to the financing-cost portion of total costs. Interest exposure is therefore particularly important in those capital-intensive industries in which interest costs account for a relatively high proportion of total costs.

The vunerability of capital-intensive industries to interest rate exposure is highlighted when companies are deciding whether or not to embark upon major capital expenditures. The uncertainty concerning future interest costs can be explicitly recognised by the use of sensitivity analysis when selecting the rate at which to discount future income streams which will accrue to a company as a result of an investment. Any project or production process which does not involve a high proportion of imported raw materials or machinery and is not very dependent on export markets is likely to be more exposed to interest rate than to currency fluctuation. For example, a proposal to build a new hotel should be evaluated against a range of fixed and floating interest rate forecasts whereas currency exposure — if at all relevant — may only be as an economic exposure affecting the occupancy rate.

Our examples have illustrated the effects of high or rising interest rates on borrowing companies. The opposite exposure, to the risk of low or falling interest rates, is faced by companies which have a large liquid surplus or for which the investment of funds is a major part of their business. The exposures of investing companies are often overlooked but are obviously a serious matter when most of a company's income comes in the form of interest.

It was stated earlier that companies have become more aware of interest rate exposure following the economic disruptions of the 1970s and 1980s. The magnitude of potential interest rate risk can be gauged from Figures 14.2, 14.3 and Table 14.3. These illustrate the variability of both short- and long-term UK interest rates during the last decade. Figure 14.2 also shows short-term Eurodollar interest rates, this being the predominant source of foreign currency finance for UK companies. It can clearly be seen that, even though the data is averaged, absolute movements of 2% — equivalent to up to 25% of the interest rate level itself — are not uncommon and can occur at short notice. Indeed, in some periods, interest rates are substantially more volatile than exchange rates. As demonstrated in the examples in this section, such movements can have material effects on short-term cash flows, budgets and profit and loss account. In the longer term, movements can have dramatic effects on the financial viability of projects and major investments or indeed can undermine the financial credibility of the company itself.

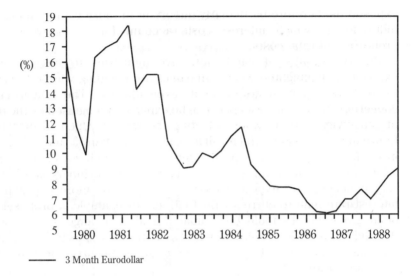

Quarterly averages (%) ⸻⸻ 3-month Eurodollar

Figure 14.2   Dollar interest rates in the 1980s

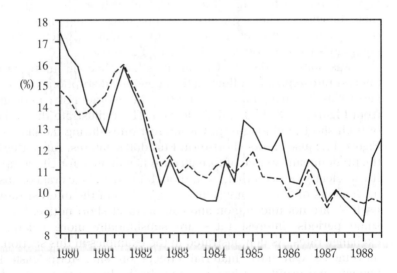

Quarterly averages (%) ⸻ 3-month LIBOR – – – – – Long gilt yield

Figure 14.3   Sterling interest rates in the 1980s

Table 14.3
Interest rates in the
1980s (quarterly averages, %)

Period		Base rate	UK sterling 3-month LIBOR	Long gilt yield	US $ 3-month Euro $
1980	1	17.00	17.68	14.44	15.96
	2	17.00	17.15	14.02	12.77
	3	16.05	16.12	13.34	10.58
	4	15.22	15.53	13.34	16.36
1981	1	13.56	13.32	13.84	16.97
	2	12.00	12.48	14.17	17.30
	3	12.34	14.25	15.27	18.37
	4	15.16	15.62	15.68	14.30
1982	1	13.83	14.36	14.68	15.03
	2	12.87	13.36	13.74	14.98
	3	11.35	11.46	12.28	11.69
	4	9.68	9.93	10.83	9.69
1983	1	10.82	11.18	11.36	9.15
	2	9.98	10.16	10.53	9.30
	3	9.50	9.83	10.90	10.03
	4	9.00	9.37	10.42	9.82
1984	1	8.91	9.27	10.31	10.08
	2	8.89	9.25	10.83	11.45
	3	10.90	11.14	11.14	11.83
	4	10.01	10.14	10.49	9.78
1985	1	13.11	13.02	10.97	8.96
	2	12.68	12.62	10.75	8.19
	3	11.72	11.69	10.40	8.08
	4	11.50	11.61	10.35	8.08
1986	1	12.30	12.41	10.20	7.84
	2	10.44	10.18	9.00	6.92
	3	10.00	9.99	9.58	6.22
	4	10.86	11.21	10.70	6.06
1987	1	10.81	10.64	9.69	6.31
	2	9.36	9.16	8.95	7.10
	3	9.60	9.80	9.71	7.16
	4	9.18	9.22	9.55	7.88

Table 14.3 (continued)
Interest rates in the
1980s (quarterly averages, %)

Period	Base rate	UK sterling 3-month LIBOR	Long gilt yield	US $ 3-month Euro $
1988 1	8.75	9.00	9.36	6.83
2	8.15	8.41	9.24	7.60
3	11.08	11.34	9.53	8.48
4	12.39	12.49	9.33	9.04

Sources: Central Statistics Office; Bank of England; Barclays Bank PLC, Economics Department.

Internal adjustment mechanisms

Earlier, it was observed that the precise effect of interest rate movements on individual projects or companies will depend upon the relative importance of interest costs in total costs. Over and above this, interest rate exposure depends upon how a company has chosen to fund its fixed assets and working-capital requirements. Therefore, in assessing a company's interest rate exposure, consideration has to be given to capital as well as the debt structure of the company. Indeed, although the bulk of shareholders' funds will be non-interest bearing, items such as debentures and preference shares may carry fixed-rate coupons and will therefore reduce the company's dependence on floating-rate debt finance.

To calculate interest rate exposure it is necessary to extract a substantial amount of information relating to every individual borrowing and, where relevant, holdings of income generating and rate-sensitive investments.

To start with, it is necessary to determine the frequencies with which interest rates on each borrowing and investment are reset. Some sources of finance — for example shareholders equity — do not incur any interest costs. At the other extreme the cost of base rate linked borrowings can be altered at very short notice. The borrowings should be grouped into individual currencies.

The next step is to produce a profile showing the volume of borrowing and investment subject to interest rate changes within particular intervals. This profile will stretch from those items which have no sensitivity whatsoever and hence will never change through long-term, fixed-rate borrowings and investments right through to overnight borrowing and surplus funds deployed overnight where rates can change almost immediately. Any quoted investments which are dependent on interest rates, such as gilts, and which are included in the balance sheet at their market valuation should also be included in the earliest timeband. Throughout the above procedure, it is important to note that items should be classified into timebands according to the time remaining to the interest rate reset date and not the original period. For example, if a loan had been rolled over for 12 months but this occurred nine months ago, the next interest reset is in three months' time and this would be the correct timeband in which to place this particular loan.

The above comments immediately suggest several straightforward methods by which companies can reduce their exposure to interest rate changes without the need to resort to more sophisticated financial products. First, the need for external finance can be reduced by adjusting dividend policy. Naturally, other considerations will be brought to bear on this matter (and are discussed elsewhere in this book) but a reduced dividend would allow more funds to be retained within the business and therefore reduce the company's dependence on variable rate debt. Secondly, the capital structure can be investigated for opportunities to augment equity with fixed rate finance such as debentures or preference shares. Thirdly, economies in the use of working capital may be effected by increasing the period of credit taken from suppliers and reducing that allowed to customers thus reducing the need for interest-bearing borrowings. This is the equivalent of 'leading' and 'lagging' currency payments and receipts mentioned in the earlier section on managing exchange rate exposure (see p.249).

Even if it were the case that a company could or would not alter any of the above, perhaps because they had already been optimised, it is still possible to vary the terms of existing bank borrowing facilities and the interest rate sensitivity of investments. Many bank facilities permit borrowers to switch between, for example, 3, 6 or 12 month LIBOR as the basis from which to calculate total cost at each roll over. Furthermore, there are increasing opportunities for borrowers to fix their interest cost for up to 10 years using bank facilities or even longer using bond markets.

Similar opportunities are available to investing companies. Having analysed the interest reset dates of their existing investments, any new cash or reinvestment of maturing amounts can be allocated in accordance with the company's strategy and interest rate expectations. A company with most of its investments in short-term deposits would lose income if interest rates were to fall and hence might choose to reduce its exposure by placing some of its funds in a one-year deposit or buying a longer-dated bond. Conversely, a company with a high proportion invested in gilts would miss an opportunity to gain income if rates rose (and could also suffer a capital loss). It could reduce its exposure by increasing the proportion of its funds invested in short-term deposits.

Even without resorting to sophisticated modern techniques, provided companies have access to fixed-rate financing, either through commercial bank or capital market products, or to markets for term deposits, there will be considerable scope to alter the fixed/floating rate mix of equity and investments. Whether or not companies actually avail themselves of these opportunities depends on the company's agreed policies, chosen strategies and views of the future course of interest rates. It is to these considerations that we now turn before elaborating on particular currency and interest rate exposure management instruments in Chapters 15 and 16.

To Hedge Or Not To Hedge

The above sections have illustrated how currency and interest rate exposures in all their forms can arise, have shown what information is required to quantify those exposures and have provided examples of the substantial effects those exposures can have. It has also been demonstrated that many financial products and internal techniques are available to assist companies in their control of those exposures. Whether or not they actually use those techniques and products depends upon the company's attitude to risk, view of future rates and the costs/benefits of pursuing different strategies.

'Hedging' is the term used to describe actions taken to offset the exposure to risk that a company faces. The development of a coherent policy for hedging should be a priority for any company. Small and inexperienced companies may have no policy at all on currency and interest rate exposure management, and at the least sophisticated level they may not even recognise the existence of these risks. At the next level of development, companies may be sufficiently worried about their exposures to take hedging action against all of them. This is a valid strategy for companies where the resources available for exposure management are limited or where the exposures are so large that the company cannot afford to run the risk of unexpected loss.

Well-run and experienced companies are aware of the risks to their business and have clearly stated policies as to the levels of acceptable risk. Multinational companies with large and sophisticated treasury departments have become sufficiently confident of their skills and experience in managing exposures as to designate their treasury operations as profit centres in their own right. They are risk takers and are aggressive in the hedging strategies adopted and, typically, such companies now employ dealers who are permitted to run modest short-term interest and foreign exchange positions independently of the company's financing needs with the objective of making a profit. Again, once a future cash flow is identified it is not automatically hedged; instead the exposure implications are analysed in the light of the view of rates.

Thus a company which has decided that it is a risk taker retains the potential to profit from favourable movements in interest or exchange rates. The price for taking such risks is that there is also a significant potential for losses. However, the important element in all this is that there is a clearly-formulated policy and strategy and that there are limits to the risks that the company is prepared to take.

The limits beyond which risks become unacceptable can be expressed in a variety of ways. Examples might be as follows:

(a) The Treasurer may be given complete freedom to arrange borrowings and invest surplus funds, etc. up to a certain period in the future (say one year) depending on his view of interest rates. Thus a known cash in- or outflow in nine months' time may or may not be hedged in terms of both currency or interest rate exposure.

(b) Limits may be expressed quantitatively — currency open positions may not exceed a certain fixed amount in total and/or by individual currency; maximum amounts that can be borrowed with interest rate resets greater/less than one year or other frequency are specified.

(c) Other constraints may be stated proportionally — for example 'up to a half of forecast cash flows up to six months may be left uncovered'.

(d) Other decisions may have to be referred to the company's board or finance sub-committee, e.g. borrowing or investment over one year.

Some companies which are fully aware of their exposures and experienced in the techniques of hedging choose to leave potentially adverse positions uncovered on the grounds that they are of such a fundamental nature that to offset them would change the nature of the company itself. A company is ultimately responsible to its shareholders and it can be argued that the shareholders of a company with a major investment in, say, Australia have chosen to invest in that company and as a corollary are willing to take on that exposure. For the management of the company to hedge the exposure away might therefore be contrary to the shareholders' wishes. This argument has some merit for large and obvious exposures but it would not be reasonable to assume that shareholders had full knowledge of, and fully acquiesced in, every day-to-day exposure of the company, nor would it absolve the directors from their duty to act in the best interests of the shareholders.

In conclusion, companies should have policies which incorporate a statement as to the level of acceptable exposure. The risk-averse company will adopt policies which state that all exposures have to be covered, where possible, within a limited time frame and when known with reasonable certainty. An aggressive policy will be stated in such a way that there is considerable discretion to retain what is perceived as being desirable exposure. This can lead to competitive advantages but, if judgment is poor or the profit and loss effects of the retained exposure are large relative to the company's earnings, it can be disastrous. There are many instances of companies that have run into serious difficulties as a result of poor exposure management.

The next two chapters provide descriptions of the many instruments that can be provided by bankers and other financial intermediaries to Corporate Treasurers to assist them in that task.

Further Reading

References on currency and interest rate exposure management will be found at the end of Chapter 16, p.292.

CHAPTER 15

Currency Exposure Management Instruments

Robert Hudson and Nicholas Tonkin

Introduction

There are few areas of risk management where the choice of available management instruments is as great as is the case for currency exposure. In the years since the collapse of the Bretton Woods agreement for fixed parities the foreign exchange markets have developed a wide range of techniques which permit the Corporate Treasurer to protect himself against the effects of currency fluctuations. This chapter explains the particular features of each instrument and concludes with a summary of their application to the types of risk identified in Chapter 14.

Forward Exchange Transactions

A forward exchange contract is an agreement entered into by two parties to exchange a specified amount of one currency for another at a future date but at a rate of exchange which is set today. For example, a British company expecting to receive 500 million yen in three months' time could agree with its bank to sell 500 million yen in exchange for sterling at a rate of 250 yen = £1. The company then knows that it will ultimately receive £2 million (provided the commercial contract is settled as expected) no matter what the spot exchange rate for yen against sterling is when it receives the yen.

Banks quote forward exchange rates for many currencies for periods up to one year and in some cases even further forward. The rate quoted for forward dates will not be the same, normally, as today's spot rate, nor will it be based upon any forecast of future rates. The calculation of forward rates is in fact quite a mechanical process and is based on the Fisher Interest Parity Theorem. This theorem gives rise to an equilibrium rate of exchange which is derived from principles of arbitrage. Given two currencies which can be bought and sold spot and borrowed or lent for say three-month periods, the three-month forward rate of exchange is uniquely determined by today's interest and exchange rates. The formula is as follows:

$$F = S \times \frac{(1 + if)}{(1 + id)}$$

where F is the forward rate, S is today's spot rate, if is the foreign rate of interest, and id is the domestic rate of interest. Suppose that at today's rates DM3 = £1 and that Deutschmarks can be borrowed or lent at 5% p.a. and sterling at 10% p.a. The one year forward rate for marks against sterling will then be:

$$F = 3 \times \frac{(1 + 0.05)}{(1 + 0.10)} = 2.8636$$

If a bank is not quoting 2.8636 as the forward rate then it will lose money. Suppose it is quoting 2.5. Then we can borrow £1 million, sell it spot for DM3 million which we deposit for one year at 5%. At the end of the year, we receive DM3.15 million which we sell at DM2.5 = £1 to receive £1.26 million. We repay our £1 million borrowing plus £100,000 interest and we are left with a completely risk-free profit of £160,000. If the bank had been quoting DM3 = £1 as its forward rate then, by borrowing DM3 million, selling for sterling and buying back at the forward rate, we could have made a profit of DM150,000. Only if the forward rate is exactly 2.8636 will there be no way to make a risk-free profit from dealing against the bank. As no bank will willingly lose money in this way, the Corporate Treasurer can be sure that forward rates are fairly determined by market forces and that in dealing in the forward market he is not trying to outguess the banks as to what the forward rate should be.

Conventionally, forward rates are expressed as premiums or discounts to the current spot rate. In our example above, sterling would be said to be at a discount of 13.64 pfennigs whereas the Deutschmark would correspondingly be at a premium. (For a full explanation of the conventions of quoting foreign exchange rates see the *Financial Times Guide to Statistics*.)

It follows from the construction of forward rates that forwards will only be available for currencies and periods where there is a fairly free market for loans and deposits. Three months DM/$ is therefore no problem but the Corporate Treasurer should not expect to obtain a very competitive quote for, say, 13-month drachma/peseta. Nevertheless, for the majority of transactions, the forward exchange market will offer the most liquid and cheapest form of cover.

One criticism of forward exchange is that it appears relatively inflexible. If a company agrees to sell 250 million yen for £1 million at a date three months in the future (say, 1 June) then what will happen if the 250 million yen do not arrive until 1 July, or do not arrive at all? In practice there are well established procedures for handling such eventualities which do not penalise the customer unfairly. In the case of late arrival, an extension of the contract will be calculated as if the bank had sold the customer the yen he needed to complete the original contract at the spot rate and then entered into another one-month forward contract at the then prevailing one-month forward rate. In the absence of any major changes in interest rates (and hence in premium/discount) the total cost to the customer will be little different from that of entering into a four-month forward contract initially, and sometimes he may even make a small gain.

Procedures for closing out contracts are similar. If, two months after entering into a three-month forward deal to sell yen for sterling, the customer discovers that his funds will not be arriving after all, he can effectively close out by entering into a one-month forward deal to sell sterling for yen maturing on the same date as the original transaction. Only the net difference, if any, would then need to be paid at settlement of the two matching deals, but in this case the customer would pay the cost (or receive the benefit) of any change in spot rates between the dates of entering into the forward deals.

There is one other feature of the forward market which adds further to its flexibility. This is the existence of 'option date forwards' (not to be confused with 'foreign currency options' which are covered later in this chapter). These are specifically designed to cover the common situations in international trade where the trader does not know exactly when his foreign currency will arrive. The trader could enter into a fixed date forward and close-out or extend as need be but this exposes him to some slight risk of a change in forward rates. He may prefer the certainty of rate offered by the options date forward. What this enables him to do is to agree a rate of exchange for a fixed amount of currency with the delivery to take place at any time between two specified dates. For example, sell $5 million for £3.2 million (exchange rate 1.5625) at any time between 1 August and 1 September. In setting its rate the bank will quote the fixed forward rate for *either* 1 August *or* 1 September, whichever is the least favourable to the customer. (In rare cases there may be a less favourable rate applying in the middle of the option period in which case that would be quoted.) Thus if the forward rate for 1 August is 1.5580 and for 1 September is 1.5625, the bank will *buy* dollars at 1.5625 for this option period but would *sell* dollars at 1.5580.

Currency Futures

Currency futures are an adaptation of the long-established principles of commodity futures. The two parties to the futures contract commit themselves to deliver (if the seller) or to take delivery (if the buyer) of a specified amount of a given currency in exchange for the counter currency at a specified future date. A principal feature of futures markets is that they trade standard units (referred to as 'a contract') so as to facilitate the development of a secondary market. Thus a sterling currency futures contract on the London International Financial Futures Exchange consists of £25,000 worth of US dollars for delivery on the third Wednesday of March, June, September or December. In practice, it is still possible to obtain good cover even when there is a clear mismatch with regard to the size or date. Different sizes can be matched by trading multiples of the standard contracts and the first delivery month after the date required would be selected. When required, the trader can sell the contracts back into the market and be left with a profit or loss reflecting the movement in rates in the meantime.

An example may help to clarify the operation of the market. Figure 15.1 illustrates the case of an exporter who agrees in January to sell goods worth $150,000 to an importer in the USA. Payment will be made on 19 April. If payment were made today, the exporter could immediately sell his dollars at the spot rate of exchange for £100,000. He fears that sterling will strengthen before he is actually able to effect the exchange, so to cover his risk he buys four sterling currency futures contracts. The futures market price for June delivery is currently 1.4950 (futures prices are determined in the same way as forward prices, i.e. by interest parity conditions).

2 January   Exporter agrees to sell goods for $150,000 to US
                  customer
                  Current spot rate $1.50 = £1
                  June futures contract price 1.4950

19 April   Exporter receives payment of $150,000
                  Current spot rate $1.65 = £1
                  June futures contract price 1.6460

Underlying transaction:

Receipts at 2 January rate	£100,000.00
Actual receipts	£ 90,909.09
Loss	£ 9,090.91

Futures transaction:

Buy four contracts at 1.4950	$149,500.00
Sell four contracts at 1.6460	$164,600.00
Profit	$ 15,100.00

Net position:

Underlying transactions loss	£ 9,090.91
Futures profit	£ 9,151.51
Net windfall gain	£ 60.60

Figure 15.1 Currency futures

On 19 April the spot rate has indeed risen to 1.65 so that when the exporter takes his $150,000 to his bank he receives only £90,909.09 for them rather than the £100,000 he had hoped for. However, he can now sell his futures contracts at the new price of 1.6460 obtaining a profit of $15,100 which, at the current spot rate, is worth £9,151.51. This offsets his loss on the underlying deal and, indeed, leaves a small windfall profit. Note that this could have easily been a small loss and, as futures and forward markets can be arbitraged against each other, there is no reason to expect any systematic price advantage in using one rather than the other.

The mechanics of currency futures markets are very different from those of the forward market. Trading is done through brokers who must be members of the recognised exchange where the contracts are registered. On buying or selling a contract the trader does not have to pay the full face value but is required to deposit only a small proportion of the face value of the contract (perhaps as little as 2%) with his broker who in turn deposits it with a central clearing house. This is referred to as the 'initial margin'. Thereafter, positions are revalued every day and any losses must be made good immediately (on most exchanges profits are also paid out immediately). Thus, in the example shown in Figure 15.1, if on 3 January the price of the June future had moved to 1.4930 the company's position would have worsened by $200 (0.0020 × 100,000) and that 'variation margin' would have to be paid to the clearing house on the next business day. The purpose of this margin system is to prevent any trader from building up a large loss in a position which he subsequently was unable to meet. In this way the creditworthiness of the market is guaranteed.

The first currency futures contracts were introduced in 1972 in Chicago as a response to the abandonment of fixed exchange rates in the previous year, and the explosive growth of financial futures markets has been a major feature of risk management in the late 1970s and early 1980s. Their development must be viewed in the context of the United States banking system which is fragmented into many small banks often with no foreign exchange capabilities at all. In the absence of contact with one of the major banks, a United States Corporate Treasurer might find that the futures market offered as good a service in covering his foreign exchange exposures as anything, although the same is unlikely to be the case in Europe. Currency futures were first traded in London in 1982 by which time a liquid, cheap and efficient forward exchange market was well established. The currency futures market is therefore likely to be less relevant to European traders than it is to their United States counterparts, although there are some special situations which may justify the use of futures rather than forwards. These are discussed in the concluding section of this chapter.

Foreign Currency Options

One problem with both forward cover and currency futures is that the trader is committed to the rate agreed no matter what happens thereafter. In other words, he is protected from adverse currency movements but he no longer has the chance of benefiting from favourable movements. Foreign currency options offer greater flexibility in that the customer agrees a rate for a forward transaction with his bank but can then choose whether or not to deal at that rate depending on whether or not it proves to be favourable to him. In return for this option, the customer pays a non-returnable fee.

The reader who is not familiar with the jargon of options trading should study the glossary on p.276 before proceeding further. Essentially, an option confers on the purchaser the right, but not the obligation, to deal at an agreed price. The seller, conversely, *must* deal if the buyer so demands. As the buyer is only likely to wish to deal when it is to the disadvantage of the seller, a fee known as the premium is paid by the buyer to the seller in order to compensate for this asymmetric risk. Options are traded in standardised form on a number of exchanges but there is also a flourishing over-the-counter market whereby options can be purchased direct from the major banks. Tailor-made options are readily available to cover the exact risks which a company fears most.

For example, a British company expecting to receive $3 million in three months' time could sell the dollars forward at a rate equal to today's spot rate of, say, $1.50 = £1 in which case it would know with certainty that its sterling proceeds would be £2 million. Alternatively, it could buy an option to sell $3 million for sterling at $1.50 (dollar put, sterling call). If the spot rate on receipt of the dollars is $2 = £1 then the company will exercise its option to sell the dollars at 1.50. If, however, the rate is $1 = £1 it will ignore the option and convert at the spot rate.

In deciding whether to use options a company will have to balance its desire to retain the chance of gain from a favourable rate movement against the cost of the premium. Using options every time is unlikely to produce a better return than choosing forward cover. The premium paid for an option is derived from mathematical models which have as their main ingredients the current spot and forward rates, domestic and foreign interest rates, the length of time to expiry of the option, the exercise price of the option and, most importantly, an estimate of the volatility of the exchange rate concerned. Each bank is likely to have its own variation of the basic model and will aim to price the options it sells in such a way as to make a certain minimum return. The models also give rise to 'hedge ratios' which are an estimate of the sensitivity of the bank's option portfolio to movements in the spot exchange rate. By balancing its position in the underlying currencies and its option portfolio in accordance with the hedge ratios a bank can minimise the risk it takes in adopting the potentially unlimited exposure of the option seller. Option premiums are not therefore based on guesses about future trends but, like forward rates, are determined in a neutral way.

One very important feature of option pricing is that the premium required for an option reduces the further out-of-the-money it becomes. This gives an extra dimension of flexibility in that a company can choose the rate at which it wants protection. Whereas with a forward or future a company will obtain whatever is the market rate for the period concerned, with an option it can choose the rate. To illustrate the value of this consider the company described above that expected to receive $3 million in three months' time. Suppose that the company really felt that there was very little chance of the dollar weakening and so would really like to leave the position uncovered in the hope of benefiting from a favourable currency movement. But if $3 million represented a big sum for this company it simply might not be able to take the risk of running an uncovered position. It could, therefore, buy an at-the-money option, as illustrated above, and pay perhaps 5% of the face amount for it ($150,000) or, alternatively, it could choose to take some of the risk itself whilst still protecting against a catastrophic misjudgment and buy an out-of-the-money option for a lower fee. For example, an option at 1.60 rather than 1.50 might cost only 2% ($60,000). If the company chose this then it would stand to gain if the dollar strengthened from 1.50, would lose if it weakened as far as 1.60 but would be protected thereafter. In this way the company could take an active view of the management of its currency exposures whilst also having cheap disaster insurance in place in the event that its forecast proved completely wrong.

Using Options

Figure 15.2 illustrates the choices that a company can make in covering its short-term currency exposures. Figure 15.2(a) illustrates the nature of the exposure for a UK exporter selling to the USA in dollars. If the exchange rate, shown on the horizontal axis, rises, the sterling value of his fixed dollar receipt (say $15 million) falls. He can cover this by entering into a forward contract, to sell dollars at a fixed rate. The effect of forward cover is to insulate him completely from the effects of exchange rate changes (Figure 15.2(b)). No matter what the spot rate is at the time he receives the dollars, he will get the same amount of sterling for them under his forward contract. This is shown by the horizontal dotted line. Using futures would produce a similar result.

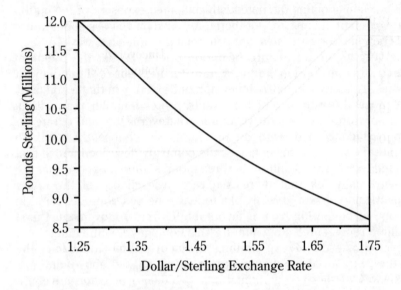

Figure 15.2(a)   Uncovered

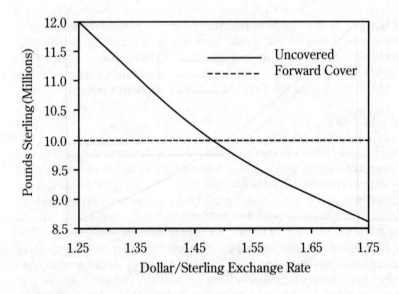

Figure 15.2(b)   Forward cover

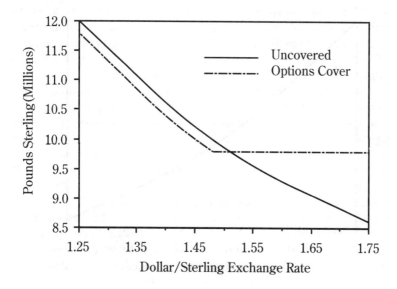

Figure 15.2(c)   Options cover

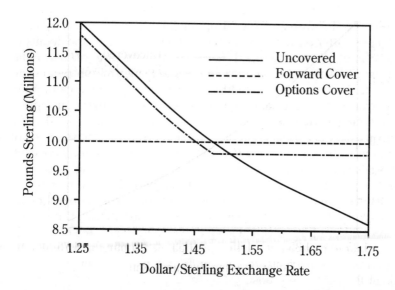

Figure 15.2(d)   Cover compared

Figure 15.2(c) shows the cover given by a sterling call option. As the exchange rate rises above the exercise price, the value of the option rises, offsetting the declining value of the uncovered position so as to give a fixed sterling value. Below the exercise price the option has no value, only a fixed cost represented by the premium paid. The broken line in the figure shows this relationship, running parallel to the uncovered position (but below it by the amount of the premium) when the exchange rate moves favourably, but having a guaranteed minimum sterling value when the exchange rate moves unfavourably. The line therefore has a pronounced kink in it at the exercise price of the option. Figure 15.2(d) shows the three alternatives of uncovered, forward and option cover. Note that with the benefit of hindsight, option cover is *never* the best solution, nor is it usually the worst solution (it will only be the worst solution where the spot rate at maturity is very close to the forward rate). It will always prove better to have covered forward or to have left the positions uncovered, the reason being that a premium has to be paid for the option. The company's choice is therefore whether to accept this known second-best solution or to try to guess which of the others will prove to be a winner.

To increase the choice available many banks now offer combinations of options and forwards which give rise to a growing lexicon of terms such as range forwards, zero cost options, participating forwards and so on. These offer particular tax or cash-flow advantages the details of which cannot all be included here. Two cases are of particular importance however, the cylinder option and tender-to-contract cover.

The cylinder option is created by the customer buying a call option on a currency from his bank and simultaneously selling a put option back to them (or vice versa). He therefore pays a premium for the call but receives one for the put and it is possible for the exercise prices of the options to be set in such a way that the two premiums cancel each other out leaving a zero cost. For example, by buying a sterling call/dollar put at 1.50 and selling a sterling put/dollar call at 1.40 the exporter described above would know that if rates rose above 1.50 he could exercise his option to give a maximum rate of 1.50; if rates fell between 1.50 and 1.40 he would keep the benefit; if rates fell below 1.40 the bank would exercise its option giving him a minimum rate of 1.40. This permits companies to take a quite detailed view of future rate trends at limited or zero cost.

The second special type of option is designed to cover the case of companies tendering for a contract. The exchange rate cover arranged is made contingent upon the customer being successful in winning the contract and a reduced option fee is charged to reflect the fact that the chances of success are not 100%. If the customer wins the tender, he receives exchange rate cover appropriate for his contract whereas if he loses the tender, he receives nothing. He does not, therefore, have the opportunity for windfall gains but does have a guaranteed rate if he needs it. Schemes of this type are run by the Export Credit Guarantee Department and at least two major banks.

Parallel Loans and Currency Swaps

Forwards, futures and options are usually only available for short-term covering of foreign exchange exposures, say up to two years. Companies with longer-term exposures, particularly those of a structural nature such as translation exposure, will need to consider other techniques if they are to obtain adequate cover.

For example, a German parent company with a British subsidiary may find that it needs to borrow sterling to support its subsidiary in the UK. It could borrow Deutschmarks, sell them for sterling and lend them to its subsidiary, but that would create a foreign exchange exposure when interest on the Deutschmark loan has to be paid and at maturity. If this is several years into the future then forward cover may not be available. An alternative is to borrow Deutschmarks and lend them to a British company which has a subsidiary in Germany and consequently has the opposite need. This exchange of borrowing to the mutual benefit of two companies is the idea behind a variety of differently named techniques which all achieve the same end but with slightly different legal status. A *back-to-back loan*, for example, would be created by the German parent lending Deutschmarks to the British parent at the same time as the British parent lent sterling to the German parent. A *parallel loan* would be created by the respective parent companies lending to the subsidiaries in their own country. This technique is particularly valuable therefore where exchange control prevents cross-border currency flows.

A currency swap can involve the full exchange of principal amounts at the beginning and the end of the agreed period or may simply be an agreement to exchange interest payments with no principal changing hands. Most commonly, the agreement will have a similar effect to a back-to-back loan although its legal status is as a purchase and sale of currency rather than a loan. Figure 15.3 illustrates the cash flows which take place in a simple currency swap. At the start of the deal, Company

A sells dollars to Company B in exchange for Deutschmarks at an agreed exchange rate which will be something close to the prevailing spot rate. In our example, the rate of exchange is assumed to be DM2 = $1 and the principal amounts are $50 million and DM100 million. During the life of the deal, Company B will pay interest on the dollar principal at an agreed rate to Company A, whilst Company A pays interest on the Deutschmark principal to Company B. The interest payments may be netted at the agreed exchange rate so that only the difference changes hands. At the end of the deal, the principal amounts are re-exchanged, at the original rate.

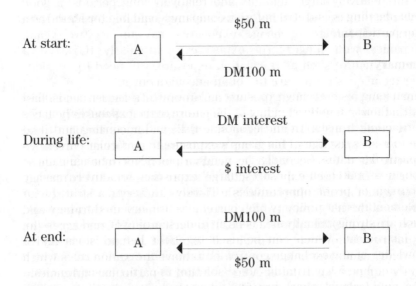

Figure 15.3   Cash flows in a currency swap

Currency swaps are highly flexible and, if the two parties agree, the interest payments can both be at a fixed rate, both at a floating rate, or one floating and one fixed. Interest on one or both sides can be set at zero with an adjustment to the principal amounts exchanged and so on. This ability to negotiate mutually-beneficial terms makes currency swaps valuable in making long-term alterations to a company's structural exposures and also opens up the possibility of exploiting cheap funding alternatives in other currencies. These opportunities are a major influence on activities in the international bond markets.

Markets for parallel loans and currency swaps are far less liquid than are the shorter-term foreign exchange markets. Although banks do act as market makers in currency swaps it is usually necessary to wait for the right counterparty to emerge before a swap for a particular amount and maturity can be arranged. Minimum amounts would usually be $5 million, preferably more, with maturities of three to ten years or occasionally up to 15 years. Swaps where the US dollar is one of the currencies are readily available but, say, French franc/sterling swaps would be relatively rare and swaps involving anything other than the major currencies very unusual. It should also be noted that, as swaps are for relatively large amounts and relatively long periods, a good credit standing is essential before a company would be considered as a swap participant.

Summary

In managing his currency exposure, a Corporate Treasurer needs, first of all, a thorough understanding of the nature of the exposures he faces (transaction, translation and economic risk) and adequate data to be able to assess the size of his group's exposure in particular currencies at particular dates. Secondly, he needs a policy for managing these exposures (match all exposures, 'large' exposures or actively manage in pursuit of profit opportunities). Thirdly, he needs a strategy for implementing that policy (which currencies are expected to be weak, which are strong). Finally, he needs an understanding of, and access to, the instruments which can be used to effect his decisions and a knowledge of any exchange control limitations or taxation rules which may force him away from his ideal solution in particular currencies.

As noted above, there are few areas that are as well served by alternative instruments as is the field of currency exposure management. It would be wrong to be dogmatic about which instrument should be used for which situation as there is almost always a choice, and selection will depend upon relative price at the time as well as upon the strategy being followed. As a brief guide, however, we would suggest that forward contracts are the best antidote to transaction risk; that translation risk is best covered with currency swaps, and that economic risk is best limited by structural change such as changing the currency mix of the company's assets and liabilities either with physical deals or perhaps currency swaps. Currency futures are of limited value given an efficient forward market whilst options are likely to prove expensive for the unsophisticated but of limitless scope to the active exposure manager, and are uniquely valuable in tendering for contracts. Given the size, scope and efficiency of the foreign exchange markets there is very little excuse for any Corporate Treasurer who does not cover his company's currency exposures.

Options Glossary

Call option	The right to buy at an agreed price
Put option	The right to sell at an agreed price
Exercise price/ strike price	The agreed price at which the option may be completed
Premium	The fee paid by the purchaser of the option
Expiry date	The last day upon which an option may be exercised before lapsing
American option	An option which can be exercised at any time between purchase and expiry
European option	An option which can only be exercised on its expiry date
At-the-money	The current spot price is equal to the option's exercise price
In-the-money	The currency spot price is less favourable than the option's exercise price (i.e. higher for calls, lower for puts)
Out-of-the-money	The current spot price is more favourable than the option's exercise price (i.e. lower for calls, higher for puts)

Further Reading

A selection of references for more detailed analysis of this topic will be found at the end of Chapter 16, p.292.

Interest Rate Exposure Management Instruments

Robert Hudson and Nicholas Tonkin

Introduction

Although perhaps the range of instruments available to manage interest risk is not quite as wide as is the case for currency risk, it is nevertheless extensive. This chapter provides a description of the most important and common of these instruments.

Short-Term Rate Fixing Techniques

Chapter 14 described how companies could alter their interest rate exposures by changing the interest rate basis of loans or deposits at roll overs. Thus if rates were expected to rise then many bank facilities would permit a borrower to lengthen the maturity of his borrowing from, say, three to 12 months, or alternatively, if rates were expected to fall, a shorter borrowing period would be chosen and so on.

The question arises as to what can be done between roll overs if, for example, there is a sudden change in the company's view of future interest rates. Similarly, the company may identify an increase or decrease in its projected cash flow and may wish to manage the interest exposure thereon. This section addresses questions of precisely this nature.

Naturally, a company could make use of remaining headroom within existing bank facilities. It could borrow relatively long and deposit the surplus for a shorter period until such time as a tranche of borrowing matured or was due to be rolled-over, but this is an inefficient use of the company's credit lines and balance sheet and will attract a cost in terms of the bid-offer spread. Fortunately, better short-term rate fixing techniques are available so as to achieve exactly the same effect as the above but in a much more efficient and cost-effective manner.

Just as a forward foreign exchange contract enables a company to exchange one currency for another at a future date at a known rate, so a *forward/forward loan and deposit* enables the two parties involved to borrow from or lend to the other for known periods, commencing at some fixed date in the future, at predetermined rates. No fee or premium is involved although there is a bid-offer spread which enables banks to cover their costs in the same way as in conventional deposit/loan transactions.

Using this technique, a company can protect itself from a rise in short-term (up to one year) rates. For example, suppose a company forms an opinion that short-term rates are about to rise and that they will remain at the higher level at least until a loan is scheduled to roll over in three months' time. The company can insulate itself from the exposure to a rise in rates for one year from today by contracting now to borrow nine months' money, three months forward. The lender in such a forward/forward transaction is fixing the rate in advance and the borrower is committed to borrow at that rate for nine months, commencing in three months' time. The rate will be determined by the relationship between three and 12 months borrowing and lending rates and/or the price of financial futures contracts (discussed in greater detail later). The forward/forward therefore achieves exactly the same protection as actually borrowing for 12 months and redepositing for three months. Arbitrageurs will ensure that the rates achieved are virtually identical and the forward/forward has the added advantage of avoiding balance sheet expansion and the utilisation of credit lines. Figure 16.1 illustrates the mathematics of a forward/forward transaction.

A customer wants to borrow £10m for nine months, commencing in three months' time.

To cover this forward loan, a bank could raise funds in the interbank market for 12 months and deposit the proceeds for the intervening three months until the customer drew down the forward loan.

We can now calculate the rate which the bank needs to charge its customer on the nine-month loan in order to recover its funding cost for 12 months after allowing for the benefit of the deposit in the first three months. Say the 12-month cost of raising funds is 11% and the rate at which the bank can deposit funds for three months is 10%. For every £1 raised from the interbank market today, the bank will need to repay £1.11 in 12 months. For every £1 deposited today, the bank will receive £1.025 in three months' time. The break-even rate (R) for the forward/forward loan can then be calculated as follows:

$$\left(1 + \frac{11}{100}\right) = \left(1 + \frac{10 \times 3}{100 \times 12}\right) \times \left(1 + \frac{R \times 9}{100 \times 12}\right)$$

Therefore

$$R = \left(\frac{(1.11)}{(1.025)} - 1\right) \times \frac{4 \times 100}{3} = 11.057\%$$

In general, the following formula would apply:

$$R = \left(\frac{1 + A \times C}{1 + B \times D}\right) \times \frac{1}{E} \times 100$$

where

A is the interest rate, as a decimal, at which the bank can raise funds for the period from now to the ultimate maturity of the loan.

B is the interest rate, as a decimal, at which the bank can deposit funds until they are drawn by the customer.

C is the period, as a proportion of a year, from now to the ultimate maturity of the loan.

D is the period, as a proportion of a year, from now until the drawing of the customer's loan.

E is the period, as a proportion of a year, for which the customer wishes to borrow funds.

Note: The calculation and formula excludes the bank's credit margin and any margin for dealing costs.

Figure 16.1   Example of calculation of a forward/forward rate

---

Forward/forward loans and deposits are available in all major currencies, normally in minimum amounts of $1 million, or equivalent, and for periods generally up to one year or two years — and occasionally longer — for sterling, Deutschmarks, US dollars and Swiss francs.

The key disadvantages of forward/forwards are that they are rather cumbersome for banks to construct and the customer is committed to undertake the transaction. If interest rates do not move as expected the customer can only reverse the earlier transaction to which he was committed and the cost of so doing is such that he will not benefit from current rates.

A more flexible off-balance sheet instrument is the *forward rate agreement* (FRA) which does not involve any transfer of principal. This enables a customer to protect himself from interest rate movements commencing on a specific future date and for a specific period and agreed nominal amount. However, there is no commitment to an underlying loan or deposit, the customer merely agrees to pay or receive the difference in interest between the contracted rate and the actual market rate at the start of the contract period, this difference being applied to the notional amount. Thus, the FRA achieves exactly the same objective as a forward/forward with the essential difference that no physical transfer of principal is involved. Companies can therefore divorce the rate protection element from the basic transaction and could obtain a loan from one bank but an FRA from another. The British Bankers Association has produced a standard document for FRAs which are consequently traded on similar terms by all banks in London.

Figure 16.2 presents an illustrative calculation. Continuing the earlier example, the company could fix the rate in three months' time by entering into a 'three month versus 12 month' FRA, at say 11⅛%. At this stage no premium or fee is involved but in three months' time the loan itself is rolled-over and settlement on the FRA occurs. If nine-month LIBOR is higher than 11⅛%, say 11½%, the bank providing the FRA would pay the company the difference between the actual nine-month LIBOR and the agreed 11⅛% applied to the notional principal for nine months.

Today:
Company enters into '3 versus 12' month FRA at $11\frac{1}{8}\%$ on a notional amount of £10 million.

Three months' time:
(a)   Nine-month LIBOR is $11\frac{1}{2}\%$. Therefore the bank pays $11\frac{1}{2} - 11\frac{1}{8} = \frac{3}{8}\%$ on £10 million for nine months. This is discounted at the nine-month rate for nine months as the FRA is settled at commencement, whereas loan interest is paid in arrears.

Therefore the bank pays:

$$£10 \text{ million} \times \frac{3}{8 \times 100} \times \frac{9}{12} = £28,125$$

discounted at $11\frac{1}{2}\%$ for nine months = £25,892

(b)   The above sum is invested at LIBOR for nine months.
(c)   The loan itself is rolled over at $11\frac{1}{2}\%$ (excluding credit margin)

12 months' time:
(a)   Loan interest is paid:

$$£10 \text{ million} \times \frac{11.5}{100} \times \frac{9}{12} = £862,500$$

(b)   The FRA settlement amount, invested at LIBOR* is then worth:

$$£25,892 \left(1 + \frac{11.5}{100} \times \frac{9}{12} \right) = £28,125$$

Result:
This gives a net cost of £834,375 which is equivalent to $11\frac{1}{8}\%$ for nine months on £10 million.

*Note that this amount could not realistically be invested at LIBOR but this assumption is made here in order to illustrate the theory of FRAs.

Figure 16.2   Example of a forward rate agreement

This sum is paid at the beginning of the contract period and is discounted, as interest on the loan would normally be payable in arrears. The overall effect is to offset exactly the higher cost of the loan roll-over. If nine-month LIBOR were lower than the agreed rate the exact opposite happens and the customer is contracted to pay the difference, calculated in the same way, to the bank. The net effect is to raise the cost of the loan roll-over back to the agreed 11⅛% rate.

The availability of FRAs is very much the same as with forward/forwards and also achieves the identical result of fixing the company's borrowing cost in advance. The greater flexibility of FRAs now means that they have largely supplanted forward/forwards and the market for the latter is very much in decline. However, there is also the same disadvantage that if rates do not move as expected then any benefits have to be foregone. To obtain the advantages of even greater flexibility, the company would have to look to using interest rate options which are discussed in detail in the next section.

Before moving on to options, mention should be made of interest rate futures. It was pointed out earlier that banks have some natural cover for their forward/forward or FRA exposures through a bid-offer spread because they both 'buy' and 'sell'. Residual exposures can be covered in the interbank FRA market or by the bank itself helping the interest rate risk through appropriate activities in *interest rate futures*.

Interest rate futures operate in the same way as that described in the section on currency futures in Chapter 15, see p.265 (the reader should refer to that section for an outline of the operation of futures markets). The only difference is that the futures contract is defined in terms of delivery of specified deposits (for short interest rate contracts), or a notional fixed interest rate security (e.g. a UK government gilt), rather than the delivery of a specified amount of one currency in exchange for another currency.

For example, the short-term sterling interest rate contract traded on the London International Financial Futures Exchange (LIFFE) is specified in terms of a £500,000 three-month sterling deposit at one of a list of banks in London. Delivery months are March, June, September and December and, again as with currency futures, different principal amounts can be hedged by using multiples of the futures contract and good, though not perfectly accurate, cover for non-delivery dates can be achieved by buying or selling futures in the delivery months either side of the date for which cover is required.

The operation of the market can be illustrated (see Figure 16.3) using the position of a company where there is known to be a loan of

£1m rolling over in three months' time, say 19 April. The exposure to an interest rate rise between now and the roll-over date can be removed by selling two of the short sterling interest rate futures for June delivery. The current price of those futures contracts is, say, 90.37 which implies a three-month interest rate of 9.63% (contract pricing for the short-term interest rate contracts is defined very simply as 100 − LIBOR). The company is then protected from a rise in three- month rates because, as a result of arbitrage, the futures price will closely mirror movements in the three-month money market rate. Thus, if the latter rate rises to 10½%, the futures price will fall to approximately 100 − 10.50, i.e. 89.50, and the company's obligation to deliver £1 million of sterling deposits can be discharged at a lower cost. Note that there is no complete certainty that the futures price will be exactly 89.50 (except on futures delivery days) so some residual risk remains. Our example assumes that the price settles at 89.52. The profit earned by the company by selling the futures at 90.37 and then being able to buy them at 89.52 almost exactly offsets the increase in borrowing costs on the loan itself. The net result is therefore to lock-in the interest cost of the loan roll-over at the rate implied by the futures contracts sold on 2 January.

2 January   Company decides to hedge the interest rate exposure on a
             loan that rolls over on 19 April.
             Sells 2 June futures contracts at 90.37.
19 April   The company rolls over its £1m loan for three months at a
             LIBOR rate of 10½% (excluding the bank's credit
             margin).
             At the same time, the company closes out its futures
             position by buying 2 June futures contracts at 89.52.

Interest cost:
$$£1,000,000 \times \frac{3}{12} \times \frac{10.5}{100} = £26,250$$

Futures transaction:

Sale $£500,000 \times 2 \times \dfrac{3}{12} \times \dfrac{90.37}{100} = £225,925$

Purchase $£500,000 \times 2 \times \dfrac{3}{12} \times \dfrac{89.52}{100} = £223,800$

Profit   £2,125

Net position:
Interest cost reduced to £24,125, which is equivalent to 9.65% on the
£1m loan.

Figure 16.3   Short-term interest rate futures

If, as in our earlier example, the company is concerned about a
sustained rise in rates, then it should also cover itself against this risk
before subsequent roll-overs by adopting the same futures strategy but
with contracts deliverable in September, December, etc. The only
limitations to a company adopting such a strategy are that futures
market delivery dates rarely exceed 18 months to two years forward
and even for some of these dates there is limited liquidity in the market.
For this reason there is a limit to how far ahead one can hedge and the
amount one can cover reduces progressively.

Futures markets offer a limited range of contracts, LIFFE, for
example, providing only three short-term interest rate contracts, these
being based on three-month sterling, three-month Euromark and
three-month Eurodollar interbank rates (at the time of writing there

are plans for a fourth contract in ECUs). Hedgers wishing to cover exposures to five-month sterling CD rates, for instance, can apply certain weighting techniques to the available futures contracts to provide some cover, but this is a specialised area and anyone less than a highly-experienced Corporate Treasurer would be well advised to cover such risks with a tailor-made FRA from his bank. The banks will probably cover their own risks in the futures markets, but they have more experience and a greater spread of risks to enable them to cope with the residual exposures. Futures markets are really for the large-scale, professional interest rate manager and most corporates will find FRAs more suitable for their needs.

One area where FRAs tend not to be available is in covering long-term interest rates. Futures can therefore be very useful when planning and preparing an issue of corporate debt. For example, a company might decide that the rates currently obtainable on a sterling bond issue are very attractive. However, the company may have to join a queue of such issuers and also it might take several weeks to obtain various internal approvals and make other preparations. The company could protect against a short-term rise in bond rates by selling the requisite number of LIFFE's long gilt future which provides a hedge of 15–25 year sterling interest rates. Again this is a specialised area best left to experts. Interested readers should refer to the recommended reading at the end of this chapter.

Before concluding this section it is worthwhile noting that banks themselves are active in markets for futures, FRAs and forward/forward business and are major if not the most important participants in all of them. It is not surprising therefore that the prices of all these products are interrelated and that professional arbitrageurs, often working for banks, ensure that any pricing anomalies exist only for a second. Modern computer technology has been deployed to seek out and profit from pricing anomalies and this, together with the potential for rapid execution of transactions, ensures efficient pricing. The corporate customer choosing between these markets will rarely find any significant difference in prices quoted by major banks active in this market. Convenience and suitability for the purpose will be the main criteria of choice.

Interest Rate Options and Related Products

A common feature which emerged from all the instruments discussed in the previous section was the borrowers' (or lenders') commitment once agreements or contracts had been entered into. In all cases the customer was fixing, by various means, future interest rates, thereby achieving the objective of removing his exposure to potential adverse movements in interest rates. However, the drawback common to all these instruments is that if rates move in his favour, a borrower cannot benefit from lower rates nor can an investor benefit from higher ones. This is not to say that those products are inflexible — FRAs can be reversed and futures contracts can be closed out — but rather that the customer is fixing rates with virtual certainty. If the customer wants to avoid a loss when rates move adversely, but retain the chance to benefit if they move in his favour, then he should consider an interest rate option. As was seen with currency options in the last chapter, options do not entail a commitment or obligation on the part of the option purchaser to exercise his option. In return for an up-front fee, the purchaser obtains maximum flexibility of cover for future rates.

The terminology and operation of interest rate options is very similar to that for foreign currency options and will not be repeated here. To assist in understanding how they work we return to our example of a company wishing to protect itself from a rise in interest rates before the next loan roll-over in three months' time, 19 April.

The company asks the bank for an option on three-month LIBOR which can be exercised on the loan roll-over date at a strike price of 10%. The bank, therefore, sells to the company a European Option to borrow at 10% in return for a non-returnable fee quoted as a percentage of the notional amount. If LIBOR exceeds 10% on the roll-over date, the bank will pay the company the difference between the borrowing cost at the prevailing LIBOR and the agreed 10%. If LIBOR is below 10%, the borrower will not obtain any compensatory payment nor will he be called upon to make one himself. He retains the benefit of the lower rate.

Figure 16.4 illustrates the choices available to the company in our earlier example (Figure 16.3) when deciding what to do about the next roll-over date. If three-month LIBOR, shown on the horizontal axis, rises between now and the roll-over date, the effective interest cost, on the vertical axis, will obviously rise if the company leaves the exposure unhedged. The company could fix its interest costs in advance, by means of forward/forward, FRA or futures transaction. In this example, all such transactions fix the roll-over rate at, say, 9.63%. Options provide another alternative. If the company perceives the risk, but is not wholly or sufficiently convinced that rates will rise, then it could decide to retain flexibility by purchasing an option on three- month LIBOR in three months' time to cover such an event.

In this example a 'ceiling' has been chosen at 10% for which a premium of, say, 0.2% is charged. If three-month LIBOR on 19 April is less than the agreed exercise or strike rate of 10%, the option is worthless and the option premium is a sunk cost. The overall cost of borrowing is therefore higher because of the option premium than it would have been had the interest rate exposure on the loan roll-over not been hedged in this way. However, the other side of this coin is shown in the graph. If interest rates did rise as originally feared by the company, the option ensures that the borrowing cost is limited to 10%, plus the option premium, and the bank reimburses the company for the excess cost. As with FRAs the underlying loan or deposit and interest-rate option are entirely separate transactions, but should be viewed in combination when the intention is to cover or remove interest rate exposure.

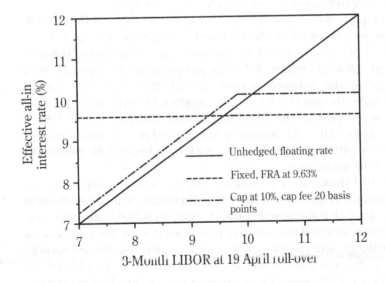

Figure 16.4 Example of options compared with fixed- and floating-rate finance

The pricing, hedging and operation of interest rate options are similar to those of currency options, as are the factors that the company has to consider before embarking on an options strategy rather than using alternative instruments to protect itself. Thus, the company has to weigh up the potential benefits of retaining the opportunity to gain from favourable rate movements and the chances of this occurring, against the option costs themselves. The company can be certain of one thing — the option strategy is rarely the best or worst when viewed in retrospect. It is always best to have correctly anticipated rate movements and acted accordingly, by either continuing the exposure to short-term movements if rates move down (for borrowers) or up (for investors), or to fix rates, using the techniques discussed in the first section of this chapter, if rates rise/fall. Options, however, provide insurance against being wrong.

Before leaving the subject of options, a few comments on the types and availability of them are in order. The example above was a 'ceiling' on an interest rate at one date. A series of ceilings is called a 'cap'. Thus, two consecutive three-month ceilings become a six-month cap. Floors are also available, and if a borrowing company is prepared to concede the benefits of a fall in rates below an agreed level, it can lower its borrowing costs by selling a floor option and collecting a premium. The combination of a ceiling and a floor is commonly known as an interest rate 'collar'. The reader may recognise this as nothing more than the interest rate equivalent of the cylinder currency option which was mentioned in Chapter 15. In some cases the interest rates of the ceiling and floor can be combined in such a way as to reduce costs to nothing. Companies wishing to protect the future value of interest income will obviously take the opposite actions, buying 'floors' and perhaps selling 'ceilings'. The combination of different types of options leads to many alternative strategies.

Interest rate options are available for the same major currencies and periods as forward/forwards and FRAs. However, they are also available as a proprietary over-the-counter instrument and it is occasionally possible to negotiate 'caps' and 'floors' for much longer periods, and in currencies of lesser importance.

Interest Rate Swaps

All the products described in this chapter so far are usually only available up to one or two years, though occasionally longer dates are obtainable. Longer-term interest rate risks, particularly those of a structural or capital nature, have to be managed using other techniques and products. Chapter 14 provided an introduction to how a company might be able to fix its borrowing costs by managing its capital resources. This section describes how the same advantages can be obtained using the technique of interest rate swaps.

For example, a company might not have access to fixed-rate finance. Many capital markets are limited to blue-chip companies and bank fixed-rate debt may be expensive or unobtainable by smaller companies. By making use of an *interest rate swap* such companies may be able to obtain fixed-rate finance. Even blue-chip companies which are able to issue bonds may not wish to do so, or might be able to obtain finer rates by using an interest rate swap. Consider a blue-chip company that can obtain relatively cheap fixed-rate finance, but would prefer floating-rate borrowing to meet its own exposure objectives, or because of its view of rates. Suppose that its cost of fixed-rate funds would be 10%, whilst floating-rate funds would cost LIBOR + ½%. However, a smaller company might be prepared to pay 10¾% for fixed-rate funds, and be able to borrow at LIBOR + ¾% as a floating rate.

Figure 16.5 shows how the blue-chip and smaller companies can be brought together to their mutual satisfaction. Effectively, via the financial intermediary, the smaller company assumes the unwanted fixed-rate obligations of the blue-chip company. Similarly, the blue-chip company assumes the floating-rate obligations of the smaller company. Each of them therefore obtains the interest payment type they really want on mutually advantageous terms.

In the example, the blue-chip company agrees to issue a bond (or may already have an outstanding issue) at a fixed rate of 10%. The financial intermediary pays the blue-chip 10% for these funds and passes them on to the smaller company at 10¾%. The floating-rate funds raised by the smaller company at LIBOR + ¾% are passed to the financial intermediary at the same rate and then to the blue-chip company at LIBOR + ¼%, enabling the smaller company to obtain the fixed-rate funds it wanted; the blue-chip company to cut its floating-rate borrowing cost by ¼%, and the intermediary to derive a margin of ¼% per annum in return for taking on the credit risk of guaranteeing the interest payments.

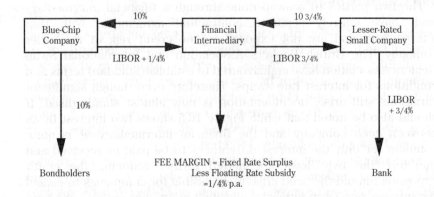

Figure 16.5   Interest rate swap

Note that only the interest payments actually change hands in an interest rate swap. The principal amounts remain with the original borrowers and it is therefore the responsibility of the blue-chip company to redeem its bond issue at maturity, even though the interest payments are being matched by flows from the smaller company. It is the fact that only the interest element is at risk which permits companies of lesser creditworthiness access to fixed-rate funds through swaps, when they would not be an acceptable risk for the full principal amount.

Interest rate and currency swaps evolved from the parallel loan market as explained in the previous chapter. It was not until the 1980s that the swap mechanism was refined sufficiently to create a standardised product. However, since this was achieved, growth in the volume of US dollar interest rate swaps has been explosive and has spread to sterling, yen and Deutschmarks. Other major currencies are likely to experience similar rapid development. Liquid markets exist for swaps in the four currencies mentioned, although US dollar swap liquidity dominates and extends out to 10 years and occasionally beyond. Sterling swaps are much less liquid but are also available out to 10 years and, occasionally, out to 15 years. Minimum amounts are normally $5 million or £3 to £5 million, with $50 million deals being quite common. The availability of swaps gives companies full flexibility in managing their interest rate exposure independently of the underlying loan or deposit, and enables them to switch freely between fixed and floating rates on their borrowings or investments.

The two parties to a swap done through a financial intermediary each have entirely separate contractual agreements with that intermediary and are not exposed to the credit risk of the other company. The British Bankers Association and International Swap Dealers Association have endeavoured to establish standard terms and conditions for interest rate swaps. Therefore even though significant variations still arise, documentation is now almost standardised. It should also be noted that while Figure 16.5 shows two interest flows between each company and the financial intermediary, it is quite common for only the interest differences to be paid or received and therefore the two flows are netted further reducing the credit exposure. Should the need arise it is possible for companies to cancel the interest rate swap either by engaging in another entirely opposite transaction or by closing-out the original swap. The standard documentation incorporates clausing to calculate the amount payable/receivable by the company to or from the financial intermediary. Payment of this termination sum absolves the company of its contractual obligations to the intermediary but without any effect on the other company. These features make swaps a very flexible and secure tool for interest rate management.

Summary

The basic requirements of a Corporate Treasurer in managing interest rate exposure are identical to those for currency exposure management. He needs an appreciation of the nature and potential impact of the risks, adequate data on existing exposures and accurate forecasts of future cash-flows and investments. These ensure he knows where he is starting from and that he also has a good idea of any likely additional exposure that will arise. Next a policy framework and guidelines have to be agreed, preferably at board level. This assists the Corporate Treasurer by defining the limits of his responsibility and thereby facilitates control. He then needs to form a view of both short- and long-term interest rates in the various currencies the company may borrow or invest in. This view should ideally include not only the direction of expected changes of interest rates and future levels, but also some measure of how likely those changes are. This is particularly important when considering option strategies. Finally, he needs an understanding of, and access to, the various instruments described in this chapter so as to be able to select the appropriate instrument to implement strategy decisions.

Having implemented decisions, exposures have to be continuously reported and monitored. This provides feedback on performance relative to policy objectives and also serves as a control on the corporate treasury's activities. Evaluation of performance may lead to revised policies and strategies and also to use of different instruments.

It is impossible to make dogmatic comments as to which instruments or products to use in which situations. Every endeavour should be made to ensure that internal transactions and cash-flow management assist in meeting interest rate exposure objectives. If it is decided to commit to fixing a short rate, FRAs will probably be the most flexible of the instruments described, and have the additional benefits of leaving existing obligations undisturbed and not excessively utilising bank credit lines. Futures can be cumbersome to operate and, with reasonably efficient markets, any benefits are passed on at negligible additional cost to corporate customers through products such as the FRA. If the Corporate Treasurer has significant doubts as to the future path of interest rates, then a strategy using options or option-based products is likely to be appropriate. Options are particularly appropriate for use in situations where future cash-flows are uncertain as to timing or amount. Generally speaking such contingent exposures are best hedged with contingent liabilities such as options.

It is always important to monitor the position and reassess one's view of the future and this is particularly relevant to strategies which employ options as they are readily resaleable. This implies that options are most suitable to active and sophisticated exposure managers — but could prove expensive and unsuitable for the unsophisticated. Their great advantage is flexibility as they can be deployed in combination to achieve almost any exposure objective. The range of products available and the efficiency of major-currency money markets inevitably leads to the conclusion that companies can cover, and should actively consider covering, their interest exposures. As has been explained, 'doing nothing' can be a valid strategy in certain circumstances, but it should be a conscious decision and not because one does not know what to do.

Further Reading

Useful insights into practical difficulties and decision-making in multinational companies can be found in Zenoff (1980). Kenyon (1981) provides a good general introduction to currency exposure management.

Detailed and comprehensive descriptions of specific instruments are provided in the series of Euromoney books (Antl (1986), Fitzgerald (1983, 1987)), whilst the *Financial Times Guide to Statistics* (1984) gives details of many market conventions. Thorough coverage of exchange-rate arithmetic is given in many sources, for example Whiting (1986).

Useful background on corporate debt and capital structure can be found in Henning (1978), Samuels & Wilkes (1981) and Watson & Altringham (1985).

Occasional articles in *The Treasurer* magazine are also recommended.

1   B. Antl, *Swap Finance*, Euromoney Publications, 1986.

2   M. Dickson, Ed., *A Guide to Financial Times Statistics*, revised ed., *Financial Times*, 1987.

3   M. D. Fitzgerald, *Financial Futures*, Euromoney Publications, 1983.

     M. D. Fitzgerald, *Financial Options*, Euromoney Publications, 1987.

4   C. N. Henning, *International Financial Management*, McGraw Hill, 1978.

5   A. Kenyon, *Currency Risk Management*, Wiley, 1981.

6   J. M. Samuels and F. M. Wilkes, *Management of Company Finance*, 4th ed., Van Nostrand Reinhold, 1986.

7   A. J. W. Watson and R. Altringham, *Treasury Management: International Banking Operations*, The Chartered Institute of Bankers, 1986.

8   D. P. Whiting, *Finance of Foreign Trade*, Pitman 1986.

9   D. B. Zenoff, *Management Principles for Finance in the Multinational*, Euromoney Publications, 1980.

CHAPTER 17

Electronic Banking and Cash Management Services

Michael Meltzer

Editor's Notes

Having reviewed methods of financing in earlier chapters, the reader's attention is now drawn to other considerations impacting on the financial decisions of the corporate and its financial well-being, commencing with a discussion on the important part played by transmission services in moving funds to and from the bank accounts of the corporate and providing the Treasurer with information about the balances.

Introduction

How can money be transferred from one organisation to another? Why move the money, and when is there a need for information about the arrival or departure of that money? This chapter addresses these fundamental questions.

In this chapter, therefore, we are interested in any form of trade where there is a need for value to move from one party to another. The form that the underlying transaction takes can have a major impact both on the speed with which that money needs to move and the need for certainty of arrival on a specific date with good value. We are interested in the means of movement and the flows of information rather than the transaction itself.

It is outside the scope of this book to review all the workings of the various clearing/settlement systems in the world. We will concentrate on the services offered by various institutions in the United Kingdom and United States.

As might be expected from a leading financial centre such as London, one of the world's most sophisticated systems for moving value (between parties) exists in the UK. The systems currently available in the UK evolved fairly slowly till the advent of the computer and, latterly, the greater use of telecommunication networks.

Although cash and cheques remain a major medium for the purchase and sale of small items, in this chapter we are more concerned with the movement of value from one *organisation* to another.

Domestic Transfers

Cheque clearing

The principal ways of moving value are the cheque and to a lesser extent giro credits. The period for clearing this paper item varies between same day and three working days after presentation (usually two in the case of large corporates) to the clearing system with slightly longer periods for cheques drawn on Scottish and Irish branches.

Town clearing

Within the City of London a further means of clearing has evolved for items above £100,000 (formerly £10,000), (a) to meet the needs of the City as a financial centre for 'same-day' funds, (b) to be available to settle a wide variety of transactions where title to securities or goods requires 'cash' settlement, or (c) where the amount is significant in interest value terms.

The town clearing operates within the City of London based on cheques being drawn on, and paid in at, one of the 100 or more town clearing branches before 3 p.m. for same-day value. All the branches are within, say, a ten-minute walk of the bankers clearing house to facilitate the clearing process.

The town clearing cheque remained unique in its ability to transfer funds from one party to another on the same day until the advent of systems like CHAPS (Clearing House Automated Payment System). Even with the advent of CHAPS there is still a large volume of high-value cheques and bankers payments being processed via the town clearing.

High-value electronic systems

CHAPS was devised as a means of electronically replacing the paper-based town clearing cheque for items above £7,000. With effect from February 1990, this limit will be lowered to £5,000. There are suggestions that it may be lowered to zero at a future date. It was established by the UK's settlement banks, and based on the same type of central computers using a standardised means of input and output.

Payments are input by means of a terminal and once released the recipient is guaranteed cleared funds. This service is not restricted by location within the UK or abroad as it interfaces with international payment systems as well. A broadly similar system runs in New York called CHIPS but funds movement remains conditional upon settlement at close of business. The current comparable service to CHAPS is a domestic United States-based system called Fedwire in which funds are guaranteed at the moment of release, with debits and credits being posted to accounts that United States domestic banks hold at the Federal Reserve Bank.

In Japan, for example, the comparable system is the Zengin. All institutions that provide payment services are connected to Zengin's computer in Tokyo, through which transfers can be made with no value limits throughout the country.

The CHAPS system can be viewed in the UK as the precursor to terminal-based money transfer services, electronic funds transfer (EFT), now routinely offered to customers. Banks each have or share a computer system that houses gateway software for both accounting and audit trail purposes so that funds can be transferred easily and securely between banks. Access to CHAPS can be via SWIFT, bank developed terminals and computer links which are developing rapidly as banks realise that customers require increasing technological sophistication in the ways information is relayed to them so that they may respond.

Customers must normally deliver their payment instructions before the 3.10 p.m. cut-off time to enable the system to process the payments. The gateways close automatically at 3.10 p.m. Due to the large amounts involved, security features and reliability have to be of a high standard, and CHAPS messages are both authenticated and encrypted on transmission between settlement banks and, in many cases, from user to settlement bank.

Automated Systems

BACS (Bankers Automated Clearing System)

For a large proportion of trade payments and receipts many organisations now use BACS. It was one of the earliest forms of electronic banking originally established as the Inter-Bank Computer Bureau in 1968 and renamed BACS in 1971.

BACS Ltd is owned by the clearing banks whose shareholding is broadly in proportion to the volume that each bank generates, and its main work is the bulk processing of credit transfers, standing orders, direct debits, payroll and other trade payables. The minimum time to process instructions to give the recipient good value is three days as the system is based on batch processing.

When BACS was started all input had to be by magnetic tape, but in 1981 cassette tape and floppy disk were accepted. In 1983 BACSTEL was introduced, which allowed direct telecommunications linkage to pass detailed instructions. A more recent innovation has been the ability to give telephonic payment instructions, based on a set of pre-established procedures.

The ease with which users can now move value through BACS will see its utilisation increase. Given the capabilities of current computer and telecommunication software/hardware the opportunity to offer real-time, same-day BACS might also be possible in the future.

Corporate Treasurer's options
For amounts of £100,000 and above:

(a)   Cheques, including those drawn in the town clearing
(b)   CHAPS payments
(c)   BACS payment
(d)   Bank Giro credit transfers (BGC).

For amounts £99,999.99 or less:

(a)   Cheques
(b)   BACS
(c)   Bank Giro credit transfers (BGC)
(d)   Cash
(e)   CHAPS (for items in excess of £7,000; this limit will be lowered to £5,000 in February, 1990).

For all amounts the telephone transfer system is still in use, though its usage is actively being discouraged.

Assuming the Corporate Treasurer maintains a zero balance approach to bank accounts, the CHAPS payment or town clearing cheque can be effected three days after the due payment date (two in the case of large corporates), giving him three days longer before funding with no loss of value to the beneficiary (two in the case of large corporates). Of these two methods, CHAPS is irrevocable once transmitted, while town clearing cheques remain revocable up to the opening of business on the next banking/business day.

Regular cheques, BACS and BGCs require input to the system three banking days before the beneficiary receives cleared value funds.

Provided the beneficiary does not bank at the paying branch, three days' deferred funding can be operated. However, this payment method is not precise, except for BACS. Under BACS, predefined value dates for simultaneous debit and credit are specified.

Consequently, a Corporate Treasurer can optimise his balance management by choosing one of the above listed instruments.

International Transfers

International money movement

Value transfer occurs by cheque (or draft) and/or by electronic funds transfer via SWIFT (Society for Worldwide Interbank Financial Telecommunication). In the case of non-SWIFT banks it is usual to utilise an authenticated cable or a signed mail payment order. Transfers made by cheques incur deferred good value to the beneficiary commensurate with the clearance procedure for cheques. Wire transfer payment made via SWIFT with cover advices enable Corporate Treasurers to remit funds later than otherwise required, but for the beneficiary to receive cleared funds earlier than had a cheque been used in settlement. From a cash management perspective this is beneficial to both parties.

With more and more banks becoming members of SWIFT, the ultimate settlement of cheque proceeds interbank would be effected via a SWIFT message to the collecting bank's correspondent.

Automation of international funds movement

SWIFT was set up by a number of international banks as a means of transmitting instructions relating to money movement between themselves.

SWIFT has simplified the means of transferring value by providing a fast and secure telecommunications switching system based on a private network. Messages are passed in standard format which facilitates fully-automated handling by computers. An overview of how an instruction flows is provided in Figure 17.1. SWIFT handles bank and customer-to-bank transfers, foreign exchange details, loan and deposit confirmations, collections, securities transactions, account statements (NOSTROs) and special messages. It does not, however, allow non-bank membership. Companies can, therefore, only access SWIFT through the banking system, although there is a possibility of also letting securities/broking houses have access, in the near future. In many ways SWIFT acts as the bank's own cash management/information reporting network.

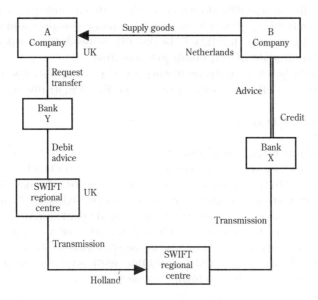

Figure 17.1 SWIFT (Society for Worldwide Interbank Financial Telecommunication)

Cash Management

The modern concept of 'cash management' developed in the USA and spread to Europe in the early 1980s; the catalyst in the UK being the introduction by banks of computer accounting systems. In addition, the abolition of UK exchange controls in 1979 extended the concept to offshore branches and subsidiaries and, hence, international cash management techniques evolved.

In the early stages of the development of what we know today as 'cash management', companies recognised that they could reduce their borrowing costs and improve cash flow if they could speed up their cash collections whilst delaying their payments.

Taking the United States, for example, cheques drawn on a bank in Arizona sent in payment to a company in New York could take up to three weeks to be cleared. This delay before cheques are debited to the account of the drawer is normally termed 'float'. This term needs further clarification, however, as between 'bank float' — that is between the collecting bank and the paying bank — and the 'customer's float' between organisations trading as debtor and creditor. Within the UK system, 'bank float' is very limited and even BACS is 'bank float' free, as the beneficiary and the payee are respectively credited and debited on the same day. In other countries this varies by convention or banking practice, or geography and distance.

Lockboxes
With thousands of United States banks and the numerous ways of disbursing funds, 'customer float' could extend to many days. The 'float game' was further refined over time and extended internationally. As an extreme example, payment for goods imported from Scandinavia was made by cheques — posted from the United States and drawn on an obscure United States regional bank. The time taken to collect these could be up to two months so that the creditor suffered a considerable cash-flow disadvantage and sometimes exchange losses when the cheques were converted to local currency.

One of the first institutions to attempt to reduce this excessive float was RCA in 1947, which asked one bank in Chicago and another in New York to collect payments directly from a post office box and deposit the money in RCA's accounts. This service promoted by banks has become known as the 'lockbox' and cuts the delay in turning receivables into cash by reducing clerical, post and cheque collection time.

The United States has developed the use of lockboxes with the objectives of reducing collection 'float time' and costs. Due to existing United States banking laws, companies often have to use different banks in different cities, i.e. a regional basis.

Lockbox services are offered in the United States by many banks on a regional basis. Instead of cheques being sent to a company's office they are posted to a specific bank's post office box number. The bank collects the cheques at regular intervals throughout the day, processes and then clears them by presentation to the paying bank. The customer's accounts are credited and the customer advised of the amount at the end of each day. Customers and other banks using the service can also receive a full reconciliation service to assist in their accounting procedures. Today many of these are computer based and will interface with a company or bank's internal computing system.

In Europe, few see the need for lockboxes given the relative sophistication of clearing systems and the geographical proximity of most drawer and drawee banks. Each United States bank tends to provide a schedule of availability (value date) regarding cheques collected on behalf of its customers. This will tell the customer the day on which he will receive value regarding cheques drawn anywhere in the United States. To overcome the discrimination on out-of-state cheques various types of lockbox have been developed:

(a) *Bank affiliation* — where a number of interstate banks offer the service, allowing anyone to act as the concentration bank with the others acting as processing banks. Correspondent bank charges are eliminated/waived.

(b) *Mail intercept* — where a bank sets up its own localised mailbox which is cleared by an express courier company each day and the cheques couriered to the centralised processing office.

(c) *Joint venture* — where banks collect the proceeds and large corporates with branch office networks process the cheques on the banks' behalf.

(d) *De novo* — where the bank sets up its own processing centres in key cities with the daily details being transmitted to one focal point.

Advantages

(a) Reduces 'mail float' time.

(b) Improves the cash flow for both the bank and its clients.

(c) Centralised processing reduces costs such as account maintenance fees, wire transfers, deposit charges (by avoiding superfluous accounts) and clearing local cheques by eliminating the Federal Reserve Bank's per item clearance costs.

Risks

(a) Because of delegated control, loss of one day's funds availability can occur if a clearance 'deadline' is missed.

(b) By using correspondent banks double charges may be incurred.

(c) Potential liquidity problems if the correspondent bank exceeds its Federal Reserve Bank balance sheet requirements which would result in cash resources being frozen and therefore the lockbox holder's account not receiving its funds.

Growth of Cash Management and Corporate Treasury Management

After the success of RCA's venture in reducing float and improving the process of cash collection, other companies adopted the practice which soon became prevalent throughout the United States. To overcome the problems of corporates that were multi-banked because of state laws (Glass Steagall Act), other cash management techniques have developed such as electronic funds transfer and balance/ transaction reporting.

United States banks have also been largely responsible for the development of electronic 'cash management' services globally, but their introduction into Europe was not without its problems. Few United States banks recognised the need to adapt their products to meet the needs of the European corporate, and in many cases the products on offer were United States systems with the programmes adjusted simply for the currency of the country concerned. Local clearing arrangements and the European value dating procedures had not been catered for. This required fundamental changes to the systems and a fresh approach to their marketing strategies. The typical services now offered by both European and United States banks are money movement via terminal/personal computer and balance/ transaction reporting. Many elements of so-called cash management services have been available for some years, i.e. sweep (automatic balance investment) accounts, netting facilities, etc., although it is only in the 1980s with the advent of the personal computer that these functions have been more accessible to the Corporate Treasurer. Sweep accounts are so called because at a predetermined time each day the aggregated balance is automatically transferred to an overnight investment fund. The principal is returned to the main account on the next business day with the interest being paid monthly (if the account is located in the United States) or daily (if in Europe).

The receipt of timely and accurate information on account balances has become an early morning necessity for today's Corporate Treasurer. It provides him with the essential information on funds availability to cover payments, make investment decisions and other operational needs. In some instances it enables the slow payers to be identified earlier. The ability to effect payments in advance, in the certain knowledge that value will be received on the required payment date, facilitates the funding process and cash management procedures. Few treasurers other than in the financial services sector have taken advantage of some of the latest innovations such as 'real-time' reporting, primarily due to internal company budgetary restraints and the high cost of accessing real-time systems.

The real-time facilities tend to relate to activities such as electronic funds transfer in sterling, for example, CHAPS. Tracking cross-border currency transfers in real-time is still difficult, however, due to time-zone differences, third-party correspondent processing procedures, confirmation of receipt of cover, etc.

Many other electronic services are now being offered to the corporate and personal customer, for example, letters of credit, commercial paper, securities purchase and sale, etc. Additionally, the current availability of decision support and management information systems is making the highly sophisticated corporates more demanding in their requirements for electronic banking services.

Cash management and corporate treasury management
The banks are realising that their customers' needs are global and not just limited to their home base, and therefore they must develop international communication networks and a high degree of technical expertise.

It follows from this that there is an increasing need for specialist electronic banking and cash managers to support the more traditional generalist corporate account manager. Banks are now in the business of selling technology as well as the traditional lending and treasury products.

Traditional banking relationships are, therefore, at risk from banks supplying superior electronic banking services. Defending multi-national relationships requires a service to the customer across a wide spectrum of electronic operational products. With greater opportunities for corporates to raise funds through the securities markets at prices that are not attractive to banks, the need for operational revenues which these products can generate is of increasing importance.

The ability to manage funds on an international basis through modern international cash management systems allows treasury departments to be centralised and on occasions take on the characteristics of an in-house bank. Some of the most sophisticated corporates have gone as far as to purchase computer software originally designed for banks. BP Finance is, to all intents and purposes, a bank and carries out many of the functions of a bank dealing room. Further changes are likely as the larger corporate makes greater use of its own internal computer/communication capabilities and closer links with banks' computer systems are established.

Future developments will allow corporate customers to largely eliminate paper-based correspondence with banks. This is happening now as personal computers and mainframes are linked to the customer's own personal computer/systems through secure communication links. They not only provide the basic balance and transaction reports but additional services such as letters of credit, electronic mail, bank bulletins, interest/forex rates, electronic data interchange (EDI), etc.

Corporate Treasurer's view

A group Treasurer is one of the few people in a company to be able to take a 'bird's-eye view' of the overall position. This global perspective enables him to make decisions on:

(a) hedging methods, i.e. to protect the company from market fluctuations in currency or interest rates;

(b) offsetting, i.e. a net daily debit or credit position across all accounts within the same currency for interest accrual purposes; and/or

(c) leading and lagging techniques, i.e. whether to advance or retard settlement of international commitments to take advantage of interest rate differentials and forward currency rates.

To optimise the benefits from these decisions, multi-bank reporting systems into a separate spreadsheet-type package are sought. Armed with this information, the type of funding, its currency and its timing all contribute additionally to a company's profitability. Corporate Treasurers in the future will react to market changes in direct competition to current bank treasury departments. Consequently, they will utilise the same resources for financial movements currently available to banks and therefore total electronic links will be the norm.

A further requirement of corporates will be a download capability of financial (bank) information direct into corporates' mainframe computers without rekeying. Already the larger corporates have developed their own internal systems to meet this requirement.

Corporate Treasurers are rapidly expecting the banks to eliminate float totally by use of value dating and at the same time insisting on transaction costs being reduced to nominal levels. The future will see Corporate Treasurers negotiating flat rates for global banking relationships/business. Failure to provide the excellent service demanded will result in global relationships being terminated.

Deadlines currently imposed upon banks will be identical with those applicable to the large corporations. Those banks unable to supply 'state of the art' electronics will not only be redundant in the global arena but will become subservient to larger corporations. As these companies grow, and the level of electronic usage increases, it is probable that large corporations will institute net settlement between themselves, eliminating banks as the intermediaries. In order for banks to protect their own interests they must at all times be aware of corporates' financial needs and be able to supply new products to meet this ever more sophisticated market. An increasing tendency is for pseudo-joint ventures to be conducted between market leaders in financial products and the financial institutions (banks). These enable tailormade packages to be devised which service both financial institutions' needs exactly.

CHAPTER 18

Taxation and Overseas Investment

Peter Davies

Editor's Notes

Over and above day-to-day financing problems, the Corporate Treasurer must never lose sight of the impact of taxation, and an outline of some of the more fundamental aspects is given before a discussion on the impact of investment overseas, which many companies find difficult even though they take domestic investment in their stride.

Introduction

The objective of this chapter is to draw the reader's attention to a number of other factors which influence the financial decisions of the major corporate. Concepts such as currency and the interest rate exposure management have already been dealt with in earlier chapters and specific instruments are available for dealing with them. However, in the case of the factors discussed in this chapter there are no mechanical devices available to help out the Corporate Treasurer.

It should be stressed at the start that many companies are likely to have a different approach to these problems and even the same company may change its approach over time, particularly as its business changes or the company becomes less or more liquid.

It should also be stressed that this chapter does not attempt to give the reader a comprehensive description or treatment of these various subjects. What it does do however, is to point the student in the direction of a few basic principles.

Taxation

Because a multinational usually has companies operating in different tax regimes and subject to a wide variety of different conditions it has opportunities to achieve the optimisation of its tax position. In order to achieve this a company's tax planners inevitably have access to a vast amount of data regarding the tax position, projected profits, cash flows and inter-company payments in each of their group companies. This is necessary because, among other things, they are operating in different tax regimes with different rates of tax and different fiscal year-ends (indeed some of the subsidiaries may have different accounting periods from that of the parent). In addition, different tax treatment may obtain for the same particular operation (e.g. in some cases certain items are chargeable to tax where in others they are not), and the ever-present uncertainty that regulations may change, will mean that a company by adopting different practices may or may not have to pay more or less tax.

It is generally accepted that the objective of any tax planning shall be the maximisation of post-tax cash flow and in addition the Corporate Treasurer will wish to achieve this maximisation of cash flow in currencies which are relatively strong as opposed to weak ones.

It should also be accepted that there are times when the Corporate Treasurer will not necessarily pursue a policy which will be in-line with the recommendation of his tax planners. He may decide that in the long run it is better perhaps to pay slightly more tax in order to achieve greater liquidity in the short run. This must always be a consideration since it is part of the finance function to support the business objectives of the group and to define ways of financing these at the optimum cost, but within such provisos there are certain general principles which influence corporates in their tax planning, for example:

(a)   It is generally considered desirable to maximise any borrowing in high tax areas because, provided the company is making profits or alternatively can carry forward tax losses for reasonable periods, the tax concession on interest is potentially valuable. In this context it should be remembered that whilst in almost every tax regime interest on borrowings is allowable for tax purposes many tax regimes restrict the amount which may be charged against tax in those cases where a company has a relatively small capital in relation to its borrowings. This restricts the opportunities to be gained by non-resident controlling shareholders from 'thin capitalisation', i.e. the policy whereby the shareholders' stake in the company is minimised and borrowings maximised, which in countries with high interest rates is a much used tactic employed by many companies. It is not illogical therefore for a company with a relatively small capital in relation to its financial needs, to be interested in leasing as much of its equipment as possible rather than to buy, since that would doubtless impact upon the borrowing levels.

(b)   From the taxation point of view, it is usually considered desirable to maximise borrowing in high interest rate weaker currencies than in lower rate strong ones, partly because of the point made above, namely that interest can usually be offset against tax, but more importantly capital losses on revaluation of foreign currency liabilities are not normally chargeable to tax. There were numerous examples in the 1970s where UK companies borrowed Swiss francs under the impression that the low interest rate would be an advantage to them, only to find that on repayment they were not allowed to charge the cost of the parity changes to tax.

(c)   The fact that a country may have very high tax rates is not normally a reason for deciding against investment in that particular country. This is because many countries with high taxation levels have an extremely well-developed social infrastructure, e.g. hospital, schools, etc., which saves the company spending additionally on this over and above what is already paid to its expatriate workers. In addition, most such countries normally have available well-developed transport and communication facilities as well as an educated workforce. These factors usually outweigh by a considerable margin any apparent advantage which a lower tax structure might suggest.

(d)   Where interest rates on delayed tax payments are less than current interest rates (this has frequently been the case in the UK) it is to the advantage of the company to delay such payments.

(e)   In countries where there is an annual tax on net worth it is important to distribute as much as possible from profits and to increase borrowings to the greatest possible extent.

(f)   It is normal to use tax havens in order to accumulate surplus income and dividends in order to avoid tax overspill. By pooling dividends before transmission to the parent this can be achieved and is particularly important if the parent is established in a tax regime with relatively low tax rates as has been the case recently in Britain where the tax rates from corporates have, over the last few years, been reduced from 52% down to 35%.

(g)   Tax havens should be used to raise loans etc., for example Eurobonds on which interest can be paid without deduction of tax. Interest on marketable securities issued *outside* tax havens is normally paid after tax has been deducted, thus making such bonds less attractive to the investor. It should be remembered that tax havens have only a limited advantage to a corporate since in almost every case as soon as profits are remitted from the tax haven to any of the countries in which the corporate is operating, those remittances become taxable income on the part of the recipient.

(h) Corporates are intensely concerned with the taxation rules regarding new financial instruments. It is of little benefit to a Corporate Treasurer to be offered a sophisticated financial instrument only for him to discover subsequently that its tax treatment is more onerous than he expected and that the marginal saving in interest cost is more than outweighed by the additional cost incurred because the cost of the instrument is not allowable for tax purposes. In this context, banks have been criticised justifiably by corporates in marketing financial products without knowing what the reaction of the Revenue is likely to be.

(i) It is fundamental that a multinational will try to ensure that it allows its untaxed profits to accumulate in a country which has the lowest rate of tax.

(j) Double taxation agreements covering reduced rates of withholding tax on such items as dividends, royalty payments and interest exist between many countries (the UK has such mutual arrangements with over 80). In addition UK domestic tax legislation provides for relief in respect of foreign tax levied on profits in those countries with which no formal double taxation agreements exist. It should be noted however that taxes related to turnover or capital and net worth are not included. As far as the UK is concerned these concessions ensure that whilst such payments may be taxed twice, none are in effect taxed at a higher rate than the total which obtains in the UK (currently 35%) unless the overseas country's tax rate is higher, in which case no additional UK tax is deducted.

The banker is never in a position to know the whole picture of a multinational company's tax position. Nevertheless there are a number of other factors which ought to be known to him such as the dates on which taxes are due to be paid, for example in the UK post-1964 companies must pay their tax nine months after their financial year (i.e. a company whose financial year ends on the 31 December has to pay its mainstream corporation tax on 1 October following). The concession enjoyed by pre-1964 companies will disappear following changes in the 1988 Budget and, ultimately, they will have to pay tax in-line with the nine-month rule. The banker should also know when advance corporation tax (ACT) is payable as this is on an identifiable date following the end of the quarter in which the dividend is paid. Whilst ACT is deducted from the mainstream tax it should not be overlooked that this is normally payable well before the mainstream tax is due. (Similarly the dates on which value added tax has to be paid should also be known.) Any well-run company makes provision for these payments of tax and ensures that adequate liquidity is available. It should be noted that the recent introduction of schemes by corporates in Britain whereby they enable shareholders to receive their dividends in the form of shares reduces the amount of ACT payable, and gives the corporate the use of that amount until mainstream tax is due.

Investment Overseas

It is outside the scope of this chapter to comment on, let alone analyse, all the reasons why corporates decide on expansion overseas as opposed to further domestic activity but it is appropriate to identify and comment on financial issues related to the implementation of the decision to invest offshore. Many of these are similar to those arising in a purely domestic situation, but are rather more difficult to resolve.

Financial problems attaching to investment overseas can, to a great extent, be avoided by good planning, a process which should commence long before the start of any negotiations, since any decision to invest is a strategic one, and whether offshore or in the domestic environment, planning is an essential and integral part of it. To decide on an overseas investment with neither a careful examination of the alternatives, nor within a previously agreed strategy, is usually an expensive gamble. Within the strategic planning process therefore based on a SWOT analysis (an analysis of the organisation's strengths and weaknesses, the opportunities offered by the former and the threats and dangers arising from the latter) and such questions as, for example, 'where should our company be in 5 to 10 years' time?', the company will decide on sectors of business it should pursue and in which markets. From these a logical decision should flow as to which countries would provide the best opportunities and probably also the form of investment which might be made, for example, a sales office; a sales, service, and distribution organisation; or a manufacturing plant. Such an analysis would also point to whether the expansion should be by way of an acquisition or by the establishment of a subsidiary or branch of the company's own organisation.

As part of an examination of the alternatives the likely financial requirement can be gauged with any acquisition likely to be, at least in the short run, more expensive than any going-it-alone policy.

If the acquisition path is chosen it is normal to draw up a profile of the desired investment, from which certain potential target companies can be identified. Should a more detailed analysis confirm the desirability of making a bid an appropriate strategy should be drawn up in order to facilitate the acquisition process. This strategy may include the delegation of specific authority to certain named people and set down both the financial limits, and precisely how the operation is to be funded. Where this requires increased capital the shareholders' authority for its raising should be obtained well in advance.

The establishment of a limit for the cash element of the bid which the company will not, in any circumstances, exceed is essential since the acquisition must be well within the company's resources so that additional sums can still be made available to meet unexpected needs in other parts of the business and hopefully to retain something in reserve. Any amounts beyond that specified figure of cash to be available should be met by providing for the purchase price to be partly in the form of shares usually in the parent (or possibly in the company acquired).

There is grave danger whenever influential persons within the corporate become enthusiastic about a 'once in a lifetime opportunity' which requires an immediate decision or which does not allow a proper investigation and analysis. Usually such opportunities are a little outside the scope of the company's plan and there is strong temptation to revise the strategy or amend the criteria in order to justify the decision to go ahead. It is in such cases that the financial requirements usually increase rapidly and the need to exercise close control of the acquired organisation and for its effective management becomes even more acute. One only has to consider the effect of the acquisition by Midland Bank of the Crocker Bank in California to recognise how easily foreign adventures can prove costly not only in monetary terms but also in terms of reputation and market share, especially where inadequate control is exercised.

Well-tried methods exist for avoiding trouble when acquiring a privately-controlled company, and these are equally applicable whether the acquisition is overseas or in the domestic market. Provided that the acquisition fully meets the criteria laid down for expansion, and adequate research has been completed, the investing company should be willing to agree to pay a reasonably generous amount for the purchase, subject to certain specific conditions, for example, the following are typical in the case of agreed bids

(a)   Payment to be made partly in shares and partly in cash.
(b)   Half the purchase price should be paid immediately and the balance in two/three or even more equal instalments only when specific profit forecasts have been achieved, with additional amounts being payable to the vendors if these profit targets are exceeded by agreed amounts.
(c)   The more useful members of the existing management team should be retained with the offer of attractive profit-sharing incentives.
(d)   The vendors must take responsibility for discharging all existing contracts (including those with personnel).
(e)   Unless the debtors' figure is of modest proportions there should be a condition that the purchase price is reduced by that amount and the vendors be left to collect these items for their own account. As an alternative to this any shortfall on collection of debtors should be deducted from later instalments of the purchase price. A similar practice should be adopted regarding estimates of tax payable which turn out to be rather less than is subsequently required.

In the case of contested bids, other more complicated issues are involved which are outside the scope of this book.

The imposition of vigorous overall management will be needed from the start and there must be no delay in the identification and solution of the problems which will doubtless exist within the company acquired. It is often said that no company worth selling is ever put up for sale and for this reason alone the buyers must expect to find some skeletons in the cupboard and therefore adopt a determined cleansing operation from the first day. This is usually achieved rapidly if retained executives are encouraged by good performance related bonuses, etc.

The importance of financial planning of the acquisition process cannot be underestimated since the immediate impact on the cash flow of a purchase price payable in instalments is considerably reduced as is the situation in which a significant proportion of the price is payable in the form of shares. The Finance Director of the company will wish to see these factors reflected in the terms finally agreed, and furthermore the board should have decided beforehand, in conjunction with the Finance Director, precisely what methods are to be used to find the available cash.

That the acquisition is on a relatively small scale does not mean that the planning process and the identification of criteria to be applied (including the maximum amount payable in cash) can be neglected, or that vigorous management will be unnecessary.

The alternative of setting up the company's own operation overseas offers choices ranging from a local sales office right up to a fully-integrated manufacturing enterprise, with commensurate variations in cost. At one extreme the possibility that the sales office can operate from rented premises with leased office equipment and motor vehicles is one which will reduce the level of working capital required, an advantage not only in the minimal impact on the cash flow of the parent but equally important there will be no adverse effect on the balance sheet due to potential translation losses, nor will there be problems as regards the loss of capital if the sales office has to be closed down.

A sales service and distribution network could also be set up with relatively little impact on cash flow by means of leased premises, equipment and vehicles, but the relatively larger stock which such an organisation would have to maintain has to be financed somehow, but frequently by the parent and other group companies with a corresponding adverse impact on their individual liquidity, and often on that of the group as a whole.

At the other end of the scale, a production plant is likely to require considerable capital investment and here again whilst some plant, equipment and premises can be leased a considerable working capital to finance wages, local purchases and debtors will be needed until proceeds of sales begin to exceed outgoings, and this may be a lengthy process even though generous credit periods may be negotiated with some suppliers to help the cash flow. It should not be overlooked that extended credit periods granted by other group companies can have a seriously adverse effect on their liquidity and restrict their flexibility and scope for expansion.

Many companies establishing overseas operations pursue a policy to maximise local domestic borrowing rather than to provide adequate capital or loans from group sources, or to borrow internationally especially where they regard the local currency as being weaker than their own. Even though this may be relatively expensive it avoids translation losses in the balance sheet and if any form of ex-appropriation by the host country should take place the parent is likely to lose considerably less than if it had itself provided finance either in the form of capital or loans. Similarly, any guarantee given by the parent to secure the borrowing will become less onerous if the local currency weakens in relation to its own. This practice of protecting the parent company's position at the expense of the overseas subsidiary has from time to time been pursued with such ruthlessness by some multinationals that they have earned a bad name for MNCs as a whole, and many countries now operate credit or exchange control restrictions on companies controlled from overseas so as to ensure that they are properly capitalised, and tax legislation frequently exists which makes it relatively expensive for the parent if it is unwilling or unable to provide adequate finance for its subsidiary. The tax aspects of this, usually called, 'thin capitalisation', are mentioned earlier in this chapter.

Branch or subsidiary
A broadly similar legal environment controlling commercial activity exists in most countries including those LDCs where legislation imposed by former colonial powers usually continues relatively unchanged, and most countries recognise the concept of the limited liability company as distinct from its shareholders. Differences in corporate legislation for example may include:

(a)   The imposition of minimum capital requirements.
(b)   Registration locally with chambers of commerce as opposed to State registration in the USA or central registration as in Britain.
(c)   The requirement that named individuals have specified levels of responsibility and liability.

Nevertheless, there may be good reason why an organisation prefers to set-up overseas by establishing a branch rather than a subsidiary quite apart from any requirements of the authorities either in its own or in the host country.

The taxation can be the deciding factor, as in those cases where the profits of a branch attract lower rates of tax than those applicable to locally-incorporated companies or in those countries where there is an annual tax on net worth. Similarly, in some countries there may be significant disadvantages in having a locally-incorporated company, since whereas dividends are taxed, remittances from a branch to its parent are often not treated as dividends.

Experience shows that except in the case of a small sales operation most companies' expansion overseas is in the form of locally-incorporated companies which suggests that on balance there are usually greater benefits from so doing, and among the more obvious advantages are:

(a)   It may avoid restrictions on local borrowing due to thin capitalisation. Adequate capitalisation is also necessary to provide business confidence and, because there can be considerable difficulties in proving that a branch is actually employing a specified amount of capital, the formal capitalisation which is an essential characteristic of a corporate places this matter beyond doubt.

(b)   It avoids direct legal involvement of the parent for the liabilities of its subsidiary whereas its liability in respect of a branch's debts could involve the parent in uncertainty and expense.

(c)   It facilitates the inclusion of local partners or at worst the disposal of the whole.

(d)   Whilst from time to time there may be advantages in the tax position of a branch as opposed to that of an independently-incorporated subsidiary, tax regulations over a period can change considerably which might nullify any earlier advantage of adopting the other policy.

Protecting one's overseas investment

Companies with investments and subsidiaries overseas use a variety of mechanisms in order to protect both the value of their investment and to ensure that adequate proportions of the earnings of the subsidiary are remitted back to the parent.

The most common methods of extracting profits from a subsidiary are:

(a)   *To raise the price of all goods supplied from other members of the group to that particular subsidiary* (transfer pricing). However, where there are significant customs duties added to the price of goods imported, this practice can add considerably to the ultimate market price of the product and make it uncompetitive when offered for sale in the country where the subsidiary is operating. In addition, some tax regimes may assess the subsidiary for additional tax on the assumption that its purchases from its parents are priced so as to minimise profit and tax payable.

(b)   *To charge royalty, licence or management fees on an annual basis.* However, many tax regimes regard such payments as disguised dividends and these are often taxed as such. This reduces the effectiveness of such practices except that the regular payment of these fees tends to be made at an earlier date than would have been the case if they had been paid in the form of a dividend, and it would be by no means abnormal for licence and even management fees to be paid in advance. In addition, such fees are payable regardless of whether a profit has been made by the subsidiary.

(c)   *To maximise two-way trading.* Where an overseas subsidiary or sales office is both importing and exporting it is usual for the parent company to take a large proportion of its subsidiary's exports and market them in its own name thereby providing it with the opportunity to make more profit from the subsidiary, and indeed sometimes it would pay the subsidiary at a discounted rate for the goods taken. Similarly, there is no reason why a sales office should not act as an export agent for other host country products using the group's network to provide sales outlets.

(d)   *To control credit periods.* Another method is to allow the subsidiary minimal credit periods on items supplied. This could be done by the drawing of sight bills in respect of each shipment from the parent. A similar practice would be to include substantial interest rate clauses on any such bill. Another method would be for the subsidiary to open letters of credit in favour of its parent but this is a relatively expensive process.

Tax authorities in every country are concerned to ensure that non-resident controlled enterprises at least pay a reasonable amount of tax in comparison with the scale of operations conducted by similar indigenous companies. Methods developed by these non-resident controlled companies to minimise tax they pay are usually countered by changes to the local tax legislation at regular updating intervals.

Summary

From the foregoing it will be noted that companies operating on an international scale as opposed to a purely domestic one face rather more complicated problems in order to optimise the cash flow and profitability of their operations overall. Only by having available comprehensive information as to the position of the various group companies throughout the world, together with a sound understanding of the various financing mechanisms available to him, can the Corporate Treasurer hope to achieve a successful balance between the demands of the situation and the resources available to the group.

Further Reading

The Treasurer: October 1987, 'Mergers, Acquisitions and Disvestments', January 1989, 'Mergers and Acquisitions'.

CHAPTER 19

Trade Finance Instruments

John Bateman

Editor's Notes

Although a number of the financing mechanisms discussed in this chapter have been considered earlier, an opportunity is taken to reconsider them from the viewpoint of the importer and exporter.

Overview

Over the past decade we have witnessed great changes in the price of energy, a worldwide recession, and the debt crisis in Latin America which, coupled with the development and liberalisation of financial markets, have all led to interest rate and exchange rate volatility. These factors have added to the problems facing the exporter while simultaneously increasing the competition for a declining pool of contracts.

In the face of such difficulties it may seem surprising that companies continue to export. However, world trade is expanding at about twice the rate of the global average domestic GDP and just as importantly many national markets are too small to allow competitive production of most products. These factors drive companies to trade on an international basis so that they can continue to grow at a profit and so secure continued employment and wealth for themselves and their nation.

The major problems that affect the exporter are:

(a)   The buyer's requirement for extended credit terms.
(b)   The exporter's need to manage both his balance sheet and cash flow to ensure the most efficient use of financial resources.
(c)   The exporter's requirement to protect the quality of the earnings stream through the mitigation of risk.

The key feature in this situation is the respective parties' perception of any particular risk and their willingness or otherwise to accept that risk. Risk may take many forms, but central to all trade transactions is the failure of either the buyer or seller to fulfil their obligations — either in terms of equipment performance or payment default. To this is added a further dimension in the form of political risk where changes in foreign government policy cause trade disruptions. Therefore, broadly speaking, the risks can be categorised as follows:

(a)   Commercial credit risk
(b)   Performance risk
(c)   Political risk.

Risk can be reduced in a number of ways but one of the most common is through the introduction of third parties, not central to the essentially bilateral nature of a trading relationship, to remove or reduce the level of risk or recourse to buyer or seller. Third parties are usually either export credit agencies or the banks.

For many centuries the world's banking community has acted as the conduit through which funds have flowed to allow goods to move in the opposite direction. Over time, however, the demand for credit has grown and the banks have responded typically with recourse to one of the parties — most commonly the exporter himself or the supporting government agency (usually a credit insurer).

In recent years, however, the world's banks have needed to provide non-recourse funding and this has prompted them to move into areas which were formerly the preserve of the specialist risk-takers known as export finance houses, confirming houses and the like. This transition has called on a multi-disciplined and multi-skilled approach demanding a knowledge of a far wider range of techniques than before. Nowadays the banker is to be seen beside the corporate right at the outset of the contract negotiations using his knowledge to help the client secure a profitable contract.

Notwithstanding the buyer's requirement for credit, it should be remembered that a large proportion of world trade is conducted on a cash or near cash basis with no credit term involved. Demands for credit are however still escalating, fuelled by two powerful and conflicting market forces. Firstly, there is simple competition. Exporting countries are competing ever more fiercely to sell their goods and services and this has made the finance package a vital and indispensable part of the product mix. The second force exacerbates the competitive pressure. It is the regression of the markets, the dwindling of good quality market opportunities as in real terms many countries become poorer and are in need of extended credit. In fact many countries now find themselves unable to service their debts and they are teetering on the brink of opting out of the world monetary system altogether. This has given rise to the sudden and dramatic growth in non-money payment solutions such as countertrade.

The requirement to offer extended credit to a potentially weaker quality of risk has led the exporter to consider more seriously the implications for his future earnings, balance-sheet strength and cash flow. To hold a five-year, or perhaps longer, receivable of doubtful quality is clearly less favourable than having the cash immediately, without recourse. Against this benefit must be offset the charges made by the party which removes the risk having given due consideration to the cost of capital savings and the opportunity cost/benefit derived from improving the cash-flow cycle.

In the preceding paragraphs we have outlined the forces shaping the demand for credit and the impact this can have on the exporter and his balance sheet. As stated previously it is the role of the banks, government and private credit agencies and development organisations to offer a means of improving the exporter's position in respect of one or more of the factors involved.

To simplify our analysis of the various trade finance techniques, we can identify two different types of trade finance mechanisms; the first under the heading of 'with recourse' to the exporter and the second 'without recourse'. This is an over simplification but it does provide us with a framework for discussion.

With Recourse Finance

A broad definition of 'with recourse' would be 'the provision of finance in a manner such that in the event of non-payment of the underlying trade debt the lender has a right to claim for recovery of the debt either in whole or part against the borrower'. We will now go on to discuss some of the possibilities.

Overdraft facility

The exporter can finance his export sales through his existing overdraft facility with the bank. This is simple, quick and convenient because it enables the exporter to drawdown funds from the overdraft without additional documentation to finance construction and work-in-progress with replenishment coming from the sale proceeds. However, there are some obvious disadvantages. First, the size of the facility is based on the exporter's balance sheet strength so there may not be room within the credit facility to support the particular transaction or series of transactions. Secondly, and perhaps more importantly, the financier has full recourse to the exporter and the risk is not therefore mitigated.

The need to provide working capital for the export contract could restrict the amount of funds available or result in a poorly-managed balance sheet. Moreover, the overdraft can only be used to finance short-term trade debt because of its 'on demand' nature. As a result, as business increases it is unlikely that an exporter can finance overseas sales entirely from overdraft. Finally, it should be noted that it will often be more expensive to finance exports by this mechanism than by other methods.

Advance against bills of exchange
Provided that the only document required for payment is a bill of exchange the exporter could arrange finance against this instrument. In this case the exporter would obtain an advance from his bank against the face value of a bill of exchange drawn by him on an overseas buyer under the terms of the supply contract. In practice, the exporter would take the bill to the bank which would advance an agreed percentage of the face value immediately and undertake to present the bill to the overseas buyer for collection through the banking system. In the event of non-payment on the maturity date the bank has full recourse to the exporter for the loss so the exporter carries the risk on his balance sheet. The exporter does benefit from improved cash flow and more efficient use of financial resources but there are other disadvantages in addition to the risk aspect. For instance, interest is typically charged at a margin over base rate which does not necessarily relate to the quality of either buyer or supplier.

Bill negotiation facility
An alternative method is a bill negotiation facility whereby the exporter's bank agrees to purchase the bills on presentation. The bank will send the bills for collection overseas and reimburse itself when the funds arrive. However, despite the apparent assumption of risk implied by this structure, the facility is with recourse because the bank will require the exporter to make reimbursement in full should any difficulty arise. The advantages and disadvantages are similar to an advance against bills, and both methods can be used with documentary collections.

Documentary collection

The documentary collection provides a link between with recourse and non-recourse finance because it offers the exporter some degree of security, or at least the ability to obtain some degree of security, in that he can maintain title to the goods through the bank. Release of the documents of title can be contingent upon the buyer's acceptance of the bill of exchange, or indeed the buyer's cash payment. However, the bank only undertakes to collect the payment on the exporter's behalf and while it will act upon the exporter's instructions it does not undertake to ensure payment. More importantly, the bank disclaims liability for any failure on the part of the bank overseas to carry out its instructions.

Documentary credits

The documentary credit, on the other hand, is normally drawn up so as to guarantee payment and as such is the first stage in a movement to non-recourse finance. A documentary credit is structured so that a bank, typically domiciled in the buyer's country, will agree to make payment to the exporter subject to compliance with its terms. Moreover, if the supplier does not feel satisfied with this first assurance of payment he can request that a second bank, typically domiciled in his own country, add a further conditional guarantee of payment (confirmation).

The documentary letter of credit begins therefore to address some of the major concerns of the exporter in that a bank will stand in the buyer's shoes. The exporter is relieved of the considerations of buyer risk and with confirmation he is also relieved of country risk. However, the undertaking which the banks make to the exporter is conditional. Notwithstanding this the exporter is left with the problem that he has to comply exactly with the terms of the letter of credit and if he cannot meet the terms as laid down then he should negotiate a suitable amendment. This can cause quite a few problems including time delay. It should also be made clear that there is a limit to the availability of both risk mitigation (through confirmation) and finance. The financing agent bears the risk himself without recourse to the exporter once he has added his conditional guarantee, and this means that risk mitigation and finance may not be available in those markets for which they are most desired. The pricing of these two aspects may be dependent upon the quality of the bank requesting confirmation and the country risk involved. It would be for the contracting parties to determine how these charges are to be met.

From the importer's perspective the documentary credit is a means of ensuring the quality of goods he has purchased and may also provide him with a short-term credit period. It should be noted, however, that banks deal in documents and not the goods themselves and, therefore, banks can only be responsible for the correctness of the documents presented under the credit.

So the documentary credit can provide short-term credit to the buyer while mitigating risk and protecting cash flow and earnings for the supplier.

Credit Insurance

Another means of mitigating risk is insurance, which in fact falls into two categories, government-backed credit insurance and private market insurance.

Government-backed insurance cover

The British Government established the Export Credits Guarantee Department (ECGD) to provide and administer insurance cover for British companies trading overseas. By using this cover the risks of selling abroad can be greatly reduced.

ECGD divides risk into two categories, commercial and political, and it is possible for the exporter to include the majority of his potential risk under both of these categories. The commercial risks relate to non-payment of a debt because the buyer fails to pay for various reasons which could include insolvency.

The political risks, as implied, relate to non-payment of a debt for political reasons, for example, a general moratorium on external debt decreed by the government of the buyer's country. ECGD usually provides 90% cover for commercial risks and 95% for political risks. This means that in most cases at least the cost of production and shipment will be recovered. It should be noted that a claim by a policyholder on ECGD for a loss due to commercial reasons may affect future premiums, but this will not apply to losses relating to political risk. Furthermore, the percentage of cover may be reduced for policyholders with poor track records, which helps to ensure that the exporter will exercise care in his choice of buyer. It is also possible for the exporter to offer credit and yet obtain cash on shipment against the protection of these insurance policies, thus satisfying his two other major needs. This aspect is considered in the next section.

However, it should be noted that the supplier is not protected against the risk of his own non-performance. A point emphasised by the fact that ECGD requires the exporter to enter into a recourse agreement prior to issuing the policy. This recourse would be for 100% of the debt in the case of the exporter's own non-performance or for the residual 5 or 10% in the case of non-payment for commercial or political reasons. In view of this the finance available against this type of insurance is considered to be limited recourse finance.

Limited Recourse Finance

Short-term credit

As stated earlier, it is possible for the exporter to make use of ECGD insurance cover to enable him to obtain finance usually from his bank. In the case of short-term regular trade for consumer goods, the exporter could pass over full administration to the bank under a joint policy arrangement or maintain his own policy. In both instances the exporter would need to offer ECGD and the bank a reasonable spread of the total export turnover.

The exporter has to be acceptable to ECGD because of the recourse aspect mentioned earlier and the buyers must also be approved prior to insurance cover or finance being made available. Once these steps have been taken the exporter has only to submit a bill of exchange or invoice to receive 90% finance on shipment with the balance paid on receipt of debt. The costs to the exporter are interest charged on the daily outstanding balances plus the cost of the insurance premium.

Clearly these schemes have advantages:

(a)   They remove the majority of commercial and political risk subject to performance of contract.
(b)   They facilitate the provision of finance on shipment.

However, there are certain disadvantages:

(a)   There is an element of recourse.
(b)   Some facilities may be inflexible, requiring the exporter to offer a good spread of turnover.
(c)   There are time delays should a claim ensue.

Medium-term finance

In the case of semi-capital and capital goods, ECGD can provide a guarantee to the banks to secure advances made to finance goods and services sold on credit terms of two years or more. The guarantee covers the full amount of the bank's loan and so the bank will normally offer to provide finance to the exporter. This type of finance is provided at a fixed and preferential rate of interest for the life of the loan.

There are two broad mechanisms by which medium-term credit is made available to the overseas buyer:

(a)   Lending to the supplier who passes the credit terms on to the buyer in the terms of his contract of sale (supplier credit).
(b)   Lending direct to the importer (buyer credit).

Like all risk assessors ECGD does not consider all markets to be creditworthy and it will also take a view on the quality of the borrower. The other major caveat is that ECGD will only grant a limited range of credit periods and will always seek to match the credit period with the nature of the goods.

However, this method of finance has the advantage of providing fixed funding and concessionary rates of interest while mitigating the majority of the payment risk. However, one should consider the overall cost to the borrower, once the insurance premium and the bank guarantee premium have been taken into account, when determining the cost of this form of finance.

As before, the exporter will retain a contingent risk on his balance sheet, and the associated capital cost and the impact upon balance sheet strength should be considered.

If ECGD is agreeable to issuing the bank guarantee, the guarantee will support an agreed deferred portion of the UK element only of the contract, unless ECGD is prepared to guarantee on a selective basis a minor portion of non-UK goods or local costs. Such a deferred portion of the contract would usually be 80 to 85%. It will be seen that the establishment of facilities under this scheme differs from short-term financing in that a separate facility and bank guarantee is established for each contract.

This type of finance would typically be used for a simple supply contract involving the sale of capital goods to a buyer requiring medium-term credit in a situation where the supplier is viewed as a satisfactory credit risk by ECGD.

Medium-/long-term buyer credit
As stated earlier it may be possible to provide finance directly to the overseas buyer or other approved borrowers in the buyer's country.

Such buyer credit financing may be preferable to the exporter, apart from possibly being preferred by the buyer, for the following reasons:

(a) ECGD recourse requirements are more limited than in the case of supplier credit because the supplier is released from his obligations to ECGD when it is known that he has satisfactorily completed the performance of his contract. When the supplier has been paid in full, having received the deposit on order, the payment on shipment and the balance under the loan agreement guaranteed by ECGD, the continuing relationship is between the UK bank and the borrower with the bank guaranteed by ECGD.

(b) It may be possible for the exporter to obtain, under the financial agreement, progress payments at agreed stages in the manufacturing period. This is provided the buyer, who will be accepting liability for repayment of interest charges on these progress drawings, is agreeable to such payments.

(c) Under certain types of buyer credit an exporter can obtain protection in cases where a contract is terminated or where there is resort to arbitration. This lies in the interaction between the supply contract and the loan agreement. For this protection to be available there is a need to establish the exporter's right to make drawings from the bank.

It is therefore in the exporter's interest that the contract allows him to terminate in the event of default or *force majeure* and to claim for all the work-in-progress and costs already incurred. The arbitration clause must also provide a fair means of resolving disputes, and the working of the loan agreement should give proper access to the loan for the payments of these amounts in such circumstances.

However, there are a few potential drawbacks. ECGD will only consider buyer credit arrangements for contracts in excess of £1 million. Negotiation of buyer credit facilities are more detailed and usually lengthier than those for supplier credit and it is important that the exporter applies for support to ECGD and the banks at an early stage. Finally, it should be recognised that the payment terms must be suitable to ECGD (i.e. 15% with order and a maximum of 85% on credit) and that repayments will be in equal semi-annual instalments. This inflexibility can pose a problem with some more project-related contracts.

In most instances a buyer credit will be used for contracts which involve supply and installation of capital equipment either for a complete project or for a particularly large order. The buyer would normally be a first-class risk within the country concerned and the mechanism could also be used for a contract involving one or more suppliers.

Pure Non-Recourse Finance

It is this whole area that has generated the major interest in recent years as recession in major manufacturing and exporting countries has imposed cruel strains upon companies' balance sheets while driving them either to export or cut back the scale of operations. Non-recourse finance offers an exporter the ability to sell his goods on credit terms without in any way restricting the rest of his business growth or incurring significant risks. However, it must be recognised that the growing procession of defaulting buyers and countries has caused banks to look with a jaundiced eye at financing exports without recourse to the exporter at the very time when the exporter's own balance sheet may be under the greatest pressure.

Export finance house

The major export finance houses, many bank owned, have representation in a number of countries and operate several national and international credit insurance schemes. The prime function of these institutions is the provision of finance to the buyer on a non-recourse basis.

The advantage to an exporter will depend upon his own circumstances and needs but the following are some of the more important potential benefits:

(a)   The export finance houses can remove completely the financial risks from exporting. All the exporter has to do is deliver and perform according to his contract.
(b)   The exporter receives cash, usually against shipping documents, with the resulting cash flow and liquidity benefits.
(c)   The export finance house will assume full responsibility for funding, credit insurance (if applicable), foreign currency risks and subsequent collection of the debt.
(d)   There is often only minimal documentation required.

This means that the exporter is free to take on export business without needing to worry about his own balance sheet and may expand his business both at home and abroad more easily. However, the export finance house has to take a commercial view of the risk involved and this does impact upon price and credit availability.

It is a method of finance which is more frequently used for trade of a regular and short-term nature and fulfils a broadly similar requirement to short-term ECGD schemes and export factoring.

Export factoring

If his export business meets the necessary criteria an exporter can shift all the burdens of debt collection to an export factor. The exporter effectively sells his trade debts and receives in return 80% of their face value on shipment. The factor handles the sales accounting and collects the debts from overseas. The factor monitors the export sales ledgers, and when he receives payment in full from the overseas buyer he credits the exporter with the remainder less service charges. There are obvious advantages in the reduction of administration costs and the freeing of management time but the value of this has to be offset against the cost of the factoring company's charges. In making this judgment it should be recognised that the factor's costs will vary in direct proportion to sales. Here the factor prefers repetitive business with credit periods of no more than 180 days, and usually shorter.

In the event of default there is no recourse to the exporter and on the due date the remaining balance less charges is still paid over. It follows, therefore, that before agreeing to an arrangement, the factor will make a careful assessment of the exporter himself, his overseas portfolio and the countries of risk. In practice, a factor will operate within the majority of OECD countries but is less able or willing to do so in countries where he considers the infrastructure or legal system inadequate. This is a disadvantage but one which can only be expected.

Forfaiting

One area of trade finance that is expanding rapidly and is enjoying considerable publicity of late is forfaiting. This technique has in the past been confined to capital goods transactions of between two and seven years, but more recently there has been a marked tendency for short-term a forfait business, particularly in commodities.

Furthermore, although the technique evolved in Switzerland particularly to serve the needs of West European exports to Comecon countries, there is little question that London has now become the world centre of this trade.

The mechanism is fairly simple, the forfaiter purchases without recourse to the exporter, a bill, promissory note or strip of bills. These bills will have been drawn by the exporter, accepted by the importer and will in the majority of cases carry the aval or unconditional guarantee of a major and acceptable bank in the importer's country. These bills will usually mature at regular intervals during the agreed credit period and are bought at a discount. Forfaiting effectively uses free market funds to provide fixed-rate supplier credit.

The principal benefits to the exporter of using forfaiting finance can be summarised under six headings:

(a)   It turns a credit sale into a cash transaction.
(b)   It relieves the balance sheet of contingent liabilities as it is 100% without recourse.
(c)   The forfait company can give a quick decision. If the trade paper is guaranteed and verified, the financing terms can be agreed within hours.
(d)   The forfaiting company handles all the funding of the finance, taking on board all the attendant currency risks and interest rate movements.
(e)   An a forfait transaction can be arranged for a single export order and does not require the whole of an exporter's turnover to be financed.
(f)   Because the finance is based on one piece of trade paper the documentation is extremely simple.

There is no restriction on where the goods are sourced, which permits a multinational to source the product in the most appropriate manner to ensure the optimum use of resources. The exporter can also decide whether or not to include all, or some, of the finance costs in the cash price. The forfaiter will then be able to calculate the new contract price and bill amounts, for him to quote. The prime disadvantage stems from its major selling point which is the fact that forfaiting relies on the existence of a market and in particular a demand for the paper under consideration. The result is that paper from difficult markets can only be sold on a best-efforts basis once the bills are in the forfaiter's possession. This removes the element of certainty from the exporter and hampers products and cash-flow management. In addition some countries will not allow their paper to be traded. The pricing of forfaiting is based upon a commercial assessment of risk but it can still be very competitive with consensus finance in many markets.

Countertrade

It is ironic that this latest and much discussed phenomenon should do no more than take us back to our trading origins before money economics emerged. This whole area of swapping exported goods for products manufactured elsewhere for conversion into hard currency by whatever means is attracting considerable attention and there is hardly a major bank or multinational company in the western world that is not at least examining the opportunities provided by countertrade to develop further business opportunities.

We need to understand firstly why we are seeing this resurgence of interest in forms of non-cash trading. Is it that there is loss of confidence in the major trading currencies of the world? Are we on the verge of going back to the years between the two world wars when confidence collapsed and goods became currency? Or is it a repeat of history when the imbalance between economies was so great that cash transactions were not even possible?

The impetus has in fact come from the would be importing nations and the pressure has been put on western exporters to enter into various forms of compensation arrangement. This pressure emanated principally from the Comecon countries which have always been unable or unwilling to generate enough hard currency to meet their import requirements.

More recently however there has been a number of other countries, particularly less developed ones, which seek to maintain the flow of goods without adding to their already considerable burden of debt. The most recent notable entrants into this market have been Indonesia and China.

This development is thoroughly unpopular with governments and companies in the west as it completely distorts the free market forces which ought to determine how goods are bought and sold.

Paradoxically, it is also becoming unpopular in some quarters in the state-controlled economies as the effects of compensation trading can destroy the markets for the normal export of their goods and depress price structures. It does not matter what has triggered this upsurge in demand; it could be laid at the door of OPEC in 1973, it could be greedy western bankers overlending to developing economies, or it could be the eastern bloc's inability to manage its economies properly, but the fact is that the demand is there and in current circumstances few exporters can afford to ignore it.

The most usual form of trading in goods today is said to be compensation trading whereby the value of the delivered goods by a foreign country is offset by an export of the importing country's goods to the foreign country. In this manner the necessity of one country extending credit to the other is avoided, only if such transactions are concluded over a clearing account.

Full compensation requires 100% mutual transfer of goods but the two transfers are paid for independently of each other. The character of the transaction derives from the fact that the western exporter commits himself to purchase goods equivalent in value to his own deliveries with the option to transfer his purchasing obligation to another party. This third party pays the exporter the value of the exports minus a subsidy.

In partial compensation situations the western exporter receives part-payment in cash and the remainder in goods. Frequently in this form of transaction there is no intermediary and the original exporter has the burden of finding a purchaser for the goods he has to take in part-payment. This is the fundamental drawback with compensation trading — the goods often are not totally acceptable in the market-places available to the exporter and there are frequent quality problems. As a result when striking a deal the exporter must build into his price an additional margin which will have to be used to subsidise the sale at lower prices of the imported goods that he has agreed to accept, so that they can be converted into cash as soon as possible. This has the nonsensical result of increasing the price of the supply contract to the original importing country, while at the same time virtually guaranteeing that the goods that they export will be sold at very low prices in the western country concerned.

A much simpler form of transaction is the simple parallel deal or counterpurchase. Here the western exporter delivers his goods and receives payment for them but at the same time enters into a commitment to purchase a percentage of the value of the deal in imports. He then must look around to find suitable imports and a suitable market. If he fails to fulfil his obligation he is required to pay a penalty. Whereas only one contract is drawn up for a compensation transaction, two contracts are negotiated under a parallel deal; one relating to the export and a separate agreement for the import.

In conclusion, most deals involving the transfer of goods rather than the use of straightforward cash or credit only really work successfully when there is an obvious mutual advantage to both parties.

Conclusion

A Corporate Treasurer, from a cash and risk management point of view, must seek to optimise the position of his company in an export transaction. As has been explained this should embrace three major features:

(a)   The need to offer competitive credit periods at competitive rates.
(b)   The need to manage both balance sheet and cash flow.
(c)   The need to protect the quality of the earnings stream through the mitigation of risk.

UK manufactured exports are falling and the country is now a net importer of manufactured goods. To reverse this situation, exporters will have to become far more professional in their commercial attitudes and the financial institutions which serve them will need to be more aware of exporter problems and quicker to react to new market demands. The past comfortable practice of looking to ECGD for support and accepting both ECGD's instructions and credit judgments will have to disappear and finance directors and bankers alike will have to work as a team in order to compete successfully with West Germany and Japan.

The Corporate Treasurer has to balance his objective against the requirements of the other party. As an exporter, the Corporate Treasurer requires, in order of priority:

(a)   certainty of payment, without recourse;
(b)   payment at the earliest possible date;
(c)   payment at the lowest possible cost.

In this sense the Corporate Treasurer is an integral part of the sales function.

As an importer the Corporate Treasurer's objectives are different. His priorities are:

(a)   assurance that the goods he receives will be in accordance with the terms of contract;
(b)   the longest possible credit period;
(c)   the minimisation (or elimination) of the cost of credit.

As both an importer and an exporter he is also concerned to ensure that he protects himself against parity changes but this is not a matter dependent solely on the type of instrument he uses.

Clearly it is the intention of the Corporate Treasurer to harness the various alternative trade finance instruments to produce the optimum benefit for himself and his company. The instruments and techniques he uses must take into consideration not only the desires of the other party but also the type of transaction involved.

CHAPTER 20

Financial Packages

Gilly Webb-Wilson

Editor's Notes

Any corporate involved in major projects inevitably needs to draw on a wide variety of financial mechanisms and the final two chapters provide a practical background in which many of these techniques come together.

Introduction

Large financing needs for major contracts and projects or anticipated corporate capital expenditure programmes frequently require specialised funding techniques. By using several different financing alternatives to create a package of liabilities, able to support significantly large expenditure, corporates and project sponsors can expect to lessen interest costs, to minimise gearing and to acquire long-term funding suited to the life of the asset purchased or to the construction and payback periods of a project. Project financing is examined in greater detail in the next chapter but loan packages for such financing may well include several of the alternative techniques examined below, particularly 'soft' financing and grants from bilateral and multilateral agencies, mixed credits (i.e. export credits plus aid), as well as the more familiar banking products of Eurocurrency loans and export credits. This chapter considers not only these last topics but also the traditional sources of funds open to a borrower (i.e. equity, near equity, conventional loans and leasing) and financing alternatives such as countertrade.

Funding Corporate Capital Expenditure

Equity and debt instruments

Quoted corporations with good stock-market ratings may consider tapping the equity markets to support a major capital expenditure programme, deciding that the loss of the tax advantage of loan interest deductibility and the post-tax dividend costs are compensated by the cost advantage in raising fresh equity and the overall strengthening of the balance sheet. In the 1980s (up to 1987) bull equity markets, we have seen significant share placings and rights issues, the proceeds of which have funded acquisitions, modernisation programmes and specific fixed assets. Such needs can also be financed through medium- and long-term bank loans, quoted debt instruments such as debenture stock and unsecured loan stock or through capital market instruments, e.g. via the bond markets, thus enabling the borrower to access long-term, fixed-rate finance in his domestic currency or in foreign exchange. The number of debt instruments available to a corporate are now multifarious (see Chapters 10–13 on recent developments in financing techniques) and choice will depend on the borrower's interest rate management policy and balance-sheet position. For instance, a UK corporate with a major US$ capital expenditure need may choose to raise US$ funding by a conventional long-term bank loan (to match the asset purchased with a corresponding liability) or to enter into a currency swap as a hedge (maybe in addition to an interest rate swap which has already reduced the cost of borrowing). Alternatively it may rely on continued availability of funding from shorter-term global commercial paper and multi-option facilities or from straightforward bankers acceptances (N.B. Only bankers acceptances relating to trade transactions are eligible for finest rates of discount at the Bank of England, but a corporate may choose to release alternative financing for capital expenditure by increasing the use of acceptance credits to fund stock and debtors.)

Off-balance sheet financings

Corporates are always concerned that their balance sheet shows the right picture and some may not wish to burden their balance sheets with debt for specific income-producing projects but may want to retain a gearing capacity or a certain level of return on assets. Off-balance sheet transactions may then supplement direct balance sheet funding. Previously, UK corporations have often adhered to the Companies Acts and Accounting Standards by careful drafting of financial agreements and contractual arrangements such that the parent's access to the economic use of the assets being financed off its balance sheet was unimpaired. Whilst leasing has always been heralded as the prime example of such financing its off-balance sheet advantages have declined in Britain (see below).

Historically the most widely available financing schemes have involved:

(a) Using the Companies Act definitions of subsidiary to create subsidiaries which remain unconsolidated in group accounts and where the debt does not impact group gearing. The recent changes to the Companies Act may affect these kinds of structures.

(b) Buy-back agreements covering the sale of assets to third parties, for example so that stock does not appear on the balance sheet at the end of a financial year. Recent changes to the Companies Act will also affect these structures.

(c) Changing a capital obligation to a smaller revenue one (see operating leases).

Off-balance sheet financings have been used for transactions as diverse as the financing of retailers' debtors arising from the purchase of goods by use of in-house credit cards, the financing of whisky stocks during the long maturing process and the funding of properties used in its mainstream business by a company which wishes to utilise bank debt based on the current yield on the properties and their market value without recourse to the user's own balance sheet. The degree of recourse to the 'economic beneficiary' of the transactions will depend on the structures but it may well also affect the pricing of the deal in that traditionally the less the recourse to parent company, the higher the cost of debt will be.

Regulatory and accounting authorities (not only in the UK) are increasingly anxious to expose the true 'credit impact' of off-balance sheet financings (e.g. in some cases SEC filing requirements may already require greater explanations than those available in published UK accounts). The aim is to ensure that transactions are accounted for according to their substance and their economic effect and that corporate entities effectively controlled by another are consolidated into the latter's accounts. Thus, in order to show a 'true and fair view' the accountancy profession believes that the often large liabilities and balancing assets that can be found in 'off-balance sheet vehicles' should be consolidated. Measures are already being taken (through amendments to the Companies Act and through the publication of Exposure Draft 42 by the Accounting Standards Committee) to implement this disclosure policy. Some corporates are already reacting to criticism of their financial reporting by publishing far greater details than before of their unconsolidated assets and liabilities.

The Role of Equity and Debt in Project Financings and Buy-Outs

The financing alternatives examined previously are suited to large corporates in mainstream activities such as manufacturing, property and retailing which either wish to use their balance sheet in fund raising for capital expenditure by accessing several different structures, or who wish to hive off a particular asset from the balance sheet. In project financings and buy-outs the risks absorbed by investors and lenders are often greater than those encountered in supporting ongoing corporate activities with a proven management and profit track record, and the structure of debt and equity will differ from that described above.

On the equity side in buy-outs and project financings, investors may aim to achieve some return even whilst profits are low but will also look to realising maximum return from growth in the capital value of their investment. Typically, therefore, relevant corporate structures will have an equity mix of ordinary and preference shares. Investors in the former will expect a high return on 'exit' (e.g. on flotation of a company conceived through a buy-out) and/or on high dividend payout when the entity is generating healthy distributable profits. Investors in the latter can share in the capital growth particularly if the preference shares are convertible, but can also access a fixed income from net earnings earlier than the former. The level of dividend income from preference shares may also depend on whether the shares are cumulative (i.e. dividend obligations from one year, not met due to lack of net profits, are carried forward to next or even subsequent years) and participative (i.e. subject to participation in an additional dividend after receipt of the preference dividend). Bank debt of varying tenors relating to the operating and investment needs of the entity may form the bulk of the debt liabilities. This debt will usually be secured in recognition of the credit risks, and may be supplemented by further unsecured borrowings. Subordinated lenders will obviously seek a higher return than unsubordinated, typically through higher fees and margins and an 'equity kicker' (e.g. through provision of debt by convertible loans).

The mix of debt and equity will vary according to the borrower's perceived gearing capacity, the level of risk in the success of the buy-out or project, tax implications and dividend remittance restraints.

Leasing as an alternative funding strategy
Leasing used to be seen as an excellent means of acquiring the use of assets with long-term, fixed-rate funding in place. Advantageous tax allowances in the UK permitted funding at rates which were often well below comparable bank debt. Although these allowances were reduced

in the UK by the 1984 Finance Act there exist still many reasons why leasing continues to be worth considering for capital expenditure. In the international field some countries, such as Germany and Japan, still offer opportunities for tax-based cross-border leasing. The main advantages of leasing are:

(a)   Long-term debt at competitive rates.
(b)   Cost and cash flow savings due to the lack of an up-front cost (i.e. no need to make large front-end payments).
(c)   Flexibility — for example, rental payments can be tailored to match cash flows and can match contract-related progress payment structures by being staggered rather than being payable in fixed equal periods and instalments; and rental agreements can allow for currency switches.
(d)   Operating leases may guard against asset obsolescence.
(e)   Balance sheet impact — for example, the off-balance sheet nature of operating leases.
(f)   The reduction of dependency on and the avoidance of use of existing bank lines — leaving these available for other funding needs and avoiding the possibility that gearing loan covenants might be breached.
(g)   Certainty of cost — rentals are usually priced at fixed rather than floating rates of interest.
(h)   Administrative ease — documents are standardised, relatively short and easily amended, for example a new lease can be attached to an original lease document.

To understand leasing it is necessary to examine the two types of leases — operating and finance — and the advantages to both lessor and lessee which each affords.

The basic concept of leasing is similar to the principle of hire purchase (HP). Unlike an HP contract, an agreement for a UK tax-based lease never permits the user to be able to purchase the asset from the owner. Ownership is vested in the lender (lessor) and the borrower (lessee) has the right of use. The two categories of leases as defined in the UK, finance and operating, have different accounting treatments in that the former must be capitalised on the balance sheet of the lessee (i.e. the asset and corresponding rental liabilities must be shown on the balance sheet) whilst the latter is off-balance sheet and annual rentals over the contracted lease period are simply deducted from the profit and loss account. SSAP 21 defines the acid test for determining whether a lease is finance or operating by stating that the former is one which 'transfers substantially all the risks and rewards of ownership of an asset to the lessee'.

Under a *finance lease* the lessee will specify the type of equipment and can even order it as agent for the leasing company or financial institution acting as lessor. The lessee will be responsible for all operational and repair costs in addition to the rental payments. Such finance leases are an ideal alternative to funding the purchase of an asset needed in the ordinary course of business (e.g. a specialised machine for motor vehicle manufacture, a particular crane for a construction company), as although rental payments cover full cost (plus interest) of the asset, there is a cash-flow saving because the initial capital expenditure is made by the provider of the funds. Further, rental payments can be structured to follow cash-flow streams related to use of the asset. Also fixed-rate funding of a longer term than that found in usual bank loan financing is often achievable.

Under an *operating lease*, it is assumed that the asset will have a substantial and quantifiable residual value so the rentals should be lower since they are amortising not 100% but 90% or less of the asset. Thus the lessor purchases an asset to be leased at a rate and term which will not be expected to cover all three elements of capital cost, interest and profit since the lessor will expect either to lease the asset for further periods at the end of an initial lease or will earn cash from the sale of the asset after its use by the lessee (i.e. will gain from its residual value). Aircraft leasing must be a prime example of operating leases. There is a well-developed market for secondhand aircraft and ones which usually have high resale (residual) values. In any event, regular servicing of the asset will have been undertaken to ensure continued airworthiness and the lessor therefore should have a well maintained asset.

Finally, it should be mentioned that despite the reduction of tax incentives in the UK and USA, leasing is still a growing industry. The big-ticket market is still very competitive and banks are able to fund large projects such as aircraft and major factory developments. Some entire projects are still subject to leasing structures (for example, the part financing of an ethylene plant in Scotland by a partner in the joint-venture using leasing techniques), and the government has encouraged leasing in Enterprise Zones (e.g. London's Dockland) by giving 100% first-year capital allowances on new building developments there. At the other end of the market, since current tax legislation favours leases of a period of under five years, UK corporations are finding that tax-based leases over three to four years are still attractive, and the growth of non-tax based operating leases of computers and cars continues unabated.

Financial Packages for Exporters

Previous examples in this chapter have concentrated on financing techniques for long-term major capital expenditure or for the purchase of a particular asset. Any exporting corporate or project sponsor will also regard incentive finance for exports and concessional funding from bilateral and multilateral sources as important financing techniques to support large contractual commitments.

Incentive Finance

Export Credits Guarantee Department (ECGD)

ECGD is the UK's government department briefed to insure exporters against non-payment by their overseas customers whether this occurs due to commercial (e.g. insolvency of the buyer or delays in transfer of funds) or political reasons. By administering an 'interest make-up' scheme on behalf of the Treasury, ECGD also provides the vehicle whereby commercial banks can provide subsidised long-term buyer credits to overseas buyers, in accordance with OECD consensus rules. (See the next section below.)

ECGD's range of policies is extremely wide and perhaps only matched by the export insurance system available in France. Detailed information is best found in ECGD's own publications but, broadly speaking, the exporter's pure insurance guarantees fall into two categories, namely comprehensive and specific guarantees, and their period of cover divides mainly into short term (i.e. credit given to a maximum of 180 days) and medium term (i.e. credit given for over 180 days but for a maximum of five years). The comprehensive guarantees, whether they be the comprehensive short-term guarantee (CSTG) or its medium-term equivalent the supplemental extended terms guarantee (SETG), are designed to cover continuous exporting of primarily consumer goods in the former case and capital goods in the latter case. The CSTG is expected to cover all an exporter's business in all countries accepted by ECGD but ECGD can demand a higher premium, accept less than 100% of turnover or exclude some countries. The SETG is made available on a case-by-case basis and will frequently be supplemented by pre-credit cover, running from the contract date, since the main cover is only effective from date of shipment. ECGD's level of cover available always depends on the type of guarantee purchased by the exporter, for example the CSTG usually offers 90% cover of commercial risk and 95% political risk cover. The premium payable will vary according to valuation of the risk inherent in the term of credit given, the amount of business and the spread of country risk.

ECGD supported bank finance

Whilst the cover described above removes the effect of losses due to non-payment from the importer, it still leaves the exporter the onus of providing credit from his own balance sheet. Several schemes are available to remove this debt burden which may also enable an exporter to offer a buyer competitive financing. An assignment to the bank of policies will encourage financing but it is likely to be with some recourse to the exporter; to keep the debt off the balance sheet it is preferable for an exporter to arrange for ECGD to issue guarantees direct to the bank which then provides financing. There are three such medium- and long-term guarantee-backed funding structures summarised as follows:

(a)   *Specific bank guarantee* covers deferred payment of two to five years for single contract for capital goods construction, production goods and services. The financing is at consensus rates available via ECGD's interest make-up scheme which allows banks to fund themselves at short-term floating rates whilst offering fixed rates to the buyer. Sums are advanced to the exporter after purchase without recourse of *accepted* bills of exchange drawn on the buyer or of promissory notes issued by him. Finance is available only on completion of the commercial contract, e.g. shipment of goods, construction works accepted by client.

(b)   *Comprehensive extended terms banker's guarantee (CXBG)* covers a number of specific contracts insured by SETG with same credit terms etc. as (a) above. Essentially a revolving facility to refinance supplier credit.

(c)   *Buyer credit guarantee* — available for contracts for goods and services with value of £1m plus in sterling or approved currencies and used for major contractual projects and large exports of capital goods. Financing rates in accordance with

OECD rules — loan usually limited to maximum of 85% of contract value and exporter paid direct from drawdown of loan. The cover is available over five years; longer periods can be negotiated on a case-by-case basis and cover can be combined with a Supplemental Specific Guarantee to cover the exporter during the manufacturing period.

(N.B. These schemes are not available for exports to EEC member states.)

In two other financing schemes often accessed by exporters the financing bank may not be the exporter's own. The first, the lines of credit scheme, enables payment for relatively low contract value exports (as low as £25,000) on cash terms at advantageous rates to the buyer, i.e. a buyer credit structure is used. Lines of credit are either project related, financing a number of goods and services needed for a particular scheme in the buying country, or are general purpose lines, in which case a bank will usually be the borrower and will approve both buyer and contract before financing. Lines of credit, being in place prior to contract, encourage easy access for buyer and supplier. Under the second scheme ECGD makes a CETG available to specialist export finance institutions (e.g. confirming houses) and banks acceptable to ECGD which under a 'finance contracts (overseas banks) endorsement' (FINCOBE) or 'associated borrower endorsement' (ABE), if the borrower is an associate of the institution, provide loans to overseas borrowers (usually overseas banks) in support of UK exports. A FINCOBE only covers 95% of political and commercial risk, whilst an ABE covers 95% of political risk only.

In all the instances above, consensus rules on maximum credit periods, country classifications and interest rates will apply. As from July 1989 the matrix of minimum interest rates was as follows (rates are reviewed six monthly):

	Category II (intermediate) %	Category III (relatively poor) %
Two–five years credit	9.15	8.30
Five years credit and over	9.65	8.30

For Category I countries (the relatively rich) maximum rates have been abolished. For these markets a separate system of Commercial Interest

Reference Rates (CIRR) now applies. These concensus rates reflect commercial market rates and include standard currencies as well as low-interest rate currencies (the so-called LIRCS). Thus, exporters can still offer fixed rate finance to Category I countries, but not at heavily subsidised rates.

Flexibility of ECGD

Only the main guarantees which open avenues of financing to buyer and supplier have been discussed above. It should be remembered that an ECGD support package for an exporter can include facilities as diverse as a foreign-exchange guarantee for financing contracts in foreign currency in approved currencies (US$, yen, DM), guarantees against unfair calling of bonds, cover against insolvency of joint-venture partners and political risk cover for investments overseas such as equity capital and loans. ECGD's flexibility also extends to allowing some foreign content in a contract (reciprocal arrangements in the EEC allow the placing of subcontracts of up to 40% of contract value with another member state), to providing cover for a UK exporter as a subcontractor although the buyer's relationship is only with the main contractor, and to covering sales from a UK corporate's overseas stocks.

All these different guarantees and financing schemes combine to offer an exporter maximum flexibility and to enhance competitiveness.

Three alternatives to ECGD supported transactions

A UK exporter may wish to seek alternatives to ECGD either for price reasons, i.e. to reduce premia, or for cover reasons, or to gain cover for territories which ECGD will not cover, or simply in order to leave existing bank lines undisturbed by accessing different sources of funding. Firstly, the simplest method would be to find a bank prepared to make a clean risk Eurocurrency loan to a buyer, the proceeds of which enabled an exporter to be paid cash.

Secondly, the forfait market could be used. In a forfait transactions, a bank purchases bills of exchange or promissory notes without recourse to the exporter. This 'paper' will sometimes be avalised by a bank. The bills or promissory notes are discounted at a fixed rate applied to the face value of the bills. An exporter will obviously try to build this interest cost into the commercial contract. A forfait is used for medium and large transactions involving the direct shipment of goods (i.e. not for projects) and is a useful means of avoidance of interest rate risk for the exporter (since the bank commits to purchase notes to be issued in the future) and of alleviation of commercial and political risk.

Risks can also be covered by the third alternative, commercial insurance market. In practice, cover from Lloyds or specialised insurance companies has been more readily available for the political risks of expropriation and confiscation than for non-transferability of funds. However, non-payment cover, usually for three years maximum on an annual revolving basis, has been seen. In some instances banks have been prepared to finance exports following the assignment of insurance policies, particularly when the exporter agrees to cover the interest cost during the waiting period prior to payment of a claim.

Incentive finance for multi-sourced export contracts

In OECD countries the aim of all export support agencies is to provide protection to the exporter against default of a buyer whether for political or commercial reasons. Additionally, most OECD countries have developed preferential re-financing and interest support schemes to enable tenderers to offer financing packages at lower than market sourced costs. Structures differ from country to country but in all cases insurance is available either direct to the exporter or to a financing institution and financing is either provided direct from a bank or through an intermediary such as government agencies themselves. To illustrate the different approaches one need look no further than western Europe. In Switzerland only pure insurance cover is available and funding is sourced from the domestic capital markets. In Austria the Oesterreichische Kontrollbank (OKB) administers the official export credit guarantee scheme on behalf of the state and will also refinance some credits. Generally, however, the banks provide buyer credit financing but with some interest rate protection. Italy adopts a bipartite scheme with insurance being provided by SACE (Sezione Speciale per L'Assicurazione del Credito All'Esportazione) whilst Mediocredito Centrale, a state financial institution, provides an interest rate subsidy or discounts credits at consensus rates. Belgium has an even more complicated tripartite scheme with a state-guaranteed public agency providing insurance and underwriting some risks for its own account and some for the government, another agency providing interest rate subsidies and a further institution, owned mainly by the banks, providing re-financing opportunities.

Banks specialising in export finance packages today must be familiar with all OECD export credit structures and their access to them if their customers are to maximise funding opportunities in support of an export contract. Multi-sourced export finance packages are increasingly popular; one of the advantages being that a buyer can be offered greater financing. For example, for countries where export credit insurance limits are scarce, support from a number of agencies can be pooled, if a buyer is prepared to purchase goods and services from differing territories, thereby achieving a larger total loan package than if only one sourcing territory were involved. A buyer may also be able to hedge his currency exposure by taking finance in traditionally weaker currencies. As tendering for large-scale contracts and projects becomes more complex and bids are therefore made on a consortium basis so do multi-sourced buyer credit packages increase — the keen price competitiveness of which is expected as borrowers, too, become more sophisticated.

Mixed credits and aid packages
When large contract-related amounts need to be funded, ECGD or multi-sourced buyer credit facilities may not satisfy the interest cost and credit period criteria of the buyer or indeed even be suitable to the construction period of the project itself. By accessing bilateral aid schemes, such as the UK mixed credit budget, the aid and trade provision (ATP) administered by the Department for Trade and Industry, packages can be created which, when mixed with more traditional export credits, consist of very long-term, fixed-rate funding, softened by aid funds. In 1986 two such special soft loans from the UK to Indonesia and China allowed the countries 25-year credit at 5%. Much criticism has been levelled at mixed credits (particularly if the aid is tied) in that the system encourages infusion of aid to a level which enables tenderers to be just price competitive on financial rather than commercial terms and that, in the past the OECD formula for calculating the aid component favoured low interest rate countries, e.g. Japan. In 1987 measures were taken to raise, in two stages, the minimum permissible aid component in mixed credits from 25 to 35% and in the case of least developed countries to 50%, thus forcing a more onerous aid commitment from donor countries' budgets and, further, the notional interest rate for calculation of the cash value of a grant was amended thus abolishing the advantage available to low interest rate countries which enabled them to spread their aid budgets further.

Projects financed entirely by aid should not be excluded when considering incentive-based financial packages. Although the banking community may see the funds emanating from such grants or long-term low interest rate loans, only at disbursement (i.e. via a transfer of funds from donor to beneficiary or donor to contractor) banks will be used for all ancillary banking needs such as contractor-related bonding, letters of credit for importation of machinery and local current accounts for working capital needs.

Financing from multilateral agencies and specialised funds
The cost of major infrastructural projects and the restricted access of lesser developed countries (LDCs) to conventional sources of funds from the international capital markets, and at times even from official export credit agencies, have highlighted the need for the sophisticated collation of varying financing sources to achieve an overall package of very long-term (say 15 years plus), low interest rate funding. Such concessional soft loans are most readily available from bilateral aid, the major multilateral agencies (e.g. the World Bank) and development banks (e.g. the Asian Development Bank). These agencies and banks are of varying size depending on membership criteria (the largest being the World Bank) and have consequent fund raising and disbursement capacity but common aims and strategies are apparent. With the exception of some specialised situations (e.g. the OPEC fund balance of payments loans and the World Bank's adjustment loans designed to support policy changes essential to a country's economic growth), the aims are to provide long-term loans at commercial rates to the more creditworthy countries, long-term soft loans and grants to poorer LDCs and latterly to encourage private sector direct investments in LDCs. The World Bank's own objectives could be echoed by most of the development banks and similar multilateral agencies:

To promote economic progress in developing countries by providing financial and technical assistance, mostly for specific projects in both public and private sectors. (*Source:* The World Bank and International Finance Corporation.)

Projects supported are obviously key to the economic growth of the borrowing country, the agricultural sectors receive most assistance together with infrastructural projects such as in the energy, transportation, telecommunications, mining and water treatment sectors. Assistance (unless granted under specific schemes for direct investment in the private sector) is only available to governments or borrowers with a government guarantee.

Applications cannot be made by tendering corporates wishing to win a contract by constructing a concessional finance package. The availability of such financing, however, is of importance to the corporates in that evidence of a buyer entering into a contract with, say, multilateral agency funding support and other funding sources can offer the exporter the security of knowledge that the total cost of the contract in question can be financed and that close supervision of the project will be exercised. Further, co-financing structures (see below) mean that the contractor/exporter's own banks will often be working closely with the agencies. Lastly, since procurement policies tend to restrict equipment and sourcing largely to member countries of the agencies and development banks, any exporter should be aware of the contracts funded under the umberella of such entities as a potential source of business which some competitors may not be able to access.

The World Bank

The World Bank is a multilateral development agency. It has two main arms, the International Bank for Reconstruction and Development (IBRD) owned by the governments of more than 150 countries and the International Development Association (IDA) whose membership includes most IBRD member states. The IBRD lends for 'economically productive purposes' to developing countries, mainly for specific projects, whereas the IDA lends on concessional terms to the poorest countries. Typically, the former will raise its funds in the global capital markets and generally will lend for 12 to 15 years with three to five year grace periods at a rate linked to the average cost of the pool of the IBRD's borrowings plus a margin. The latter raises funds mainly as grants from governments to be on-lent as 35-year and 40-year credits with grace periods of up to 10 years, the interest rate being nil but commitment fees and services charges being payable. Feasibility and technical studies as well as projects themselves can be financed so long as the procurement rules stipulating international competitive tendering are obeyed. The International Finance Corporation (IFC) plays a far smaller role but it aims to encourage private enterprises or government organisations that assist the private sector. Loans average 7 to 12 years maturity and are priced at market rates. The need to support this sector more by promoting the flow of international investment to developing nations has led to the idea of the World Bank creating a Multilateral Investment Guarantee Agency (MIGA). MIGA covers transfer risk, loss from legislative or administrative action by a host government causing loss of investor control, contract repudiation and war and civil disturbance and focuses on protecting equity interests, near equity financing and direct investment through, for instance, management and service contracts. Target countries are LDCs whose payment problems cause a reluctance for direct investment.

The multinational development banks

The multinational development banks are regional, that is they concentrate on financing developing member countries (DMCs) within their own geographic sphere, usually denoted by the bank's title, for example The Asian Development Bank (ADB) and the Inter-American Development Bank (IDB). Member countries usually include most OECD territories, with the major powers, especially the USA and Japan, contributing significant capital. These agencies are modelled on World Bank lines in respect of types of sectoral activities supported and in types of financing available. The greater percentage of loans will be on terms similar to the IBRD's and will be funded from capital resources but specific funds, for example the Asian Development Fund, will offer very long-term funding at low interest rates. Co-financing (see below) is encouraged as the development banks are unlikely to fund 100% of project costs and expect other financing sources to be associated. Like the World Bank, assistance to the private sector is also being developed through specialist wings such as the IDB's Inter-American Investment Corporation which will participate via structures such as equity participation rights in small- and medium-sized companies. These operations will not require government guarantees but security may well be taken by the lenders.

The European Investment Bank (EIB) and the European Development Fund (EDF)

The EIB is a project financing institution owned by the EC member states. Set up under the EEC Treaty, it finances capital investment projects that promote the balanced development of the Community, with the major part of its lending in the Community's less-favoured regions. The EIB, the largest international borrowing and lending institution after the World Bank, raises most of its funds on capital markets, mainly through bond issues (AAA), for on-lending on a non-profit basis to investment projects meeting Community priorities.

It may support only economically, technically and financially viable investment. Loan maturities range from 4 to 12 years for industry and up to 20 or more years for infrastructure, with repayment of principal and interest normally in equal six-monthly instalments and with grace periods of several years possible. Loans may be in a single currency or a mix of currencies. Its rates, set for each currency borrowed, follow closely the cost of its borrowings taking into account a 0.15% margin for operating costs. The traditional product is fixed-rate loans, though adjustable fixed-rates and variable-rate loans are also available. The bank is a complementary source of finance, normally never financing more than up to 50% of a project's capital.

Less than 10% of the EIB's total financing operations are outside the Community, within aggregate ceiling amounts laid down in cooperation agreements between the EEC and the 12 countries in the Mediterranean region, and under the Third Lomé Convention for the 66 African Caribbean and Pacific states. Under these arrangements the bank also manages risk capital operations (highly concessionary finance) provided from budgetary resources, by the Community in the case of the Mediterranean countries, and the European Development Fund (funded by the EEC member states) under the Lomé Convention. Loans from the bank's own resources in these countries are usually 'softened' with interest rebates from budgetary resources and are made directly to the project promoters.

Other bilateral agencies and aid funds

The list of international agencies and funds providing soft loans and grants is exhaustive and will not be discussed in detail here. Suffice it to say that the aid is usually untied, that is funds may be spent in any country without restriction as to origin of goods or services but all the agencies differ in financial terms and on target sectors, and have limitations on amounts available to any one name according to their charters and rules of incorporation. Like the other agencies above, only approaches on a government to government basis are encouraged and administrative structures tend to be similar to the World Bank.

Co-Financing

The term co-financing largely describes a collaboration between different sources of finance to provide the means to fund high priority large contracts and projects and is best illustrated by the schemes encouraged by the World Bank. The World Bank can only provide a small element of the needs of member countries, and borrowers are therefore encouraged to augment resources with other external sources of funds, appropriate to the borrower's own economic situation. Such sources are, firstly, state bilateral aid programmes, development banks and multilateral funds, secondly, export credit agencies and, thirdly, commercial banks. The poorer LDCs will only be able to access the official agencies providing concessionary loans whereas countries able to fund from the international markets will access export credits and Eurocurrency loans.

World Bank arrangements with co-financiers are structured for individual cases but will typically allow for the sharing of information, for agreement on the appraisal and implementation of a project, and procedures relating to the solution of problems in the event of difficulties with the project or its debt service. If the procurement procedures of agencies are similar then funds from them can be apportioned easily for payment of a common set of goods and services (this method is called 'joint financing') but, in practice, most agencies have different rules on sourcing, making such a method infeasible. 'Parallel financing' is then encouraged, allowing each lender to finance a parcel of goods and services. The World Bank will ensure that the price and quality of these goods as well as the financing terms are acceptable to it.

Historically, the official agencies and development banks have been the main co-financiers since they share with the World Bank common aims and similar financing structures. More recently, export credit financing associated with the World Bank has increased (in the fiscal year 1988 nearly half of the $6.6 billion World Bank assisted projects attracted some co-financing). Borrowers gain the advantage of longer debt maturities but again careful packaging of purchases is needed to ensure no conflict over procurement rules arises. Although commercial banks are encouraged to enter co-financing schemes by the presence of export credit agencies, this source remains the smallest, due partly to the nature of the borrowers, and despite access to an 'optional' cross-default clause linking a commercial loan to a World Bank loan. Recent developments, however, should stimulate an increase in commercial bank involvement in co-financing. The World Bank (since early 1983) has three new co-financing instruments:

(a)   in addition to making its own loan it will participate in the commercial loan ('parallel financing') by methods such as participation in the later maturities to extend the tenor of a loan;

(b)   it will guarantee the later maturities, thus encouraging their funding from commercial sources in the first instance, or it will allow a 'put' option to achieve similar comfort for bank lenders;

(c)   it will take a contingent participation in the final maturity of a loan with a fixed level of instalments that combine floating-rate interest and variable principal repayments. If the interest rate rises above a certain figure then the amortisation schedule is not adhered to and the World Bank will, on request, finance the final repayment if the commercial lenders are not willing to finance the balance of principal outstanding.

It is hoped that these methods of involving the World Bank will offer comfort to a commercial lender's assessment of country risk such that borrowers can extend the tenor of commercial loans to a maturity consistent with the type of project being financed.

Countertrade as a Financing Method

All the financial packages discussed so far have a commonality in that they involve disbursement of funds as payment for goods and services purchased. It is not unusual today to find buyers, particularly from countries with hard currency payment problems, seeking to pay for imports by countertrade methods (i.e. by forcing foreign exporters to accept goods in lieu of payment or by insisting on local content and manufacturing as part of a contract). Countertrade not only improves the balance of payments situation in the importing country but also helps promotion of its own exports and opens new markets for them. Countertrade is a generic term covering several mechanisms (the terminology of which can vary), commonly known as barter, counter purchase, buy-back, co-operation and offset transactions. Additionally, the term covers payment for goods and services through bilateral agreements by using 'clearing accounts' or 'switch transactions'.

Barter

Straightforward barter, goods for goods, is rarely seen today due to the complications of matching exact values etc.

Counterpurchase

Counterpurchase introduces an element of cash payment not found in barter and covers two types of transaction. Firstly, in a 'parallel' deal the exporter receives payment for goods supplied but he enters into a separate contract with the importer committing himself to the purchase of goods from the exporter's country for a given percentage value of the underlying trade contract. This commitment can usually be on-sold to a third party at a discount (the 'disagio') but, if unfulfilled, triggers penalty clauses. Secondly, by 'compensation' transactions an exporter will be involved in two trade deals which are not directly linked. Goods move from exporter to importer and vice versa, the sale proceeds of the latter deal satisfying the former for 100% value. It is not unusual to find triangular compensation deals with the original exporter eventually receiving hard currency although the discount needed to on-sell goods at an attractive price to a third party may be high, thus the exporter will not receive 100% payment. Counterpurchase transactions become more onerous when the goods offered by an importer as payment are limited in scope and when restrictions are placed on the ultimate buying country of the goods so that existing export markets are not disturbed.

Examples of counterpurchase (E = original exporter I = importer):

Parallel deal:

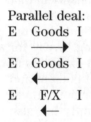

Triangular compensation:

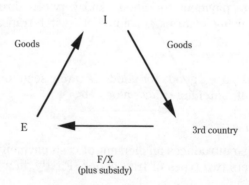

Buy-back

In this instance, the exporter will be paid for a major project or a piece of high-value plant in the form of the goods being produced by the project or equipment itself. It is vital that the products involved are saleable and have defined market prices or the exporter will suffer and will encounter severe difficulties in even constructing a sale price.

Co-operation

This is a sophistication of the buy-back principle. Traditionally, the exporter will transfer the manufacture of products to an entity in the importing country as a *quid pro quo* for the latter making certain purchases from the exporter.

Off-set

Off-set contracts are complicated and require the exporter to agree to a package of techniques. The exporter may have to use goods and services from the importer's country in the final product and may have to make direct investments in the importing territory or transfer technology to it, in addition to entering into more regular counterpurchase transactions.

Clearing and switch transactions

Bilateral agreements covering payment for goods between two countries not in freely convertible currencies but via book entries at respective central banks have existed for several years — particularly in relation to trade with Comecon (e.g. Finnish/Russian clearing accounts). Clearing accounts can be accessed for payments to third countries in 'switch' transactions so 'soft' clearing currencies are then converted, at a cost to the original exporter, into 'hard currencies'. For example:

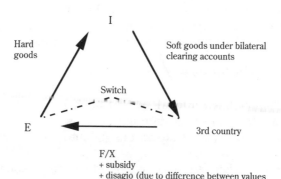

The role of banks and specialised institutions in countertrade should not be overlooked. The latter's strength will lie in their ability to take on, often as principal, an exporter's countertrade obligations at a subsidy cost and to match sources and needs to use bilateral clearing accounts effectively. The former can achieve earnings by providing performance bonds for parties concerned and by holding the escrow accounts which enable funds from the sale of goods from the importer's country to be accumulated for use by the exporter.

Traditionally the province of post-war trade between the West and Comecon, countertrade is now a major financing method. In the early 1970s only 15 countries insisted on such techniques but the figure had risen to 50 by the mid-1980s and it is now estimated that up to 10% of world trade is financed this way. Countries such as Indonesia have well-developed policies, Singapore is encouraging five-year tax holidays for countertraders and, in 1987, India announced that the two big state-owned trading companies handling 18% of the country's foreign trade must aim to cover 50% of imports by countertrade. In any countertrade deal, the goods and services in the main export contract and the goods available from the importer will dictate methods used. To illustrate, counterpurchase will typically cover exports of commodities, consumer goods, chemicals, pharmaceuticals and some capital goods against consumer goods or commodities. The most effective goods as payments are commodities with a stable price and market. Higher-value contracts, particularly those related to the export of large-scale industrial equipment or turnkey projects, are more suited to buy-back, co-operation and off-set, a prime example of the latter being Boeing's sale of AWACs to the UK whereby the latter offered to spend 130% of the contract value in Britain.

Despite the complicated deals countertrade requires and the inevitable distortions in the market it creates, such financing techniques are expected to grow as debt service problems and depressed prices for some commodities continue.

Which Financial Package to Choose?

This chapter has outlined several financing methods which involve using a combination of different sources to satisfy an overall need. Broadly speaking the transactions fall into three categories:

(a) those that support major domestic expenditure such as corporate capital expenditure plans funded by a debt/equity mix;

(b)   those that are export related and enable an exporter to release himself from non-payment risk or from burdening his own balance sheet with incremental debt whilst receiving cash payments upfront or on a stage payment basis; and

(c)   those that offer a buyer a means of covering the total cost of a contract or project.

No one package is exclusive and the skill of the banker and adviser lies in creating a mix of financing opportunities suitable to the needs of both parties.

Further Reading

1   D. Bowen, et al, *Guide to Export Finance*, Euromoney, 1987.
2   G. Holmes and A. Sugden, *Interpreting Company Report and Accounts*, 3rd ed., Woodhead-Faulkner, 1986, Chapters 10–11.
3   A. Watson, *Finance of International Trade*, 4th ed., The Chartered Institute of Bankers, Chapters 15–16.
4   Information publications from ECGD, The World Bank, etc.
5   The leasing file held at The Chartered Institute of Bankers' Library, which contains articles available for loan to members.

CHAPTER 21

Project Finance

Gilly Webb-Wilson

Introduction

The term project finance can be misleading since project financings can be split into two basic groups. First there are financings that rely on the cash flow from the project itself to provide the lenders with a first and often only source of repayment (non-recourse financing). Secondly, there are those that cover the financing of large infrastructural projects undertaken by a single contractor or a contracting consortium where repayment is sought directly from the buyer (sometimes called the sponsor) and/or his host government and where the credit risks associated with the contractor can be as high as those found in non-recourse project financing.

This chapter aims to examine these two types in the light of the risks encountered by buyer, supplier and financier in such projects. It is further intended to explore how, by using the products, knowledge and expertise available to him, the banker can bridge the wide gap between the supplier's and buyer's divergent needs.

What Is Project Finance?

Non-recourse financing

In its purest sense, project finance should be non-recourse with the lenders seeking debt service from the cash flow of the project without requiring any direct legal recourse to and credit support from the sponsors. Lenders will protect their credit risks by ensuring the assets of the project act as loan collateral and by structuring a debt and equity package which not only ties in the project sponsors to the project but which also ensures that the latter's interests are subordinated to bank debt. The long-term aim would be to hand over the project to the sponsors and investors once bank debt is repaid.

Non-recourse project financing is attractive to sponsors and contractors in that, correctly structured, it need not affect the credit standing or balance sheet of any party; debt does not impact balance sheet ratios, covenants are not affected and security can be given without breaking negative pledge clauses. It is chosen as a financing route when the size of a transaction and its obligations are too large for any buyer/supplier to bear. It is particularly suited to some industries, e.g. mining and energy, where an underlying commodity is extracted to be on-sold to generate cash. Equally, infrastructural projects, often being supported by a host country due to their ability to provide import substitution, are natural candidates for project financing, for example the construction and operation of a sugar refining plant or pulp mill, or the erection of a cement factory.

Today, the purest form of non-recourse financing is not common but from it have developed the much used techniques of limited recourse financing and contractual obligation supported financing where the debt package is still expected to be serviced from cash flow but where the project sponsors and other parties are legally contracted to ensure that the project is completed and that debt is serviced. Lenders will use covenants and undertakings to ensure the commitment of further shareholders' funds and will acquire completion guarantees (e.g. to provide additional finance in the event of cost overruns) and working capital guarantees (e.g. during a start-up phase). Contractual obligations include:

(a) The provision of throughput agreements (for example, in pipeline financing, whereby the owners of the oil or gas field guarantee to pass a minimum amount of oil and gas through the pipeline at an agreed price or to pay a cash penalty).

(b) The assignment of 'take or pay contracts' to the lenders (such contracts will typically involve a third party who has agreed to purchase the commodity being extracted by the project but is not a project sponsor).

(c) Forward oil (or gas) purchase agreements (FOPA) and similar structures, which are popular since the underlying obligation is a trading one rather than balance sheet debt. In this instance, a specific non-consolidated finance company would be set up to borrow funds for advance purchases of oil under a FOPA. The producer will obviously commit to deliver oil on future dates such that revenue will be generated on its sale to service debt.

Contract-related project financing with direct credit recourse

Non-recourse financing is the province of specialists, and banks heavily involved in such financing have departments staffed with industry and technical experts with considerable expertise in creating funding packages designed as off-balance sheet financing. Non-specialist bankers, especially those with customers in the civil engineering and construction sectors, will also encounter the term project financing where the repayment credit risk will usually be centred on the buyer or promoter of the project. Typically, such projects would be capital-intensive and motivated by the infrastructural needs of the buyer (for example, improvement in a country's road systems, the modernisation of a telecommunications system, development of a power system by the commissioning of hydroelectric power stations or the construction and equipment of a hospital complex). In recent years the developing nations and, in particular, the oil-rich Middle East governments have been the typical commissioners of such projects and also the main credit risk in buyer credit financing to support them.

Although the lenders will have direct legal recourse to the buyer or its guarantor as cover for their term funding, the project risks themselves and the risks connected with the contractor will be similar to, and indeed often as high as, those associated with non-recourse financing. An analysis of the risks identifies opportunities for bankers to use their products to alleviate the risks, thereby helping both buyer and supplier to satisfy their differing needs by what is often innovative 'financial engineering'.

Risks Common to All Project Financings

Risks in project financing can be categorised broadly into four groups. The country risk, the completion risk, the operating risk and the financial risk.

Country risk

The acceptance of country risk is fundamental to the success of a project and thus to the safe repayment of credit facilities. Country risk embraces the social, political and economic environment of a country, which factors, if unstable and volatile, could threaten the viability of a project.

The inherent political risk may be defined as the politically-motivated actions which adversely affect:

(a)   the contractor's ability to perform;
(b)   the operation of a structurally completed project at the time when lenders are looking to the cash flow for repayment; or

(c)   most importantly, the transferability of foreign exchange for debt repayment.

A boycott or an embargo unilaterally imposed on a contractor would obviously affect the contractor financially since start-up and pre-construction costs are high. Similarly, expropriation and confiscation of a complete plant or indeed just of equipment and machinery can lead to the contractor encountering operational and financial problems resulting in dispute and debt moratorium. In some countries, these political risks will be higher than in others. Banks are unwilling, for instance, to accept the country risk of territories where governments change rapidly, and where there is a history of reneging on contracts. The transferability risk is closely linked to the country's own economic situation and since the 1982 Latin America debt crisis banks have become more aware of this risk, spreading their country risk exposure with greater diversification between territories.

The economic risk is linked to political risk but in project financing it is examined in the light of the project's fundamental suitability to the country's own socio/economic situation. The more a project will benefit the wealth of a nation, either by providing import substitution, or by creating a source of revenue (e.g. the extraction of oil for on-sale) or by improving the infrastructure of the country itself (e.g. an urban transport system), the more likely it is the project will be supported both politically and economically.

Completion risk
This risk is essentially that of the contractor being unable to perform and satisfy the technical requirements of the contract. Delays are almost inevitable in capital projects and they invariably lead to cost overruns and expose the project to the threats of downturn in market risks such as reductions in the pricing of the commodity being extracted (see below). Additionally, completion delays mean the income stream available for debt service is pushed further into the future, finance costs are increased as the interest burden is greater and contractors run the risk of missing key delivery dates.

Technical problems are a major cause of delay. The lenders and the project sponsors must feel confident that the contractors are technically suited to the job contracted, and have the management to control the project during start-up, construction and the operating phases.

Operating risk

The operating risk is encountered primarily by those involved in non-recourse or limited recourse funding, except to the extent that a bank is on risk due to the continued existence of a retention or maintenance bond (see below) after completion date. For a cash-flow lender or investor it covers the period of maximum risk not only since revenue stream from the ongoing operation of the project is vital but also because at this stage third party and sponsor guarantees may well have expired.

The main operating risks hinge on the demand and supply (and thus the price levels) of the project's revenue generating sales. For example, the success of a project involving the erection and operation of a pulp mill is entirely dependent on the market risk that the pulp milled locally will not be more costly than imported pulp. If world prices of pulp collapse then it is possible that even with the help of local protectionism (e.g. import tariffs on imported pulp) pulp from the new plant being financed cannot be sold at prices high enough to satisfy debt service. The problem of market risk was seen in the mid-1980s as the oil price sank, putting the economic viability of several energy projects at risk thus prompting the shelving or delaying of some projects. Market risk at its most virulent has been seen in the mid-1980s in the oil sector where many energy projects and financings collapsed due to low oil prices. Market risks include not only the threat of competition but also simple demand factors such as market location and access to it. Operating risk is also a feature of turnkey projects where the contractor may be obliged to operate the plant for, say, 12 months and to train local staff during that period.

Lastly, the degree of operating risk will be lessened by strong management of the project. Sponsors and lenders have to be completely satisfied that the requisite industry experience and technical skills, marketing ability and financial expertise are present in management and can support ongoing operations. The evaluation of management remains the project financiers' most difficult task in that no matter how sophisticated and tailormade banking products may be, weak management exposes a project to delay and cost overruns at the construction stage and to suspect revenue stream thereafter.

Financial risk

Identification of this risk is simple. It includes the possibility of non-repayment of financing, the unforeseen costs of incremental financing needs in the start-up and construction period, and a foreign exchange mismatch risk.

The foreign exchange risk occurs when financing payments and receipts are denominated in different currencies and mismatched positions occur. The mismatch can occur for several reasons, for example sales of the project's output are denominated in a different currency from that which the cash-flow revenue stream is expected to service, equipment is sourced from several territories and priced in local currency, a project cannot be funded from local markets but is financed from the international capital markets in a freely convertible currency.

The 'Needs Gap' Between Buyer and Supplier in Project Financing

Even a brief examination of the inherent risks in project financing highlights the gap which will occur between the terms on which the supplier can safely undertake a contract and those which a buyer is prepared to accept in awarding and paying for a contract. The commonality of needs is slender and probably limited to a desire, in 'pure' project financings, to keep the debt burden as far away from a balance sheet or public expenditure plan as possible and to see that the contracted project is structurally complete as soon as possible.

The contractor or supplier will be particularly interested in:

(a)   being paid quickly and in cash (e.g. no barter, countertrade);
(b)   receiving maximum payment in advance to cover pre-construction and start-up costs;
(c)   ensuring full payment will be received and that monies will be disbursed regularly to cover the costs of work as stages of the project are completed;
(d)   taking no credit risk on the buyer and equally avoiding credit recourse falling on himself (e.g. via supplier credits or onerous equity participation);
(e)   being paid at best in a currency suitable to his own financial position, such that foreign exchange risks are avoided, or at worst in a freely convertible currency; and
(f)   having discretionary control over the sourcing of his equipment.

The buyer's needs are likely to be diametrically opposed to those of the supplier and can be more complex in that they will be influenced by his political and economic environment. In particular, there is strong political and economic motivation in less developed countries (LDCs), which obviously provide strong demand for large infrastructural projects, to insist that any contractor tendering must use local labour and equipment as much as possible to avoid unnecessary payments in valuable foreign exchange. In some territories the conditions of local involvement required will be more stringent, and tender specifications may stipulate that only tenders involving joint ventures with acceptable local partners will be considered. Equally, the buyer will be seeking tenders which offer the most attractive credit terms, whilst still satisfying the underlying problems that the contractor will not wait to be paid and that the project must be completed in accordance with the terms of the contract.

A summary of the buyer's concerns and needs shows he is primarily interested in:

(a)   receiving credit terms from the supplier;
(b)   beneficial credit terms — i.e. minimum costs but with maximum length grace period and extended amortisation period;
(c)   certainty of interest cost — i.e. a strong preference for fixed-rate funding, and for aid-supported packages;
(d)   minimisation of foreign exchange risk, e.g. by maximising the use of local resources and local funding;
(e)   successful completion of the project with as little cost overruns as possible;
(f)   possible reduction of the hard currency payment obligations by using countertrade techniques;
(g)   avoiding recourse to himself by demanding non-recourse project finance structures with debt service dependent on income stream.

The 'needs gap' between buyer and supplier is difficult to bridge without a third-party involvement in an advisory role in both technical and financial matters. The banking community is well-placed to satisfy this needs gap by the provision of both advisory and direct services to the buyer and supplier such that both parties feel the risks they are shouldering in the project are reduced to acceptable levels. The fee-earning opportunities in project financing are attractive and the need for high levels of direct financing provides high-interest income. The risk : reward ratio for banks is at its highest in project financing, particularly in non-recourse and limited recourse funding or where the country risk itself is high.

The Banker's Role in Project Financing

There are perhaps four different roles a bank can play in bridging the 'needs gap' identified above. These involve:

(a)   providing an advisory service in drafting the feasibility study for the project and continuing to advise during the lifetime of the project;

(b)   arranging a financial structure and the provision of funding for all parties;

(c)   providing specific non-funds based banking products (e.g. F/X lines, bonding);

(d)   making available ancillary banking services (e.g. insurance, countertrade).

No single role is mutually exclusive nor will the contractor or project sponsors necessarily seek to use just one bank to play all four roles. It is not unusual to find a bank which specialises in providing project advisory services being only an arranger of the funds and non-funds based banking products. It requires a bank with a large capital base, a good international network and much experience in project advisory work to satisfy the criteria governing all four roles. A project co-ordinator, however, pulling all the threads of the banking community's products together is often a key player.

The banker's different roles need to be broken down and examined in greater depth to show how the needs of the buyer and supplier can be satisfied.

The Advisory Role

The advisory role is an ongoing assignment, beginning with assistance in the preparation of a feasibility study (which would incorporate, *inter alia*, topics as diverse as recommendations regarding the funding structure for the project and an assessment of technical aspects), moving to advice and support at the bidding stage and to the arranging of the funding itself and any ancillary banking products that may be needed. The adviser's task will not be fulfilled until the project is completed and financing is repaid. An adviser is often at his most useful as an intermediary and negotiator when a project runs into difficulties (e.g. when delays occur affecting cost overruns) and either the repayment schedule is thereby jeopardised or, at worst, client and contractor enter into disputes which affect the viability of the project itself.

Bank assisted funding structures are examined below but it is worth considering in greater detail, at this stage, the key areas which need to be covered in a feasibility study and an adviser's role in the bidding process.

Feasibility study
It is important to realise that any bank providing advisory services at an early stage in the conception of a project will be working closely with contractors and will recognise the gap in technical knowledge and understanding between contractor and banker. To close this gap, banks usually employ the services of independent specialist consultants whose aims are to provide the banks with an impartial third-party assessment of the technical viability of the project and to highlight the areas of 'sensitivity' which could have a dramatic effect on the payback potential of a project. Any feasibility study or project appraisal requires an analysis of five discrete areas:

(a) the technical risk
(b) the country risk
(c) the market risk
(d) the quality of management
(e) the financial structure

so that each financial participant can have enough information to decide how and to what level they will participate.

(a)   *Technical risk* — An appraisal of the technical risk includes the project description (the products and anticipated volume output) and assesses the quality of plant design and the sophistication of the process in the light of the environment in which the project is situated. Close attention is paid to geographical and infra-structural influences (e.g. the adequacy of road/rail access to the site, the adequacy and reliability of energy supplies, the suitability of the terrain) and the availability of manpower and raw materials. The bank will tend to be little involved in the collation of the above facts but will need to consider the imputed risks in order to draft proposals on financing structures with relevant protections acceptable to all parties.
(b)   *Country risk* — Whilst every participant in project financing decides to participate at its own risk after independent analysis

of the risks, any feasibility study whether it is part of a published prospectus or of an in-house credit analysis should address the country risks mentioned previously. Particular attention is frequently paid to the economic evaluation of the project (that is an assessment of the economic and social benefits made available by it) and to the political support necessary to ensure smooth-running of the project. Without the latter, the risk of non-payment or slow payments tends to be higher.

(c) *Market risk* — In so far as market risk affects the demand for, and pricing of, the end products from the successful completion of a project, a feasibility study will evaluate such risk in the light of financing requirements (e.g. level of payback period in non-recourse project-financing, break-even point determining grace periods). Both in the local context, if products are being produced for the domestic market, and in the global context in the case of production for export, an assessment of the competition, such as the effect of similar projects coming on stream the same time as the one being proposed, will also be prepared. Attempts will be made to indicate possible effects of direct intervention (e.g. by governments imposing taxes and levies or price controls). A bank with good local knowledge of the territory in which the project is planned can make a valuable advisory contribution at this stage.

(d) *The quality of management* — Assessment of management is, by its very nature, subjective. However, examples of past and current operations illustrate marketing and technical successes and failures and show whether management experience is such that the intended project would not stretch its ability or know-how. The management failure risk would tend to be higher, for instance, in cases where a contractor used to domestic, local work only finds himself now working overseas in an LDC where control problems are different and more complex.

(e) *Financial structure* — In order to identify the correct banking and funding mix of products, a feasibility study will address the financing sources and requirements, that is the liabilities structure of a project, in parallel with debt service requirements. The study will approach the financial risk differently depending on the degree of country risk involved and on whether the project structure is to be on a limited or non-recourse basis or whether the credit risks fall more directly on the buyer and supplier.

In the case of limited or non-recourse financing, care is taken to establish the cash-flow position of the project with attention being paid to earnings generated not only from the more obvious sale of products but also from licence fees, royalties and management fees. The downside of revenue projections must also be considered and assessed in cash-flow sensitivity analyses. This technique is the main bankers' tool for illustration of the impact, say, of falling profit margins, rising inflation and interest rates, foreign exchange rate fluctuations and changes in tax legislation. Without such sensitivity analyses it would be impossible to forecast levels of financing required, in the pre-production phase and in the medium term. The need for working capital will also be highlighted by examining 'worst and best case' scenarios based on cash-flow projections. An advisor to a project will have to consider other areas too, apart from debt, in particular (where appropriate) a liabilities structure of debt and equity. In this instance the level of equity will be influenced by the desire to tie in the sponsors' commitment to the project.

If the equity contribution is low it may be recommended that guarantees from shareholders are provided. The total of the equity and near-equity could well include as wide a mix as ordinary and preference share capital, convertible loan stock and subordinated debt; in each case the effect of legal factors, exchange controls, taxation, foreign currency exposure and the return on investment requirement of the various participants determines a recommended liabilities structure.

Attention to these latter points will also help the advisers determine the appropriateness of a project finance vehicle company structure in that it may be decided to create a limited company, a joint venture or a partnership, to establish a subsidiary or associate of a larger company or for accounting and tax reasons to establish a non-consolidated subsidiary or associate the liabilities of which are well separated from those of the parent. At this stage too, an adviser will consider the effect of foreign exchange mismatch positions.

The feasibility study will be used by the advising bank in its attempts to guide the project sponsor and it will make recommendations as to choice of structures and financing packages. It will probably also be used by the Lead Managers in their efforts to draft an information memorandum supporting the raising of suitable finance. During the bidding period (a stage when constructive financial advice can mean the gain or loss of a contract) it is usual for the niceties of financial, technical and production contracts and the final agreed pricing of the project to be established.

Financial advice on bidding for a contract

The period between a tender date and award of contract for any substantial project is unlikely to be less than six months and can stretch to several years as the buyer negotiates over financing offered as well as project costs. In non-recourse financing the negotiations will be between sponsors and financiers as each party attempts to minimise its risks whilst remaining price competitive. It is common practice today for tender documents to require the provision of a financing package to accompany the technical and costings tenders.

Cases have occurred where an adviser has played several roles such as convincing a buyer that a project is viable and in its economic interests, negotiating with the UK government such that soft-loan policy is amended to suit the needs of a particular buyer and introducing aid elements from multilateral agencies, identifying certain overseas funds to support particular causes.

Not all such causes have their origins at the pre-bid stage and some may well arise due to particular points being raised during the bid period. The adviser's skills lie in his flexibility of approach to the financing and his knowledge and experience which stimulate the creation of tailormade packages which can be sold to the financial markets. Additionally, an adviser with good local knowledge will frequently be able to lessen the 'burden' of import levies on equipment etc. by suggesting structures which take advantage of local regulations, for example it may be cost-effective for a local company rather than the contractor to import machinery.

The financial adviser's contribution to a successful project financing cannot be underestimated. It is a contribution which is expected to last from a feasibility study to completion of the project and in most instances to the final repayment date of associated projects. Like a banker lending direct to buyer or supplier in a project where no specific financial adviser is contracted, the adviser must always keep himself fully aware of the status of the project being financed by regular site visits and the maintenance of close contacts between buyer and supplier so mediation constructive to all parties occurs rapidly when required.

Financial Structures in Project Financing

The financial structures provided by the banking and financial community fall broadly into:

(a)   those that accept pure cash-flow risk (i.e. non- or partial-recourse financings),
(b)   those that accept a buyer's credit risk, and
(c)   those that hinge on a supplier's credit risk.

It is not intended to examine non-recourse financing further except to stress that such financing depends on the creation of a suitable security package which captures the commitment of the sponsors and provides lenders with tangible comfort. Typically such lenders' requirements would include legal access to revenues (by assignment of contracts or receivables), charges over assets of the financing vehicle and/or the project itself, charges on the shareholders' stakes in the project and restrictions on ancillary funding as well as the obvious right to first place in the repayment schedule (i.e. other providers of finance are subordinated to bank lenders). Like direct financings, non-recourse loans will have tailored drawdown schedules to dovetail into construction phases, and repayment schedules will recognise the need for grace periods during the pre-commissioning period and for the maximum term thereafter. Lastly most non-recourse financing will be accompanied by banking packages similar to those serving as the mainstay in contractor-related direct recourse project financing. Such packages would include buyer and supplier credits with and without export credit agency support, aid and soft loan packages, working capital loans, standby facilities to fund cost overruns and even more complex structures, for example standby letters of credit which cover the project risk whilst the borrower gains the finest margins in the international capital markets (e.g. via FRNs, United States commercial paper) due to the collective rating of the banking syndicate.

Buyer credits
Where UK companies are the main contractors, the majority of project financing is satisfied by the provision of buyer credits, of which the greater percentage (usually 85% of the contract price under OECD consensus guidelines) is covered by export credit agency guarantees or insurance (e.g. ECGD buyer credit guarantees which remove the risk of the buyer defaulting to that of the UK government). Such loans are usually long-term, fixed-rate and subsidised by the exporting country's authorities (again at rates in accordance with international consensus rules). Thus the buyer benefits from low fixed interest rate funds for a term usually not available commercially and the supplier acquires the certainty of payment for work undertaken since he is paid through

direct disbursement by the bank providing the loan. If the buyer does not represent pure sovereign risk or is generally not wholly acceptable to the credit insurers, first-class bank guarantees of the risk may be sought by the insurer. For those banks prepared to accept direct credit exposure on the buyer this enables them to increase fee earnings by guaranteeing the buyer and thereby giving the latter access to long-term fixed-rate, low coupon funding. Export credit insured loans can be supplemented and their attractiveness enhanced by joint packages involving aid monies or grants and loans from development funds which will often be available for longer periods (up to 20 years in extreme cases) thus increasing the average life of the buyer's fund raising. The skill of the banker lies in creating the relevant package of 'mixed credits' soft loans and co-financing.

The 'uninsured' portion of a buyer credit (usually 15% of the project costs and often referred to as the 'commercial loan') can only be covered by direct acceptance of the buyer's credit risk by international commercial bank lenders. As in the insured loan, a buyer may succeed in persuading a group of banks to guarantee his credit and country risks in order to make his risk more widely acceptable to an international banking syndicate. In practice, however, it is more common for lenders to take the direct risk of the buyer or its host state (e.g. Électricité de France, guaranteed by the Republic of France). The repayment schedule of the commercial loans is generally shorter than that of the insured financing as the credit risk is usually greater and interest rates have traditionally been on a floating-rate basis except in low interest rate currencies where the opportunities for longer-term fixed-rate funding are greater. As an alternative to seeking commercial loans tied to a project, a buyer or sponsor may choose to use today's fertile and divergent capital markets and undertake a major fund-raising exercise as part of its general foreign currency funding requirements from the international markets. Cash can then effectively be paid for the 15% balance. Typical instruments would be FRNs, Euronote facilities, commercial paper transactions or bond issues. In these cases the funding is not project related and the banks would have no role in disbursements of the proceeds of the loan to any third party. As pricing gets keener, in the capital markets creditworthy and market-acceptable names are increasingly tapping these sources of financing to fund major projects. Such fund-raising exercises, however, do not alleviate the supplier's risk of non-payment and will form part of the host country's external borrowing requirements.

Supplier credits

The supplier is nearly always reluctant to provide credit to his buyer due to the credit risk and cash-flow implications. At times the buyer will insist on supplier credits being offered either in respect of a particular item of equipment or in respect of an entire contract. The buyer will usually forego the advantage of the long-term funding when insisting on supplier credits (in that the latter tend to have a shorter maturity than the former) but will avoid the commensurate bank debt on its balance sheet. A provider of supplier credit can protect its position by acquiring export credit agency guarantees or insurance but it can also alleviate its risk further and can improve its cash flow by being paid up-front rather than in accordance with the payment schedule of the credit by banks prepared to re-finance a supplier credit itself. The re-financing would usually be without credit recourse to the supplier, in that promissory notes or bills of exchange are purchased outright from the supplier on a non-recourse basis. Unlike a forfait transactions, paper purchased under a supplier credit will not necessarily be avalised nor be discountable at fixed rates of interest. Interest rates will follow the terms of the supplier credit itself, and purchasers of the debt instruments may choose to take a direct credit risk on the buyer without bank guarantees against the risk. The banks re-financing such credits do tend to consider such transactions, however, as riskier than those with a direct risk on the buyer as the re-financing is superimposed on an underlying contract between supplier and buyer. The costs can therefore be high on uninsured risks.

In a buyer credit such 'third party transactions' are avoided as the bank does not have the imputed performance risk on the supplier and is not dependent for fulfilment on the commercial terms of the supply contract as is an integral feature of the supplier credit.

Letters of credit

Letters of credit are discussed in the section on non-funds based banking products but these instruments can also form the base for alternative funding. A supplier may be required, under his contract, to provide certain equipment for payment under a letter of credit which can have a lengthy payment structure. Banks can unburden the contractor/supplier of the credit risks concerned by confirming the letter of credit and by re-financing drawings under it so that the supplier is paid immediately rather than on the deferred terms specified in it. The interest costs will be a matter of negotiation between supplier and the bank; in some cases the bank may require the supplier to make-up and increase the interest charge contracted between buyer and supplier as it represents terms which may be well below market financing rates but which are considered commercial between the supplier and buyer. (This 'interest make-up' feature will also occur in re-financings of straightforward supplier credits.)

Working capital facilities

Such financing essentially divides into hard currency and local currency loans; both tend to be medium-term to cover the construction period of the project and are designed to ensure that a cushion of financing is available over and above the long-term funding structure, to cover unforeseen contingencies which could have a serious delay impact on the project and to cover everyday needs. 'Standby credits' are usually made to cover the hard-currency safety cushion required, typically these will be medium-term floating-rate revolving loans attracting a commitment fee. Credit recourse is likely to be direct to buyer or supplier and if the borrower is a project finance vehicle, the lenders may seek guarantees from involved third parties rather than add the standby commitments to the non-recourse funding. Any contractor will need local currency facilities in the host country which, for practical reasons, are unlikely to be offered by anyone else other than a local bank.

The local facilities a contractor would require range from wages and salaries accounts (perhaps with small overdraft limits to cover remittance delays if the account has to be funded from overseas), to current accounts for expatriates and to working capital loans and overdrafts to cover payments to local suppliers. All such facilities would be subject to local banking and foreign exchange regulations. It is not unusual in countries with strict regulations (particularly in the developing world) to find that local facilities have to be secured or guaranteed by external third parties, are subject to mandatory interest rates and are governed by bureaucratic procedures. A procedural mistake with local facilities can cost a contractor dear and local banks can provide a valuable service in preventing international contractors from falling foul of local bureaucracy.

Leasing — an Alternative Funding Structure

Leasing as part of financial packages is discussed in the previous chapter but it is important to see its application in project financing. The benefits to all parties of the leasing route are primarily access to off-balance sheet long-term fixed-rate funding, the ability to structure lease rentals to fit in with a progress payment schedule in the construction period and cash-flow projections, the ability for lessor and lessee to share in the residual value of the asset if they so wish and to achieve an interest rate cost lower than commercial rates.

A leasing structure can be used to finance multi-million dollar projects (although lessors will not usually accept the project risks), or alternatively it can be more straightforward and apply to an individual piece of equipment. A contractor needing a specific machine for one project and which will not be used again, may choose to lease it from a leasing company rather than have direct ownership of the asset. Obviously, in both instances, leasing enables the lessee to avoid utilising bank lines for the funding although the leverage of its balance sheet may still be impacted if leases are capitalised — as are such finance leases in the UK and USA.

Non-Funds Based Banking Products Necessary in Project Financing

Today, as banks are more conscious of the need for return on assets and capital adequacy, the realisation has emerged that providing loan facilities alone does not necessarily generate sufficient return on risk or represent an adequate reason for gearing up the bank's own balance sheet. Consequently, bankers are very conscious of the ability to augment the return on risk (i.e. the return on any name to which facilities are being provided) by generating fee and commission income from non-funds based banking products. The opportunities to earn such income from project financing are considerable due to the high levels of equipment and material being shipped (letters of credit can cover this requirement), the level of bank guarantees required to bridge the confidence gap between supplier and buyer (i.e. the need for one party to feel sure it will be paid and for the other to be confident of satisfactory project completion), the need for foreign exchange services, and the desire to minimise financing costs through use of interest rate management products.

Letters of credit
Letters of credit are one of the most traditional and trusted forms of trade financing and are widely used as the payment instruments for capital goods exports. If a supplier can negotiate immediate or fast payment from a buyer for a shipment of essential goods a sight or

maybe usance letter of credit with credit periods of up to 180 days will often be used. The supplier feels it is safe to ship and that payment will be made and the buyer can expect delivery of goods specified in the documents. Deferred letters of credit with medium- to long-term payment structures are more likely to be re-financed than sight or short-term usance credits but all types will offer banks the chance of earning opening, advising and maybe negotiating fees. Confirmation of a letter of credit by a leading bank will normally satisfy the beneficiary's doubts over payment and also lead to incremental non-funds based earnings. In many cases it may be impossible for the buyer to acquire import approvals and gain access to the foreign exchange required for payment without opening a credit. This enables the authorities to supervise the pricing of imports (transfer pricing becomes more difficult) and to control allocation of foreign exchange. Letters of credit will not only be used for simple transactions but can be used to bridge other gaps between buyer and supplier, between financiers and the project sponsors, and to help a supplier's own cash flow. To illustrate:

(a)   A bank can access the cash flow of a project by structuring letters of credit as the financing means for 'take or/and pay contracts'; thereby achieving close control over the revenue stream by routing payments through the financing bank.

(b)   A supplier can avoid using his own cash flow to pay sub-suppliers by a back-to-back letter of credit structure routed from buyer to sub-supplier or by seeking payment by transferable credit. Such credits may also protect the supplier from additional exchange risk as equipment from a sub-supplier to be paid for in DM, for instance, could be paid for by a DM denominated credit opened by the buyer. The buyer who has agreed a sterling price with the supplier will not be happy to do this in every case.

Guarantees

Guarantees are used in project financing to allow the transfer of certain risks such that parties need not necessarily become directly involved in a project and can benefit from their liability being only contingent and therefore off-balance sheet. Examples have already been given in relation to project finance structures (e.g. sponsors' working-capital guarantees). Any major contract will also require 'contract-related' guarantees to support both the suppliers' and buyers' positions. Often such guarantees are collectively referred to as 'bonding requirements' and the bank uses its credit rating by assuming its client's (the obligor's) payment obligations under the bonding terms and honouring any beneficiary's calls on bonds issued by the bank. The bank opening the bond obviously takes credit risks on the obligor and will ensure that a suitable counter guarantee/counter indemnity from the latter enables recourse to the obligor following payment under a bond and allows calls for cash cover of bonds outstanding in certain instances (e.g. if the obligor is in default of its financial obligations). Further protection can be gained from the use of ECGD's or the commercial insurance market's policies covering the unfair calling of bonds. The types of guarantee that may be required are discussed below, individually. The list is not exhaustive and in each case local requirements may determine the actual wording and structure of the bonds.

Tender bonds (bid bonds)
As an indication of their seriousness, contractors tendering for contracts have to lodge with their tender a guarantee stating they will not withdraw from the contract if awarded it and that requisite follow-on guarantees bonds will be issued, e.g. performance and maintenance bonds. The validity of a tender bond is usually the period required to assess tenders (e.g. three to six months) but bonds are frequently extended as the evaluation of tenders becomes protracted. The sum guaranteed is usually between 5 to 10% of the contract price but may be a fixed sum in mega-sized contracts.

Performance bonds
Again, these are usually related to contract price (typically between 5 to 10%) but are for a longer period than tender bonds as bonds must be current during the whole contract period. Banks and buyers/sponsors favour unconditional 'on demand' bonds which do not force them into any disputes on the legitimacy of a call but such a bond is obviously more dangerous for the obligor. The purpose of the bond is essentially to guarantee a contractor's financial soundness (that is, that the supplier will not cease trading or performing in the middle of a contract) and to provide a sum which could be used to pay another contractor if the first defaults — although the occasions when this scenario occurs are rare; the costs of bringing a new contractor on site being prohibitive.

Advance payment guarantees

It is unusual for a contractor to operate without an advance payment from the buyer to cover initial start-up costs and raw materials. An advance payment will obviously reduce a contractor's financing costs and thus his overall price — but a buyer is reluctant to part with such cash without an ability to redeem the sum if things go wrong. A bank guarantee for the sums advanced covers this contingency — this will typically be for an amount of 5 to 25% of the contract price. Normal practice is for the advance payment to be repaid over the period of the contract, i.e. if the advance is 5%, then 5% is deducted from each progress payment to repay the advance and the bank's liability is reduced accordingly. The bank will seek to ensure payments are made through it to monitor reductions and thereby earns extra fees if the sums are then transferred overseas, and it also benefits from increased deposits.

Maintenance bonds

These bonds cover a maintenance period after the completion of the contract (say 12 months) often referred to as the 'snagging period'. Only at the end of the maintenance period when the project is formally handed over will retention monies be released. The sum guaranteed usually represents 5 to 10% of the contract value.

Retention bonds

It is practice for amounts to be withheld from progress payments due to a contractor with often half the retention being released on completion of the contract and the remainder at the end of the maintenance period. It may be possible for a contractor to secure early release of the retention against a bank guarantee and thereby improve cash flow and reduce finance costs.

Duty deferment guarantees

These cover the importation into the host country of equipment linked to a project's construction. The authorities may relax import duty requirements usually levied if a bank guarantees the sum in question. If at the end of the construction period, the equipment is not then removed from the host country, the guarantee is called. Such guarantees are relatively cheap and avoid the supplier suffering unnecessary cash-flow costs.

The above examples illustrate how the use of guarantees helps a contractor's cash flow whilst offering the buyer the comfort of a bank credit risk rather than direct supplier risk and direct access to cash compensation. To a contractor the pricing of guarantees (lower than direct financing costs) is attractive and by using bonding to its best limits a contractor can avoid gearing up his balance sheet unnecessarily since his counter-guarantees to the bank issuing the bonds are only contingent liabilities.

Foreign Exchange Services

Foreign exchange (F/X) fluctuations during the financing or payment period of a project's completion can severely increase the cost to the buyer or wipe out the supplier's/contractor's profit margin. Most major contracts will be priced in hard currency and since large-scale financing will be most readily available from the liquid international capital markets, funding will be denominated also in hard currency. A buyer will attempt to lower the foreign exchange costs as much as possible by accepting tenders which use local goods and services as much as possible (the contractor would then expect to receive some payment in local currency to meet local costs) but would still need to meet significant foreign currency obligations. The contractor/supplier, the recipient of this foreign exchange, may well find himself with an exposure problem too if the pricing of the contract is not in a currency suitable to his balance sheet or if he has ordered from overseas sub-suppliers. The extent to which the exposures of both buyer and supplier can be hedged will be governed by local exchange controls but the banking products that can be offered to fulfil the task are common to both parties except in the instance of specialist cover available to exporters through export credit agencies and recent innovative products designed to protect parties at the bid stage. Chapters 14 and 15 cover the mechanisms available to both buyer and seller, and reference should be made to these.

Hedging loans

In the absence of long-term foreign exchange cover, or as an alternative to conventional forward cover, a contractor/supplier may decide to hedge its receivables (i.e. progress payments) by taking out a matching foreign currency loan. There may be balance sheet reasons for doing so, particularly if there is a fear of translation losses on balance sheet consolidation. This method of hedging would not necessarily relieve the contractor of all translation differences, due to the problem of synchronising borrowings and receivables, but it may alleviate a potential risk. In the late 1970s, for instance, a practice arose in Saudi Arabia to denominate contracts in Saudi riyals and until measures were taken to curb offshore riyals, some contractors chose to borrow that currency through offshore centres such as Bahrain. With the Saudi riyal then moving in line with the US$, this method was considered a suitable hedge against receivables. Today cross-currency swaps will also be used to hedge translation exposure where there is an active market in the currencies.

Banking products to cover foreign currency tenders
Banks can provide products which will not necessitate conventional forward cover and which can be less cumbersome and cheaper. Options can be structured, at a lower cost than usual, which are only exercisable if a tender is successful. Solutions have also emerged which move the option purchase from supplier to buyer (e.g. shared currency option under tender) but which benefit all parties, for example the buyer takes out one option contract to cover the tender period and sells it, pro rata, to each tenderer. Ultimately the option cover is transferred to the successful tenderer. This enables tenderers to acquire options at a cheaper premium cost by sharing in one option and can be used to cover a situation where tenders are coming from several countries — for example, a $/ECU option would act as a proxy hedge, if several European contractors were bidding; the latter would suffer only an ECU/local currency risk.

Interest Rate Management

Protection from interest rate movements to enable certainty of obligations and costs is as important as foreign exchange management. Fixed-rate buyer credits are obviously the prime means of achieving this but a buyer or supplier can also fix rate costs by using the swap market to swap floating-rate obligations into fixed-rate ones. The swap markets are sophisticated enough to cope with the cash-flow problems of staggered drawdowns and stage repayments but care is needed to ensure that timing differences do not destroy the swap structures. Swaps will also be used to change the interest rate obligation from a high coupon currency to a low one, for example in a Chinese power project a series of swaps changed the dollar obligation to a yen one. Other means are available to all borrowing parties to fix interest costs at an early stage (e.g. to secure a true all-in cost of the project) such as the use of forward rate agreements (FRAs) prior to drawdown of a loan.

Ancillary Banking Services Useful in Project Financing

With the banking community becoming an increasingly diverse service industry, opportunities also arise to provide fee earning ancillary services. Two completely different services are probably most readily available. The first is insurance cover — several major banks now have insurance broking arms which would be able to arrange cover ranging from confiscation and expropriation insurance to cover political risks, to contractors all risks insurance (covering, for instance, damage to works and plant during construction) to business interruption insurance and to cover against 'unfair calling of bonds'. Secondly, as foreign exchange resources in the developing world become scarcer bids increasingly call for financing options to include an element of (or indeed 100%) countertrade proposals. Specialist banks will help satisfy these obligations and can provide useful advisory services.

The Opportunities and Risks in Project Financing

The analysis above of the advisory work a bank can undertake in assisting the development and satisfactory completion of any contract or project and of the earnings potential from funds and non-funds based banking products illustrates the immense opportunities project financing offers a banker. The enormity of the risks involved, however, cannot be overemphasised as the banker is essentially acting as a filler of the 'needs gap' between buyer and supplier by assuming diverse risks to avoid the contracting parties themselves assuming them. Banking history is rife with tales of failed project financings due to reasons as diverse as changes in market risks (e.g. project financings relying on high oil prices) or unsuitable financial structures. In nearly all cases incorrect assessments of the risks have been made at an early stage (one of the greatest such risks being the management risk), or control by the lenders has been weak due to lack of current knowledge on the status of the project. It is essential that any project, whether non- or limited-recourse or contractor-related, is monitored carefully. This can be done in a variety of ways:

—   by site visits to confirm progress and to build up background knowledge by discussions with engineers;

— by insisting on regular progress certificates to compare work completed with price and period and to relate borrowing levels to certificates held and unpaid;
— by discussing projects regularly with consultants to the project;
— by appointment of independent consultants to monitor a project, when necessary.

If a mix of these techniques and the credit analysis skills expected of the project banker are used then a project should run smoothly, and all parties, buyers, suppliers/contractors and providers of financial products should be satisfied.

Index

Page numbers in **bold** refer to tables, in *italics*
to figures. Textual matter may occur on the
same pages.